Radiomics and Its Clinical Application

THE ELSEVIER AND MICCAI SOCIETY BOOK SERIES

Advisory Board

Titles

Balocco, A., et al., Computing and Visualization for Intravascular Imaging and Computer Assisted Stenting, 9780128110188.

Dalca, A.V., et al., Imaging Genetics, 9780128139684.

Depeursinge, A., et al., Biomedical Texture Analysis, 9780128121337.

Munsell, B., et al., Connectomics, 9780128138380.

Pennec, X., et al., Riemannian Geometric Statistics in Medical Image Analysis, 9780128147252.

Trucco, E., et al., Computational Retinal Image Analysis, 9780081028162.

Wu, G., and Sabuncu, M., Machine Learning and Medical Imaging, 9780128040768.

Zhou S.K., Medical Image Recognition, Segmentation and Parsing, 9780128025819.

Zhou, S.K., et al., Deep Learning for Medical Image Analysis, 9780128104088.

Zhou, S.K., et al., Handbook of Medical Image Computing and Computer Assisted Intervention, 9780128161760.

MICCAI

Radiomics and Its Clinical Application
Artificial Intelligence and Medical Big Data

Jie Tian

CAS Key Laboratory of Molecular Imaging, Chinese Academy of Sciences; Beijing Advanced Innovation Center for Big Data-Based Precision Medicine, School of Engineering Medicine, Beihang University, Beijing, China

Di Dong

CAS Key Laboratory of Molecular Imaging, Chinese Academy of Sciences; School of Artificial Intelligence, University of Chinese Academy of Sciences, Beijing, China

Zhenyu Liu

CAS Key Laboratory of Molecular Imaging, Chinese Academy of Sciences; School of Artificial Intelligence, University of Chinese Academy of Sciences, Beijing, China

Jingwei Wei

CAS Key Laboratory of Molecular Imaging, Chinese Academy of Sciences; School of Artificial Intelligence, University of Chinese Academy of Sciences, Beijing, China

ACADEMIC PRESS

An imprint of Elsevier

ELSEVIER

Academic Press is an imprint of Elsevier
125 London Wall, London EC2Y 5AS, United Kingdom
525 B Street, Suite 1650, San Diego, CA 92101, United States
50 Hampshire Street, 5th Floor, Cambridge, MA 02139, United States
The Boulevard, Langford Lane, Kidlington, Oxford OX5 1GB, United Kingdom

Notices

Knowledge and best practice in this field are constantly changing. As new research and
experience broaden our understanding, changes in research methods, professional
practices, or medical treatment may become necessary.

Practitioners and researchers must always rely on their own experience and knowledge in
evaluating and using any information, methods, compounds, or experiments described
herein. In using such information or methods they should be mindful of their own safety
and the safety of others, including parties for whom they have a professional
responsibility.

To the fullest extent of the law, neither the Publisher nor the authors, contributors, or
editors, assume any liability for any injury and/or damage to persons or property as a
matter of products liability, negligence or otherwise, or from any use or operation of any
methods, products, instructions, or ideas contained in the material herein.

Library of Congress Cataloging-in-Publication Data
A catalog record for this book is available from the Library of Congress

British Library Cataloguing-in-Publication Data
A catalogue record for this book is available from the British Library

ISBN: 978-0-12-818101-0

For information on all Academic Press publications visit our
website at https://www.elsevier.com/books-and-journals

Publisher: Mara Conner
Acquisitions Editor: Tim Pitts
Editorial Project Manager: Chiara Giglio
Production Project Manager: Prasanna Kalyanaraman
Cover Designer: Victoria Pearson

Working together
to grow libraries in
developing countries

www.elsevier.com • www.bookaid.org

Typeset by TNQ Technologies

Contents

Biographies

Dr. Jie Tian received his PhD (with honors) in Artificial Intelligence from the Chinese Academy of Sciences in 1993. Since 1997, he has been a Professor at the Chinese Academy of Sciences. Dr. Tian has been elected as a Fellow of ISMRM, AIMBE, IAMBE, IEEE, OSA, SPIE, and IAPR. He serves as an editorial board member of Molecular Imaging and Biology, European Radiology, IEEE Transactions on Medical Imaging, IEEE Transactions on Biomedical Engineering, IEEE Journal of Biomedical and Health Informatics, and Photoacoustics. He is the author of over 400 peer-reviewed journal articles, including publication in *Nature Biomedical Engineering*, *Science Advances*, *Journal of Clinical Oncology*, *Nature Communications*, *Radiology*, *IEEE Transactions on Medical Imaging*, and many other journals, and these articles have received over 25,000 Google Scholar citations (H-index 79). Dr. Tian is recognized as a pioneer and leader in the field of molecular imaging in China. In the last two decades, he has developed a series of new optical imaging models and reconstruction algorithms for *in vivo* optical tomographic imaging, including bioluminescence tomography, fluorescence molecular tomography, and Cerenkov luminescence tomography. He has developed new artificial intelligence strategies for medical imaging big data analysis in the field of radiomics and played a major role in establishing a standardized radiomics database with more than 100,000 cancer patients data collected from over 50 hospitals all over China. He has received numerous awards, including 5 national top awards for his outstanding work in medical imaging and biometrics recognition.

Dr. Di Dong is currently an Associate Professor at the Institute of Automation, Chinese Academy of Sciences. He received his PhD in Pattern Recognition and Intelligent Systems from the Institute of Automation, Chinese Academy of Sciences, China, in 2013. Dr. Dong is a member of the Youth Innovation Promotion Association of the Chinese Academy of Sciences, an active member of the American Association for Cancer Research (AACR), and a corresponding member of the European Society of Radiology (ESR). Dr. Dong has carried out long-term research work in the field of tumor radiomics and medical big data analysis. In recent years, Dr. Dong has published nearly 50 peer-reviewed papers in SCI journals, e.g., in *Annals of Oncology*, *European Respiratory Journal*, *Clinical Cancer Research* (three publications), *BMC Medicine*, etc. These articles have received over 1,600 Google Scholar citations (H-index 24). He has 6 ESI highly cited papers. He has applied for more than 20 patents and 10 software copyright licences in China.

Dr. Zhenyu Liu is currently a Professor at CAS Key Laboratory of Molecular Imaging, Institute of Automation. He received his PhD in Pattern Recognition and Intelligent Systems from the Institute of Automation, Chinese Academy of Sciences, China, in 2014. Dr. Liu got the outstanding youth fund of the Natural Science Foundation of China (NSFC) and is a member of the Youth Innovation Promotion Association of the Chinese Academy of Sciences. His research focuses on medical imaging analysis, especially radiomics and its applications in oncology research.

In recent years, Dr. Liu has published nearly 30 papers in peer-reviewed journals, e.g., in *Clinical Cancer Research, Theranostics, EBioMedicine, Radiotherapy and Oncology*, etc. These articles received over 1,300 Google Scholar citations. He also holds more than 10 patents in China.

Dr. Jingwei Wei is currently an Assistant Professor at the Institute of Automation, Chinese Academy of Sciences. Her research focuses on radiomics and its clinical application in liver diseases, liver-specific feature engineering, traditional pattern recognition classifiers, and deep learning methods implemented towards liver disease-oriented research. Her primary work includes pre-operative prediction of microvascular invasion in hepatocellular carcinoma (HCC), prognosis prediction in HCC, and non-invasive imaging biomarker development for pathological factors prediction in liver diseases. Dr. Wei has published over 20 peer-reviewed papers in SCI journals, e.g., in *Liver Cancer, Liver International, Clinical and Translational Gastroenterology*, etc.

Preface

With the expeditious growth of medical imaging data and the rapid advancement of artificial intelligence techniques, image-derived diagnosis and prognosis of multi-fold diseases has broken through the scope of conventional computer-aided diagnosis. Toward the era of intelligent analysis, a new product that combines big data of medical imaging and artificial intelligence, radiomics, has emerged.

In 2012, Professor Philippe Lambin and Professor Robert Gillies first proposed the concept of radiomics, which converts medical images such as computer tomography, magnetic resonance imaging, positron emission tomography, and ultrasound into excavable data, mines massive quantitative imaging characteristics related to diseases, and builds intelligent analysis models by artificial intelligence techniques to assist clinical diagnosis and prognosis. Radiomics originates from clinical issues and eventually returns to clinical guidance applications. It is currently one of the most important research hotspots with cutting-edge directions and has definitely shown great clinical application prospects. Up to now, many mainstream international imaging conferences, such as those of the Radiological Society of North America, the International Society for Magnetic Resonance in Medicine, and the World Molecular Imaging Congress, and clinical oncology conferences (such as those of the American Association for Cancer Research, American Society of Clinical Oncology), have set up special sessions for radiomics. There is also a trend of rapid growth in international research papers related to radiomics year by year.

We have been following the research hotspot of radiomics for many years and have participated in the international radiomics seminars hosted by Professor Robert Gillies for six consecutive years. While witnessing the rapid development of radiomics and the endless novel methods and clinical applications, we are deeply concerned about the lacunae of books dedicated to radiomics in China. In view of this, we have systematically sorted out the radiomics technique procedures and typical clinical applications and compiled this book, hoping to attract more domestic clinical and scientific researchers to jointly launch radiomics researches and provide a potential technical tool for promoting the precise diagnosis and treatment of cancers and other diseases.

The publication of this book has received much help and support. We appreciate the National Science and Technology Academic Publication Fund (2017-H-017), the National Key Research and Development Program of China (2017YFA0205200), the National Natural Science Foundation of China (81930053), and the Science Press for their long-term strong support. This book is based on radiomics research studies accumulated over years by the Key Laboratory of Molecular Imaging of the Chinese Academy of Sciences and the preliminary work of many doctoral students, master's students, postdoctoral fellows, and young teachers. We are especially grateful to three authoritative experts in the field of radiomics, Robert Gillies, Philippe Lambin, and Sandy Napel, for writing prefaces to this book and supporting the research of radiomics in China. We thank Di Dong, Zhenyu Liu, Jingwei Wei,

Zhenchao Tang, Shuo Wang, Hailin Li, Siwen Wang, Lianzhen Zhong, Mengjie Fang, Lixin Gong, Runnan Cao, Caixia Sun, Kai Sun, Dongsheng Gu, and Shuaitong Zhang for participating in the writing and organization of this book. They contributed a lot to the final completion of this book.

Jie Tian
October 2020

Introduction

1

Chapter outline

Medical imaging began in 1895 when German physicist *Wilhelm Konrad Rontgen* discovered X-rays. In 1978, *G.N. Hounsfield* published computed tomography (CT) technology, which is considered to be one of the great achievements of science and technology in the 20th century. Since then, medical imaging has developed rapidly, and various new medical imaging devices and technologies have been continuously presented. Especially medical imaging has played a vital role in cancer screening, diagnosis, and treatment for patients. On the other hand, the rise of modern artificial intelligence in recent years has led to breakthroughs in computer vision and patter recognition, and the growth of massive medical big data provides an excellent opportunity for artificial intelligence applications in medical imaging analysis. Especially, the multiple molecular events represented the intrinsic progress in the micro scale, which can be possibly uncovered by artificial intelligence analysis on medical imaging. In this context, radiomics emerges as a new research area that integrates artificial intelligence and machine learning to extract pathophysiological information of tumor images, thus enabling tumor staging classification, therapeutic evaluation, and prognosis assessment. The content of this chapter is focused on the background of medical imaging, multidimensional complexity of biomedical research, concept of radiomics, value of radiomics, workflow of radiomics, and the clinical applications of radiomics.

1.1 Background of medical image analysis in cancer

According to the 2014 World Cancer Report published by the International Agency for Research on Cancer of the World Health Organization on February 3, 2014, there were 14.1 million newly diagnosed cancer cases and 8.2 million cancer-related deaths worldwide in 2012. The incidence of young patients is increasing year by year [1]. *Wanqing Chen* and *Jie He* of the National Cancer Center of China estimated there were 4.292 million newly diagnosed cancer cases and 28.14 million cancer-related deaths in China in 2015 [2]. Cancer has become a major disease that seriously affects the quality of human life and threatens human life. Early diagnosis of cancer and accurate prognosis assessment via imaging plays an important role in providing personalized treatment plans.

CT, magnetic resonance imaging (MRI), positron emission tomography (PET), and ultrasound are widely used in clinical practice. Thus, the results of relevant examinations provide assistance and reference for cancer staging and assessment of cancer patients' prognosis. Medical imaging is an important tool for evaluation of the tumors and the curative effects. The diagnostic value of CT for cancer is that it can observe the changes of morphology and density of cancerous tissues and the extent of tumor invasion from CT images, thus achieving staging of the tumor. But it is difficult to diagnose early tumors with inconspicuous morphology. MRI has a high advantage in multidirectional imaging and soft tissue contrast ability, which can clearly show the size and location of the tumor and the degree of invasion of surrounding tissues. MRI has good clinical value for the diagnosis and staging of cancer, and can also provide information on the spread of tumors to help develop surgical plans.

As a noninvasive method for tumor diagnosis, medical imaging has been widely used in the auxiliary diagnosis of various cancers:

Firstly, the use of image information for clinical diagnosis often relies on the subjective experience of doctors, and imaging features are connected to corresponding diagnosis. However, medical imaging contained valuable information to reveal both intra- and intertumor heterogeneity. For example, based on standard medical images (e.g., CT, MRI, and PET), clinicians can only obtain concise diagnostic information related to tumor shape, size, image contrast, and tumor metabolism. However, these information may not fully reflect the pathophysiology or diagnosis and treatment of the entire tumor, and thus it is impossible to provide an effective means to quantify the imaging finding soft tumors' pathological staging or tumor changes after treatment [3]. Medical images are not just images, in addition to providing visual information, they also contain a large amount of potential information related to tumor pathophysiology and tissue cell microenvironment [4]. Such information has not been effectively utilized for a long period of time in clinics. The deep exploration of medical imaging data will provide more information, including tumor morphology, potential pathological mechanism, and tumor heterogeneity toward the precise diagnosis and personalized treatment of patients.

Secondly, medical imaging has evolved from single X-ray imaging to a multimodal medical imaging technique. Currently, medical imaging is routinely used for clinical evaluation of tumors, diagnosis of tumor staging, and evaluation of the therapeutic effect [5,6]. However, most of the applications of these medical images only focus on the evaluation of tumor anatomical structure (e.g., tumor size) in the standardized clinical diagnosis. This measurement limits the application of medical imaging in the study of extensive tumor heterogeneity. The advantage of medical imaging is that the appearance phenotype of the tumor can be obtained in a noninvasive way, such as macroscopic intratumoral heterogeneity. Alternatively, tumor-related information can be obtained by invasive biopsy by extracting selected cancer tissue, therefore the heterogeneity of the tumor tissue cannot fully reflect the internal pathological information of the tumor. Furthermore, repeated invasive biopsies are a heavy burden for high-risk patients. Conversely, the imaging phenotype of the tumors provided by medical imaging provides a wealth of information on tumor genotypes, tumor microenvironments, and potential therapeutic effects [4]. At the same time, the information provided by the images can complement the genetic information. Therefore, the role of the tumor image phenotype based on medical imaging in precision medicine opens new possibilities for clinical research. Moreover, the clinician can quantitatively evaluate the patient's tumor phenotype at each follow-up. Therefore, analyzing tumor heterogeneity by quantitative imaging has a great potential for precision oncology applications.

Thirdly, in current clinical practice, physicians from the radiology department use quantitative indicators for tumor evaluation. In axial CT imaging, tumor size can be described by one- or two-dimensional methods. In molecular imaging, there is less quantitative information extracted and used for clinical application. In PET imaging, only the maximum or average intake is used to quantify the metabolism. Although these indicators are highly meaningful biomarkers, a large number of potential imaging characteristics were yet to be elucidated from quantitative tumor imaging. In addition, semantic features can also be obtained from medical imaging. The semantic features refer to the tumor characteristics obtained by visual evaluation of medical images via radiologists. By definition, semantic features are qualitative judgment of the tumor in clinical practice. The extraction of semantic features highly depends on professional medical imaging knowledge and is subject to subjective influence by different human evaluators. The benefit of establishing a unified terminology standard is that the terminology defined by experienced radiologists can establish a uniform measure of tumor characterization. Moreover, radiologists can evaluate low-quality or low-resolution medical images and give diagnostic results.

1.2 Multidimensional complexity of biomedical research

Multidimensional complexity is an important problem in biomedical research, which is mainly divided into spatial complexity and time complexity.

In terms of spatial complexity, human cells contain about 20,000 protein-coding genes, about 360,000 mRNAs, and about 1,000,000 protein molecules [x]. Their biological functions and activities are difficult to measure and estimate. The human body contains about 30 trillion cells, 79 key organs, 13 major organ systems, and their phenotype and function are still difficult to estimate. The composition of the human body has a strong spatial complexity from micro to macro levels. The existing data processing methods are difficult to effectively analyze such a large amount of biomedical data.

In terms of time complexity, the interaction of each person's behavior from birth to death to the external environment is incalculable. The tissues, organs, proteins, RNA, and DNA of an organism change over time, and are also affected by the external environment and various behaviors. Similarly, existing data processing methods are difficult to make an effective analysis for such a large amount of biomedical data.

For the above reasons, analyzing the multidimensional and complex biomedical data needs to overcome many challenges, and biomedical research usually needs to choose a simplified and controllable research direction. For example, medical big data come from various sources including gene sequencing, protein sequencing, electron microscopy, optical microscopy, etc. At the molecular cell level, medical data are generated by clinical examination, medical imaging, surgery, autopsy, etc. At the tissue and organ level, medical big data are generated by environmental monitoring, smart cities, smart homes, wearable devices, etc. At the behavioral level, we can solve specific problems in a local dimension. However, the local dimension study based on medical imaging big data cuts in from the macroscopic tissue organ dimension, and can reflect the microscopic dimension information through image features. A patient's CT image can contain 52,428,800 voxels, which contain between 1000 and 100,000 image features, while 1000 patients contain between 1 million and 100 million image feature big data. Such a large amount of data lay the foundation for artificial intelligence in medicine. In the spatial dimension, the relationship between medical image features and pathological gene analysis results is constructed from macro to micro. In the time dimension, the association between medical imaging features and treatment follow-up results was constructed from treatment to prognosis. This joint analysis can help achieve assisted precision diagnosis and treatment planning for patients. Molecular events represent the intrinsic molecular activities in the micro scope. The massive collection of molecular events in the micro scale is reflected in the macro scale as the medical image. The pathological changes are usually related to multiple abnormal molecular event. The massive amount of multiple abnormal molecular events would display as abnormal regions in the medical images. Though medical images are macro representation of the massive amount of multiple abnormal molecular events, it is still difficult to associate the macro images characteristics with the micro abnormal molecular events. Nevertheless, with the help of artificial intelligence, the potential information in the macro images can be mined in the approach of quantitative analysis. Then, the multiple molecular events can be analyzed by the quantitative information explored by artificial intelligence. In the earlier research, Michael Kuo et al. analyze the diversity of genetic and protein activities with the diverse radiographic features extracted from CT images [7]. They found that the combination of 28 radiographic features can reconstruct 78% of the global gene expression profiles. The radiographic features are also related with cell proliferation, liver synthetic function, and patient prognosis. The finding of Michael Kuo and his colleges indicate the substantial relation between the macro quantitative information and the multiple molecular events. Furthermore, Sun et al. extracted quantitative features from contrast-enhanced CT images to investigate the relationship with the CD8 cell tumour infiltration [8]. It was found that the quantitative features combined with RNA-seq genomic data can be used to assess the tumour-infiltrating CD8 cells and predict the response to anti-PD-1 or anti-PD-L1 immunotherapy. The macro image biomarker can directly reflect the micro changes of CD8 cell tumour infiltration, which is an important marker for tumor response. Sun's work shows that the relationship between the macro images and the micro multiple molecular events cannot only be explored but also can be used to assess the clinical manifestation of the patient, such as the therapy response. Their findings are also validated in three independent cohorts, which indicating that the image biomarker is promising in predicting the immune phenotype of tumours. Similarly, Haruka et al. extracted quantitative image features capturing the shape, texture, and edge sharpness information of the glioblastoma [9]. They found three distinct phenotypic "clusters" are related to unique set of molecular signaling pathways, which were directly related to differential probabilities of survival. So, the macro image phenotypes are related to different prognosis by associating with the micro multiple molecular events. Thus, the distinct phenotypes of the images can provide as a noninvasive approach to stratify GBM patients for different targeted therapy and personalized treatment. In a recent study, Mu et al. analyze the relationship between the quantitative F-18-FDG-PET/CT image features and the EGFR mutation status, which is related to the longer progression free survival in patients treated with EGFR-TKIs [10]. They construct an EGFR deep learning score significantly and negatively associated with higher durable clinical benefit, reduced hyper progression, and longer PFS.

1.3 Concept of radiomics

In recent years, due to the advancement of storage and information technology, the medical image information of patients has been well preserved digitally. Compared with previous simple image processing based on small samples, the ever-growing number of medical images brings new research opportunities: (1) Based on a large amount of imaging data, a more accurate statistical model can be established to improve the level of diagnosis and detection of computer-aided diagnosis systems, so that its accuracy is comparable to human-level diagnosis; (2) More complex and expressive machine learning, pattern recognition, and statistical methods can play a better role with the big data, thus mining more potential laws and information from massive imaging data. The accumulation of medical image big data and the rapid development of artificial intelligence technology directly promote the new comprehensive analysis method in medicine.

Radiomics generally refers to the use of CT, PET, MRI, or ultrasound imaging as input data, extracting expressive features from massive image-based data, and then using machine learning or statistical models for quantitative analysis and prediction of diseases [4,11–13]. Compared with the traditional practice of using only manual viewing, radiomics analysis can extract high-dimensional features that are difficult to quantitatively describe in human visuals from massive data and correlate them with clinical and pathological information of patients to achieve the prediction of certain diseases or genes. Using advanced bioinformatics tools and machine learning methods, researchers are able to develop potential models that improve the prediction accuracy of diagnostic and prognostic approaches [4].

Radiomics is an emerging medical image analysis proposed by *Lambin* et al. [12] in 2012, which refers to the high-throughput extraction of a large number of image features from radiological images. In the same year, *Kumar* et al. supplemented the definition of radiomics to high-throughput extraction and analysis of a large number of advanced quantitative image features from CT, PET, and MRI [11], expanding the imaging modality and adding quantification analysis. In 2014, *Aerts* et al. published a breakthrough application in *Nature Communications*, pointing out the prognostic ability of radiomics [13], which caused widespread concern in the scientific research community. In general, radiomics refers to the extraction and analysis of highly representative quantitative image features from clinically large-scale imaging data, that is, using a large number of automated data feature description algorithms, the imaging data were transformed into high-dimensional extensible feature space, and the disease diagnosis and prediction of the case data were completed by comparing and analyzing the imaging data with clinical information. Furthermore, the radiomics analysis is based on the assumption that the quantitative image–based parameters have a certain correlation with the molecular phenotype or genotype of the tumor. Radiomics postprocesses the medical images that need to be collected in clinical diagnosis and treatment, extracts information that is difficult to see with the naked eye, and combines with other genomic data, metabolic data, and protein data to improve the efficacy prediction and prognosis of the tumor. Thus, personalized treatment of the patient is achieved.

1.4 **Value of radiomics**

Due to the pathological characteristics of different tumor types, they have different imaging performances. Different tumor image features also indicate completely different treatment methods, which directly affect the prognosis. At present, based on the subjective clinical experience of the doctor, prejudgment of the tumor is achieved through medical images. Based on the existing medical image feature analysis, some multidimensional texture features can accurately reflect the pathological information of the diseased tissue, which has important research value for the realization of individualized medical treatment. Therefore, a complete feature database can filter the subsequent key features and provide more comprehensive data support. The use of radiomics methods to assist in the predictive analysis of tumors and to give credible recommendations is of great practical significance.

Radiomics analysis mainly extracts and quantifies the features associated with a diagnosis from images. For example, in the CT images of tumors, there are differences in the tumors' shape, size, and texture with different pathological grades. These features are often used by doctors as a basis for manual diagnosis, but the diagnostic results are subjective and relevant to the radiologists' experience, which makes it difficult to realize objective and repeatable diagnosis results. However, in the analysis of radiomics, the features of these doctors' qualitative descriptions can be quantitatively described by mathematical expressions from the perspective of images, thus providing an objective and repeatable diagnosis. Radiomics attempts to extract image features associated with diagnostic results through a large number of medical images, and directly analyzes results via the images, rather than just simple image processing. For example, researchers extracted high-dimensional image features by radiomics and found that these features were highly correlated with the prognosis survival of lung cancer, patients could be divided into different risk groups according to different values of these features, and different treatment plans could be implemented [13].

In addition to the use of imaging data, radiomics has introduced genetic analysis to improve diagnostic accuracy. In the traditional genetic analysis, whether a gene is mutated is determined by gene sequencing of tumor tissue sampled from a certain location of the tumor. However, due to the heterogeneity of the tumor, genetic mutations may occur in other parts of the tumor that are not sampled. Therefore, traditional genetic analysis may have sampling errors [4]. The mutated gene affects the growth of the tumor and is thus expressed in the imaging data [14]. Radiomic features can be extracted from the overall tumor image, which contains complete information. The genetic analysis in radiomics can complement the traditional genetic analysis to improve diagnostic accuracy.

1.5 **Workflow of radiomics**

Radiomics includes the following steps of data acquisition, lesion detection, lesion segmentation, feature extraction, and information mining for clinical decision support. An automatic algorithm can be used to detect the lesion area after acquiring the imaging data. Manual or automatic segmentation is performed for the detected lesion area to obtain an accurate tumor area. High-dimensional features can be extracted for the tumor area by an image processing algorithm. Finally, the relationship between the feature and the pathological result is analyzed by machine learning or statistical methods to predict the pathological result through the imaging data.

Radiomics analysis mainly includes the five key technologies [11] described in 1.5.1−1.5.5.

1.5.1 Image acquisition and reconstruction

Due to the different reconstruction methods and slice thickness of different scanners, the parameters (such as resolution) of images are also greatly different. In order to reduce the differences, on the one hand, it is possible to reduce the difference in parameters as much as possible by formulating a series of clinical medical image acquisition specifications. On the other hand, it is possible to select features that have high reproducibility between different patients, sufficient dynamics range [15], and are insensitive to image acquisition protocols and reconstruction algorithms in the analysis process.

1.5.2 Image segmentation

Radiomics analysis extracts features from the region of interest (ROI), including tumors, normal tissues, and other anatomical structures. The accurate segmentation of the ROI is very important for feature quantification, feature extraction, and statistical analysis. The manual segmentation results of experienced radiologists are often used as the gold standard, but this method is very time-consuming and has very large subjectivity. Therefore, it is not suitable for radiomics analysis based on large data volume medical images. The research of robust automatic or semiautomatic segmentation methods is a very important part of radiomics analysis.

1.5.3 Feature extraction and selection

Radiomic features extraction can be performed after the tumor area is determined. Classical features include the description of characteristics of tumor gray histograms (high or low contrast), tumor shape (circular or needle-like), texture features (homogeneous or heterogeneous), and relationship between tumor location and surrounding tissue.

A large number of radiomic features can usually be extracted based on the extraction methods described above. The dimension of the features may be much larger than the sample size, but for a specific analysis target, not all features are valuable, so reducing the feature dimension and selecting the most valuable features is very important. Feature selection can be implemented either using machine learning or statistical analysis. In the selection process, in addition to considering high information volume and nonredundancy, high repeatability is also an indicator that needs to be considered.

1.5.4 **Database and data sharing**

The ultimate goal of radiomics is to establish the relationship between image features and tumor phenotypes or molecular features. It is necessary to establish a complete database of images, features, clinical data, and molecular data (Fig. 1.1). In the establishment of this database system, it is necessary to protect the patient's privacy and hide the individual information of the patient in the Digital Imaging and Communications in Medicine (DICOM) data header file.

1.5.5 **Informatics analysis**

One of the most important aspects of the radiomics analysis is to propose appropriate, identifiable, reliable, and reproducible features that have potential applications in clinical diagnostics. The employment of existing bioinformatics analysis tools can be the first step in the analysis of the features, which can reduce the trouble of developing new analytical methods, as well as use widely accepted methods. On this basis, the improved methods specifically for the radiomics analysis mainly involve the following: (1) Multivariate validation problem; (2) Supervised or semi-supervised analysis; (3) Classification for biomarker verification, etc. It is also very important to combine clinical and patient risk factors, as these risk factors may be related to medical image characteristics, or they may be statistically significant for the prediction analysis. Therefore, the combination of biostatistics, epidemiology, and bioinformatics is necessary to establish robust clinical predictive models that relate high-dimensional features to tumor phenotypes or gene protein markers. It is believed that when the database shown in Fig. 1.1 is established, the development of targeted analysis methods will be further promoted.

In addition, due to the rapid development of natural image processing and artificial intelligence, deep learning models with feature self-learning capabilities have also been broadly applied in medical image analysis. Unlike the traditional radiomics process, deep learning does not require precise tumor boundary segmentation and artificially defined feature extraction but automatically learns the features associated with the pathological diagnosis from imaging data by self-learning. This is an end-to-end learning approach that has achieved remarkable success in the field of artificial intelligence and has also been gradually accepted in medical imaging processing. Deep learning techniques will also be explained in detail in this chapter as a new radiomics technique.

1.5.6 **Medical image acquisition**

A large amount of data are the consolidated foundation for reliable conclusions, especially in the field of radiomics, because radiomics seeks to mine the correlation between clinical data and high-dimensional quantitative features extracted from a great number of medical image data. However, collecting and integrating large-scale medical image data are difficult. Firstly, most medical images are scattered at institutions or hospitals in various regions, and the number of medical images

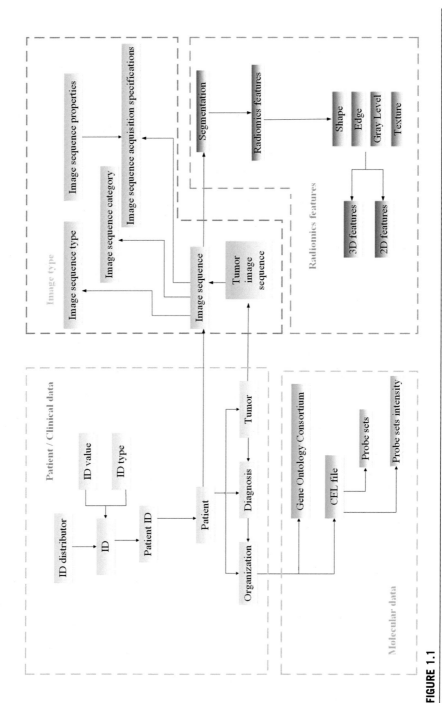

FIGURE 1.1

Framework for the radiomics database. Mainly composed of four parts: patient/clinical data (*blue*), medical image type (*orange*), Radiomic features (*purple*), and molecular data (*green*).

depends on the size of the local patient population. All of these factors make data resources markedly scattered. Secondly, it is very time-consuming to collect medical images. For example, it often takes several years to follow up on patients to determine their survival time when performing a prognostic analysis. Lastly, the instruments and scanning parameters and methods used by various hospitals or institutions are different, which may result in inconsistent or incomplete image formats, which would affect the accuracy of the analysis. Therefore, it is our priority to allow institutions and hospitals to start to creating large medical image datasets with consistent and rich diagnostic information.

Recently, The Cancer Imaging Archive (TCIA) established a medical image data sharing platform, providing publicly available medical images and metadata for specific cancers from various institutions and hospitals around the world [14]. Based on these datasets, researchers and engineers can develop new medical image analysis methods and tools to validate their hypotheses or assist radiologists in making clinical decisions. For example, a large dataset that constitutes TCIA is the Lung Image Database Consortium image collection (LIDC-IDRI) [16,17]. The dataset contains the original CT image and four radiologists' markers on the tumor boundary. It also provides some diagnostic information and detailed annotations of the lung nodules, including the location, benign and malignant information of the nodules, which provide good resources for verification of nodule detection and segmentation methods [18−21]. In addition, many researchers use this database for classification of benign and malignant pulmonary nodules.

Since these medical images are obtained from different institutions and hospitals, different software and coding protocols are required for the reconstruction. Researchers using these datasets need to consider these differences to avoid potential unexpected effects.

1.5.7 Segmentation of the tumor

Tumor segmentation is a fundamental step in the radiomics analysis because it converts the original medical image into an image that can be extracted. Although the segmentation algorithm has been studied for a long time, the fully automatic segmentation algorithm still needs to be improved, especially in the field of medical image analysis. This is mainly due to the following difficulties in the existing segmentation algorithm: (1) There is no consented gold standard for nodules or tumor boundaries because there is adhesion between the tumor and surrounding tissues, and the definition of tumor boundaries has certain subjectivity. Due to subjective varieties, it is difficult to obtain consistent segmentation results [16]. This poses a challenge to the machine learning−based segmentation method because the segmentation labels of the training set are not necessarily true or robust. (2) It is very time-consuming for doctors to manually segment the tumors. Doctors must mark the tumor slice by slice, while larger nodules are usually distributed over many slices. Finally, nodules are not in regular geometric shapes, so it is difficult to model them. (3) Due to the influence of adhesions and other conditions, the tumor boundary will be unclear, which also brings difficulties to segmentation. (4) The repeatability of segmentation is also very important because the following feature extraction procedure is performed on the segmented tumors, and repeatable segmentation ensures that the extracted features are stable and reliable. Despite the above difficulties and problems in the segmentation algorithm, researchers are still perfecting the segmentation method for specific situations [22,23].

At present, the segmentation methods of tumor images can be divided into three categories: manual segmentation, semiautomatic segmentation, and automatic segmentation. The commonly used segmentation algorithms mainly include threshold segmentation, image segmentation based on fuzzy theory, region-based image segmentation, and edge-based image segmentation. Although there have been a large number of tumor image segmentation algorithms, there has been no consensus on how to choose the right algorithm in different situations, how different segmentation algorithms affect postfeature quantization and feature extraction, what kind of segmentation method will be more consistent with the gold standard, and whether there is a general segmentation method.

1.5.8 Tumor image phenotype

The most crucial part of radiomics is to extract high-dimensional features to quantify the tumor. Based on the automatic feature extraction algorithm, radiomics can extract high-dimensional features from medical images [4,11−13]. Feature extraction is a bridge connecting images and clinical results, which can be divided into semantic features and nonsemantic features.

Semantic features refer to the characteristics of qualitative descriptions by doctors, such as uniformity and edge spurs, which often lack effective mathematical expressions. Nonsemantic features can be quantitatively described as mathematical expressions. Currently, the general method for generating nonsemantic features is extracting them from segmented nodules based on mathematical expressions. Firstly, segmented markers can be used as a mask to extract shape-related features such as volume, surface area, and compactness. Secondly, the gray intensity of each pixel can be used to construct a large number of features, such as first-order, second-order, and high-order statistical features [4]. The first-order features are mainly related to the gray distribution in the tumor area, such as the minimum value of the grayscale, maximum value, median value, entropy of the gray histogram, and the characteristics of kurtosis and skewness; the second-order features mainly describe the statistical correlation between the current pixel and surrounding pixels, such as texture features, which can be used to describe the heterogeneity of the umor. In the radiomics analysis, texture analysis can employ texture analysis to reflect intratumoral heterogeneity by a gray run-length matrix and gray function matrix. In addition, heterogeneity is often seen as a feature of malignant tumors, and it is reflected in many levels of genes to the macroscopic level. As an effective means to evaluate heterogeneity, using texture parameters to evaluate the treatment output or assess prognosis has been valued by researchers [24]. Texture analysis has been used as a new tool for assessing intratumoral heterogeneity in medical images, especially in PET images. Moreover, since it reflects the relative change between adjacent pixels, the disadvantages of not being robust in SUV analysis can be overcome. Although texture analysis has not been widely used in clinical practice, more and more studies have demonstrated its important role in prediction of diagnosis or evaluation of prognosis. Some studies have demonstrated that texture parameters are superior to gray values in predicting treatment outcomes and overall survival in many cancers. Higher-order features such as wavelet and spectral analysis are often used to characterize repeated or nonrepetitive potential patterns [4]. In addition, there are shapes, positional features, and features that reflect the three-dimensional features of the tumor, such as sphericity, spikiness, position, and attachment characteristics.

There are still many studies devoted to extracting more quantitative features from medical images. In an earlier study [11], 182 texture features and 22 semantic features were extracted from CT images of lung cancer; in recent research [13], researchers extracted 662 radiomic features based on the Laplace transform analysis of the Gaussian kernel, including 522 texture features and fractal features. Obviously, the number of radiomic features can be very high, so there is a risk of overfitting in the subsequent modeling analysis. Thus, a reasonable feature reduction must be performed. The common method is to first remove the redundant features. A highly correlated cluster of features can be dimensioned to a more representative feature. This feature usually requires the largest interindividual variability and dynamic range. After reducing the correlation between features, feature selection can be performed by some statistical methods, such as a two-sample T-test or an F-test, to select features that are statistically different between different patient populations. In addition, the features' selection approach, such as Lasso [25] or Elastic-net [26] regression, can be used to select features useful to predicting benign and malignant tumors, staging, and prognosis. In general, feature extraction can produce hundreds of features; however, most of the features are correlated, so there is redundancy between the features, and feature selection is required to remove redundant features. In Ref. [15], the authors first selected features that were highly reproducible in multiple experiments and then used hierarchical clustering to extract highly dependent features. They also proposed a "dynamic range" metric function to characterize changes between different patients to rule out small variations between different patients. In the article [13], the author used a similar procedure to construct a radiomics label from four types of features. The feature dimension after feature selection is usually less than 100, which is much less than the feature dimension before selection.

1.5.9 Clinical prediction for tumor

The clinical prediction of tumors is also the process of knowledge mining of medical images, where the goal is to find the correlation between radiomics and clinical information. In many applications, this is converted into classification problems.

For example, the association between images and gene mutations can be converted into image classification problems (gene mutations and gene nonmutation). This step trains the classifier to learn the difference of the features between the two types. Feature mining related to patient survival is also an application of data mining. Machine learning and artificial intelligence algorithms play a very important role in this step.

Since the tumor area and the infected tissue have similar gray values on the tumor image, it has always been a challenging clinical problem to distinguish them from each other. Yu et al. used the K-nearest neighbor classification (KNN, K-nearest neighbor) to classify the head and neck cancer from infected tissue based on texture features, which provide a basis for quantifying infection in future cancer diagnosis [27]. In addition, some research work focuses on assessing the malignant degree of the tumor. Chen et al. used image retrieval methods to extract texture features from breast cancer ultrasound images and predicted the benign and malignant tumors [28]. Acharya et al. extracted texture features from breast cancer thermal imaging and used the support vector machine method in classifying benign and malignant tumors [29]. Although many studies have shown that the texture features have significant differences between the different prognoses of cancer, it has not yet been established as a perfect prediction system. In addition, various prediction methods have their own advantages and disadvantages, and there is currently no universal method. This requires us to compare different classification methods to get the best effect on the specific classification prediction of certain types of cancer.

The combination of radiomic features related to tumor diagnosis is similar to the cohort combination of biomarkers, based on which quantification and validation can be performed. Quantification is used to show that the data have a predictive effect on the predictor; and verification is used to demonstrate whether the predictive performance of the features is stabilized. That is, we need to identify the distinctive features, and verify whether they have predictive effects in the independent validation set. In the construction of the model, features are entered into the model to predict the patient's diagnosis or prognosis. The choice of model depends on the label to be predicted. Generally, multiple models can be used to verify performance, and then a model with the best predictive performance will be selected. A simpler model can be more easily applied to an independent verification set, so it will also be the first choice for model construction. After the model is built, model performance verification must be performed on an independent validation set. When the number of subjects is small, cross-validation—based internal verification are also acceptable [30]. In addition, it is also necessary to judge the benefit from the decision-making of the model, evaluating whether the radiomics model can provide more clinical benefits than the judgment of the clinicians.

Although the output of the radiomics model can determine the final predictive performance, successful establishment of the model lies in the availability and interactivity of the model, which can decide whether the model can be clinically accepted. If the model's predictions cannot be reasonably explained, even if the radiomics model is established by a large patient population and successfully validated on an independent validation set, this model still cannot be clinically accepted. In addition, the radiomics model needs to be visualized. A typical visualization method is the nomogram. Nomogram is a graphical display method proposed in the early 20th century. It can easily apply the radiomics model to clinical practice for decision-making assistance.

1.5.10 New technology of artificial intelligence

Artificial intelligence, especially deep learning, has the potential to study clinical tumor imaging. Artificial intelligence algorithms can quantify data patterns that have made significant advances in autonomous driving and speech recognition [x]. Radiomics is the application of artificial intelligence in medical imaging, which can provide quantitative imaging characteristics for tumor tissues. This information can be used to predict diagnosis and assist clinical decision-making, as well as to evaluate treatment efficacy. Radiomics has attracted wide attention in recent years due to its huge potential for clinical application, and more research results are expected in the near future. At present, many studies have made robust and meaningful findings, but there are still some studies that have problems with unreasonable laboratory design, such as lack of model validation, failure to perform good variable control, etc. These problems not only lead to unreasonable results but also cause other studies to make the same mistakes. The enormous potential of artificial intelligence has led to many related studies on medical imaging. With some research on abnormal situation monitoring or automatic disease quantification, others focus on the mapping between imaging phenotypes and genes. Given the positive results of the current study, radiomics research will continue to make progress in the near future.

Deep learning is under rapid development recently with various applications. Convolutional neural network (CNN) is one of the most widely used models in the image applications. The first successful application of CNN dates back to the 1990s, when LeCun used the LeNet-5 model for handwritten digit recognition [31]. The second wave of development is that the CNN model won the first place in the Imagenet Large-Scale Visual Identity Competition in 2012 [32]. Due to the development of hardware technology (such as the graphics processor GPU), researchers can now design larger networks to solve more complex problems. Many applications in medical image analysis focused on improving the performance of existing CAD systems, such as improving nodule detection accuracy [33] and diagnostic accuracy [34]. In recent years, Kumar et al. introduced the concept of "exploration Radiomics" for lung cancer detection of CT images [35]. Their proposed radiomics framework uses a deep CNN model to determine the phenotype of the tumor, which extracts abstract image—based features. There are two main advantages in using the CNN model: (a) Since CNN is an end-to-end machine learning architecture, its input can be the original segmented images [36]; (b) discriminative features are automatically learned during training. These advantages are very important to improve the classification accuracy of the model. As mentioned earlier, there are many difficulties in segmentation, but it is inevitable for the current radiomics process operation. Unreliable segmentation can affect feature extraction and even produce wrong predictions. In the feature selection step, the features associated with the disease or prognosis remain unknown. Therefore, a lot of unrelated features are extracted before feature selection, and deep learning can greatly accelerate this time-consuming feature extraction process.

Although deep learning has many advantages, there are still many difficulties in related research. For example, the features selected by deep learning are not directly interpretable, and the association of these features with diagnostic data is unknown. In other words, the deep learning features are conceptually similar to black boxes for researchers. Making deep learning features more interpretable and friendly useable for clinicians will be the center for deep learning applications in medicine.

In the field of natural image processing, there is a good research environment for everyone to share their well-trained deep neural network. In this way, other researchers do not need to spend a long time to retrain the model. In the field of medical imaging, deep learning development is still in its early stages. Many researchers prefer to use existing models for reproduced results and rapid development. Therefore, creating open source communities is of great significance for the application of deep learning in the field of medical imaging.

1.6 Prospect of clinical application of radiomics

Radiomics is a rapidly developing field in radiology and oncology. In the past few years, extensive studies have shown that image features are associated with cancer diagnosis and gene expression [13,37−39]. At present, the clinical application of radiomics mainly includes auxiliary diagnosis, treatment evaluation, and prognosis prediction. With the development of medical image big data, more abundant image data will enable the application of artificial intelligence methods. At the same time, excellent clinical manifestations obtained by various advanced pattern recognition methods also enable the application of radiomics in auxiliary diagnosis, treatment evaluation, and prognosis prediction. Now, more researchers are entering the field of radiomics clinical applications [39−44]. The current research results show the promise that radiomics can be used as an auxiliary and complementary tool for doctors' diagnosis. More radiomics applications, implementation details, new opportunities, and challenges are covered in the following chapters.

References

[1] Stewart BW, Wild CP, editors. World cancer report 2014. Cancer worldwide. International Agency for Research on Cancer; 2014.
[2] Chen W, et al. Cancer statistics in China, 2015. CA Cancer J Clin 2016;66(2):115−32.
[3] O'Connor JPB. Rethinking the role of clinical imaging. eLife 2017;6:e30563.

[4] Gillies RJ, Kinahan PE, Hricak H. Radiomics: images are more than pictures, they are data. Radiology 2016;278(2):563–77.

[5] Buckler AJ, et al. A collaborative enterprise for multi-stakeholder participation in the advancement of quantitative imaging. Radiology 2011;258(3):906–14.

[6] Kurland BF, et al. Promise and pitfalls of quantitative imaging in oncology clinical trials. Magn Reson Imag 2012;30(9):1301–12.

[7] Segal E, et al. Decoding global gene expression programs in liver cancer by noninvasive imaging. Nat Biotechnol 2007;25(6):675–80.

[8] Sun R, et al. A radiomics approach to assess tumour-infiltrating CD8 cells and response to anti-PD-1 or anti-PD-L1 immunotherapy: an imaging biomarker, retrospective multi-cohort study. Lancet Oncol 2018;19(9):1180–91.

[9] Itakura H, et al. Magnetic resonance image features identify glioblastoma phenotypic subtypes with distinct molecular pathway activities. Sci Transl Med 2015;7(303).

[10] Mu W, et al. Non-invasive decision support for NSCLC treatment using PET/CT radiomics. Nat Commun 2020;11(1).

[11] Kumar V, et al. Radiomics: the process and the challenges. Magn Reson Imag 2012; 30(9):1234–48.

[12] Lambin P, et al. Radiomics: extracting more information from medical images using advanced feature analysis. Eur J Cancer 2012;48(4):441–6.

[13] Aerts HJWL, et al. Decoding tumour phenotype by non-invasive imaging using a quantitative radiomics approach. Nat Commun 2014;5:4006.

[14] Gatenby RA, Grove O, Gillies RJ. Quantitative imaging in cancer evolution and ecology. Radiology 2013;269(1):8–15.

[15] Balagurunathan Y, et al. Reproducibility and prognosis of quantitative features extracted from CT images. Transl Oncol 2014;7(1):72–87.

[16] Armato III SG, et al. The Lung Image Database Consortium, (LIDC) and Image Database Resource Initiative (IDRI): a completed reference database of lung nodules on CT scans. Med Phys 2011;38(2):915–31.

[17] McNitt-Gray MF, et al. The Lung Image Database Consortium (LIDC) data collection process for nodule detection and annotation. Acad Radiol 2007;14(12):1464–74.

[18] de Carvalho Filho AO, et al. Automatic detection of solitary lung nodules using quality threshold clustering, genetic algorithm and diversity index. Artif Intell Med 2014;60(3): 165–77.

[19] Diciotti S, et al. Automated segmentation refinement of small lung nodules in CT scans by local shape analysis. IEEE Trans Biomed Eng 2011;58(12):3418–28.

[20] Orban G, Horvath G, IEEE. Lung nodule detection on digital tomosynthesis images: a preliminary study. In: 2014 IEEE 11th international symposium on biomedical imaging; 2014. p. 141–4.

[21] Song J, et al. Lung lesion extraction using a toboggan based growing automatic segmentation approach. IEEE Trans Med Imag 2016;35(1):337–53.

[22] Gu Y, et al. Automated delineation of lung tumors from CT images using a single click ensemble segmentation approach. Pattern Recognit 2013;46(3):692–702.

[23] Song J, et al. Lung lesion extraction using a toboggan based growing automatic segmentation approach. IEEE Trans Med Imag 2015;35(1):337–53.

[24] Tomasi G, Turkheimer F, Aboagye E. Importance of quantification for the analysis of PET data in oncology: review of current methods and trends for the future. Mol Imag Biol 2012;14(2):131–46.

[25] Friedman J, Hastie T, Tibshirani R. Regularization paths for generalized linear models via coordinate descent. J Stat Softw 2010;33(1):1−22.

[26] Tibshirani R. Regression shrinkage and selection via the Lasso. J R Stat Soc Series B Stat Methodol 1996;58(1):267−88.

[27] Yu H, et al. Automated radiation targeting in head-and-neck cancer using region-based texture analysis of PET and CT images. Int J Radiat Oncol Biol Phys 2009;75(2): 618−25.

[28] Chen D-R, Huang Y-L, Lin S-H. Computer-aided diagnosis with textural features for breast lesions in sonograms. Comput Med Imag Grap 2011;35(3):220−6.

[29] Acharya UR, et al. Thermography based breast cancer detection using texture features and support vector machine. J Med Syst 2012;36(3):1503−10.

[30] Moons KGM, et al. Risk prediction models: II. External validation, model updating, and impact assessment. Heart 2012;98(9):691−8.

[31] LeCun Y, et al. Gradient-based learning applied to document recognition. Proc IEEE Inst Electr Electron Eng 1998;86(11):2278−324.

[32] Krizhevsky A, Sutskever I, Hinton GE. Imagenet classification with deep convolutional neural networks. In: Advances in neural information processing systems; 2012.

[33] van Ginneken B, et al. Off-the-shelf convolutional neural network features for pulmonary nodule detection in computed tomography scans. In: Biomedical imaging (ISBI), 2015 IEEE 12th international symposium on 2015. IEEE; 2015.

[34] Shen W, et al. Multi-scale convolutional neural networks for lung nodule classification. Inf Process Med Imag 2015;24:588−99.

[35] Kumar D, et al. Discovery radiomics for computed tomography cancer detection. arXiv preprint arXiv:1509.00117. 2015.

[36] Shen W, et al. Multi-scale convolutional neural networks for lung nodule classification. In: Information processing in medical imaging. Springer; 2015.

[37] Ozkan E, et al. CT gray-level texture analysis as a quantitative imaging biomarker of epidermal growth factor receptor mutation status in adenocarcinoma of the lung. Am J Roentgenol 2015;205(5):1016−25.

[38] Coroller TP, et al. CT-based radiomic signature predicts distant metastasis in lung adenocarcinoma. Radiother Oncol 2015;114(3):345−50.

[39] Parmar C, et al. Radiomic feature clusters and prognostic signatures specific for lung and head & neck cancer. Sci Rep 2015;5:11044.

[40] Leijenaar RT, et al. The effect of SUV discretization in quantitative FDG-PET radiomics: the need for standardized methodology in tumor texture analysis. Sci Rep 2015;5:11075.

[41] Grove O, et al. Quantitative computed tomographic descriptors associate tumor shape complexity and intratumor heterogeneity with prognosis in lung adenocarcinoma. PLoS One 2015;10(3):e0118261.

[42] Cameron A, et al. MAPS: a quantitative radiomics approach for prostate cancer detection. 2015.

[43] Parmar C, et al. Robust radiomics feature quantification using semiautomatic volumetric segmentation. 2014.

[44] Cook GJ, et al. Radiomics in PET: principles and applications. Clin Transl Imag 2014; 2(3):269−76.

Key technologies and software platforms for radiomics

Chapter outline

The key technologies of radiomics include the automatic segmentation of tumors, the extraction of radiomic features, and the construction of radiomics models. In order to measure the performance of the radiomics model, a unified quality assessment system is also needed to measure the clinical value of the developed model. In radiomics research, it is necessary to use artificial or automatic algorithms for tumor segmentation (detection); then massive radiomics feature extraction for the tumor ROI region; since the extracted features contain high-latitude irrelevant information, feature dimensionality reduction of radiomic features is needed to identify key radiomic features; and finally, a small number of key radiomic features are used for the modeling analysis to provide clinically available radiomics models. At the end of this chapter, we will introduce the radiomics platform and software developed by relevant teams to facilitate radiomics research.

2.1 Tumor detection

For the past decades, researchers have been developing computer-aided diagnostic systems (CAD) to improve the diagnostic efficiency and accuracy. As the most common cancer, early screening for lung cancer is of great significance in CAD development. Due to a large number of CT image sequences and relatively small pulmonary nodules, it is common to have missed diagnosis frequently. Therefore, the CAD system for the detection of pulmonary nodules is of great clinical value. A typical pulmonary nodule detection system consists of three parts: (1) data preprocessing, (2) detection of candidate pulmonary nodule, and (3) reduction of false-positive rate. Data preprocessing is used to standardize data, limit nodule search space in the lungs, and reduce noise and artifacts. In the detection of candidate pulmonary nodules, the algorithm will detect suspected pulmonary nodules with a high sensitivity to improve recall rate, which usually has a high false-positive rate. Subsequently, a large number of false-positive nodules will be removed during the phase of reducing false positives. A typical CAD system for detecting pulmonary nodules is described in detail as follows.

2.1.1 Data preprocessing

Data preprocessing plays an important role in many deep learning algorithms. In an actual situation, many algorithms likely achieve optimal performance after data are normalized and whitened. Thus, finding suitable parameters of prepressing analysis becomes an important focus for medical image analysis.

The scanning parameters of medical image data such as layer thickness and layer spacing have great influence on the algorithm. Medical images usually were generated from different parameters and protocols in different medicine centers, and algorithms should design for mitigating the difference of multicenter data variance. Reproducibility and quality of the extracted features of CT, PET, MRI, and US, caused by variant image acquisition parameters, are crucial for radiomics research. It was essential for researchers to overcome the interference of variant image acquisition parameters toward building reliable and accurate radiomics models. Standard imaging protocols or algorithms for overcoming interference of acquisition parameters were necessary to be considered.

Therefore, before target detection, data resampling is needed to keep all the data resolution consistent. At the same time, the pixel value of CT images needs to be preprocessed to ensure that it is within a reasonable range, for example: (1) The lung window or mediastinal window is used to limit the amplitude, and only the lung tissue is retained. (2) Perform z-score normalization on CT images to make the mean value and standard deviation of the images 0 and 1, so as to facilitate subsequent algorithm processing. (3) Suppress outliers in CT images, such as removing pixels, which are 3 times the size of the standard deviation except for the mean value and removing noise.

1. Data normalization

   In data preprocessing, the first step of the standard is data normalization. While there are a number of possible approaches, this step is usually chosen based on the specific situation of the data explicitly. Common methods of feature normalization include the following:

   (1) Simple scaling

   (2) Per-example mean subtraction

   (3) Feature standardization (making all features in the dataset have zero mean and unit variance)

   In simple scaling, the goal is to resize the values of each dimension of the data (which may be independent of each other) so that the final data vector falls between [0, 1] and [−1, 1]. This is important for subsequent processing because many default parameters (such as epsilon in principal component analysis (PCA) whitening) assume that the data have been scaled to a reasonable range. In dealing with natural images, for example, we obtain the pixel values in the interval [0, 255], the commonly used treatment is the pixel values divided by 255, making them zoom in [0, 1]. In per-example mean subtraction, if your data are smooth (each dimension data statistics are subject to the same distribution). Example: Normalization removes the average intensity of the image. In many cases we are more interested in the image contents than the illumination of the image, so it makes sense to subtract the mean values of pixels for each data point. Note: although this method is widely used in dealing with images, extra care should be taken when processing color images because pixels in different color channels do not all possess specific smooth properties.

2. Feature standardization

   Feature standardization is the most common approach to normalization, which enables each dimension of data has a zero mean and unit variance. In practice, feature standardization is done by calculating the mean value of the data on each dimension (using the whole data) and then subtracting the mean value on each dimension. The next step is the data of each dimension divided by the standard deviation of the data in that dimension.

3. PCA/ZCA whitening

After simple normalization, whitening is usually used as the next step of pre-processing, which makes our algorithm work better. In fact, many deep learning algorithms rely on whitening to get good features. In PCA/ZCA whitening, Zero-centered is necessary which makes the $\frac{1}{m}\sum_i x^{(i)} = 0$.

It should be noted that this step needs to be done before calculating the covariance matrix (the only exception is that the per-example mean subtraction has been done and the data are flat across dimensions or pixels). Next, in PCA/ZCA whitening, appropriate parameters need to be selected. Selecting appropriate parameter values plays an important role in feature learning.

2.1.2 Detection of candidate nodules

Candidate nodule detection is the use of a rectangular frame in CT images to detect possible nodule areas. This stage is designed to ensure that a nodule is not missed with high sensitivity. At present, the commonly used region detection algorithm of interest can be realized by image processing. The lung area was first segmented using CT thresholds and potential candidate nodules were then detected in the lung area. In this method, the window width of 300HU to 750HU was first used to remove the CT values of blood vessels and trachea. Then, morphological corrosion operations were used to remove the noise generated by blood vessels and other tissues. Finally, all voxels were clustered using connected component analysis to obtain regions of interest.

These steps result in a large number of regions of interest, most of which are not pulmonary nodules. Therefore, feature extraction is required for all regions of interest to screen for true pulmonary nodules. Commonly used features include the following categories: intensity features, texture features, and morphological features [1].

Intensity features: for voxels in the candidate nodule region, using 50HU group spacing to calculate the normalized histogram of image intensity, and calculating the following statistics: entropy, mean, average histogram spacing, kurtosis, skewness, peak, and histogram spacing of 5%, 25%, 50%, 75%, and 95%. In addition, standard deviations, minima, and maxima can also be used to describe the intensity distribution.

Texture features: texture features mainly use a local binary pattern [2] (LBP) and 2D Haar wavelet. Both describe local spatial texture information and have been widely used in CT image texture analysis. These features can help eliminate false positives in ground glass areas caused by motion artifacts.

Shape features: the shape characteristics of most pulmonary nodules are ellipsoid but not tumor areas such as blood vessels, which may appear as a strip. Thus, shape becomes an important feature in distinguishing true and false positives. Shape features mainly include spherical degree, compactness, radius, and so on.

After extracting the above features for all candidate nodules, we used a classifier to classify each candidate nodules and finally determined whether it was a real pulmonary nodule. Because different machine learning algorithms have their own advantages and disadvantages, it is necessary to choose a classifier that matches the features. In the process of classifier selection, 5-fold cross-validation or 10-fold cross-validation is often used on the training set to select the best parameter for the classifier. Here are some common classifiers and their advantages and disadvantages.

1. Naive Bayes algorithm: The principle of Bayes classifier is to use the prior probability of each category, then use Bayes formula and independence assumption to calculate the likelihood and posterior probability category of the object, namely the probability category of the object to which the item belongs, and then select the object with the highest posterior probability as the category of the object. Its advantages are as follows: (1) Solid mathematical foundation, stable classification efficiency, easy to explain; (2) Estimation requires few parameters and is not sensitive to the lost data; (3) There is no need for a complex iterative solution framework for large datasets. However, it has the following disadvantages: (1) It may not satisfy the assumption of independence between attributes; (2) It is necessary to know prior probability, and the classification decision has a specific error rate.

2. Logistic regression algorithm: Binomial logistic regression model is a classification model, expressed by conditional probability distribution $P(Y|X)$ in the form of parameterized logistic distribution. The random variable X is a real number, and the random variable Y is 1 or 0. Model parameters can be estimated by supervised learning. The model has the following advantages: (1) low computational cost, easy to understand and implement; (2) applicable to numeric and subtype data. But it also has the following disadvantages: (1) easy to underfit; (2) classification accuracy may not be high.

3. Support vector machine (SVM) algorithm: For two types of linearly separable learning tasks, the SVM finds a hyperplane with the most considerable interval to separate the two types of samples. The most considerable break can ensure that the hyperplane has the best generalization ability. In the case of small samples, the model shows good performance, but it is sensitive to missing data and depends on the choice of specific and function of nonlinear problems.

4. Decision tree: Decision tree is a heuristic algorithm, in which each node selects features by using criteria such as information gain, and then constructs a tree classifier recursively. The computational complexity of the model is not high, and it is easy to understand and explain. It can handle both data type and subtype characteristics. However, for the data with an inconsistent number of samples, the result of information gain tends to the class with more samples, thus reducing the classification performance. In addition, too deep trees are prone to overfitting problems.

5. AdaBoost algorithm: AdaBoost algorithm is from a weak learning algorithm, gets a series of weak classifier (namely basic classifier) by learning repeatedly, and then combines these weak classifiers to be a strong classifier; the most ascending method is changing the probability distribution of the training dataset (the weight distribution of training data) according to different training data distributions, and the weak learning algorithm is used to learn a series of weak classifiers. This kind of integrated classifier usually has high classification accuracy. Moreover, various methods can be used to construct subclassifiers and is not easy to cause overfitting.

2.2 Tumor segmentation

When the location of the tumor is detected, accurate tumor segmentation is further essential for quantitative/pixel-wise analysis of tumor images, which includes manual, semiautomatic, and automatic segmentation methods. However, it was difficult to segment tumors because of the extensive heterogeneity of tumors and their similarity of the visual features to the surrounding environment. Firstly, there are no golden standard methods for accurate tumor segmentation. Each slice of each imaging sequence was inevitable to be checked and sketched by radiologists, and a tumor mask for a large tumor usually contains dozens of slices. Secondly, it was difficult to overcome differences between existing numerous morphological variations and geometric objects during segmentation modeling. Thirdly, tumor margins could be blurred by the partial volume effect or noise, which was not precisely defined in medical images.

The following sections will detail the relevant technologies of tumor segmentation, such as pulmonary nodules segmentation, pulmonary nodules segmentation based on the central pooling convolutional neural network [3] (CF-CNN), and tumor segmentation based on full convolution. Tumor segmentation determines the region of interest that will be analyzed in subsequent steps of radiomics.

Since feature extraction is based on segmented tumors, the segmentation method can ensure the reproducibility and reliability of radiomics features. Intraclass correlation coefficient (ICC) is used to assess inter-reader and internal agreement. Some studies recommend the use of acceptable ICC to detect ROI so that further extracted features can be used. Many automatic or semiautomatic segmentation methods have been developed to reduce labor costs and increase the reproducibility of tumor segmentation.

In CT image analysis of a tumor, the cost of obtaining clinical labels or labeling data is relatively high, which leads to a relatively small amount of normalized tumor CT image data. If it is directly analyzed in hundreds of samples, it is difficult to train the deep learning model and give full play to the advantages of deep learning. Although the volume of CT data for patient-grade tumors is small, a CT image of a tumor typically contains a large number of voxel points. For example, a CT image of a typical lung tumor may contain $10 \times 10 \times 5 = 500$ voxels. If every voxel point in the CT image of tumor is taken as a training sample, a large number (tens of thousands) of training samples can be generated, and then more complex deep learning models can be trained. This is the idea of a voxel-level classification algorithm. In the task of medical image segmentation with a small sample size, it is a good method to transform the segmentation problem into a voxel-level classification problem. By transforming the image segmentation problem into a classification problem of every voxel point, every voxel point (pixel) can be taken as a training sample to expand the dataset.

Although the above studies generated a large number of training samples by converting the segmentation problem into the voxel-level classification problem, the CNN network they used lacked specific improvements for the voxel-level classification problem. According to the characteristics of voxel-level classification, if a CNN network structure matching the voxel-level classification can be designed, this will make the voxel-level classification method work better. In order to solve the problem of segmentation of lung tumors in CT images, the voxel-level classification method was used to expand the training samples. At the same time, according to the characteristics of the voxel-level classification method, the structure of the CNN network and the selection method of training samples are improved, and a new CNN model and training sample sampling method are proposed.

2.2.1 Segmentation of pulmonary nodules based on the central-focused convolutional neural network

Before deep learning was widely applied in the field of computer vision, TextonForest and a classifier based on random forest were generally used for tumor semantic segmentation. The Texton-based texture analysis method expresses the image as the histogram distribution of the texture image. The Texture dictionary can be a set of filter responses or neighborhood brightness. The Texton classification based on neighborhood brightness includes four parts: Texton dictionary construction, Texton histogram generation, classifier training, and classifier result prediction. The algorithm of image semantic segmentation based on random forest randomly samples a fixed-size window from the training library image as a feature, and compares the pixel values of two pixels randomly selected in the window, and quantizes these features into a numerical vector. The vector set is used to train the random forest classifier. Convolutional neural network (CNN) is not only beneficial to image recognition but also successful in image semantic segmentation. A common semantic segmentation method in deep learning is used to transform image segmentation into pixel classification. For each pixel in the image, we take the image with a fixed neighborhood size around it as the center and classify it. Finally, the label of neighborhood classification is assigned to the label of the central pixel. In other words, the image blocks around the pixel are used to classify each pixel. When the tumor is segmented by voxel-level classification, the target voxel is always located in the center of the neighborhood image. At this time, the importance of images at different spatial positions in the neighborhood image is also different. For example, the image at the center of the neighborhood image is closer to the target voxel and is more important. However, the image at the edge of the neighborhood image is far away from the target voxel and has less useful information. In view of the phenomenon that images in different spatial positions have different importance in the voxel-level classification method, researchers proposed the central-focused convolutional neural network (CF-CNN) to segment lung tumors. For each voxel in the CT image, we extracted a 3D neighborhood image centered on the voxel and a 2D multiscale neighborhood image as the input of the CF-CNN model, and predicted whether the voxel belonged to the tumor or normal tissue.

The CF-CNN model proposed by researchers is a classical segmentation algorithm of pulmonary nodules based on pixel classification [3].

The CF-CNN model uses the 2D and 3D network structure to segment pulmonary nodules. For a voxel in a CT image, the model takes this voxel as the center and extracts the 3D neighborhood and the multiscale 2D neighborhood (patch) as the input of the CNN model. A classification label is utilized to determine whether this is a pulmonary nodule or a normal tissue as the output. The model includes two training network branches with identical image structure but different image scales. Each branch consists of six convolutional layers, two central pooling layers, and a full connected layer. The six convolution layers of the CNN model are divided into three computing units, each of which is composed of two convolution layers with 3×3 convolution kernels. These layers convolve all the input feature graphs and use the activation function parametric rectified linear unit (PReLU) to obtain the corresponding output feature graphs. The structure of the CF-CNN model is shown in Fig. 2.1.

The CF-CNN network includes two branches with the same structure, which, respectively, use 2D and 3D neighborhood images for training. Each branch of CF-CNN includes six convolutional layers, two central pooling layers, and a full connected layer. The six convolution layers in each branch are divided into three convolution blocks, each of which uses the exact same structure, including two convolution layers with a convolution kernel size of 3×3. These layers convolve the input image to learn the mapping from the image to the voxel point category label. In order to speed up the training process, Batch Normalization is carried out after each convolution layer to eliminate the mean and variance drift of its output values. After batch normalization, the PReLU function is used as the activation function for nonlinear transformation. Between each convolution block, a new pooling method called central pooling layer is proposed by researchers to select a more effective subset of features from the convolution layer. After the last convolutional layer, a fully connected layer F7 is used to capture the relationship between the features of the different convolutional layers.

This network consists of six convolution layers (C1−C6), two central pooling layers (central pooling layer 1 and central pooling layer 2), and two full connected layers (Fig. 2.1, F7, F8). The size of the convolution kernel is the filter width × the filter height of the convolution filter (for example, 36@3×3 represents 36 convolution kernels with a size of 3×3). The number below each convolution layer

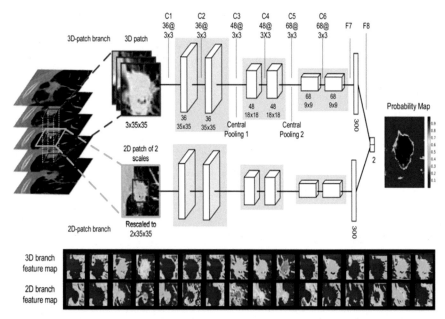

FIGURE 2.1

CF-CNN structure.

represents the size of the convolved feature graph. After the neighborhood images of all voxel points were input into the CNN model, a probability graph of the same size as the input image was obtained, in which the value of each voxel point represented the probability that it belonged to a lung tumor.

The output of the model is the probability graph of the image, in which each value is the probability that the pixel in the corresponding position belongs to the tumor. Each convolutional layer of the input image carries out the operation of $f^j = PReLU\left(\sum_i c^{ij} * f^i + b^j\right)$ in which f^i and f^j represent the feature graph of i_{th} channel and j_{th} channel, respectively. b^j is the offset of the j_{th} channel. To speed up the training process, the model uses batch normalization to normalize the output after each convolution operation. After the convolution layer calculation, the model uses the nonlinear activation function for nonlinear mapping. The nonlinear activation function is a PReLU [4], whose formula is expressed as follows:

$$PReLU\left(f^j\right) = \begin{cases} f^j & \text{if } f^j > 0 \\ a_j f^j & \text{if } f^j \leq 0 \end{cases} \tag{2.1}$$

In this equation, a_j is a training parameter, and j represents the j_{th} feature graph in the convolution layer. In this model, a_j is initialized to 0.25. When the input is a negative number, PReLU contains a nonzero slope parameter a_j, and has been shown to be more effective than the traditional ReLU function. In the middle of each block, a method called central pooling is used to select a subset of features from the convolution layer. After the last convolution layer, a full connected layer is adopted, with each output unit connected to all the input units. The full connected layer can obtain the correlation of different features. To obtain nonlinear transformations, PReLU is used as the activation function after the full connected layer. At the end of the model, the outputs of the two CNN branches are combined by the full connected layer to describe the correlation between the features of the two branches.

CF-CNN uses a two-branch network structure to learn both 3D and 2D information. 3D branching uses a voxel size of $3 \times 35 \times 35$ 3D neighborhoods image as input. Specifically, given a voxel point, we select a $3 \times 35 \times 35$ cuboid centered on the voxel as the 3D neighborhood image of the voxel and input it into the 3D branch. The 3D neighborhood image includes the CT section where the target voxel is located and the upper and lower CT sections of the target voxel. The rectangular region of 35×35 is taken from each section. The images of three CT sections are fed into the 3D branch as three-channel images. Due to the large gray value distribution range of CT images, researchers used the z-score to standardize the three-channel images.

At the same time, researchers designed a 2D branch to focus on learning more fine-grained features from axial images because axial images have a higher resolution in CT images than the other two directions (coronal and sagittal). First, two 2D neighborhood images with dimensions of 65×65 and 35×35 were selected with the target voxel as the center. They are then rescaled to the same size (35×35) using a cubic spline interpolation algorithm to form a two-channel image and feed into a 2D CNN branch. This multiscale neighborhood image strategy can use only one network to learn multiscale features without training multiple individual networks.

In addition, compared with traditional maximum pooling, the model proposes a central pooling layer. Unlike the maximum pooling layer, the central pooling layer uses nonuniform pooling operations. In the central pooling operation, a smaller pooling window is used for the image center, and a larger pooling window is used for the image edge so as to ensure that more information from the center of the image is retained after the pooling operation, while less information from the edge of the second image is retained. In the classification of pixel points, the target pixel is always in the center of the image, while the background pixel is around the image. This nonuniform central pooling operation can ensure that the target pixel of the central point is enlarged while the surrounding redundant information is taken out, so as to prevent the target information from being lost caused by multiple pooling (Fig. 2.2).

The central pooling method contains two parameters: (1) the size of each pooling window; (2) the number of each pooling window. In this study, we used three kinds of maximum pooling Windows (pooling window size s = 1, 2, 3). The number of pooling Windows of each type can be determined by the following rules: (a) similar to the traditional maximum pooling method, we guarantee that the output image after the central pooling operation is half the size of the input image in each

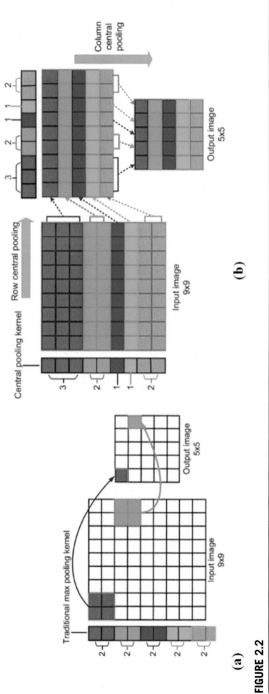

FIGURE 2.2

Schematic diagram of central pooling. (A) Traditional maximum pooling layer; (B) central pooling layer.

direction. (b) In order to avoid image distortion caused by nonuniformly distributed pooling Windows, we keep half of the pooling Windows at the size of 2×2, which is often used in a traditional maximum pooling operation. After determining the number of three kinds of pooling Windows, we make a symmetrical distribution of all pooling Windows. For example, small pooling Windows (s $= 1$) are distributed in the center of the image, while large pooling Windows (s $= 2, 3$) are symmetrically distributed near the edge of the image. Given an input image of size $O\times O$, the following equation can be used to determine the number of three types of pooling Windows $n1$, $n2$, and $n3$. In the process of central pooling, the amount of the pooling window size can be calculated automatically through the following constraint conditions:

$$\begin{cases} n_1 + 2n_2 + 3n_3 = O \\ n_1 + n_2 + n_3 = \dfrac{O}{2} \\ n_1 + 3n_3 = n_2 \end{cases} \quad (2.2)$$

In order to simplify the central pooling operation, the method stipulates that only three types of pooling Windows with sizes of 1×1, 2×2, and 3×3 are used, the number of them is n_1, n_2, and n_3 and O is the image size. After determining the number of pooling Windows of three sizes, the 1×1 pooling window is located in the center of the image, the 2×2 pooling window is located in the middle of the image, and the 3×3 pooling window is placed at the outer edge of the image to complete the central pooling operation. Fig. 2.3 shows the contrast between central pooling and traditional maximum pooling:

When using the CF-CNN model, cuboid ROI is needed to select the region of the lung tumor, and then voxel points are classified in this region to the segment. Because lung tumors are typically distributed on multiple sections, the process of

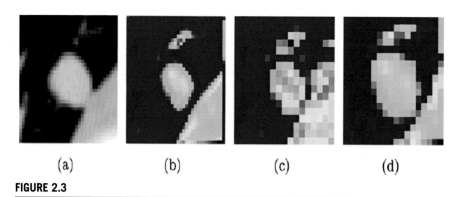

(a)　　　　　　(b)　　　　　　(c)　　　　　　(d)

FIGURE 2.3

Central pooling effect. Note: (A) input image, (B) feature map, (C) traditional maximum pooling, and (D) Central pooling.

delineating rectangular ROI regions on each section is cumbersome. So we simplify user interaction through 3D processing steps. The user only needs to specify a rectangular ROI on a CT section to mark the tumor location. The user-tagged section is defined as the starting section (S1 in Fig. 2.4). Subsequently, user-specified ROI will be applied iteratively to the sections above and below the initial section until at least one of the following two termination conditions is satisfied: (a) CF-CNN does not segment the tumor in this section (Fig. 2.4, Section S6); (b) in this section, the tumor area segmented by CF-CNN was less than 30% of the tumor area in the previous section. For example, Section S3 in Fig. 2.4 was finally removed because, in this section CF-CNN segmented the tumor to contain only four voxels, which was only 10% of the size of the previous section (Section S2). In addition, in order to eliminate noise voxels such as isolated tiny regions (R1, blue region in Section S5) in the 3D segmentation process, we carried out the following connected domain selection operation: (a) when the noise appeared in the initial section, we selected the connected domain closest to the ROI center; (b) when the noise appeared in other sections, we selected the region with the center of mass closest to the center of mass of previous sections. For example, CF-CNN segmented two independent candidate regions R1 and R2 in Section S5. The distance between the centroid of these two regions and the centroid of the tumor in the previous section (S4) is d1 and d2, respectively. Since d2<d1, region R2 is retained and region R1 (noise) is removed.

The ROI of the rectangle is first specified on the initial section and then applied in turn to the CT slice images above and below the initial slice. The number on the right of each section image is the number of voxel points contained in the segmented tumor region. The image in the left column shows the original CT slice, and the image

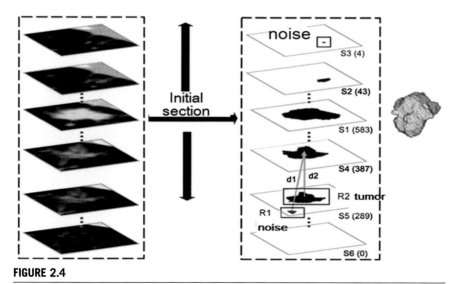

FIGURE 2.4

3D segmentation process.

in the middle column shows the segmentation results of the CF-CNN model, where the red and blue areas represent the tumor and false-positive noise, respectively (false-positive noise marked in blue is eventually removed by the algorithm). The image of the right column is the 3D visualization of the final segmentation result.

When training model, all pixels can be used as training samples. However, some pixels with lower difficulty in segmentation do not need to be selected too much, while pixels with higher difficulty in segmentation, such as those at the edge of nodules, need to be sampled massively to ensure that the model can better classify these pixels with higher difficulty in segmentation. This paper proposes a new weighted sampling method based on the difficulty of pixel segmentation. For all the pixels inside and outside the nodules, the paper proposed the following sample segmentation difficulty calculation formula:

$$PW_i = \frac{\exp(-\min_{j\in N}d(i,j))}{Z} \tag{2.3}$$

$$NW_i = \frac{I_i\exp(-\min_{j\in P}d(i,j))}{Z} \tag{2.4}$$

In this formula, PW and NW, respectively, represent the weight of the representation segmentation difficulty of nodule pixels and background pixels. $D(I, j)$ represents the Euclidean distance between voxel point I and voxel point j. Set N and set P represent the background pixels and node pixels, respectively. Z is a normalized factor, ensuring that the weight sum of all pixel points is 1. After using this new sampling method, the sampling results are shown in Fig. 2.5 below.

Using this method makes the dice of 495 cases of pulmonary nodules (82.15%) in the open dataset LIDC-IDRI, and 74 cases of pulmonary nodules (80.02%) in Guangdong Provincial People's Hospital. The effect of partial segmentation results is shown in Fig. 2.6.

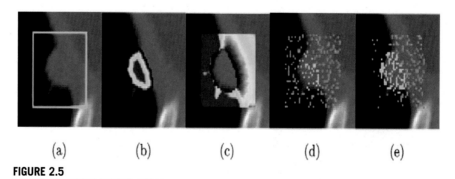

(a)   (b)   (c)   (d)   (e)

FIGURE 2.5

Rendering of the sampling method based on the difficulty of pixel point segmentation. Note: (A) input image, (B) positive sample sampling weight graph, (C) negative sample sampling weight graph, (D) random sampling results, (E) sampling results based on the difficulty of pixel segmentation.

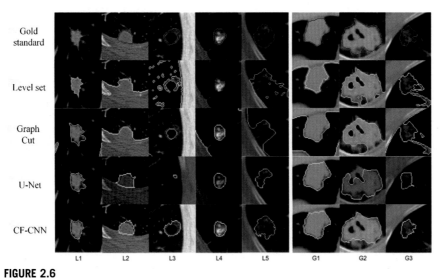

FIGURE 2.6

CF-CNN renderings.

CF-CNN model is superior to the Graph Cut algorithm and level set algorithm in the LIDC dataset. In addition, CF-CNN also achieves the best results when tested on an independent GDGH dataset, and achieves good segmentation for a variety of different types of lung tumors. In order to prove the advantages of the central pooling layer proposed in this paper, researchers compared the CF-CNN and CF-CNN-MP models. Among them, CF-CNN-MP replaces the central pooling layer in CF-CNN with the traditional maximum pooling layer, and other parameters and network structure are consistent with the CF-CNN model. The central pooling layer proposed in this paper improves the average DSC value by about 2% on both datasets. In addition, the combination of 3D and 2D branches also improves model performance. By comparing the 3D branch, 2D branch, and CF-CNN, it can be found that the performance of CF-CNN on both datasets is better than the single 3D branch model or single 2D branch model.

2.2.2 Segmentation of brain tumor based on the convolutional neural network

Brain tumor segmentation is a label-intense task that requires a significant amount of time for manual tumor delineation. Thanks to the successful application of deep learning in image segmentation, researchers proposed a CNN based on pixel classification for automated brain tumor segmentation [5].

This model proposes a two-branch cascade network structure, in which one branch is used to process local information and the other branch is used to process global information. For each pixel, the model extracts small blocks of 33×33 size and extracts local and global information with the following two-branch network. In the fine-grained branch, the 7×7 and 3×3 two-layer convolution layer and the maximum pooling layer are used for local information extraction, while the coarse-grained branch uses the convolution kernel of 13×13 for global information extraction. Finally, the feature graphs of the two branches are spliced together to fuse local and global information. After fusing the feature graph, the network uses the convolution layer of 21×21 to replace the full connected layer, which is used to fit the mapping between features and pixel labels. Meanwhile, the network parameters are reduced to prevent overfitting.

In order to further prevent overfitting, the network uses L1 and L2 regularization, as shown below:

$$loss = -\log p(Y|X) + \lambda_1 |W|_1 + \lambda_2 \|W\|_2 \tag{2.5}$$

Finally, the model obtained the result of dice $= 0.88$ in the brain glue tumor segmentation competition of MICCAI.

2.2.3 Fully convolutional networks

Long et al., from the University of California, Berkeley, proposed a structure named Fully Convolutional Networks (FCNs) in 2004, enabling neural networks to reach dense pixel-level classification without the fully connected layer, thus becoming a very popular CNN structure in pixel-level classification. As the fully connected layer is not required, the image can be semantically segmented much faster than the traditional method, whatever the size. Now, almost all of the advanced methods of semantic segmentation are developed based on this model.

By applying convolution to the input image layer by layer and extracting different features which are operated through the activation function for high-dimensional nonlinear fusion from multiconvolutional kernels, FCNs are capable of recognition of tumor contour so as to complete tumor segmentation. Each convolution layer of FCN uses $f_k = ReLU(W^k * x + b)$ to extract features. W is the learnable convolution kernel, $*$ represents convolution, and b is the bias of the model. The parameters of the convolution kernel W are obtained by automatic training of the network, which makes it possible to extract strong features. ReLU is a piecewise linear activation function. The transformation can perform nonlinear changes on convolution features, enhance the expression ability of features, and play the role of sparse features simultaneously. Finally, the features f_k are extracted from the convolutional layer.

Max-pooling layers are performed after convolutional layers in this research to promote robustness with reduced parameters of the model. After the last layer of pooling, FCN restored the segmented image to the original resolution by means of upper sampling and convolution layer stacking, so as to improve the accuracy in segmentation.

The pooling layer is another critical point in CNN semantic segmentation in addition to fully connected layers. The pooling layer is competent to enlarge the receptive field and discard the information where to aggregate the context information. However, semantic segmentation requires exact alignment of the classifying diagrams, thus reserving position information. Two different classification architectures are described below for this problem.

One is the encoder–decoder architecture. The encoder gradually reduces the spatial dimension through the pooling layer, while the decoder gradually recovers the details and spatial dimension of the object. There are usually shortcut connections between the encoder and decoder, which can better recover the details of the object. U-net is one of the most popular models in this kind of architecture.

Another type is to use the dilated/atrous convolutions [6] structure to replace the pooling layer.

Pooling can increase the receptive field and improve the performance of the classification network model. However, it is not the best semantic segmentation method as it reduces the resolution as well. Dilated convolution model uses dilated convolution as the convolution layer to achieve pixel-level prediction. Dilated convolution is able to increase the receptive field exponentially without reducing the spatial dimension.

2.2.4 Voxel segmentation algorithm based on MV-CNN

According to the characteristics of tumor CT image segmentation and voxel classification, researchers proposed the multiview convolutional neural networks (MV-CNN) model, which utilizes multiview CT images and multiscale strategy to segment lung tumors. For each voxel of CT images, we extract the multiscale neighborhood image from three orthogonal perspectives of the image as input of the MV-CNN model, then predict whether the voxel belongs to the tumor or normal background tissue.

Compared with the existing lung tumor segmentation methods, this model harbors the following advantages: (1) No needs to introduce any shape assumption or complicated parameter settings by users, which is easier to apply and is more robust; (2) In each perspective of the CT image, using a multiscale input image not only is the detailed texture information provided by the small-scale image but also the global shape information from large-scale image can be considered; and (3) Using three network branches to learn the information from three perspectives of the CT image, it's feasible to observe the tumor from three orthogonal perspectives at the same time, which is more conducive to segmentation of tumors with adhesion to surrounding tissues. In addition, as data-driven and automatic learning to distinguish the features of lung tumor voxels and background voxels, the extracted features from this model fit lung tumor segmentation better than the artificially defined features.

For each voxel in the CT image, researchers extract a multiscale 2D neighborhood image centered on it from three orthogonal image directions (axial, coronal, sagittal) as the input of three branches of MV-CNN, thus predicting whether the voxel belongs to the tumor or normal tissue.

The three branches of the MV-CNN model process CT images from axial, coronal, and sagittal positions, respectively. The three branches own the same structure and are composed of six convolutional layers (C1 to C6), two max-pooling layers (max-pooling 1 and 2), and a fully connected layer (F7). Six convolutional layers of each branch are divided into three blocks, each block containing two 2D convolutional layers with a convolutional kernel size of 3×3. The convolutional layers perform convolution on the input to learn the mapping between the images and the voxel category labels. The operation process of the convolution layer is as follows:

$$f^j = \sum_i c^{ij} * f^i + b^j \tag{2.6}$$

where f^i and f^j represent the i and j feature maps, respectively; c^{ij} represents the convolution kernel between f^i and f^j (* is a 2D convolution); b^j is the bias of the convolution kernel c^{ij}. Feature maps refer to the output or input image of the convolution layers in CNN. Between each block, a max-pooling layer with the window of 2×2 and step of 2 is applied to reduce the dimensions of the feature image after convolution. After the last convolution layer, there is a fully connected layer F7, in which each neuron remains connected to all input neurons. The fully connected layer is capable of capturing the correlations between different features from convolution layers. In aims to realize the nonlinear transformation, the PReLU is applied as the nonlinear activation function after the fully connected layer F7 and each convolution layer. It is defined as follows:

$$PReLU(f^j) = \begin{cases} f^j & \text{if } f^j > 0 \\ a_j f^j & \text{if } f^j \leq 0 \end{cases} \tag{2.7}$$

In this equation, a_j is a trainable parameter, and j represents the $j\text{-}_{th}$ characteristic graphs in the convolution layers. For this experiment, it is initialized to 0.25. When the input is less than 0, the output of the PReLU function is controlled by parameter a_j. This way of introducing a nonzero slope to the negative input is proved to be more effective than the traditional ReLU function in the classification tasks of ImageNet datasets.

Previous research revealed that multiscale features can boost the classification performance of CNN. Therefore, the input of each CNN branch of MV-CNN is a two-channel multiscale neighborhood image. Here we use the multiscale input image to extract multiscale features, instead of building two CNN models to process two scale images, which can reduce the computation and network parameters. During the selection of multiscale neighborhood images, we set the target voxel as the center, and chose two rectangular images with a size of 65×65 and 45×45, respectively. Then, the cubic spline interpolation algorithm is applied to scale the two-scale images to 45×45, thus constituting the CNN branch corresponding to the two-channel image input. As the gray value distribution range of CT image varies, Z-score is applied to standardize the neighborhood images, and the calculation formula is as follows:

$$f(x) = \frac{(x - x_{mean})}{x_{std}} \tag{2.8}$$

where x_{mean} and x_{std} represent the mean and standard deviation of neighborhood images, respectively. The multiscale strategy of MV-CNN on the input enables the model to learn multiscale features, while the CNN branches of three perspectives enable the model to learn 3D information of the tumor, which plays an important role in segmenting the tumor from adhesion to surrounding tissues. For example, it is difficult to recognize whether some voxels are tumor tissues only by axial images, but by coronal and sagittal images. At the end of the CNN model, the features extracted by these three branches are fused by the fully connected layer F8, hence predicting the class labels of the input voxel with two neurons in the output layer. The output layer of MV-CNN consists of two neurons whose output is transformed into the probability distribution of the two kinds of labels in the input image by the binary softmax function. Assuming that o_k is the output of the k_{th} neuron in the output layer, the probability that the input image belongs to the k_{th} category is calculated by the softmax function:

$$p_k = \frac{\exp(o_k)}{\sum_{h \subseteq \{0,1\}} \exp(o_h)} \tag{2.9}$$

where $k = 0$ and $k = 1$ represent background voxels and lung tumor voxels, respectively.

After the MV-CNN network is constructed, it can be trained through the training set data to get good prediction performance. The goal training is to maximize the probability of correct classification, which can be achieved by minimizing the cross-entropy loss function of each training sample. Assuming that y_n represents the real label (with a value of 0 or 1) of the n_{th} input image, the cross-entropy loss function is defined as follows:

$$L(W) = -\frac{1}{N} \sum_{n=1}^{N} \left[y_n log\widehat{y}_n + (1 - y_n) log\left(1 - \widehat{y}_n\right) \right] + \lambda |W| \tag{2.10}$$

where $\widehat{y}_n$ is the predicting probability of MV-CNN and N is the number of samples. To avoid overfitting, we apply L1 norm to regularize the model parameter W. The intensity of regularization is controlled by λ, which is set to 5×10^{-4}. In the process of training, by calculating the gradient of loss function L on network parameter W, the loss function can be minimized gradually to promote performance. During the process, the model parameter W is initialized by the Xavier algorithm and updated by the SGD algorithm, as shown in the following formula:

$$W_{t+1} = W_t + V_{t+1} \tag{2.11}$$

$$V_{t+1} = \mu V_t - \alpha \nabla L(W_t) \qquad (2.12)$$

where T represents the number of iterations of training, and V represents the updated amount of network parameters in each iteration, with an initial value of 0. When calculating the gradient $\nabla L(W)$, as it is difficult to store tens of thousands of training samples in memory simultaneously, this study applied 128 samples (batch size) for the batch operation. μ is the learning momentum of the SGD algorithm, set to 0.9, and α is the learning rate. The initial learning rate is set as $\alpha_0 = 6 \times 10^{-5}$ at the beginning of training, which speeds up the learning process of the network and makes the network parameters approach the optimal solution quickly. After every four epochs of the training process, the learning rate is reduced by 10 times, since it needs the lower learning rate to find a more precise optimal solution to help the network converge when near the optimal solution. If the learning rate keeps getting larger, it may cause network learning process concussion leading to nonconvergence.

As MV-CNN automatically learns CNN-based features from images in a data-driven way, many neighborhood images are needed as training samples for model training. In the chest CT image, the tumor area only accounts for a very small part of the whole lung tissue, and the number of voxels in the tumor area accounts for less than 5% of the total in a CT section. Therefore, choosing voxes randomly in the whole CT image of the lung as training samples will produce a large number of voxels (negative samples) from the background tissue, resulting in the imbalance of positive and negative samples.

To solve this problem, researchers first determined the external rectangular ROI of each lung tumor in the training set when generating training samples, and expanded the ROI on each axis by eight voxels to get an extended ROI. Then, voxels are selected as training samples in the way of even sampling at intervals in the extended ROI, which accounts for one voxel being selected as training samples after skipping one voxel in the row and column directions. Hence, a quarter of the voxels in the ROI are selected as training samples during this process. Because the number of positive and negative samples in the training samples is prone to be inconsistent, in order to avoid the influence of unbalanced data distribution, we guarantee the same number of training samples in the two categories by random sampling.

Finally, about 340,000 training samples were selected. For each voxel as a training sample, multiscale neighborhood images that are centered are extracted in axial, coronal, and sagittal positions, respectively, to train the MV-CNN network.

At the end of each training stage, the MV-CNN model was tested on the verification set and evaluated by DSC. After 20 epochs of training, DSC on the verification set becomes stable. Therefore, the model stops training after 20 epochs of training. Finally, the performance of the model is evaluated on the independent test set.

To compare the segmentation performance of the MV-CNN model, two widely used methods, including the level set method based on the active contour and graph cut algorithm, are implemented. The level set method and graph cut algorithm are implemented by Fiji software, and the parameters are optimized by the grid search. In the level set method, the first step is to apply fast marching to generate the initial lung tumor contour. Then, the active contour model is used to refine the segmentation results delicately, and parameters are set as the gray threshold value is 50, the distance threshold value is 0.1 when fast matching, while the advection value of the active contour model is set to 2.20, the curvature is set to 1.00, the grayscale tolerance is set to 30.00, and the convergence value is set to 0.005. Fiji software involves two parameters in the graph cutting method which are set as follows: Data prior (foreground offset) is 0.86, and edge weight (smoothness) is 0.56. MV-CNN, level set, and graph cut algorithm are all segmented and tested on 2D CT slices during the test.

The quantitative results of MV-CNN and various other methods on the test set all have good performance as it's easy to implement the segmentation relatively on isolated solid tumors (L1). However, when there is adhesion between the lung tumor and surrounding tissue, the segmentation performance of the level set method and graph cut algorithm decreased, revealing the two algorithms are incompetent in separating the lung tumor and surrounding tissue. For example, when there is adhesion between the lung tumor and lung wall (L2), the level set method and graph cut algorithm are prone to mistaking the lung wall for a lung tumor. When there is adhesion between the lung tumor and blood vessel (L3), the level set method and graph cut algorithm are also prone to dividing the blood vessel into the tumor. In contrast, the MV-CNN algorithm still maintains strong robustness in the segmentation of this kind of tumor, which shows that the MV-CNN has learned the critical features that are able to distinguish the lung tumor and adherent tissue. For the lung tumor with an internal cavity (L4), both the level set method and the graph cut algorithm mistakenly identity the cavity regions as background; however, MV-CNN correctly retains the cavity region. For lung tumors with internal calcification (L5), the level set method only segmented the calcified area, but mistakenly considered the noncalcified area as the background because of the large gray variance between calcified and noncalcified tissues. For a GGO lung tumor (L6), the tumor presented as a nonsolid state, with low contrast with the background. The level set method and graph cut algorithm tend to oversegment in this situation, prone to segmenting the nonsolid GGO tumor into many small regions, while MV-CNN maintains strong robustness.

2.3 Feature extraction

Feature extraction is a vital step in radiomics that captures the quantitative characteristics of the tumor. Therefore, there are numerous methods available for extracting rich tumor information with clinical value from medical imaging. Generally, the radiomics features can be divided into the features of the artificial design and the features of deep learning.

2.3.1 The features of artificial design

The features of artificial design are basically classical algorithms that describe image information. These features include low-level visual features and high-dimensional nonlinear features, which can reflect tumor information from multiple scales. The features of artificial design can be roughly divided into (1) intensity features; (2) shape features; (3) texture features; and (4) wavelet features, as shown in Fig. 2.7.

1. **Intensity Features**

    The intensity features are obtained by counting the gray value of the tumor image, generally including the first-order gray-scale statistics such as mean value, maximum and minimum value, kurtosis, skewness, entropy, etc. The intensity features reflect the contrast variance between the tumor and the surrounding tissue, and the heterogeneity of the internal tissue of the tumor.

2. **Shape Features**

    Shape features are generally applied to measure the shape, size, regularity, and other information of tumors. For example, the longest and shortest diameters and volume of tumor reflect the size information of the tumor. The ellipsoid degree of tumor reflects the shape information of the tumor, which contributes to quantifying whether the tumor tends to be spherical or

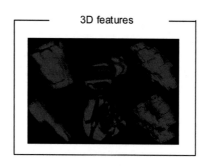

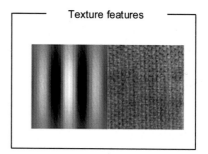

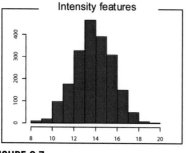

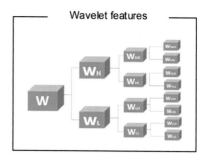

FIGURE 2.7

Schematic diagram of manually defined features.

ellipsoid. The compactness of the tumor reflects whether the shape of the tumor has a regular edge, and other shape information.

3. Texture Features

Texture features are different from shape and intensity features. Intensity and shape features reflect low-dimensional visual information, such as brightness, shape, uniformity, edge, and other image features that are easy to see. Texture features are used to quantify the texture pattern or tissue distribution inside the tumor and other information difficult to be perceived by vision. Texture features can be obtained by a variety of texture calculation matrices, such as gray-level run length matrix, which can be used to quantify gray-level run information in an image. The number of pixels with the same gray value in a certain direction is defined as a gray run. This means, in the gray run matrix $M(i,j|\theta)$, the times the element at position (i,j) repeats in the θ direction.

Gabor texture features are widely used to extract texture information of fixed patterns in some directions. Gabor filter, also known as Dennis Gabor, is a linear filter for edge detection. Gabor filter is capable of extracting multifrequency edge information in different directions. Since it contains different frequency edge information, Gabor texture shows excellent performance in most situations.

4. Wavelet Features

The features of intensity, shape, and texture reflect the low-order visual information and high-dimensional texture information of the tumor, but the amount of information is limited. In order to extract tumor information in different frequency domains [7], wavelet transform is applied to decompose tumor images into different frequency domains and then extract tumor shape, intensity, texture, and other information. Wavelet transform is capable of decomposing the tumor image into four different frequency domain images: horizontal, vertical, diagonal, and low frequency. Wavelet features reflect the multiband and multiscale information of the tumor because of the different frequency domain images generated by wavelet decomposition. In many studies, the relationship between tumor images and clinical labels is difficult to be described by simple visual features. In this situation, wavelet features, a high-dimensional abstract feature, function in capturing features that are difficult to be perceived by vision, but contain clinical information.

5. Semantic features

Semantic features could be defined as the qualitatively described empirical features proposed by radiologists. These features are beneficial for clinical settings of radiomics analysis, which cannot be related to an efficient mathematical expression directly.

2.3.2 Deep learning features

The features of artificial design have a clear calculation formula and strong interpretability but are difficult to design and lack the adaptability of different investigations. For example, the features of artificial design need the definition formula to design new features, which leads to inflexibility, dependence of expert knowledge, and weak scalability. In addition, for different clinical research, it is difficult to take different clinical labels into account. In the design of artificially designed features, research generally focuses on depicting tumor information from multiple perspectives, but designing features consistent with clinical labels or designing different features for different topics are unfeasible sometimes.

In contrast, deep learning is competent to learn features automatically from data by virtue of its powerful feature self-learning ability, rather than relying on manual feature design. Deep learning represents a class of algorithms that use the stacked neural network structure. The deep learning feature extraction commonly includes two ways: (1) training CNN model, regarding the output of its fully connected layer as a deep learning feature; (2) training self-encoder with unlabeled data, regarding the output of the encoder as a deep learning feature. When there is label data to train the supervised learning model, researchers usually train a small CNN, applying the first method to extract the deep learning feature and collect the output of its fully connected layer as the deep learning feature. In the previous study [8], researchers constructed a three-layer CNN to predict EGFR gene mutations in lung cancer. After the CNN is trained, the author extracted 30 dimensional deep learning features of the fully connected layer and trained the SVM classifier separately. In the test set, the deep learning feature reached 0.668 area under curve (AUC). When the set of labeled data is extremely small to train the supervised CNN, the self-encoders help to learn the features of deep learning automatically by unsupervised learning. In the previous study [9], a typical model of self-encoders is constructed to extract deep learning features.

The self-encoder training only needs the tumor image instead of the clinical labels of the tumor. Unlike supervised learning, self-encoders implement the encoder network to extract deep learning features; then, the decoder network is used to reconstruct tumor images from deep learning features for testing the amount of information in deep learning features. When the deep learning features reconstruct the original input images, the deep learning features contain most of the tumor image information already, therefore the deep learning features function for the construction of the model in clinical prediction.

Compared with the features of artificial design, deep learning features are acquired from data by supervised or unsupervised learning. Therefore, these features are naturally related to the clinical labels or tumor images, which is better than the artificially defined features. In addition, deep learning features do not need to define the calculation formula of features manually. Therefore, some features are difficult to be formulated but are meaningful, and they can be obtained automatically through the self-learning ability of the deep learning network. On the other hand, the design of the deep learning network structure is flexible. Only changing the network structure or training mode will realize different deep learning features.

2.4 **Feature selection and dimension reduction**

In order to describe the data more comprehensively, a large number of features will be generated from many aspects. However, too many features are not necessarily conducive to the analysis of the results. On the one hand, a large number of features need sufficient data to support training a robust and effective model; otherwise, the calculation of high complexity will lead to dimensional disaster. On the other hand, there will be interfered, redundant, and irrelevant features. Through feature selection and dimension reduction, we will reduce overfitting, promote the accuracy of the model, and reduce the training time of the model. In this section, we will introduce some widely used feature selection or dimension reduction methods in radiomics, and analyze their application scenarios.

2.4.1 **Classical linear dimension reduction**

Among machine learning algorithms, there are many basic linear dimension reduction methods including PCA, ICA, linear discriminant analysis (LDA), LFA, and LPP, but most of them are based on the projection of data, which makes data from the dimension reduction difficult to interpret. Now there are two widely used dimension reduction methods, PCA and LDA, which will be introduced in this section.

1. Principal Component Analysis
   PCA [10] is the most widely used linear dimension reduction method in machine learning with the main conception of the least square method, which is equivalent to the method of keeping the error of the least square method in high-dimensional space. The goal of PCA is to reduce dimensions with minimal loss. For example, it is equivalent to compressing points of a plane into a line. In order to minimize the loss, a line with the minimum distance from all points is the ideal model. This line is the result of compression, and the distance of each point is the error. This is shown in the Fig. 2.8.
2. Linear Discriminant Analysis
   LDA, also known as Fisher linear discriminant, is a common way of dimension reduction in machine learning. Unlike PCA, it needs to enter known labels, which means it needs supervised conditions. The concept is to find a low-dimensional space in a high-dimensional space, which can make the mean (center points) distance of two or more types of data be the farthest and the intraclasses variance of each type to be as small as possible. As shown in the figure Fig. 2.9, μ represents the center of the data classes, while the size of the red and blue circles represents the size of variance. It can be seen that by projecting the data onto the diagonal on the left, the centers of red and blue datasets can be separated.

2.4.2 **Dimension reduction method based on feature selection**

There are classical feature dimension reduction methods of machine learning such as PCA and LDA, with projecting the original data and losing some data, which outputs

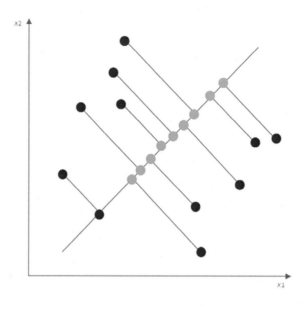

FIGURE 2.8

PCA diagram. Note: The *red dots* show the original data, and the *green dots* are the corresponding data after dimension reduction.

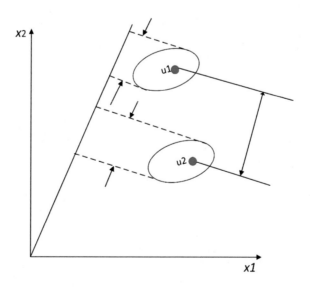

FIGURE 2.9

LDA diagram. Note: Red and blue represent the distribution of the original two datasets, μ represents the center of the data class, and the left slash is the projection target.

features with noninterpretability and weak correspondence to the ones before dimension reduction. Therefore, these algorithms have to be bound with the classification models, hence limiting applications in radiomics. We will introduce the method of dimension reduction through the selection of original features, and evaluate the importance of each original feature in this section.

1. Feature Analysis Based On a Statistical Test

In common cases, evaluating each feature information by simple statistical or test methods is helpful, so as to obtain a certain understanding of each feature. For example, in the classification cases what we are most concerned about is which features are most effectively helpful to separate the two categories. In the regression cases, what we will be concerned about is which features are most relevant. Proper features selection for specific cases promotes the performance and helps to analyze better.

For the regression cases (the target is a continuous value), correlation analysis, ANOVA, linear regression, and other methods help to evaluate the features and target value. Pearson correlation coefficient, the covariance of two sets divided by the standard deviation of two sets, is commonly applied in a correlation analysis. The absolute value of the correlation coefficient also expresses the correlation degree between the two features.

$$r = \frac{N \sum x_i y_i - \sum x_i \sum y_i}{\sqrt{N \sum x_i^2 - (\sum x_i)^2} \sqrt{N \sum y_i^2 - (\sum y_i)^2}} \qquad (2.13)$$

where r is the correlation coefficient, x_i represents the i_{th} sample of dataset X, and N is the number of samples. Linear regression is similar to a variance analysis to measure the effectiveness of the features by the error of linear fitting between the features and the target values.

For classification problems, LDA can be used, or t-test or chi-square test can be used to determine whether a significant difference exists between the two categories of data. The idea of LDA is similar to LDA, but without practical projection. The mean and variance of each category is a calculated analysis through the labels of different categories in a LDA. The degree of feature separation is evaluated by the variance of all kinds of means. T-test and chi-square test are used to test the degree of feature separation of the two categories.

$$t = \frac{\overline{X_1} - \overline{X_2}}{\sqrt{\frac{(n_1 - 1)S_1^2 + (n_2 - 1)S_2^2}{n_1 + n_2 - 2} \left(\frac{1}{n_1} + \frac{1}{n_2} \right)}} \qquad (2.14)$$

The formula above shows the t-test formula, where $\overline{X_1} - \overline{X_2}$ represents the difference between the mean values, n represents the number of samples, and s represents the standard deviation.

2.4.3 Feature selection based on the linear model and regularization

It is also mentioned above that the coefficient of the equation obtained by linear regression or classifier can judge the validity of the feature. The feature with too small of a coefficient has little effect on the overall equation. Removing such features can improve the robustness of the model and reduce the complexity of the model. However, this screening modus also requires some standards and methods. In this section, we introduce the linear model dimensional reduction through two regularization methods. Assume that the linear regression of normal use is as follows:

$$y = a_0 + \sum a_i x_i \tag{2.15}$$

In the above formula, y is the target value, a_i is the coefficient of the equation, and x_i is the i-th feature. The commonly used linear regression or classification models use the least squares rule for iterative convergence. The objective function of each iteration is as follows:

$$J = \left(y - \left(a_0 + \sum_{i=1}^{n} a_i x_i \right) \right)^2 \tag{2.16}$$

where J is the objective function, n is the number of features, y is the true value of the target, $(a_0 + \sum a_i x_i)$ represents the value obtained by the regression equation, and J is equivalent to the mean square error of the equation.

1. L1 norm regularization (LASSO)

   LASSO (least absolute shrinkage and selection operator) [11] method is an efficient feature selection algorithm, which is based on compression estimation. The LASSO method compresses some coefficients and sets some coefficients to zero by building a penalty function to get a more refined model. The LASSO method minimizes the sum of squares of residuals under the constraint, and the sum of the absolute values of the regression coefficients is less than a constant. Therefore, regression coefficients strictly equal to 0 is able to be generated, and an interpretable model can be obtained.

   LASSO regression is sometimes called L1 regularization of linear regression, that is, by adding the L1 norm in the objective function of a linear regression, which is the sum of the absolute values of the coefficients of the original equation.

$$J = \left(y - \left(a_0 + \sum_{i=1}^{n} a_i x_i \right) \right)^2 + \lambda \sum_{i=1}^{n} |a_i| \tag{2.17}$$

$\lambda \sum_{i=1}^{n} |x_i|$ added in the equation is the L1 norm, and λ is a parameter used to adjust the proportion of the L1 norm. Due to the existence of the regular term, the constraint that minimizes $\sum_{i=1}^{n} |a_i|$ is also added, so that some a_i are reduced to 0, and finally, the purpose of dimension reduction is achieved.

As shown in Fig. 2.10, when the LASSO program is called on in general, the corresponding effect is tested according to different λ(Lambda), and the penalty coefficient that can effectively classify and effectively cancel the coefficient is selected.

2. L2 norm regularization (ridge regression)

Ridge regression is similar to LASSO except that the L1 norm is replaced by the L2 norm, which is the sum of the squares of the coefficients. Since the L2 norm is a square term, the curve is smoother than L1, and there is no LASSO strict coefficient compression. The obtained coefficients are closer to zero but not zero, and the amount of information stored is greater.

$$J = \left(y - \left(a_0 + \sum_{i=1}^{n} a_i x_i \right) \right)^2 + \lambda \sum_{i=1}^{n} |a_i|^2 \qquad (2.18)$$

Fig. 2.11 is a graphical diagram of the L1 and L2 norms. It can be seen that L2 is much smoother than L1, which leads to more points to select when returning. The shape of the L1 norm is similar to a diamond, and the regression is more likely to approach the position of the four corners farthest from the center resulting in more characteristic coefficients being reduced to zero. So, L1 will be more effective than L2 for effect, while L2 will retain more detail.

3. Elastic net

Elastic net regression analysis is an extension of LASSO regression analysis. Elastic net was proposed by Hui Zou in 2005. It overcomes the shortcomings of LASSO and ridge regression. The degree of compression coefficient is between LASSO and ridge regression. Although LASSO regression analysis can solve the feature selection problem when the feature number is much larger than the sample number, LASSO randomly selects one of the features and sets the others to zero when the correlation between multiple features is strong. In medical image processing, there is a strong correlation between the extracted features. In some case, LASSO regression analysis will eliminate much useful feature information, which is not conducive to the later construction of clinical auxiliary diagnostic models. Compared with the LASSO regression analysis, the L2 norm is the penalty term, which makes the coefficients between related features closer to each other and is not compressed to 0. But ridge regression analysis cannot select the feature effectively. In the elastic net regression analysis, the penalty term is a linear combination of the LASSO penalty term and the ridge penalty term, so that the elastic net regression analysis can solve the feature selection problem with strong correlation between features.

The shape of the elastic net constraint domain is between a square and a circle. It is characterized by the trade-off between arbitrarily selecting an independent

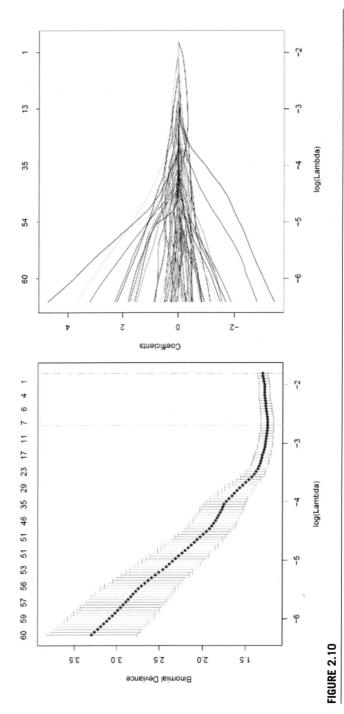

FIGURE 2.10

Recursive schematic of LASSO penalty factor coefficient [12]. Note: The left side is the change of the residual term with Lambda change, and the right picture shows the change of the coefficient.

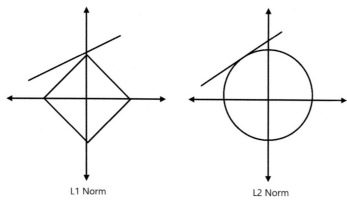

L1 Norm   L2 Norm

FIGURE 2.11

Norm diagram. Note: The left picture is the L1 norm, and the right picture is the L2 norm.

variable or a set of independent variables. It shows the advantages of LASSO and ridge regression, and can realize variable selection. It can avoid the influence of a strong correlation between independent variables.

LASSO, ridge, and elastic net is implemented in Matlab 2016a (MathWorks, Natick, MA, USA) via the Glmnet toolkit.

4. Feature selection using a tree model and min-redundancy and max-relevance

The decision tree model and the min-redundancy and max-relevance (mRMR) method are different from the linear analysis. The feature selection is based on the change of the degree of chaos in the system. The existing features are sorted by the entropy information nonpurity evaluation index, and finally the characteristics of the model penetration are selected.

(1) Tree model

The tree model currently includes decision trees, random forests, gradient trees, etc. The evaluation indicators also include Gini factors, entropy gains, residuals, etc., but the basic idea is to expand the direction of the model improvement, and gradually make the model more refined and effective. This section mainly introduces common criteria information gain and information gain ratio.

Entropy is a measure of disorder. In information theory and statistics, entropy represents the measure of the uncertainty of a random variable. Suppose X is a discrete random variable with a finite value, its probability distribution is as follows:

$$P(X = x_i) = p_i, i = 1, 2, ..., n \tag{2.19}$$

Then, the entropy of the random variable X is defined as follows:

$$H(X) = -\sum_{i=1}^{n} p_i \log p_i \tag{2.20}$$

Among them, it can be seen from the above formula that entropy only depends on the distribution of X, and has nothing to do with the value of X. The greater the entropy, the greater the uncertainty of the random variable. With a random variable (X, Y), its joint probability distribution is as follows:

$$P(X = x_i, Y = y_j) = p_{ij}, i = 1, 2, ..., n; j = 1, 2, ..., m \qquad (2.21)$$

The conditional entropy $H(Y|X)$ represents the uncertainty of the random variable Y under the condition that the random variable X is known.

$$H(Y|X) = \sum_{i=1}^{n} p_i H(Y|X = x_i) \qquad (2.22)$$

The information gain is the importance of feature X, in which the information uncertainty of class Y is decreased. The information gain $g(D, A)$ of A to the training data D is defined as the inconsistence between the empirical entropy $H(D)$ of data D and the empirical conditional entropy $H(D|A)$ of D under the given condition A:

$$g(D, A) = H(D) - H(D|A) \qquad (2.23)$$

Features with large information gains have stronger classification capabilities. For the training dataset D, calculating the information gain of each feature, comparing their sizes, sorting all the features, and selecting the top features.

When selecting features by information gain, it is preferred to select features with more values. Using an information gain ratio to correct this problem, the information gain ratio $g_R(D, A)$ of feature A to the training dataset D is defined as the ratio of the information gain $g(D, A)$ to the entropy $H_A(D)$ of the training dataset D with respect to the value of feature A:

$$g_R(D, A) - \frac{g(D, A)}{H_A(D)}, \ H_A(D) = -\sum_{l=1}^{n} \frac{|D_i|}{|D|} \log_2 \frac{|D_i|}{|D|} \qquad (2.24)$$

As shown in Fig. 2.12, the higher the general entropy gain, the higher the point splitting number and the splitting depth, which indicates the degree of improvement of the classification effect after obtaining the information.

(2) mRMR, min-redundancy and max-relevance

The min-redundancy and max-relevance method is a filtering feature selection method. A common feature screening method is utilized to maximize the relevance between features and labels. That is, to select the top k variables with the highest relevance of the categorical variables. However, in feature selection, the integration of a single great feature depends on the high relevance of features, which may cause redundancy of the feature variables. So eventually, mRMR is employed to maximize the correlation between features and labels, and minimize the correlation between features and other features.

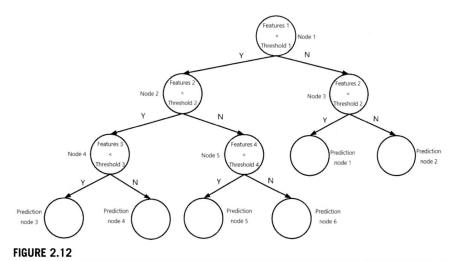

FIGURE 2.12

Schematic diagram of the tree model.

The common measurement method in the mRMR method is mutual information:

$$I(\mathrm{x},\mathrm{y}) = \int\int p(x,y)\log\frac{p(x,y)}{p(x)p(y)}dxdy \qquad (2.25)$$

This can be seen as a knowing y, and x is the loss in entropy, and p is the probability of events:

$$I(\mathrm{x},\mathrm{y}) = H(\mathrm{X}) - H(\mathrm{X}|\mathrm{Y}) \qquad (2.26)$$

Then, the maximum correlation can be defined as follows:

$$\max D(S,c), D = \frac{1}{|S|}\sum_{x_i \varepsilon S} \mathrm{I}(x_i; c) \qquad (2.27)$$

where x_i is the i-th feature, c is the categorical variable, and S is the feature subset. Min-redundancy is as follows:

$$\max R(S), R = \frac{1}{|S|^2}\sum_{x_i, x_j \varepsilon S} I(x_i; x_j) \qquad (2.28)$$

When using mRMR, D and R are generally combined by addition, subtraction, or multiplication and division into an equation as an objective function to optimize and obtain valid feature ordering.

5. Recursive feature elimination, RFE

The main idea of recursive feature elimination is to repeatedly build models (such as LR, SVM of linear models, random forests of tree models, gradient trees, etc.) to evaluate the features that have the worst (or best) performance improvement effect on the model. The resulting feature takes the dataset and repeats the process on the remaining features until all features are taken out. The order in which features are eliminated in this process is the ordering of features. Therefore, this is a greedy algorithm for finding the optimal subset of features. The specific algorithm is as follows:

(1) Input the feature vector and target value.

(2) Use the selected classifier to rank the states in which each feature is eliminated.

(3) Take the feature with the lowest score.

(4) Repeat steps 2 and 3 until the features are removed.

(5) Determine the importance of a feature in the order in which it is taken out, the more backward the more important.

The stability of the RFE depends to a large extent on which model is used at the bottom of the iteration, since it evaluates the features, especially the models used. It inherits the characteristics of the model selection features. For example, the regression coefficient of a linear model requires a penalty term or a different loss function to maintain the stability of the model, while the tree model needs to select a corresponding function for evaluation, etc.

2.5 Model building

After the completed feature selection and dimensionality reduction, a radiomics model needs to be established to describe the correlation between the feature and the predicted tag. This section focuses on the models commonly used in radiomics and the application of models.

The models commonly used in radiomics include basic linear classification models, tree models, linear regression models, and deep learning models developed in recent years. Next, each type of model will be introduced.

2.5.1 Linear regression model

Linear regression models are generally used to fit a regression curve. Unlike a classifier, the objective function of a regression model can be a continuous value, not necessarily a categorical variable. Therefore, linear regression models are often applied to the prediction of continuous values, such as survival, risk index, etc.

1. Linear regression

Linear regression is the most common regression model. Its formula is very simple. The relationship between each feature and the target value is obtained by multiple features. Finally, the offset is added.

$$y = a_0 + \sum a_i x_i \qquad (2.29)$$

where y is the target value, x_i is the ith feature, a_0 is the offset, and a_i is the coefficient of x_i. There are usually two ways to solve linear regression, least squares fitting or iterative function−based iteration. The least squares method refers to finding a set of parameters to minimize the square of the difference between the target value and the regression value. When it is iterated as the objective function, the function is as follows:

$$J = \left(y - \left(a_0 + \sum_{i=1}^{n} a_i x_i \right) \right)^2 \tag{2.30}$$

J is the objective function, n is the number of features, y is the target real value, and $(a_0 + \sum a_i x_i)$ represents the value obtained by the regression equation.

2. Proportional hazards model (Cox)

Cox regression analysis is a semiparametric analysis method for survival analysis. It proposes a concept of a proportional hazard model, which can effectively deal with the problem of multiple factors affecting survival time. The advantage is that it can ignore the distribution of survival time and effectively use censored data. Its formula is as follows:

$$h(t) = h_0(t)e^{\sum a_i x_i} \# \tag{2.31}$$

where a_i is the regression coefficient and $h(t)$ is the risk rate, which represents the instantaneous mortality of the patient who survived at time t and after time t. $h_0(t)$ indicates the risk rate when x_i is all zeroes. Due to the existence of the hidden variable $h_0(t)$, the formula is difficult to calculate. Therefore, when calculating the objective function of the **Cox** function, you need to go through the $h_0(t)$ term.

The objective function takes into account the ratio of the risk of a certain characteristic population at t time to the death risk of all people at time t, obtained by the maximum likelihood formula:

$$J = \prod_{j=1}^{n} \left[\frac{e^{\sum a_i x_{i,j}}}{\sum_{k \in R(t_j)} e^{\sum a_i x_{i,k}}} \right]^{\delta_j} \tag{2.32}$$

where t_j represents the jth time, $x_{i,j}$ represents the jth x_i, and δ_j is whether the data are censored, that is, whether the follow-up is interrupted. By this formula, a_i can be estimated without knowing $h_0(t)$.

The Cox regression application mainly analyzes various factors in the aspect of survival analysis. The regression coefficient a_i indicates the degree of danger of the factor, $a_i > 0$ indicates that the covariate is a risk factor, and the larger it is, the shorter the survival time, and $a_i < 0$ indicates that the covariate is a protective factor, and the larger it is, the longer the survival time. The standardized a_i absolute value reflects the relative magnitude of this factor's impact on lifetime. After finding the valid features, the Cox model is also used to evaluate the sample risk. The Fig. 2.13 shows the comparison of the survival curves of

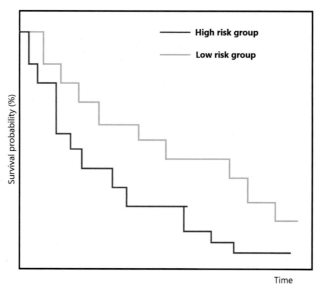

FIGURE 2.13

Schematic diagram of the survival curve.

the high and low risk groups by the median score of the Cox regression risk coefficient score.

After training the parameters in the Cox proportional hazard model, the survival probability of the patient at the specified time point can also be calculated by the following formula:

$$S(t|X) = e^{-\int_0^t h(s|X)ds}$$

$$= e^{-\int_0^t h_0(s)e^{\beta^T X}ds}$$

$$= e^{-(H_0(t))^{e^{\beta^T X}}}$$

$$= S_0(t)^{e^{\beta^T X}} \tag{2.33}$$

where $H_0(t) = \int_0^t h_0(s)ds$, $S_0(t) = e^{-H_0(t)}$. $S_0(t)$ is the baseline survival function, and the baseline survival function can be estimated by the following formula:

$$S_0(t) = \prod_{t_i < t} \frac{n_i - r_i}{n_i} \tag{2.34}$$

where n_i is the number of patients at risk of survival before time t; r_i is the number of patients who occurred (Fig. 2.13) at time t.

For a patient p, given its characteristic representation X_p, the probability of survival at time point t_p can be expressed as $1 - S(t_p | X_p)$. For example, when calculating the patient's 3-year survival probability, $t_p = 3$ year can be set, at which point the patient's 3-year survival probability is $1 - S(t = 3 \, year | X)$.

Common evaluation indicators for survival analysis are as follows:

(1) Harrell's Concordance Index

For survival data with Censored, the standard evaluation method does not apply. Harrell's Concordance Index (C-index) is a commonly used evaluation method, and its calculation method is as follows:

(1) Pair all samples in pairs to form a total of $N \times (N - 1)/2$ sample pairs.

(2) Eliminate the pairing that cannot determine the order of the end events, and set the number of remaining pairs to be M.

(3) Among the remaining M pairs, the number of pairs whose prediction result is consistent with the actual result is K.

(4) C-index $= K/M$.

C-index calls the rcorrcens function of the rms package (Frank E Harrell Jr 2018. rms: Regression Modeling Strategies) in R language (Version 3.5.1, R Core Team 2018. R Foundation for Statistical Computing, Vienna, Austria. www.R-project.org). Confidence interval (CI) is achieved by 1000 times of Bootstrap.

(2) Time-Dependent ROC

Survival analysis is different from the classification problem. Survival data include survival time and status. Therefore, the receiver operating characteristic curve (ROC) cannot be directly generated. It is necessary to determine a time point and draw ROC at this point in time, called time-dependent ROC. The Coef parameter value in Cox is the regression coefficient of the corresponding feature, through which the risk function can be calculated, and then each sample can calculate its predicted value of the survival probability at a certain point in time. The subsequent steps are the same as the ROC drawing method of the classification problem. Finally, the ROC was evaluated by AUC. The statistical difference between the two ROCs is calculated using the DeLong's test.

Time-dependent ROC calls the val.surv function of the rms package (Frank E Harrell Jr 2018. rms: Regression Modeling Strategies) and the survival ROC function of the survival ROC package (Patrick J. Heagerty and packaging by Paramita Saha-Chaudhuri 2013. survival ROC; Time-dependent ROC curve estimation from censored survival data) in the R language (Version 3.5.1, R Core Team 2018. R Foundation for Statistical Computing, Vienna, Austria. www.R-project.org); DeLong's test is implemented by calling the roc.test function of the pROC package.

(3) Kaplan—Meier

The Kaplan—Meier (K-M) survival curve is a one-factor nonparametric analysis method that estimates survival probability from observed survival time. Survival analysis studies, in addition to Cox for univariate or multivariate analysis, also used K-M survival curves to demonstrate the impact of single factors on prognosis. For the n-th time point tn in the study, calculate the survival probability.

Log-rank test is widely used in survival analysis to compare two or more K-M survival curves, which is a nonparametric test, so there is no assumption about the distribution of survival probability; the null hypothesis states that there is no statistical difference in survival between the various curve groups. The comparison is the number of events observed in each group. The statistics are similar to the Chi-square test statistic.

The K-M survival curve and log-rank test are implemented in the R language (Version 3.5.1, R Core Team 2018. R Foundation for Statistical Computing, Vienna, Austria. www.R-project.org) by calling the survfit function and the survdiff function of the survival package (Therneau, 2015) [23]. The K-M survival curve is drawn by calling the ggsurvplot function of the survminer package (Alboukadel Kassambara and Marcin Kosinski 2018. survminer: Drawing Survival Curves using ggplot2).

(4) Calibration Curve

The Calibration curve is implemented in the R language (Version 3.5.1, R Core Team 2018. R Foundation for Statistical Computing, Vienna, Austria. www.R-project.org) by calling the val.surv function of the rms package (Frank E Harrell Jr 2018. rms: Regression Modeling Strategies) and the groupkm function. The Hosmer—Lemeshow test is implemented by calling the hoslem.test function of the ResourceSelection package (Subhash R. Lele, Jonah L. Keim and Peter Solymos 2017. ResourceSelection: Resource Selection Probability Functions for Use-Availability Data).

(5) Nomogram

Nomogram was originally proposed by French engineer Philbert Ocagne in 1884, and it was originally used in engineering, which can describe the relationship between different variables. Since the nomogram can be used to calculate the survival of cancer patients, it is widely used in the medical field. For detailed mapping methods, see the paper published in the 2008 *Journal of Clinical Oncology* (JCO), *How to build and interpret a nomogram for cancer prognosis* (DOI: 10.1200/Jco.2007.12.9791). A typical nomogram can be divided into four areas: (1) score; (2) variable; (3) total score; and (4) prediction results. Its method of use is

(1) The point at which the eigenvalues of the patient's imaging ensembles are found on the target axis of the prediction result, and then the vertical line is drawn up to the coordinate axis of the score, that is, the score value of the radiomic feature is obtained. Repeat the process for each variable to get the score value for each variable.

(2) Add the sum of the score values of the individual variables and find the point of the sum value on the total score axis.

(3) Draw the vertical line down to the prediction result area to get the survival probability at the corresponding time point.

Nomogram is implemented in the R language (Version 3.5.1, R Core Team 2018. R Foundation for Statistical Computing, Vienna, Austria. www.R-project.org) by calling the nomogram function of the rms package (Frank E Harrell Jr 2018.rms: Regression Modeling Strategies).

2.5.2 Linear classification model

The linear classification model is basically the same as the linear regression, but the target value is generally 1/0 dichotomous or discrete (Fig. 2.14), rather than outputting continuous values like regression. A linear classifier is an algorithm that separates two types of objects by a line or a hyperplane. Commonly used are logistic regression, SVM, and a series of variants of them. Their formula base structure is similar to linear regression, and different classification effects are achieved by changing the objective function and the objective function form.

1. Logistic regression

Logistic regression is a generalized linear model. It is more suitable for classification tasks than direct linear regression model logistic regression. It introduces the sigmoid function as an activation function to control the original output based on the linear regression model.

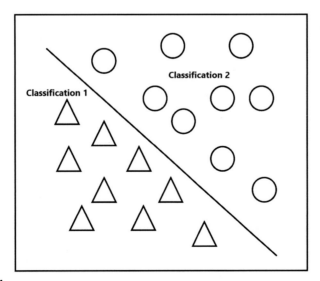

FIGURE 2.14

Schematic diagram of linear classification.

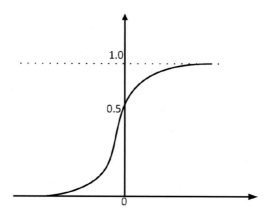

FIGURE 2.15

Schematic diagram of the sigmoid function.

$$f(x) = \frac{1}{1 + e^{-x}} \tag{2.35}$$

The above formula is a sigmoid function, the domain is in $(-\infty, +\infty)$, and the value range is between $(0, 1)$. In the neural network, it is also often used as an activation function to constrain the output, so that the original continuous and infinite range of the output is limited to a fixed small range (Fig. 2.15). Consider a vector $x_i (i = 1, 2, \ldots, n)$ with n independent variables, and let the conditional rate $P(y = 1|x) = p$ be the probability that the observation will occur relative to an event x. Then, the logistic regression model can be expressed as follows:

$$P(y = 1|x) = \frac{1}{1 + e^{-\left(a_0 + \sum a_i x_i\right)}} \tag{2.36}$$

where $\left(a_0 + \sum a_i x_i\right)$ is the same as the formula for linear regression, and the probability that the relative observation does not occur is as follows:

$$P(y = 0|x) = 1 - \frac{1}{1 + e^{-\left(a_0 + \sum a_i x_i\right)}} \tag{2.37}$$

Compare the odds of experiencing an event, abbreviated as odds:

$$\frac{P(y = 1|x)}{P(y = 0|x)} = e^{\left(a_0 + \sum a_i x_i\right)} \tag{2.38}$$

A logarithmic version of the linear regression model is also obtained. From this equation, the maximum likelihood function of the logistic regression formula can be obtained. Let the observation value be $p_i = P(y_i = 1|x_i)$, then the maximum likelihood function is as follows:

$$J = \prod_{i=1}^{n} p_i^{y_i} (1 - p_i)^{1-y_i} \tag{2.39}$$

2. **SVM**

SVM is a popular supervised learning-based method. It is a classification technology proposed by Vanpik's AT&T Bell laboratory research team in 1963. It is a pattern recognition method based on statistical learning theory and shows many unique advantages in solving small sample, nonlinear and high-dimensional pattern recognition problems. Based on the structural risk minimization theory, the optimal hyperplane is constructed in the feature space, so that the learner is globally optimized, and the expectation of the entire sample space satisfies a certain upper bound with a certain probability.

The difference between SVM and ordinary linear regression lies in the objective function. By using the hinge loss function, it uses only the sample (support vector) closest to the separation interface to evaluate the interface. The idea of SVM is to find a subinterface that perfectly separates the two categories and is equidistant from the two categories.

This formula is also based on a linear regression model, and in order to facilitate the calculation, the linear regression is rewritten as

$$g(x) = wx + b \tag{2.40}$$

w denotes a coefficient matrix, x denotes a set of feature vectors, and b denotes a bias. Through the formula, the vertical direction $\frac{w}{||w||}$ of the classifier can be obtained, and the closest distance from the classification surface is as follows:

$$d = \min_{i \in n} \frac{||wx_i + b||}{||w||} \tag{2.41}$$

Here we set $||wx_i + b|| = 1$, so there is a distance between the sides of the $m = 2d = \frac{2}{||w||}$, and get the following formula:

$$\begin{cases} wx + b > 1 \text{ , when } y_i = +1 \\ wx + b < -1, \text{ when } y_i = -1 \end{cases} \tag{2.42}$$

In this way, we can calculate the target we need, minimize $\frac{1}{2}||w||^2$, and guarantee $y_i(wx + b) > 1$, thus establishing the objective function:

$$J = \frac{1}{2}||w||^2 - \sum_{i=1}^{n} a_i(y_i(wx + b) - 1), \ a_i > 0 \tag{2.43}$$

Deriving the objective function to obtain two conditions for minimizing the function:

$$\begin{cases} \dfrac{\partial J}{\partial W} = \sum_{i=1}^{n} a_i y_i x = 0 \\ \\ \dfrac{\partial J}{\partial b} = \sum_{i=1}^{n} a_i y_i = 0 \end{cases} \tag{2.44}$$

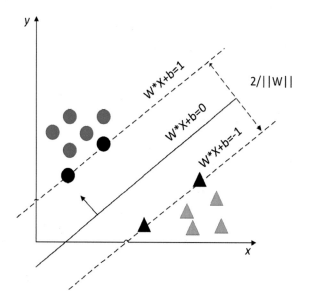

FIGURE 2.16

Schematic diagram of SVM classification.

Substituting the objective function to get the simplified objective function:

$$J = \sum_{i=1}^{n} a_i - \frac{1}{2} \sum_{i=0}^{n} \sum_{j=0}^{n} a_i a_j y_i y_j x_i^T x_j, \ a_i > 0, \sum_{i=1}^{n} a_i y_i = 0 \qquad (2.45)$$

The classifier iterated according to this objective function is the SVM. As shown in the Fig. 2.16, the triangles and circles represent the support vectors of the two types of data. It can be seen from both the formula and the graph that the iterative process of the SVM only needs the data features of the support vector, and other data points basically do not directly contribute to the classifier, so the SVM can also effectively perform the classification task for small data volumes, and at the same time, it is also more susceptible to singular support vector effects resulting in overall offset.

However, in practice, it is difficult to strictly guarantee the distance between the two sides, so there is an SVM using slack variables, and the formula changes as follows:

$$\begin{cases} \text{minimize} \frac{1}{2}\|w\|^2, \ y_i(wx + b) > 1 \\ \\ \qquad\qquad \downarrow \qquad\qquad\qquad\qquad\qquad (2.46) \\ \\ \text{minimize} \frac{1}{2}\|w\|^2 + C\sum \zeta, \ y_i(wx + b) > 1 - \zeta, \zeta > 0 \end{cases}$$

In this way, the slackness of the SVM, that is, the degree of strictness to the two boundaries, can be controlled by any small slack variable ζ and parameter C. The larger the C, the higher the fit to the data, and the easier it is to overfit. Conversely, the smaller the C, the lower the degree of fit and the more robust it is.

2.5.3 **Tree models**

There are many tree models commonly used in machine learning tasks, including decision tree, random forests, gradient tree, and so on. The basic theories of them are similar. Based on information gain or residual, the target data are classified and distinguished step by step in detail to get the final classification result.

1. Decision tree

Decision tree is a simple, efficient, and highly explanatory model, and in the field of data analysis, it is widely used. Its essence is a tree composed of many judgment nodes. The core of the algorithm is to choose the judgment node and to construct an appropriate decision tree through data learning. In general, we use GINI impurity or entropy gain on each node as we introduced in the previous section to determine whether a split is needed.

The general process of the algorithm is as follows:

(1) The input is m samples, the sample output is D, each sample has n discrete features, the feature set is X, and the output is decision tree T.

(2) Initialize the threshold value of information gain.

(3) Information gain of each feature in x is calculated to output D, and feature α with the largest information gain is selected.

(4) If the information gain of α is less than threshold value, then return the single-node tree, and mark category as the category that outputs the first sample in sample D as the category with the most instances.

(5) Repeat steps 2 and 3 until the information gain threshold cannot be reached or there are no other features.

The advantages of the decision tree lie in its fast speed, relatively small computation, easy conversion to rules, easy understanding, and clear display of which attributes are more important.

2. Random forests and gradient tree

Both random forest and gradient tree can get more comprehensive results by combining multiple tree models. Random way is used to establish random forest. Many decision trees make up the forest and they have no correlation; that is, different feature ranges are selected. After obtaining the random forest, when a new sample is input, judgment is made by each decision tree in the random forest. According to the decision made by each decision tree, the final prediction result is obtained through voting or other combined ways.

Gradient tree boosting is a combination algorithm, also called a gradient boosting regression tree. The basic classifier of gradient tree boosting is a decision tree, which can be used both in regression and classification. It typically consists of multiple regression trees, the core of which is that each tree learns from the previous residual. Regression tree is similar to a decision tree; besides the classification target value is changed from dispersed to continuous, and the evaluation method is changed from entropy gain to a residual of the regression function. It is equivalent to having done the first regression tree, and finding the direction with the greatest residual to build the next tree. Unlike the parallel structure of a random forest, the gradient tree is equivalent to tandem learning, which reduces the residual step by step and finally combines the result by weight. According to the results, random forest improves performance by reducing model variance, while the gradient tree reduces model deviation.

2.5.4 AdaBoost

AdaBoost algorithm is a lifting method, which integrates several weak classifiers by bagging and combining them into strong classifiers. AdaBoost is the abbreviation of Adaptive Boosting (Adaptive enhancement), proposed by Yoav Freund and Robert Schapire [22].

Boosting integrated classifier contains many very simple member classifiers. These member classifiers perform better in random guesses and are often referred to as weak learning machines. The typical example of weak learning machines is a single-layer decision tree. The Boosting algorithm mainly aims at samples difficult to distinguish, and the weak learning machines improve classification property of classifiers by learning on the samples with incorrect classification. Boosting differs from bagging in that the initial stage of boosting uses a nonreturn sampling to randomly extract a subset from the training samples, while bagging uses a retrieving extraction. The boosting process consists of four steps:

1. A training subset d1 is randomly selected from training set D by the no-return sampling method for the training of the weak learning machine C1.
2. A training subset d2 is randomly selected from training set D by the no-return sampling method, is added to the 50% incorrect samples of c1, and then trained to get the weak learning machine C2.
3. Training samples D3 with inconsistent C1 and C2 classification results are extracted from training set D to generate training sample set d3, and d3 is used to train the third weak learning machine C3.
4. Combine weak learning machines C1, C2, and C3 by majority vote.

The AdaBoost algorithm has been improved on the Boosting algorithm. It uses the entire training set to train the weak learning machine. The training samples are reassigned a weight in each iteration, and build a more powerful classifier based on the previous weak learning machine error. Its adaptation is to strengthen the weight of the sample of the previous weak classifier (the weight corresponding to the sample), and the updated sample of the weight is used again to train the next new weak classifier. The new weak classifier is trained with the population (sample population) in each round of training, generating new sample weights and weak classifier weights. Until the predetermined error rate is reached or the specified maximum number of iterations is reached, the iteration stops. Fig. 2.17 explains the working process of the AdaBoost algorithm:

The training sample consists of two different species. All the samples in Fig. 2.17 are given the same weight. Through the training of the training set, we can obtain a single-layer decision tree (dashed line in the figure), which divides two different types of samples by minimizing the cost function (sample impurity), in which two blue balls and one red ball are incorrectly divided. In the second training process, two mistakenly divided blue balls and one misclassified red are given greater weight (the ball becomes larger), while also reducing the weight of correctly segmented samples. In the course of this training, we will focus more on the sample with the right weight, that is, the sample that divides the error. By repeating this process, the sample is correctly divided. Then, a combination of weak learning machines is obtained, and through majority voting, the final prediction result is determined. The specific calculation process is as follows:

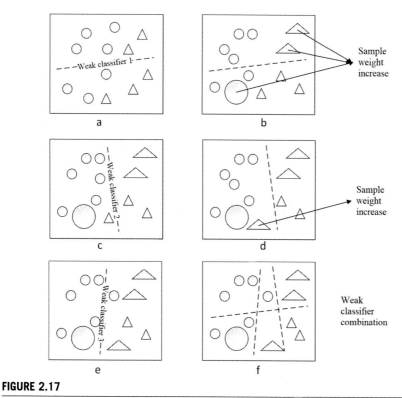

FIGURE 2.17

Adaboost classification diagram.

1. Initialize the weight ω of the sample with the same initial value, and the sum of the sample weights is 1.

$$\sum_{i=1}^{n} \omega_i = 1 \tag{2.47}$$

2. In the j-th round boosting operation, train a weighted weak classifier:

$$C(j) = train(X, y, \omega) \tag{2.48}$$

3. Forecast sample:

$$pred = predict(C(j), X) \tag{2.49}$$

4. Calculate the weight error rate:

$$\varepsilon = \omega * (pred == y) \tag{2.50}$$

5. Calculate the correlation coefficient:

$$\alpha_j = 0.5 * \log \frac{1 - \varepsilon}{\varepsilon} \tag{2.51}$$

6. Update sample weights:

$$\omega = \omega * e^{(-\alpha_j * pred * y)} \tag{2.52}$$

7. Normalize sample weights to ensure that the sum of all sample weights is 1:

$$\omega = \frac{\omega}{\sum_{i=1}^{n} \omega_i} \tag{2.53}$$

8. Complete the final forecast:

$$pred = \left(\sum_{j=1}^{m} (\alpha_j * pred(C(j), X)) \right) \tag{2.54}$$

2.5.5 Model selection

The above introduces the more commonly used machine learning classifiers. Each type of classifier has its own applicable range and the appropriate data format. It is necessary to construct different forms of data structures for each data and application scenario in order to effectively play the effect of the classifier.

For example, the linear model is derived from a classification surface whose weight is obtained by weighting multiple features. Each feature is used as the basis vector for constructing the classification coordinate system, so nonorthogonal features and complex features are less effective. That is to say, the linear model is not good for the correlation between features that are high or the variables that are controlled by multiple variables. It is more suitable for the case where each feature and objective function value are linearly related, and it is difficult to distinguish multiple related or unrelated features. Generally, the influence of these features on the model is reduced by means of deleting features and dimensionality reduction, or these features can be further processed by feature engineering, and the feature is decomposed by label coding by OneHot Encoding. Otherwise, the new feature is combined by dot product and multiplication to explore whether multiple factors work together. Overfitting problems can also be mitigated by different levels of feature grading, segmentation, and different degrees of data differentiation. Through the understanding of the data, it should be judged whether the feature should be analyzed differently as tag data or continuous data. In addition to the improvement of features and models, it also can change the learning algorithm to avoid model bias caused by extreme eigenvalues by replacing the original iterative learning with a random gradient descent method. For example, use the method of random gradient descent instead of the original iterative learning.

Compared to linear models, the tree model is less sensitive to anomalies (outside the gradient tree) and can be better handled against the label features, but is less sensitive to the relative size information in the continuous features. Therefore, the tree model is also difficult to control the degree of fitting, and it is difficult to separate the complex features. It is more suitable for the feature that can effectively separate the feature from the target value through the truncation point. It is also usually through the screening and dimension reduction of features to improve the performance of the model.

2.5.6 Convolutional neural network

The CNN is a feed-forward neural network whose artificial neurons can respond to edges of the image and have great performance for large image processing. Neurons of it include learnable weights and biases. Each neuron receives some input and performs a dot product calculation, and the output is the score for each category. CNN usually contains the following layers:

1. Convolutional layer
   The statistical properties of a part of an image are the same as other parts, which is the inherent characteristics of natural images. This also means that the features we learn in this part can also be used in another part, so the same learning characteristics for all positions on this image can be used. A more appropriate

explanation is that when we randomly select a small block from a large-sized image, such as 8×8 as a sample, some features are learned from this small sample. The features learned in the process are applied as detectors to any part of the image. Furthermore, the features learned from the 8×8 samples can be used to convolve with the original large-size image, then we can obtain an activation value for a different feature for any position on this large-size image. Each convolutional layer in a CNN consists of several convolutional units, and the parameters of each convolutional unit are optimized by a back propagation algorithm. Different types of features of the input can be extracted from the convolution operation. The first layer of the convolutional layer may only extract some low-level features such as edges, lines, and corners. Deep layers of networks can extract more complex features from low-level features. The following formula explains the detailed calculation process for convolution operations:

Given input image matrix $I = \begin{pmatrix} I_{11} & I_{12} & I_{13} \\ I_{21} & I_{22} & I_{23} \\ I_{31} & I_{32} & I_{33} \end{pmatrix}$ and convolution kernel

$= \begin{pmatrix} k_{11} & k_{12} \\ k_{21} & k_{22} \end{pmatrix}$. Convolutional layer output $F = conv(I, K)$, where $conv$ is the convolution operation. The convolution operation can be expressed by the following formula:

$$F = conv(I, K)$$
$$= \begin{pmatrix} I_{11} * k_{11} + I_{12} * k_{12} + I_{21} * k_{21} + I_{22} * k_{22} & I_{12} * k_{11} + I_{13} * k_{12} + I_{22} * k_{21} + I_{23} * k_{22} \\ I_{21} * k_{11} + I_{22} * k_{12} + I_{31} * k_{21} + I_{32} * k_{22} & I_{22} * k_{11} + I_{23} * k_{12} + I_{32} * k_{21} + I_{33} * k_{22} \end{pmatrix}$$

$$(2.55)$$

A specific example is given below: Suppose you have learned the characteristics of an 8×8 sample from a 96×96 image, and this is done by self-encoding with 100 hidden units. The convolutional feature was obtained through a convolution operation, which is required for each 8 × 8 small block image region of the 96 × 96 image. That is to say, 8 × 8 small block areas are extracted, and are marked as (1, 1), (1, 2), ... from the starting coordinates, up to (89, 89), and then to the extracted area. The trained sparse self-encoding is run one by one to obtain the activation value of the feature. In this example, it is clear that you can get 100 sets, each containing 89 × 89 convolution features.

Assuming a large-size image of $r \times c$ is given, it is defined as x_{large}. By training sparse self-encoding from a small $a \times b$ image sample x_{small} extracted from a large-size image, calculate $f = \sigma\left(W^{(1)} x_{small} + b^{(1)}\right)$ (σ is a sigmoid). The type function obtains k features, where $W(1)$ and $b(1)$ are the weights and deviations between the visible layer unit and the implicit unit. For each small image x_s of $a \times b$ size, calculate the corresponding value $f_s = \sigma\left(W^{(1)} x_s + b^{(1)}\right)$, and convolve these $f_{convolved}$ values to obtain a $k \times (r - a + 1) \times (c - b + 1)$ matrix of features after convolution.

2. Rectified linear units layer
   The activation function of this layer of nerves adjusts the output of each layer where

   $$ReLU(x) = \max(0, x) \tag{2.56}$$

   The nonlinear function performs output value transformation, and the feature extracted by the convolutional layer can be transformed into a high-dimensional nonlinear space; the activation function of ReLU can suppress the output to a negative value, achieve the purpose of feature sparseness, and prevent overfitting.
   In addition to this, there is also a sigmoid function as an activation function:

   $$f(x) = \frac{1}{1 + \exp(-x)} \tag{2.57}$$

   It can be seen that a logical regression was actually used as the input−output mapping relationship of the single "neuron."
   Also, the hyperbolic tangent function (tanh)

   $$f(x) = \tanh(x) = \frac{e^x - e^{-x}}{e^x + e^{-x}} \tag{2.58}$$

   The tanh function is a variant of the sigmoid function, which has a range of $[-1, 1]$ instead of $[0, 1]$ of the sigmoid function.

3. Pooling layer
   Usually, after the convolutional layer, features with large dimension are obtained. Cutting the features into several regions and taking the maximum value or the average value of them can greatly reduce the obtained features, and the feature complexity is reduced.
   After obtaining the features by convolution, in the next step we hope to use these features to do the classification. In theory, all of the extracted features can be used to train classifiers, such as the softmax classifier, but this is a computational challenge. For instance, for a 96×96 pixel image, suppose 400 features defined on the 8×8 input have been learned, and each feature and image convolution will get one $(96 - 8 + 1) \times (96 - 8 + 1) = 7921$ dimensional convolution feature, and with 400 features, each sample will get a $7921 \times 400 = 3{,}168{,}400$-dimensional convolution feature vector. Learning a classifier with more than three million feature inputs is inconvenient and prone to overfitting.
   In order to solve this problem, first recall that the reason we decided to use the convolutional feature because the image has a "static" property, which means that features useful in one image area are most likely to be equally applicable in another. Therefore, we can aggregate statistics on the features at different locations to describe large images. For example, the average (or maximum) of a particular feature over a region of an image can be calculated. These summary statistical features not only have a much lower dimension (compared to using all extracted features) but also improve the results (not easy to do overfitting). This

kind of aggregate operation is called pooling, sometimes called average pooling or maximum pooling (depending on the method).

If a continuous range in the image is selected as the pooled area and only the features produced by the same (repetitive) hidden unit are pooled, then these pooling units have a translation invariant. This means that even after the image has undergone a small shift, the same (pooled) features will still be generated. In many tasks (such as object detection, voice recognition), we all want to get a feature with translation invariance, because the sample (image) mark obtained in this way will not be affected by image translation.

Formally, after obtaining the convolutional features we discussed earlier, we need to determine the size of the pooled area (assuming a × b) to pool our convolution features. Then, we divide the convolution feature into a number of disjointed regions of size a × b, and then use the average (or maximum) features of these regions to obtain the pooled convolution features. These pooled features can be used for classification.

Such as assumed feature map $F = \begin{pmatrix} 1 & 5 & 2 & 8 \\ 3 & 9 & 7 & 8 \\ 1 & 0 & 2 & 6 \\ 8 & 5 & 3 & 2 \end{pmatrix}$, the size is 4×4, given a

window size of 2×2, and the maximum value of the pooling operator is 2, the pooling operation splits F into four adjacent 2×2 small matrices. The maximum value of each of the small matrices will be taken out as the result of the pooling operation $P = \begin{pmatrix} 9 & 8 \\ 8 & 6 \end{pmatrix}$.

4. Fully connected layer
   All local features are combined into global features. Integrate features in a manner similar to logistic regression, and finally complete classification.

5. Batch normalization layer
   Since the gradient of the deep network is gradually weakened during training, the batch normalization layer performs batch normalization of features after each layer of convolution, and normalizes the eigenvalues of each layer to 0 mean 1 standard deviation. It ensures that the features and gradients in the training process can be transmitted to the output and input of the network as much as possible, thus speeding up the training process of the network.

6. Output layer
   The softmax function or the sigmoid function is usually used in the output layer. In fact, the softmax regression model is a generalization of the logistic regression model on multiclassification problems. In the multiclass problem, the class label y can take more than two values.
   Our training set consists of n labeled samples in logistic regression:

$$\left\{ \left(x^{(1)}, y^{(1)} \right), \left(x^2, y^{(2)} \right), \cdots \left(x^{(n)}, y^{(n)} \right) \right\}$$

Since the logistic regression is for the two-class problem, the class is labeled $y^{(i)} \in \{0, 1\}$. The hypothesis function is as follows:

$$h_0(x) = \frac{1}{1 + \exp(-\theta^T x)} \tag{2.59}$$

We will train the model parameter θ to minimize the cost function:

$$J(\theta) = -\frac{1}{M}\left[\sum_{i=1}^{m} y^{(i)} \log h_0\left(x^{(i)}\right) + \left(1 - y^{(i)}\right)\log\left(1 - h_0\left(x^{(i)}\right)\right) \right] \tag{2.60}$$

In softmax regression, we solve the multiclass problem (relative to the two-class problem solved by logistic regression); the class Y can take k different values ($k > 2$). Therefore, for the training set $\{ (x^{(1)}, y^{(1)}), (x^2, y^{(2)}), \cdots (x^{(n)}, y^{(n)}) \}$, we have $y^{(i)} \in \{1, 2, \cdots, k\}$ (Note that the category subscript here starts at 1 instead of 0). Such as in the MNIST digital recognition task, the number of categories is 10.

For a given test input x, we want to estimate the probability value $P(y = j|x)$ for each category j using a hypothesis function. In other words, estimate the probability of the occurrence of each classification result of x. Therefore, a k-dimensional vector (the sum of the vector elements is 1) will be output through our hypothesis function to represent the probability values of the k estimates.

As the number of categories decreases, softmax regression degenerates into a logistic regression. This suggests that softmax regression is a general form of logistic regression.

The CNN is equivalent to treating each pixel in the image and the points around it as a whole by convolution, so that small images can be learned as features instead of learning from each pixel. More attention is paid to the related issues between different points in the image. With this network structure, it can approximate valid features based on the position of the data and the label oriented from the convolutional block in the picture. This allows the classifier to learn the features and methods from the picture itself, rather than providing features to the classifier by humans. On the one hand, it breaks through the limitations of human design features, and on the other hand, it completes an end-to-end device that can automatically study the problem.

Why do we want to use deep networks? The main advantage of using a deep network is that it can express a much larger set of functions in a more compact and concise way. Or, we can find some functions that can be expressed succinctly using the k-layer network (the simplicity here means that the number of hidden layer units only needs to be polynomial with the number of input units). But for a network with only the k-1 layer, these functions cannot be expressed succinctly unless it uses the number of hidden layer units exponentially related to the number of input units.

As a simple example, we intend to build a Boolean network to calculate the parity of n input bits (or XOR). It is assumed that each node in the network can perform a logical OR operation (or a NAND operation) or a logical AND operation. If we have a network consisting of only one input layer, one hidden layer, and one output layer, then the number of nodes required for the parity function is exponential with the size n of the input layer. However, if we build a deeper network, then the scale of this network can be just a polynomial function of n.

When the object is an image, we can use the deep network to learn the "partial-total" decomposition relationship. For example, the first layer can learn how to combine pixels in an image to detect edges (as we did in the previous exercise). The second layer can combine edges to detect longer contours or simple "target parts." At a deeper level, these contours can be further combined to detect more complex features.

The last point to mention is that the cerebral cortex is also calculated in multiple layers. For example, the human brain processes visual images in multiple stages, starting with the "V1" region of the cerebral cortex, followed by the "V2" region of the cerebral cortex, and so on.

CNNs have also shown good performance in the study of medical images. For example, Multiscale Convolutional Neural Networks (MCNN) for Lung Nodule Classification is very effective in the identification of benign and malignant lung cancer from unsegmented lung CT [13]. The method first extracts multiple nodule patches to capture nodule variations from the input CT images. When calculating the discriminant features, the resulting valid patch is then sent to the network.

In this paper, MCNN is used to describe the feature characteristics from different scales. The experimental results show that the image features obtained by MCNN are much better than the commonly used HOG and LBP features.

On this basis, the author also proposed an improved scheme of MCNN [14], which proposed multicrop pooling instead of the original pooling layer, thus effectively characterizing sensitive nodes. It can go out and make multiple choices for the center feature. Based on the maximum pooling layer feature of the original images, the maximum pooling layer feature of the image obtained by two center clippings are added, in which the feature proportion of the central part increases, and a more detailed feature description is obtained. Through this network, the benign and malignant discrimination effect of lung cancer can be further improved.

It can be seen from these applications that CNNs have great advantages in the processing of medical images and have great potential for improving clinical outcome prediction. With the further development, this networks design will be more widely used to lead end-to-end medical image diagnosis.

Since deep learning is an end-to-end prediction method, the prediction process is not intuitive to the common user. A visualization method is highly valuable to analyze the features extracted by the deep learning model to further understand the prediction process. The convolutional layer is the most important component of the deep learning model. Therefore, the convolutional layer can be visualized from two aspects to understand the inference process: (1) visualize the feature patterns extracted by the convolutional layer; (2) visualize the response of each convolutional layer to different tumors.

Each convolutional layer in the deep learning model consists of a number of convolution filters (convolution kernels), and each of which can extract different features. Through the filter visualization algorithm, the researchers can visualize the feature patterns extracted by the convolution filter. When visualizing a convolution filter, input a random white noise image to the deep learning model and observe the response of the filter. If the filter's response reaches a maximum value, the input image shows the feature pattern extracted by this filter; otherwise, the back propagation algorithm is used to change the input image. This process is similar to the training process of the deep learning model and will be iteratively iterated until the observed filter response reaches a maximum value. At this time, the input image is the deep learning feature pattern learned by the filter. Through this filter visualization method, the feature patterns extracted by each convolution filter in the deep learning model can be observed, and it is intuitive to understand what features each convolution layer is extracting.

Researchers can also observe the response of each convolution filter to different tumor images. For example, given a CT image of a tumor, each convolution filter in the deep learning model can generate a corresponding response map representing the distribution of corresponding feature patterns in the tumor. Define the average of the response map as the response value, where the deep learning feature is produced by the filter. A discriminative convolution filter should have different response values between classification tasks or regression tasks, such as EGFR mutations and EGFR wild-type tumors. Therefore, visualizing the convolution filter's response to different tumors can help researchers evaluate the performance of convolution filters.

2.5.7 Migration learning

Migration learning (also known as transfer learning) refers to the use of a trained model in one domain to migrate it to another domain for use. When building deep learning models, we often need a lot of data to train a deep CNN to avoid overfitting. However, in medical imaging–related topics such as radiomics analysis, the amount of data is usually small.

Small sample data are difficult to train complex deep learning networks, which is mainly due to the fact that deep learning networks are prone to overfitting in small sample cases. From the perspective of network training, overfitting occurs because the network is stuck in a local extreme point when optimizing the solution. During the training of the deep learning network, the parameters in the network are usually randomly initialized, then the network is trained using the training data. This training process is actually the process of optimizing the parameters of the network. When the network uses random initialization, the solution process starts from a random solution and gradually approximates the approximate optimal solution in the iterative process. However, when network gets deeper or the structure becomes more complex, the parametric surface becomes more rugged, and it is easy to fall into a local extreme point away from the optimal solution during the solution process.

Therefore, to solve the problem that the network is easy to fall into a bad local extreme in a small sample case, the network training process can be improved: if a better initial solution can be given to the network, the small sample data may also cause the network to converge at a better approximate optimal solution. Migration learning is applied to small sample data by changing the initial state of the network as described above. In migration learning, there are two datasets, one for the initial dataset for pretraining the CNN network and the other for the target dataset for the current problem. In general, the initial dataset has a larger amount of data, while the target dataset has a smaller amount of data.

Migration learning first uses a large number of samples on the initial dataset to train the CNN network; at this time, the CNN network has learned meaningful features, and its parameter surface will become smoother. Then, use the parameters of the trained CNN network as the initial state, and perform a refitting on the target dataset (fine tune) to obtain a new CNN model. In order to make the CNN have a better initial state, the initial dataset used for migration learning is generally a natural image dataset with a very large amount of data, such as the ImageNet dataset, which has more than 1 million images that can be used to train the CNN network. Although there are large differences between the initial dataset (such as ImageNet natural image dataset) and the target dataset (medical image dataset), many features of CNN can be shared across domains.

The characteristics of CNN learning are hierarchical, and the underlying features are generally image features, such as edges, shapes, etc. These features are versatile and applicable in medical images; CNN's high-level features are related to datasets, so you can use only the shallow network of CNN for migration during migration learning.

According to the different similarities between the initial dataset and the target dataset, migration learning has different ways to refit the CNN network as follows:

(1) Since the shallow features of CNN are general image features such as edges and shapes, they are versatile in different datasets, so the first few parameters of the pretrained network can be fixed during refitting, only training the last layers of the network, which are used to learn the features associated with the target dataset.
(2) In order to make the entire network fully adaptable to the target dataset, the entire network can be refitted to train all layers.
(3) The last layers of the pretrained CNN are replaced with newly designed randomly initialized layers and then refitted on the target dataset for the newly added layer or the entire network.

In the natural image, the ImageNet dataset has more than 1.28 million training sets, and the smaller cifar10 dataset has more than 50,000 images. Therefore, the subject of natural image processing can construct deep and complex deep learning models to get better performance. However, medical images, especially 3D tumor images (CT, MRI), have a small amount of data, usually less than 1000, which makes it difficult to directly train large depth learning models, such as CT image datasets for lung nodule segmentation. LIDC-IDRI has only 1010 patients; the MIC-CAI dataset for brain tumor segmentation has MR data for less than 100 patients.

For the problem of having a small amount of medical imaging data, migration learning is a good way to deal with it. In the multiple tasks of diabetic retinopathy, retinal fundus disease diagnosis, and skin cancer diagnosis, migration learning has shown excellent performance [15−17].

In the study of EGFR gene mutation prediction in lung cancer, some researchers constructed a new deep learning network using migration learning, and the training data based on small samples achieved good prediction performance. In natural image processing, DenseNet uses dense connections to improve the problem of gradient dispersion during network training. By introducing a layer jump connection, the gradient of the network output is directly introduced to the input, so that the input layer of the network is well trained [18].

Unlike the "radiomics" analysis method, which requires artificially defined features, deep learning is an end-to-end model whose input is the CT image of the tumor, and the output is the probability that the tumor has a mutation in the EGFR gene. First, the user selects the tumor area using a rectangular frame in each slice of the CT image, that is, it selects the ROI of the tumor. The ROI image is then scaled to a 64×64 voxel size using a cubic spline interpolation algorithm. Finally, the ROI images in adjacent three-layer CT slices are combined into a three-channel image and imported into a deep learning model to predict EGFR gene mutation. Since the CT image of a tumor contains many slice images, researchers input all CT slices of the tumor into a deep learning model for prediction, and the average of the predicted probabilities of all of the slices is taken as the mutation probability of the tumor's EGFR gene.

Drawing on the advantages of DenseNet, researchers used the migration learning method to design a new CNN based on DenseNet [19].

The DL model is based on DenseNet's network structure. In this model, two convolutional layers and two batch normalization layers make up a stack, which is defined as a group. Specifically, a group is composed of a batch normalization layer, a 1×1 convolution layer, a bulk normalization layer, and a 3×3 convolution layer stacked in order. The first six groups are stacked into the first block. In the first block, the input of each group is connected to the output of all of the groups in front of it, that is, the dense connection (Dense Connection). After the first block, the features are parameter compressed using a bulk normalization layer and a 3×3 convolution layer. For example, the first 256 feature maps are compressed to 128 feature maps using a 128 channel 3×3 convolutional layer. Subsequently, the feature map is reduced to an 8×8 size using a 2×2 average pooling layer. Then, five groups are stacked into a second block, and dense connections are also used within the block. The last convolutional layer of the second block uses the bulk normalization layer to eliminate the mean and variance drift of the feature map, and then uses global mean pooling to change all feature maps from 8×8 to one value. Finally, a 352-dimensional feature vector is generated. Next, the 352-dimensional feature vector is connected to the output neuron through the fully connected layer for EGFR gene mutation probability prediction.

The network includes subnetwork 1 and 2, wherein subnetwork 1 migrates to the top 20 layers of DenseNet, and its topology and network weight are consistent with the top 20 layers of DenseNet; subnetwork 2 is a redesigned four-layer convolution layer. During network training, subnetwork 1 is first fixed and only subnetwork 2 is trained to ensure that the weights already trained in subnetwork 1 are not disturbed. After subnetwork 2 has been fully trained, the weights of the entire network will be trained together; at this time, the migration learning weight of subnetwork 1 will also be updated, making the entire network more suitable for the current application problem. In order to expand the training samples, each layer of 2D slices in the CT image of the tumor was used as a sample to train the CNN. In the test phase, each layer of CT images of the tumor will obtain a predicted probability value. Finally, the average of the predicted probability values of all CT slices of the tumor image is taken as the final predicted value.

Subnetwork 1 has learned general image features by means of migration learning. In order for the network to learn the features associated with mutations in the EGFR gene, we constructed subnetwork 2 behind subnetwork 1 to learn the features associated with the EGFR gene mutation status for this dataset. Since subnetwork 2 is a redesigned structure, it is no longer initialized using migration learning, but is randomly initialized using the Xavier algorithm.

Deep learning model training is an iterative process. The purpose of model training is to optimize the parameters in the model and establish the correlation between CT images and EGFR gene mutation status. In each iteration, researchers used cross entropy as the loss function to measure the predictive performance of the deep learning model. Since the parameters of subnetwork 1 are obtained through migration learning, the general image features can already be extracted; but the weight of subnetwork 2 is randomly initialized, and there is no meaning at the beginning of the training, and the randomly initialized network large gradients will be generated at the beginning of the training when performing back propagation, the noise gradient generated by random initialization will destroy the trained weights in subnetwork 1 and lose the meaning of migration learning. Therefore, we first freeze subnetwork 1, and then train only subnetwork 2 with a learning rate of 1×10^{-3}. After training the model for 10 cycles, we trained the entire network (including subnetwork 1 and subnetwork 2) with a small learning rate (1×10^{-5}). At this time, the high-level image features learned by subnetwork 2 and the low-level image features of subnetwork 1 migration learning are simultaneously trained to achieve complementary effects. A total of 14,926 training sample images were generated by using a 2D CT slice image as a training sample. Therefore, subnetwork 1 was pretrained using 1.28 million natural images, and then refitted using 14,926 lung cancer CT images; subnetwork 2 was directly trained using 14,926 lung cancer CT images. Finally, after 30 cycles of training, the model converges.

In order to reduce the difference in image grayscale caused by different devices, we used z-score to normalize the tumor image, adjusted the mean of the tumor CT image to 0, and adjusted the standard deviation to 1. In addition, all tumor images were scaled to the same size (64×64).

The migration learning network was $AUC = 0.88$ on the training set and $AUC = 0.81$ on the test set by training on 631 lung adenocarcinoma CT image data.

In this study, traditional imaging and clinical models were also used as comparative experiments. The image omics model extracts image morphological features such as shape, intensity, texture, and wavelet, and uses a random forest as a classifier. The clinical model uses age, gender, and tumor TNM staging as features, using SVM as a classifier. On the test set, the AUC of the image ensemble model and the clinical model are 0.64 and 0.61, respectively, so the deep learning model has achieved better performance. Further decision curve analysis shows that the use of a deep learning model for predicting patient EGFR gene mutations can yield good clinical benefits.

Since the deep learning model is an end-to-end model, its features are combined with classifiers that cooperate with each other. After using the visualization algorithm to find the predicted focus map of the deep learning model, the deep learning model can locate each tumor in a suspicious area, providing a reference puncture location for the doctor doing the clinical puncture.

The advantage of deep learning is mainly due to its powerful feature of self-learning ability. Through migration learning and 14,926 tumor CT images, the deep learning model unearthed CT image features closely related to the EGFR gene mutation status. To better understand the deep learning features, researchers visualized several representative convolution filters in the deep learning model. It can be seen from the figure that the shallow convolution layer has learned simple image features such as diagonal edges and horizontal (Conv_2). Deeper convolutions have learned more complex features, such as tumor shape information. For example, the filters in the Conv_13 layer have a strong response to these circular or curved shapes because most lung tumors are elliptical or nearly circular. When entering a deeper convolutional layer, deep learning features become more abstract and their correlation with the mutation state of the EGFR gene is getting stronger, such as the Conv_20 layer and the Conv_24 layer.

Since migration learning uses the weights that the network trains on the ImageNet dataset, the extracted features are similar to those of natural images. In the shallow network, the convolution kernel mainly extracts the edge information, and the deeper layer extracts the shape information. As the network deepens, some complex abstract features are gradually extracted, and the visual interpretation of these features is not obvious. However, its gradual association with EGFR mutation information is more conducive to model prediction. The same convolution kernel in a CNN responds differently to different tumors. For example, a convolutional kernel has a strong response to tumors with EGFR mutations, while a convolutional kernel with EGFR nonmutation has a weak response; in contrast, other convolutional nuclei respond more strongly to EGFR nonmutated tumors. However, the tumor response to EGFR mutations is weak. The study quantified the response of the convolutional kernel, indicating that there is a significant difference in the response of the two convolutional kernels to EGFR-mutated and nonmutated tumors. In addition, unsupervised clustering of features indicates that deep learning features are highly correlated with EGFR mutations and show significant clustering in a cluster analysis.

2.5.8 Semisupervised learning

Generally, performance of supervised learning is better than unsupervised learning. Since during supervised model training, the clinical label is considered. However, supervised learning's performance is limited by insufficiently labeled data. As a trade-off between better performance and enough training data, semisupervised learning could be a good choice. A large amount of unlabeled data are utilized by semisupervised learning to mine tumor information, while small amounts of labeled data are utilized to build the relationship between features and clinical labels. In some prognostic studies, patients need long-term follow-up (such as recurrence, disease progression, and overall survival), so labeled data are very difficult to obtain. However, unlabeled data are relatively easy to obtain. For example, the number of patients with follow-up in a study available in a medium-sized hospital is usually several hundred, but the number of patients without follow-up can exceed several thousand. At this point, information extraction from unlabeled data is the key to improve the performance of the radiomics model. Semisupervised learning, as a hybrid model that combines supervised learning with unsupervised learning, can mine information from a large amount of unlabeled data while constructing predictive models with a small amount of labeled data. In general, supervised learning models have good predictive performance because they are trained to take into account the correlation between features and labels. Unsupervised learning is not directly related to clinical predictive labels during training, so its predictive performance is limited, but it can mine the information naturally found in the data. As a compromise between performance and data volume, semisupervised learning can combine the advantages of unsupervised learning to mine unlabeled data information and the predictive ability of supervised learning. In the study of the prediction of ovarian cancer recurrence time, the author proposed a framework for semisupervised learning [20].

The model is divided into two parts: (A) unsupervised feature learning; (B) supervised Cox prognostic prediction model construction. In unsupervised feature learning, the authors designed a convolutional self-encoder to learn the characteristics of ovarian cancer from unlabeled data.

1. Principle of the self-encoding algorithm
   In supervised learning, training samples are labeled with categories. Now suppose the training sample set is $\left\{ x^{(1)}, x^{(2)}, x^{(3)} \cdots \right\}$, which has no category label, where $x^{(i)} \in R^n$. A self-encoding neural network is an unsupervised learning algorithm and has a target value equal to the input value, such as

$y^{(i)} = x^{(i)}$. The aim of the self-encoding neural network is to learn a function of $h_{W,b}(x) \approx x$. In other words, it attempts to approximate an identity function such that the output $\hat{x}$ is close to input x. The learning significance of the identity function is that, when we add some restrictions to the self-encoding neural network, such as limiting the number of hidden neurons, we can find some interesting structures from the input data. For example, suppose that input x of a self-encoding neural network is a 64×64 pixels gray image (a total of 4096 pixels), and there are 100 hidden neurons in hidden layer L_2. The output is also 4096 dimensions of $y \in R^{4096}$. Since there are only 100 hidden neurons, we force the self-encoding neural network to learn the compressed representation of the input data. It must be from the 50-dimensional hidden neuron activation vector $a^{(2)} \in R^{100}$ reconstructing the 4096-dimensional pixel gray value input x. If the input data of the network are completely random, for example, each input x_i is completely independent of other features, then this compressed representation will be very difficult to learn. But if the input data imply some specific structure, such as some input features are related to each other, then these correlations in the input data can be found using the algorithm. In fact, low-dimensional representation of input data can be usually learned from this simple self-encoding neural network, which is very similar to the PCA results.

Our previous discussion is based on the number of hidden neurons is small. When the number of hidden neurons is large (possibly more than the number of input pixels), applying other constraints to the self-encoding neural network can still find the structure in the input data. Specifically, if we add sparsity constraints to hidden neurons, the self-encoding neural network can still find some interesting structures in the input data even the number of hidden neurons is large.

The concept of "sparseness" is as follows. The neuron is considered to be activated if its output is close to 1, and when the output is close to 0, it is considered to be suppressed. So the limit that causes most of the neuron's time to be suppressed is called the sparsity limit. Here we assume sigmoid function is the activation function of the neuron. If tanh function is used as the activation function, we think neurons are suppressed when the neuron output is -1. Note that $a_j^{(2)}$ represents the degree of activation of the hidden neuron j, but this representation does not explicitly indicate which input x brings this activation. So we will use $a_j^{(2)}(x)$ to indicate the degree of activation of the self-encoding neural network hidden neurons j given input x. Define the following formula as

$$\hat{\rho}_j = \frac{1}{m} \sum_{i=1}^{m} \left[a_j^{(2)} \left(x^{(i)} \right) \right] \tag{2.61}$$

This indicates the average activity of hidden neurons j (average over the training set). We can approximately add a constraint $\hat{\rho}_j = \rho$, where ρ is the sparsity parameter, usually a smaller value close to 0 (such as $\rho = 0.05$). In other words, we want to make the average activity of hidden neurons j close to 0.05. The activity of hidden neurons must be close to 0 to satisfy this condition.

In order to achieve this limitation, an additional penalty factor will be added to our optimization objective function, which will punish those cases that are significantly different so that the average activity of hidden neurons remains within a small range. There are many reasonable choices for the specific form of the penalty factor. We will choose the following one:

$$\sum_{j=1}^{s_2} \rho \log \frac{\rho}{\widehat{\rho}_j} + (1-\rho)\log \frac{1-\rho}{1-\widehat{\rho}_j} \tag{2.62}$$

Here, S_2 is the number of hidden neurons in the hidden layer, and the index j in turn represents each of the neurons in the hidden layer. If you are familiar with relative entropy (KL divergence), this penalty factor is actually based on it. It can also be expressed as follows:

$$\sum_{j=1}^{s_2} KL\left(\rho \,||\, \widehat{\rho}_j\right) \tag{2.63}$$

$$KL\left(\rho \,||\, \widehat{\rho}_j\right) = \rho \log \frac{\rho}{\widehat{\rho}_j} + (1-\rho)\log \frac{1-\rho}{1-\widehat{\rho}_j} \tag{2.64}$$

The function is relative entropy between two Bernoulli random variables, one with ρ as the mean and one with $\widehat{\rho}_j$ as the mean. Relative entropy, a standard method for measuring the difference between two distributions.

This penalty factor has the following properties: $KL\left(\rho|| \,\widehat{\rho}_j\right) = 0$ when $\widehat{\rho}_j = \rho$, and monotonically increases as the difference between $\widehat{\rho}_j$ and ρ increases. For example, when we set $\rho = 0.2$, the relative entropy value $KL\left(\rho|| \,\widehat{\rho}_j\right)$ increases as $\widehat{\rho}_j$ decreases first (Fig. 2.18).

We can see that relative entropy reaches its minimum value of 0 when $\widehat{\rho}_j = \rho$, and when $\widehat{\rho}_j$ approaches 0 or 1,the relative entropy tends to be ∞. Therefore, minimizing this penalty factor has the effect of making $\widehat{\rho}_j$ close to ρ. Now, our overall cost function can be expressed as follows:

$$J_{sparese}(W,b) = J(W,b) + \beta \sum_{j=1}^{s_2} KL\left(\rho \,||\, \widehat{\rho}_j\right) \tag{2.65}$$

where $J(W,b)$ is as defined previously, and β controls the weight of the sparsity penalty factor. The $\widehat{\rho}_j$ term also depends (indirectly) on (W,b) because it is the average activation of the hidden neuron j, and the activation of the hidden layer neurons depends on (W,b).

To perform the derivative calculation on relative entropy, we can use an easy-to-implement technique that requires only minor changes in your program. Specifically, $\delta_i^{(2)}$ has been calculated when we calculated the second layer $(l=2)$ update in the backward propagation algorithm:

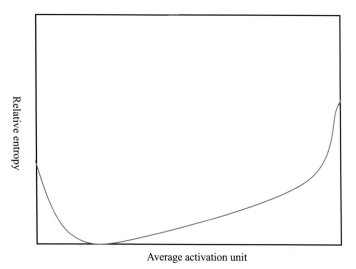

Average activation unit

FIGURE 2.18

Schematic diagram of relative entropy change.

$$\delta_i^{(2)} = \left(\sum_{j=1}^{s_2} W_{ji}^{(2)} \delta_i^{(3)} \right) f'\left(z_i^{(2)}\right) \tag{2.66}$$

Now we will replace it with

$$\delta_i^{(2)} = \left(\left(\sum_{j=1}^{s_2} W_{ji}^{(2)} \delta_i^{(3)} \right) + \beta \left(-\frac{\rho}{\widehat{\rho}_j} + \frac{1-\rho}{1-\widehat{\rho}_j} \right) \right) f'\left(z_i^{(2)}\right) \tag{2.67}$$

One thing to note is that we need to know $\widehat{\rho}_j$ to calculate this update. So before calculating the backward propagation of any neuron, you need to calculate the forward propagation for all training samples to get the average activation. If your training samples can be small enough to be stored in memory, you can easily calculate forward propagation on all your samples and store the resulting activation in memory and calculate the average activation. Then, you can use the precalculated activation to calculate the backward propagation of all training samples. If your data volume is too large to be fully stored in memory, you can sweep through your training samples and calculate a forward propagation, then accumulate the results and calculate the average activation $\widehat{\rho}_j$ (when the activation degree $a_j^{(2)}$ in the result of a forward propagation is used to calculate the average activation degree $\widehat{\rho}_j$, the result can be deleted). Then, after completing the calculation of the average activation $\widehat{\rho}_j$, it needs to resend each training sample for forward propagation so that it can calculate the backward propagation. For the latter case, it needs to calculate two forward propagations for each training sample, so the computational efficiency will be slightly lower. In this paper [20], two parts make up the self-encoder: an encoder and a decoder. The encoder compresses the image layer-by-layer convolution kernel into a 16-dimensional deep learning feature; the decoder uses the 16-dimensional deep learning features to reconstruct the original input image. When the decoder can reconstruct the original input image from the deep learning features, a large amount of tumor information is contained in the deep learning features. When the self-encoder training converges, the encoder converts the tumor CT image into a 16-dimensional deep learning feature; the decoder then reconstructs the original tumor image through the 16-dimensional feature. The reconstructed image is similar to the original input image, indicating tumor information has been completely extracted.

After learning the deep learning characteristics of the tumor through unsupervised learning, the supervised Cox proportional hazard model can use the deep learning feature to predict the recurrence time. When training the Cox model, patient follow-up information is required, so it is called a supervised learning model. After unsupervised learning with CT images of 102 patients with high-grade serous ovarian cancer, 49 patients with follow-up information were used to train the Cox prognostic model. Finally, two datasets (49 patients and 45 patients) were used to verify the predictive performance of the semisupervised learning model. This semisupervised learning model achieved a concordance index (C-Index) of 0.700 and 0.729 on both test sets. To further test the performance of the semisupervised Cox model for predicting recurrence risk, researchers used the semisupervised Cox model to predict the 3-year recurrence probability of patients. The semisupervised Cox model had the AUC = 0.833 (95% CI: 0.792−0.874) in the training set and an AUC = 0.772 (95% CI: 0.721−0.820) in Test Set 1. The predictive probability of this semisupervised Cox model was significantly different between patients with a relapse time of less than 3 years and patients with a relapse time of 3 years or more ($P < .0001$ in the train set and $P = .0010$ in test set 1). The calibration curve indicates that the semisupervised Cox model does not systematically underestimate or overpredict the 3-year recurrence probability because no significant difference between the semisupervised Cox model and the ideal model, which is tested by the Hosmer−Lemeshow test ($P = .475$ in train set, $P = .404$ in test set 1). The decision curve shows that when the doctor's decision threshold is greater than 0.3, the clinical benefit obtained by predicting the 3-years recurrence rate using the semisupervised Cox model is more than the two treatment options: treat all patients as relapsed within 3 years (treat-all) and treat all patients as relapsed after 3 years (treat-none). In the independent test set 2, the semisupervised Cox model also had similar performance (AUC = 0.825, 95% CI: 0.765−0.893). The AUC of the semisupervised Cox model is higher than the clinical model in two independent test sets (in test set 1: AUC = 0.443, 95% CI: 0.381−0.506). In test set 2, AUC $= 0.400$, 95% CI: 0.268–0.536, and there was a significant difference ($P = .0045$ in test set 1, $P = .0361$ in test set 2,by DeLong test).

2. Visualize the self-encoder training results

By visualizing the features of unsupervised learning, the intensity information of the tumor is extracted from the first convolution layer of the encoder; the second and the third convolution layers extract edge information; the information extracted by the third and fourth convolutional layers lacks intuitive visual interpretability, but it reflects high-dimensional abstraction of the tumor. Two tumors with different recurrence times were sent to the self-encoder and different responses were obtained. By further reducing the deep learning features to the 2D space, it can be found that in the deep learning feature space, patients with high recurrence and low recurrence show a more obvious clustering phenomenon.

After training the self-encoder, we also want to visualize the function to figure out what it has learned. We take the example of training a self-encoder on a 64 × 64 pixels image. In this self-encoder, each hidden unit i is calculated as follows for the function of the input:

$$a_i^{(2)} = f\left(\sum_{j=1}^{4096} W_{ij}^{(1)} x_j + b_i^{(1)}\right) \tag{2.68}$$

The function we will be visualizing is the above function that takes a 2D image as input and is calculated by hidden unit i. It is dependent on parameter $W_{ij}^{(1)}$ (temporarily ignores the offset b_i). It should be noted that $a_i^{(2)}$ can be regarded as a nonlinear feature of input x. However, there is still a problem: what kind of input image x can make $a_i^{(2)}$ get the maximum excitation? Here we have to add constraints to x, otherwise we will get a trivial solution. If we assume that the input has a norm constraint,

$$||x||^2 = \sum_{i=1}^{4096} x_i^2 \le 1 \tag{2.69}$$

The input that causes hidden unit i to get the maximum excitation should be given by pixel x_j ($j = 1, 2, 3 \cdots 4096$) calculated by the following formula:

$$x_j = \frac{W_{ij}^{(1)}}{\sqrt{\sum_{j=1}^{4096} \left(W_{ij}^{(1)}\right)^2}} \tag{2.70}$$

When we use the above formula to calculate the value of each pixel, compose them into an image, and present the image in front of us, the true meaning of the features sought by the hidden unit is gradually becoming clear.

If we train a self-encoder with 100 hidden elements, the visualization will contain 100 such images—each hidden unit corresponds to an image (Fig. 2.19).

CONV layer1	CONV layer2	CONV layer3	CONV layer4	CONV layer5

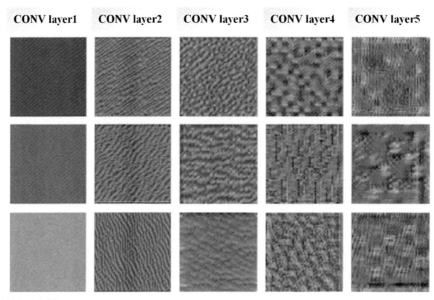

FIGURE 2.19

Schematic diagram of visual self-encoding results.

3. The principle of the self-learning algorithm

Giving the existing powerful machine learning algorithm more data can make it get better performance. There is even a saying in the machine learning community: "Sometimes the winner does not have the best algorithm, but more data."

More labeled data are always needed, but the cost is often high. For example, researchers have put considerable effort into using tools like AMT (Amazon Mechanical Turk) to get a larger training dataset. Compared to a large number of researchers building features by hand, it is an improvement to use crowd sourcing to manually label data by multiple people, but we can do better. Specifically, if the algorithm can learn from unlabeled data, then we can easily obtain a large amount of unlabeled data and learn from it. Self-learning and unsupervised feature learning are such algorithms. Although a single unlabeled sample contains less information than a labeled sample, if you can get a lot of unlabeled data (such as downloading random, unlabeled images, audio clips, or text from the Internet) and the algorithm can make effective use of them, the algorithm will achieve better performance than large-scale manual build features and labeled data.

On the self-learning and unsupervised feature learning problems, the algorithm can be used to learn a good feature description with a large amount of unlabeled data. When attempting to solve a specific classification problem, supervised learning method can be used to complete the classification based on these feature descriptions learned from labeled data. But self-learning algorithm may be most effective in scenarios where there is a large amount of unlabeled data and a small amount of labeled data. Even in the case where only the data have been labeled (when we usually ignore the class label of the training data for feature learning), the above ideas can get good results.

We have seen how to learn features from unlabeled data using an auto-encoder. Specifically, assume that there is an unlabeled training dataset $\{x^{(1)}, x^{(2)}, x^{(3)}\cdots\}$. Now using them to train a sparse self-encoder, using the trained model parameters $W^{(1)}, b^{(1)}$, given any input data x, you can calculate the activations a of hidden units. As mentioned earlier, a can be a better characterization than the original input x. The neural network in the figure below describes the calculation of the feature (activation amount a). This is actually the sparse self-encoder obtained before, and the last layer is removed here.

Suppose there is a labeled training set $\{x^{(1)}, x^{(2)}, \cdots x^{(m)}\}$ of size m. We can find a better characterization for the input data. For example, $x^{(1)}$ can be input to the sparse self-encoder to get the hidden unit activation amount $a^{(1)}$. Next, you can use $a^{(1)}$ directly instead of the original data. It can also be combined into one, using new vectors instead of raw data. After transformation, the training set becomes $\{a^{(1)}, a^{(2)}, \cdots a^{(m)}\}$. Finally, a supervised learning algorithm (such as SVM or logistic regression) can be trained to obtain a discriminant function to predict the y value. The prediction process is as follows: Given a test sample x, repeat the previous process and send it to the sparse auto-encoder to get a. Then, a is sent to the classifier to get the predicted value.

After building a radiomic model or deep learning model, the model must be validated. Only the validated model can show its potential value in clinical application. Compared with internally validated models, independent and externally validated models have higher confidence, as results from independently obtained data are usually more robust. In addition, for radiomic studies, prospectively validated models have the most credibility. Performance of radiomic models can be measured by dozens of tools. For discrimination analysis, the ROC curve is the most commonly used evaluation method, and the AUC, sensitivity, and specificity of the model can also be used to evaluate if the model can predict the clinical outcome. For survival analysis, the concordance index (C-index) and time-dependent ROC curve are usually used for validation. In addition, calibration curve is a useful tool for both discrimination analysis and survival analysis, as the agreement between the observed clinical outcomes and model predictions can obtained through it.

2.6 **Radiomics quality assessment system**

Because radiomics has a wide range of research, including research on different diseases, different diagnosis or prognostic prediction tasks, many scholars have proposed or improved the new photographic group model, the application scenarios and quality lack a unified evaluation standard. According to Professor Lammin's point of view on 2017 Nature Reviews Clinical Oncology [21], radiomics research can follow the quality assessment system below to measure the quality of the model.

Using the quality assessment system shown in Table 2.1, we can measure the reliability and clinical application value of published work, and help to further improve the quality of radiomics research and provide uniform research standards within the industry.

Table 2.1 Radiomics quality assessment system.

	Evaluation standard	Points
1	Image imaging parameters—have detailed imaging parameters (such as whether it is enhanced image, layer thickness, scan voltage, etc.) or have a public scanning protocol to ensure repeatable image acquisition	+1 (if the imaging parameters are detailed) + 1 (if using public scanning parameters)
2	Multiple segmentation—segmentation using different doctors/algorithms/software, random noise is considered in segmentation, segmentation is performed in different respiratory cycles to verify the stability of the extracted features for segmentation	+1
3	Performing a profiling experiment on all scanning instruments—detecting differences between instruments and selecting features that are insensitive to scanning instruments	+1
4	Imaging at multiple time points—collecting images of individual patients at multiple time points, testing the stability of features over time	+1
5	Perform feature selection or multiple test sets—reduce the risk of overfitting and consider feature stability when selecting features	− 3 (if neither item is available) + 3 (if there is an implementation)
6	Multivariate analysis using nonradiomics features (e.g., EGFR mutation information)—provides a more comprehensive model of fused radiomics features and nonradiomics features	+1
7	Detecting the association between discussion features and biological dimensions—demonstrating the association between subtype differences in radiomics and gene-protein levels, and explaining the association between radiomics and biology	+1
8	Cutoff analysis—use the median as a cutoff to divide risk groups	+1
9	Reporting statistics—report C-Index, ROC curve, AUC, and other statistical results. You can also use cross-validation and other methods	+1 (if both statistical and significant values are available) + 1 (if resampling is used)

Table 2.1 Radiomics quality assessment system.—*cont'd*

	Evaluation standard	Points
10	Correction statistics—report correction statistics (such as calibration curves) and their statistical values (*P* values and confidence intervals, etc.)	+1 (if the correction statistics and their statistical values are reported) + 1 (if resampling method is used)
11	Prospective study—provides the highest level of evidence to support clinical validation	+7 (proactive verification)
12	Verification—verification set is not used for training	5 (lack of verification) + 2 (concentric verification set) + 3 (verification set for other centers) + 4 (validation set from two different centers) + 4 (the study validated previously published labels) + 5 (provide validation sets for three or more different centers). The dataset must be at least the same order of magnitude as the number of features
13	Comparison with gold standards—compare radiomics models to current gold standards or better than gold standards (e.g., survival analysis using TNM staging)	+2
14	Potential clinical applications—report on current or potential clinical applications of the model (e.g., decision curve analysis)	+2
15	Cost analysis—analysis of the cost of reporting clinical problems	+1
16	Open source data—open source code and data	+1 (raw data open source) + 1 (ROI open source) + 1 (code open source) + 1 (if the radiomic feature is calculated on a representative ROI and the ROI is open source)
Total points		37

2.7 Radiomics software platform

2.7.1 Radiomics software

This software was developed by the radiomics research team of professor Tian Jie, Institute of Automation, Chinese Academy of Sciences (Key Laboratory of Molecular Imaging, Chinese Academy of Sciences) (Fig. 2.20). The major purpose of the

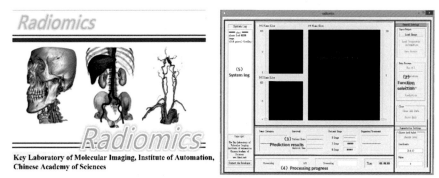

FIGURE 2.20

Radiomics Software Interface. The user can directly load the patient DICOM file by clicking "Load Image" and perform automatic segmentation of the lung nodules, benign and malignant classification, and N staging prediction.

software is to provide doctors with a set of auxiliary diagnostic systems, including the segmentation of lung nodules, the malignancy classification, and N-stage prediction of tumors (Fig. 2.21).

2.7.2 Pyradiomics—radiomics algorithm library

Pyradiomics (http://pyradiomics.readthedocs.io/en/latest/) was developed by Harvard University's Hugo team, which provides a set of open source radiomic feature extraction algorithms using Python. The algorithm library mainly includes shape, texture, intensity, wavelet, HOG, and other scale operators for feature extraction. At the same time, the library provides a very convenient unified interface and support for convenient Python function calls; it also provides a 3D Slicer plug-in, which can be imported as a 3D Slicer plug-in for visual feature extraction, suitable for imaging doctors.

There are currently four ways to install pyradiomics: 1. via pip; 2. from the source code github; 3. using the 3D Slicer Radiomics extension; and 4. using pyradiomics Docker. Pyradiomics can calculate the following characteristics:

1. Grayscale histogram feature (intensity feature/first-order feature)

   The gray histogram feature mainly uses statistics to describe the distribution of gray values in an image. Let X and X_all represent the pixel values of the previously outlined ROI, and the entire ROI has a total of N pixels. P is used to represent the probability vector of the gray histogram, and B is the center gray value. Define the following feature calculations:

   (1) Gray value intensity range:

   $$\text{gray value intensity range} = \frac{\max X - \min X}{\max X_{all} - \min X_{all}} \quad (2.71)$$

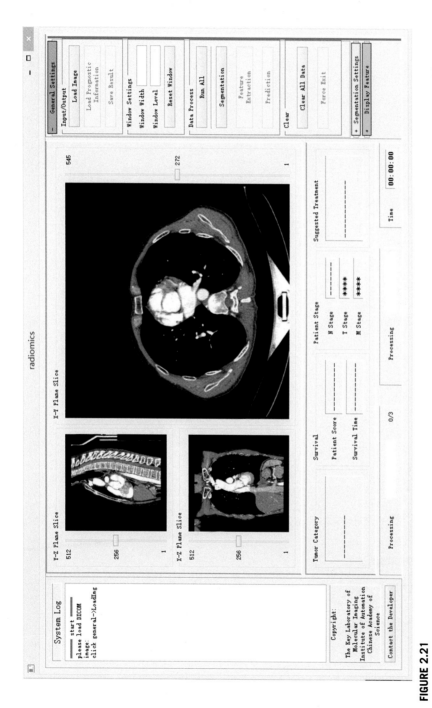

FIGURE 2.21

Radiomics work diagram.

(2) Energy:

$$\text{energy} = \sum_i^{N_l} (N * P(i))^2 \tag{2.72}$$

(3) Entropy:

$$\text{entropy} = \sum_i^{N_l} P(i) * \log_2 P(i) \tag{2.73}$$

(4) Kurtosis:

$$\text{kurtosis} = \frac{\sum_i^{N_l} P(i) * \left(B(i) - \overline{X}\right)^4}{\left(\sqrt{\sum_i^{N_l} P(i) * \left(B(i) - \overline{X}\right)}\right)^4} \tag{2.74}$$

(5) Maximum Value:

$$\max X \tag{2.75}$$

(6) Mean:

$$\text{mean} = \overline{X} := \frac{1}{N} \sum_i^{N} X(i) \tag{2.76}$$

(7) Mean Absolute Deviation (MAD):

$$\text{MAD} = \sum_i^{N_l} P(i) * \left(B(i) - \overline{X}\right) \tag{2.77}$$

(8) Median:

$$\left|\{x \mid x \in X \text{ and } x < x_{\text{Median}}\}\right| = \left|\{x \mid x \in X \text{and } x_{\text{Median}} < x\}\right| \tag{2.78}$$

(9) Minimum Value:

$$\min X \tag{2.79}$$

(10) Number of Pixels:

$$\text{number of pixels} = |X| \tag{2.80}$$

(11) Range:

$$\text{range} = \max X - \min X \tag{2.81}$$

(12) Root Mean Square (RMS):

$$\text{RMS} = \sum_{i}^{N_I} P(i) * B(i)^2 \tag{2.82}$$

(13) Skewness:

$$\text{skewness} = \frac{\sum_{i}^{N_I} P(i) * \left(B(i) - \overline{X}\right)^3}{\left(\sqrt{\sum_{i}^{N_I} P(i) * \left(B(i) - \overline{X}\right)}\right)^3} \tag{2.83}$$

(14) Standard Deviation:

$$\text{standard deviation} = \sqrt{\frac{1}{N-1} \sum_{i}^{N} \left(X(i) - \overline{X}\right)^2} \tag{2.84}$$

(15) Sum Pixel:

$$\text{sum pixel} = \sum_{i}^{N} X(i) \tag{2.85}$$

(16) Uniformity:

$$\text{uniformity} = \sum_{i}^{N_I} P(i)^2 \tag{2.86}$$

(17) Variance:

$$\text{variance} = \frac{1}{N-1} \sum_{i}^{N} \left(X(i) - \overline{X}\right)^2 \tag{2.87}$$

2. Shape feature
Shape features are primarily features used to describe the shape and size of the ROI. A is used to indicate the surface area of the ROI region, and V is used to represent the volume.

(1) Compactness1:

$$\text{compactness1} = \frac{V}{\sqrt{\pi} * A^{\frac{2}{3}}} \tag{2.88}$$

(2) Compactness2:

$$\text{compactness2} = 36\pi \frac{A^2}{V^3} \tag{2.89}$$

(3) Maximum 3D diameter:
Calculate the largest Euclidean distance between two pixels in the ROI area.
(4) Spherical Disproportion:

$$\text{spherical disproportion} = \frac{A}{4\pi * R^2} = \frac{A}{\left(6\sqrt{\pi} * V\right)^{\frac{2}{3}}} \tag{2.90}$$

(5) Spherical:

$$\text{spherical} = \frac{\left(6\pi^2 V\right)^{\frac{2}{3}}}{A} \tag{2.91}$$

(6) Surface Area to Volume ratio:

$$\text{surface area to volume ratio} = \frac{A}{V} \tag{2.92}$$

(7) ROI Volume:

$$V = N * r_{lat} * r_{cor} * r_{ax} \tag{2.93}$$

3. Texture feature
Texture features are primarily used to describe the characteristics of the pixels of the ROI and its surrounding pixels. It can be calculated by using the Gray-Level Co-occurrence Matrix (GLCM), Gray-Level Size Zone Matrix (GLSZM), Gray-Level Run Length Matrix (GLRLM), Neighborhood Gray-Tone Difference Matrix (NGTDM), and Gray-Level Dependence Matrix (GLDM). The gray values of the image are combined into N_g. Based on these combined gray values, the size of the Gray-Level Co-occurrence Matrix (GLCM) P is $N_g \times N_g$. The (i,j) th element of the matrix is defined as the pixel of the i thN_g multiplied by the distance δ, and the direction is α. The following example is a 2D image I and its GLCM, $\delta = 1, 2, 3$ in the horizontal direction:

$$
I = \begin{matrix} 2 & 4 & 1 & 1 & 2 \\ 1 & 3 & 5 & 5 & 1 \\ 2 & 3 & 4 & 2 & 3 \\ 1 & 2 & 5 & 2 & 1 \\ 5 & 3 & 1 & 3 & 5 \end{matrix} \qquad GLCM = \begin{matrix} 1 & 2 & 2 & 0 & 0 \\ 1 & 0 & 2 & 1 & 1 \\ 1 & 0 & 0 & 1 & 2 \\ 1 & 1 & 0 & 0 & 0 \\ 1 & 1 & 1 & 0 & 1 \end{matrix}
$$

Calculate 3D texture features based on GLCM. $P_{\alpha,\delta}(i,j) = P(i,j)$: The probability of GLCM pairing i,j. μ: The mean of $P(i,j)$. σ: The standard deviation of $P(i,i)$. $P_x(i) = \sum_{j}^{N_g} P(i,j)$: The probability of each line. μ_x: The mean of $P_x(i)$. σ_x: The standard deviation of $P_x(i)$. $P_{x+y}(k): = \sum_{i}^{N_g} \sum_{j}^{N_g} P(i,j),\ i+j = k.$

$P_{x-y}(k): = \sum_{i}^{N_g} \sum_{j}^{N_g} P(i,j),\ |i-j| = k.$

(1) Autocorrelation:

$$
autocorrelation = \sum_{i}^{N_g} \sum_{j}^{N_g} i * j * P(i,j) \tag{2.94}
$$

(2) Cluster Prominence:

$$
cluster\ prominence = \sum_{i}^{N_g} \sum_{j}^{N_g} (i + j - 2\mu)^4 P(i,j) \tag{2.95}
$$

(3) Cluster Shade:

$$
cluster\ shade = \sum_{i}^{N_g} \sum_{j}^{N_g} (i + j - 2\mu)^3 P(i,j) \tag{2.96}
$$

(4) Cluster Tendency:

$$
cluster\ tendency = \sum_{i}^{N_g} \sum_{j}^{N_g} (i + j - 2\mu)^2 P(i,j) \tag{2.97}
$$

(5) Contrast:

$$
contrast = \sum_{i}^{N_g} \sum_{j}^{N_g} (i - j)^2 P(i,j) \tag{2.98}
$$

(6) Correlation:

$$\text{correlation} = \frac{1}{\sigma} \sum_i^{N_g} \sum_j^{N_g} (i - \mu)(j - \mu) P(i,j) \tag{2.99}$$

(7) Difference Average:

$$\text{difference average} = \sum_i^{N_g} i * P_{x-y}(i) \tag{2.100}$$

(8) Differential Entropy:

$$\text{differential entropy} = \sum_i^{N_g} P_{x-y}(i) * \log_2(P_{x-y}(i)) \tag{2.101}$$

(9) Difference Variance:

$$\text{difference variance} = \sum_i^{N_g} \left(i - \overline{P_{x-y}}\right)^2 * P_{x-y}(i) \tag{2.102}$$

(10) Dissimilarity:

$$\text{dissimilarity} = \sum_i^{N_g} \sum_j^{N_g} |i - j| P(i,j) \tag{2.103}$$

(11) Joint Energy:

$$\text{joint energy} = \sum_i^{N_g} \sum_j^{N_g} P(i,j)^2 \tag{2.104}$$

(12) Joint Entropy:

$$\text{joint entropy} = \sum_i^{N_g} \sum_j^{N_g} P(i,j) \log_2[P(i,j)] \tag{2.105}$$

(13) Harralick Correlation:

$$\text{Harralick correlation} = \frac{1}{\sigma_x} \left[\sum_i^{N_g} \sum_j^{N_g} i * j * P(i,j) - \mu_x \right] \tag{2.106}$$

(14) Homogeneity:

$$\text{homogeneity} = \sum_{i}^{N_g} \sum_{j}^{N_g} \frac{P(i,j)}{1 + |i-j|} \qquad (2.107)$$

(15) Inverse Difference Moment (IDM):

$$IDM = \sum_{i}^{N_g} \sum_{j}^{N_g} \frac{P(i,j)}{1 + (i-j)^2} \qquad (2.108)$$

(16) Inverse Difference Moment Normalized (IDMN):

$$IDMN = \frac{1}{N^2} \sum_{i}^{N_g} \sum_{j}^{N_g} \frac{P(i,j)}{1 + (i-j)^2} \qquad (2.109)$$

(17) Inverse Difference Normalized (IDN):

$$IDN = \frac{1}{N} \sum_{i}^{N_g} \sum_{j}^{N_g} \frac{P(i,j)}{1 + |i-j|} \qquad (2.110)$$

(18) Inverse Variance:

$$\text{inverse variance} = \sum_{i}^{N_g} \sum_{j}^{N_g} \frac{P(i,j)}{(i-j)^2}; i \neq j \qquad (2.111)$$

(19) Maximum Probability:

$$\text{maximum probability} = \max\{P(i,j)\} \qquad (2.112)$$

(20) Sum Average:

$$\text{sum average} = \sum_{i}^{2N_g} i * P_{x+y}(i) \qquad (2.113)$$

(21) Sum Entropy:

$$\text{sum entropy} = \sum_{i}^{2N_g} P_{x+y}(i) * \log_2(P_{x+y}(i)) \qquad (2.114)$$

(22) Sum Variance:

$$\text{sum variance} = \sum_{i}^{2N_g} \left(i - \overline{P_{x+y}}\right)^2 * P_{x+y}(i) \tag{2.115}$$

(23) Variance:

$$\text{variance} = \sum_{i}^{N_g} \sum_{j}^{N_g} (i - \mu)^2 P(i,j) \tag{2.116}$$

The Gray-Level Run Length Matrix (GLRLM) P is defined as an image. In a given direction θ, each element (k, l) is used to describe how many surrounding pixels l in the matrix are connected to bin k. For example, there is a matrix like this:

$$
I = \begin{matrix}
2 & 4 & 1 & 1 & 2 \\
1 & 1 & 5 & 5 & 5 \\
2 & 3 & 4 & 2 & 3 \\
1 & 2 & 2 & 2 & 1 \\
5 & 3 & 1 & 3 & 5
\end{matrix}
\qquad \text{GLRLM} =
\begin{matrix}
3 & 2 & 0 & 0 & 0 \\
4 & 0 & 1 & 0 & 0 \\
4 & 0 & 0 & 0 & 0 \\
2 & 0 & 0 & 0 & 0 \\
2 & 0 & 1 & 0 & 0
\end{matrix}
$$

Calculate 3D texture features based on GLRLM. $P_{\theta(k,l)=P(k,l)}$: There are pixels k and length l and direction θ. N_g: Discrete pixel. N_r: Discrete length. N_{run}: Run length. N_p: Pixels within the ROI.

(1) Gray-Level Nonuniformity (GLN):

$$GLN := \frac{1}{N_{run}} \sum_{k}^{N_g} \left[\sum_{l}^{N_r} P(k,l) \right]^2 \tag{2.117}$$

(2) High Gray-Level Run Emphasis (HGLRE):

$$HGLRE := \frac{1}{N_{run}} \sum_{k}^{N_g} \sum_{l}^{N_r} k^2 * P(k,l) \tag{2.118}$$

(3) Long Run Emphasis (LRE):

$$LRE := \frac{1}{N_{run}} \sum_{k}^{N_g} \sum_{l}^{N_r} l^2 * P(k,l) \tag{2.119}$$

(4) Long Run High Gray-Level Emphasis (LRHGLE):

$$LRHGLE := \frac{1}{N_{run}} \sum_{k}^{N_g} \sum_{l}^{N_r} k^2 l^2 * P(k, l) \qquad (2.120)$$

(5) Long Run Low Gray-Level Emphasis (LRLGLE):

$$LRLGLE := \frac{1}{N_{run}} \sum_{k}^{N_g} \sum_{l}^{N_r} \frac{l^2}{k^2} P(k, l) \qquad (2.121)$$

(6) Low Gray-Level Run Emphasis:

$$LGLRE := \frac{1}{N_{run}} \sum_{k}^{N_g} \sum_{l}^{N_r} \frac{1}{k^2} P(k, l) \qquad (2.122)$$

(7) Number of Runs:

$$\text{number of runs} = N_{runs} := \sum_{k}^{N_g} \sum_{l}^{N_r} P(k, l) \qquad (2.123)$$

(8) Run Length Nonuniformity (RLN):

$$RLN := \frac{1}{N_{run}} \sum_{l}^{N_r} \left[\sum_{k}^{N_g} P(k, l) \right]^2 \qquad (2.124)$$

(9) Run Percentage (RP):

$$RP := \frac{N_{run}}{N_p} \qquad (2.125)$$

(10) Short Run Emphasis (SRE):

$$SRE := \frac{1}{N_{run}} \sum_{k}^{N_g} \sum_{l}^{N_r} \frac{1}{l^2} * P(k, l) \qquad (2.126)$$

(11) Short Run High Gray-Level Emphasis (SRHGLE):

$$SRHGLE := \frac{1}{N_{run}} \sum_{k}^{N_g} \sum_{l}^{N_r} \frac{k^2}{l^2} P(k, l) \qquad (2.127)$$

(12) Short Run Low Gray-Level Emphasis (SRLGLE):

$$SRLGLE := \frac{1}{N_{run}} \sum_{k}^{N_g} \sum_{l}^{N_r} \frac{1}{k^2 l^2} P(k, l) \tag{2.128}$$

The above features can be used for both the original image and the filtered image. Filtering includes wavelet transform, LoG operator, square graph, square root, logarithm, and exponent. The correlation function is inimageoperations.py. You can use enableAllImageTypes(), disableAllImageTypes(), enableImageType ByName(), and enableImageTypes() to customize the type of image.enable AllFeatures(), disableAllFeatures(), enableFeatureClassByName(), and enable-FeaturesByName() can be used to customize the calculated feature type and name. At the same time, pyradiomics can customize Image Normalization and Image Resample and Resampling Interpolation. The default interpolation method is cubic B-spline interpolation.

If using the 3D Slicer Radiomics, plugin as shown in Fig. 2.22.

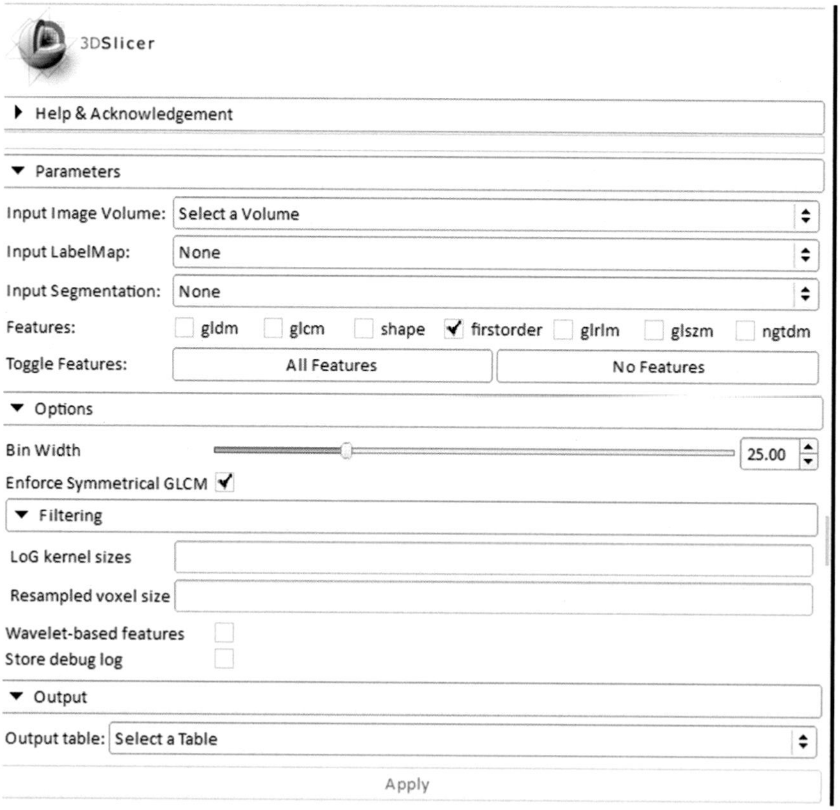

FIGURE 2.22

3D slicer extraction feature interface.

References

[1] Jacobs C, Van Rikxoort EM, Twellmann T, et al. Automatic detection of subsolid pulmonary nodules in thoracic computed tomography images. Med Image Anal 2014; 18(2):374—84.

[2] Ojala T, Pietikäinen M, Mäenpää T. Gray scale and rotation invariant texture classification with local binary patterns//computer vision - ECCV. 2000. p. 404—20.

[3] Wang S, Zhou M, Liu Z, et al. Central focused convolutional neural networks: developing a data-driven model for lung nodule segmentation. Med Image Anal 2017;40: 172—83.

[4] He K. Delving deep into rectifiers: surpassing human-level performance on ImageNet classification. In: IEEE international conference on computer vision (ICCV). IEEE; 2015. p. 1026—34.

[5] Havaei M, Davy A, Warde-Farley D, et al. Brain tumor segmentation with deep neural networks. Med Image Anal 2017;35:18—31.

[6] Chen L, Papandreou G, Schroff F, et al. Rethinking atrous convolution for semantic image segmentation. December 26, 2017. http://arxiv.org/abs/1706.05587.

[7] Aerts HJWL, Velazquez ER, Leijenaar RTH, et al. Decoding tumour phenotype by noninvasive imaging using a quantitative radiomics approach. Nat Commun 2014;5.

[8] Yu D, Zhou M, Yang F, et al. Convolutional neural networks for predicting molecular profiles of non-small cell lung cancer. In: Proceedings - international symposium on biomedical imaging. IEEE; 2017. p. 569—72.

[9] Wang S, Liu Z, Chen X, et al. Unsupervised deep learning features for lung cancer overall survival analysis. In: Proceedings of the annual international conference of the IEEE engineering in medicine and biology society; 2018. p. 2583—6.

[10] Abdi H, Williams LJ. Principal component analysis. Wiley Interdis Rev Comput Stat 2010;2(4):433—59.

[11] Tibshirani R. Regression shrinkage and selection via the lasso. J Roy Stat Soc B 1996; 58(1):267—88.

[12] Huang YQ, Liang CH, He L, et al. Development and validation of a radiomics nomogram for preoperative prediction of lymph node metastasis in colorectal cancer. J Clin Oncol 2016;34(18):2157—64.

[13] Shen W, Zhou M, Yang F, et al. Multi-scale convolutional neural networks for lung nodule classification. Inf Process Med Imaging 2015:588—99.

[14] Shen W, Zhou M, Yang F, et al. Multi-crop convolutional neural networks for lung nodule malignancy suspiciousness classification. Pattern Recogn 2017;61:663—73.

[15] Esteva A, Kuprel B, Novoa RA, et al. Dermatologist-level classification of skin cancer with deep neural networks. Nature 2017;542(7639):115—8.

[16] Ting DSW, Cheung CY-L, Lim G, et al. Development and validation of a deep learning system for diabetic retinopathy and related eye diseases using retinal images from multiethnic populations with diabetes. J Am Med Assoc 2017;318(22):2211—23.

[17] Kermany DS, Goldbaum M, Cai W, et al. Identifying medical diagnoses and treatable diseases by image-based deep learning Resource identifying medical diagnoses and treatable diseases by image-based deep learning. Cell 2018;172(5):1122—1131.e9.

[18] Huang G, Liu Z, Maaten LVD, et al. Densely connected convolutional networks. In: 2017 IEEE conference on computer vision and pattern recognition (CVPR); 2017. p. 2261—9.

[19] Wang S, Shi J, Ye Z, et al. Predicting EGFR mutation status in lung adenocarcinoma on computed tomography image using deep learning. Eur Respir J 2019;53(3).

[20] Wang S, Liu Z, Rong Y, et al. Deep learning provides a new computed tomography-based prognostic biomarker for recurrence prediction in high-grade serous ovarian cancer. Radiother Oncol 2019;132:171−7.

[21] Lambin P, Leijenaar RTH, Deist TM, et al. Radiomics: the bridge between medical imaging and personalized medicine. Nat Rev Clin Oncol 2017;14(12):749−62.

[22] Freund Y, Schapire RE. A desicion-theoretic generalization of on-line learning and an application to boosting//. Comput Learn Theory 1995:23−37.

[23] Therneau TM, Lumley T, Elizabeth A, Cynthia C. Package 'survival'. 2020. https://cran.uib.no/web/packages/survival/survival.pdf.

Precision diagnosis based on radiomics

3

Chapter outline

Radiomics and its Clinical Application. https://doi.org/10.1016/B978-0-12-818101-0.00005-7

Auxiliary diagnosis is one of the leading clinical applications of radiomics, and it can be considered as the development of the traditional medical image-based computer-aided diagnosis (CAD) method. The application of radiomics in auxiliary diagnosis revolves around specific clinical demand, explores large numbers of high-throughput features from standardized medical images, and finally establishes generalized quantitative models with high diagnostic efficiency [1,2]. Compared with traditional CAD, radiomic methods are more targeted toward the enrolled population and the clinical issues, and thus have more practical value [3]. Based on the routinely used medical images, radiomics can be widely used in the cancer diagnosis, such as screening, staging, histopathological diagnosis, gene mutation prediction and molecular subtype prediction.

One of the biggest challenges in oncology research is carrying out accurate and early screening and diagnosis of cancer patients. In the National Lung Cancer Screening Trial (NLST) involving 53,000 people, the mortality rate of lung cancer was reduced by the screening using low-dose computed tomography (CT). However, the screening using low-dose CT is proved to be too aggressive, causing a high false-positive rate and a large number of patients to receive overtreatment. The same concern could also be found in other cancers. Therefore, reducing the proportion of overdiagnosis in routine screening while maintaining high sensitivity and specificity is an important clinical issue. Radiomic techniques may provide a potential solution for precise screening.

The staging of cancer affects the determination of treatment strategies, which can help clinicians develop radical or conservative individualized treatment plans. Quantitative diagnosis based on radiomics can help improve the efficacy of clinical decision-making. Malignant tumors accompanied by lymph node metastasis (LNM) have poor prognosis. All invaded lymph nodes (LNs) should be thoroughly removed during surgery, otherwise recurrence and metastasis may occur. However, it is difficult to diagnose the presence of LNM by medical images or biopsy before surgery. Meanwhile, it is also tough to estimate the tumor infiltration degree and distant metastasis status preoperatively. Making an accurate prediction of cancer staging before surgery is a challenging problem in the current clinical management of most cancers. In response to this problem, predictive models based on radiomics showed good efficacy, which is in line with or better than traditional medical image evaluation.

Specific histopathological classification, gene mutation, and molecular subtyping of tumors are tightly associated with targeted therapy effect or the sensitivity to radiotherapy and chemotherapy. Gene mutation and cancer classification based on radiomics can act as a non-invasive, real-time, economical, and easy-to-implement detection method. Some researchers have revealed the success of radiomics in cancer histopathological classification and gene mutation, such as prediction of histopathological grade in bladder cancer, prediction of epidermal growth factor receptor (EGFR) mutation in lung cancer, and prediction of KRAS/NRAS/BRAF mutations in colorectal cancer.

In addition to the application of radiomics in cancers, its application in other diseases also achieved good results. For the coronavirus disease 2019 (COVID-19), CT-based radiomics not only helps improve the sensitivity and specificity of screening and diagnosis but also relieves the pressure of a tight clinical environment and medical resource allocation. Besides, radiomics has also been applied to liver fibrosis, portal hypertension, and cardiovascular diseases. In the following subsections, we will introduce some typical radiomic studies with practical clinical usefulness and important reference value in cancer and other diseases.

3.1 Application of radiomics in cancer screening

One of the biggest difficulties in oncology research is the exploitation of accurate and economic screening methods. Many studies have shown that the use of CAD systems improves the overall performance of radiologists using medical images for cancer detection and diagnosis. However, the current CAD systems usually allow radiologists to describe lesions intuitively, so that they are limited to subjective and qualitative characterization of lesions. Additionally, extensive evaluation of all available images by radiologists is also time-consuming. Therefore, by using more objective and quantitative methods for tumor characterization, the accuracy and effectiveness of diagnosis may be improved.

In recent years, radiomics is one of the emerging fields most relevant to quantitative cancer screening and diagnosis [1], which involves high-throughput feature extraction and thorough statistical analysis of a large number of image-derived features associated with cancer phenotypes. Radiomic methods can help improve the objective and quantitative diagnosis and evaluation of tumors. Compared with current qualitative strategies, it can significantly reduce the differences between observers and improve the performance of screening.

3.1.1 Lung cancer screening

Lung cancer is one of the most common malignant tumors. In recent years, there have been many radiomic studies on lung cancer screening [4–6]. Early screening and diagnosis can well assist in improving lung cancer patients' outcomes, especially those with a very low survival rate.

The NLST summarized the comparisons between low-dose CT and chest radiography within 3 years. Compared with chest radiography, low-dose CT could bring approximately 20% reduction in lung cancer mortality [7]. These encouraging statistics motivated the advancement of lung cancer screening. In the current clinical diagnosis, low-dose CT has already become the first-line screening modality for lung cancer, as it provides good contrast between lesion and normal lung tissue [8]. However, lots of pulmonary nodules detected by low-dose CT cannot be determined as lung cancer [9]. These indeterminate pulmonary nodules (IPNs) with a diameter of 4−12 mm were considered "suspicious", and 96.4% of them did not develop into cancers in screening or follow-up. Hence, overdiagnosis may cause severe anxiety in patients and worsen the disease condition.

In order to solve this problem, Hawkins et al. [4] aimed to investigate the potential of quantitative image features that may accurately identify whether the IPNs at baseline time (T0) would be clinically diagnosed as lung cancer at the first follow-up time (T1) or the second follow-up time (T2). They adopted demographically matched cohorts of screening CT images with IPNs that did or did not develop into cancers later. The matched scheme minimized the effects of confounding risk factors that existed between patients with lung cancer and benign pulmonary nodules (bPN). Two Low-dose CT screening cohorts from the NLST were accessed. In the cohorts, a positive screen was defined as a noncalcified nodule of 4 mm or larger in the axial plane or with other abnormalities. As shown in Fig. 3.1, both cohorts had positive screens at T0 (nodule-positive but cancer-negative), while individuals in the screen-detected lung cancer (SDLC) cohort 1 had an SDLC at T1; those in SDLC cohort 2 still had positive screens at T1, but had an SDLC at T2 (about 2 years after T0). For comparison, two control cohorts (cancer-free screening with bPNs) were enrolled, frequency-matched 2:1 to the SDLCs in terms of clinical characteristics and risk factors.

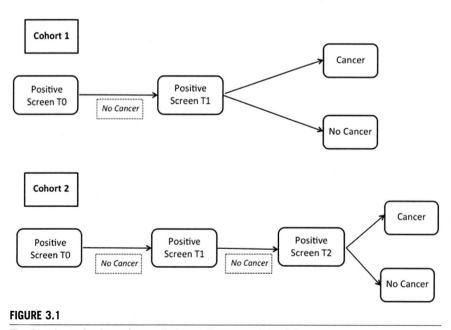

FIGURE 3.1

The flowchart of cohorts for predicting malignant nodules [4].

In this study, the SDLC cohort 1 had nodule-positive/cancer-negative screens at T0 with diagnosed SDLC at T1 in 104 patients, demographically matching 208 patients with bPNs, of which 176 were successfully segmented. SDLC cohort 2 had nodule-positive/cancer-negative screens at T0 and T1, followed by SDLC at T2 in 92 patients. These patients were demographically matched to 184 patients with bPNs, of which 157 were successfully segmented. In the statistical analysis, they found that patients diagnosed with lung cancer usually had larger nodules. The longest diameters of nodules were significantly different between SDLC cohorts and bPN cohorts.

A total of 219 three-dimensional (3D) features were extracted from the segmented regions of interest (ROIs). These features quantitatively described the size, shape, location, and texture characteristics. Models based on these features were developed to predict the occurrence of lung cancer after the baseline time (T0). All of the models were built and validated using the WEKA data mining software [10]. The modeling methods included J48, JRIP (RIPPER), Naive Bayes, support vector machine (SVM), and random forest (RF). J48 is a decision tree-based classifier and JRIP is a rule learner [11]. Before cross-validation, two feature selection algorithms were used in each fold: Relief-f and correlation-based feature subset selection. The Relief-f algorithm adopted a ranker search, and the correlation-based feature selection adopted a greedy stepwise search.

Using an RF classifier with RIDER-prioritized features [12], the best accuracy for predicting subsequent cancer occurrence at T1 from baseline scans at T0 was 80.1% (area under the curve [AUC] = 0.83; false-positive rate [FPR] = 9%). The method using SVM with a radial kernel and RIDER-prioritized features along with the Relief-f selected features showed the highest accuracy of 78.7% (AUC = 0.75; FPR = 11%) for predicting subsequent cancer occurrence at T2.

The study also compared the classification performance of different models in differentiating malignant nodules from bPNs. For example, the Lung Imaging Reporting and Data System (Lung-RADS) was established by the American College of Radiology to help standardize the lung cancer screening (malignant versus benign pulmonary nodules) from CT images. Category 3 and below were annotated as benign, and category 4A and 4B were annotated as malignant. This study performed Lung-RADS classification on screening at T0 based on 58 pre-cancer cases from the SDLC cohort 2 and 127 bPNs from the bPN cohort 2. McWilliams et al. [13] incorporated clinical characteristics (i.e., age, sex, and family history of cancer) and nodule characteristics (i.e., nodule size, solidity, nodule location, number of nodules, and spiculation) into a model to calculate the probability of lung cancer occurrence. In their model, a risk of below 5% represented a low probability of cancer development, while a risk from 5% to 10% was an intermediate level, and risk greater than 10% indicated a high probability of cancer occurrence. The study marked the first two groups as free-of-cancer and the third group as lung cancer. Model performance comparison was conducted based on the same subjects from the SDLC cohort 2 and bPN cohort 2 as Lung-RADS. Furthermore, the radiomic approach was also compared to the scheme using volume as the only feature.

The performances of the above four approaches for predicting cancer development from baseline screens are shown in Table 3.1.

The Lung-RADS model included several categories: 2 (benign appearance), 3 (probably benign), and 4A, 4B (suspicious). The McWilliams model included low, intermediate, and high risks. The radiomic model and the volume scheme included low, intermediate-low, intermediate-high, and high risks. Top performances for each method are in bold.

The results showed that the radiomic model based on pulmonary nodule features from baseline CT scans could predict the subsequent development of lung cancer or non-cancer, yielding an overall accuracy of 80.0%. Specifically, the accuracies of Lung-RADS model, McWilliams model, and the volume scheme were 71.4%, 78.9%, and 71.8%, respectively. Using McNemar's test, the radiomic model demonstrated a significantly better performance than the Lung-RADS model (two-tailed, $P = .0177$) and the volume scheme (two-tailed, $P = .025$). Moreover, the radiomic approach had an accuracy greater than 90.0% when predicting extreme benign and malignant nodule.

The long-term impact of Hawkins et al.'s work will be the application of radiomics in reducing overdiagnosis and overtreatment from lung nodule screening. Benefiting from their study design, the radiomics-predicted risk probabilities of subsequent cancer development can be used to indicate optimal follow-up scan time. For example, patients with a low risk of cancer occurrence could undergo low-dose CT examinations less frequently than those with a high risk.

Besides, Peikert et al. [5] also used the NLST dataset to carry out a radiomics study to discriminate malignant from benign pulmonary nodules. This study, however, preferred IPNs. Participants who had CT scans and did not withdraw from follow-up were selected from the NLST. Among the whole cohort, the lung cancer cases included seven subtypes. Non-cancer control cases were selected from all participants without any diagnosis of lung cancer at baseline CT screening or in the follow-up periods. Pulmonary nodules with the largest diameter from 7 to 30 mm were analyzed. Patients with multiple nodules were also included. Finally, 408 malignant nodules and 318 bPNs were included (Fig. 3.2). All of the pulmonary nodules were then manually segmented.

Most current studies suggest that multivariate models incorporating nodule texture/density, surrounding texture/density, nodule surface, and other morphological features could improve the predictive performance. Peikert et al.'s study adopted a set of predefined quantitative radiomic features that could be automatically computed and further included in multivariable model development for differentiating lung cancer from bPN. The radiomic features were divided into the following categories: (1) nodule location; (2) nodule size; (3) nodule shape; (4) radiodensity features based on the CT Hounsfield units (HUs); (5) nodule texture/density features based on the texture distributions; (6) texture/density features within a nodule surrounding region; (7) features describing the nodule surface; and (8) features capturing the distribution of the nodule surface characteristics exemplars. Univariate analysis was conducted for each feature for evaluating the discriminatory power.

Table 3.1 Model performances for predicting cancer development from baseline screening [4].

Model	Category	No. of Malignant	No. of Benign	Total	Accuracy	TPR	TNR
Overall	Total	58	127	185			
Lung-RADS (71.4%)	2	32	99	131	75.6%		
	3	13	20	33	60.6%		
	4A	10	7	17	58.8%		
	4B	3	1	4	75.0%		
	Total	58	127	185	71.4%	22.4%	**93.7%**
McWilliams (78.9%)	Low	24	98	122	79.7%		
	Intermediate	7	21	28	75.0%		
	High	27	8	35	77.1%		
	Total	58	127	185	78.9%	46.5%	**93.7%**
Radiomics (80.0%)	Low	6	80	86	93.0%		
	Intermediate-low	22	38	60	63.3%		
	Intermediate-high	17	8	25	68.0%		
	High	13	1	14	92.9%		
	Total	58	127	185	**80.0%**	**51.7%**	92.9%
Volume (71.8%)	Low	17	85	102	83.3%		
	Intermediate-low	13	20	33	60.6%		
	Intermediate-high	5	15	20	25.0%		
	High	23	7	30	76.6%		
	Total	58	127	185	71.8%	48.2%	82.7%

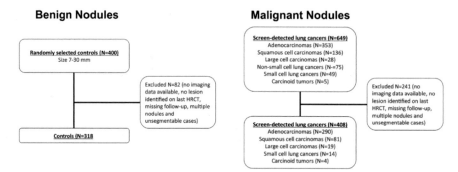

726 Nodules (318 Benign and 408 Malignant Nodules)

FIGURE 3.2

The flowchart of nodule selection [5].
HRCT, high-resolution computed tomography.

Multivariate analysis was conducted by the least absolute shrinkage and selection operator (LASSO) method for feature selection. To increase the model stability, the study ran the LASSO method 1000 times and only the features selected by at least 50% of the runs were used in the final model. Bonferroni correction was used to calculate and adjust the statistical significances [14].

Eight features were screened out, including one feature about nodule location, two features quantifying nodule shape, one feature describing nodule texture, and four features describing nodule surface, all with $P < .01$. With the eight selected features, a multivariate model was built, yielding an AUC of 0.941. After correcting the overfitting, the optimism-corrected AUC achieved 0.939. The sensitivity and specificity were 0.904 and 0.855, with the optimal threshold of 0.478 by the Youden's index method. Furthermore, the subgroup analysis of nodules with the size from 7 to 15 mm achieved an AUC of 0.9477 and an optimism-corrected AUC of 0.9409, showing good discriminative ability. This study indicated that the radiomic model had advantages over the existing clinical or radiological prediction models. Rather than replacing current clinical tools that could assess lung nodules based on nodule size or shape, the radiomic model represents an auxiliary diagnostic choice to guide clinical decision-making for IPNs.

Recently, Ardila et al. [6] proposed an end-to-end deep learning-based lung cancer screening approach using the patients' current and prior low-dose CT images to predict individual cancer occurrence risk. Their study was also carried out on the NLST database (with 6716 cases for validation) and further validated on an independent validation cohort (with 1139 cases). There were three highlights making up the key components of their study: (1) the 3D deep convolutional neural networks (CNNs) were trained on whole low-dose CT volumes with pathology-confirmed lung cancer (also called the full-volume model); (2) the features characterizing the ROI were learned automatically by deep learning methods, rather than the hand-engineered methods; and (3) both the cancer localization and malignancy probability were predicted.

Ardila et al.'s deep learning method could perform localization for predicted cancerous nodules on low-dose CT images and provide patient-level malignancy risk with impressive performance. Their tools could directly assist clinicians in lung cancer screening workflow. Low-dose CT screening is usually in a relatively early phase, so the potential for improvement in patient care in the coming stage is substantial. Thus, the model's localization function could assist in directing follow-up for specific nodules of greatest risk, including diagnostic CT examination or biopsy. In the future, the combination of hand-crafted features, deep-learning features, and clinical factors would be a research direction in lung cancer screening.

3.1.2 **Gastrointestinal cancer screening**

As one of the most common cancers, gastrointestinal cancers have posed a great threat to human health. Gastrointestinal cancer is usually diagnosed at advanced stages, and the prognosis is usually poor. Gastrointestinal cancer screening using radiomics may help to change the status quo [15].

According to previous reports, if detected early, the 5-year survival rate of gastro-intestinal cancers would be >90% [16]. The screening of gastrointestinal cancer utilizes endoscopy in most situations. However, in many less developed areas, the rate of endoscopically missed gastrointestinal cancers is still very high.

In Luo et al.'s multicenter study [15], a Gastrointestinal Artificial Intelligence Diagnostic System (GRAIDS) using endoscopic imaging data was developed for screening upper gastrointestinal cancers. This study included multicenter endo-scopic imaging data and a prospective validation cohort (Sun Yat-sen University Cancer Center, SYSUCC). None of the enrolled patients had undergone endoscopy previously, and all of them were over 18 years old and had no history of cancer. The patients were diagnosed by a pathological assessment based on the hematoxylin- and eosin-stained tissue slides. Only images with a standard white light were included, and low-quality pictures were excluded. A total of eight experienced endoscopists then participated in the image assessment and lesion segmentation. Any disagree-ment was settled by discussion.

The construction of GRAIDS was based on the DeepLab's V3+ concept [17], which consists of encoder and decoder modules. The input of the model was the endoscopic image, and the output included two elements: one was whether the image contained tumors, which was a classification task; the other was the segmen-tation of tumor areas, which was a segmentation task. The retrospective data from SYSUCC were applied to train GRAIDS. The performance of the model was validated on a prospective validation set from SYSUCC and five external validation sets from other hospitals. In the validation of GRAIDS, the intersection-over-union was calculated to assess the segmentation ability, the receiver operating character-istic (ROC) curve analysis was performed to assess the diagnostic performance of the model for upper gastrointestinal cancer prediction, and the Clopper-Pearson algorithm was applied to calculate the 95% confidence intervals (CIs) for the performance evaluation index. Two-sided statistical tests were conducted, and all significance levels were 0.05. To compare the diagnostic ability between GRAIDS and endoscopists, three endoscopists diagnosed a subset that was separated from the prospective validation set. The three endoscopists included an expert, a competent, and a trainee endoscopist with at least 10, 5, and 2 years of endoscopic experience, respectively. None of the three endoscopists participated in the image selection and segmentation.

A total of 314,726 images from 20,352 patients were obtained from SYSUCC. After reviewing the pathological reports and image quality, a total of 157,207 images, including 39,462 upper gastrointestinal cancer cases and 117,745 control images, were included in this study. The prospective validation set consisted of 4317 cancer images and 62,433 control images. In addition, 2,439, 5,244, 9,712, 7,095, and 4173 upper gastrointestinal cancer images and 73,015, 197,588, 112,185, 286,095, and 114,993 control images were obtained from five other hospitals, respectively.

Since the performance of the model GRAIDS did not improve further after 176 epochs of the training, the model training was then stopped. The results showed that the model's tumor segmentation ability was similar to that of the endoscopists, with a median intersection-over-union of 0.737 in the internal validation set. A good classification performance of GRAIDS was seen in all of the sets: the classification accuracy in the internal validation set was 0.955 (95% CI 0.952–0.957), in the prospective validation set it was 0.927 (95% CI 0.925–0.929), and in other validation sets, it reached 0.915 (95% CI 0.913–0.917), 0.949 (95% CI 0.947–0.951), 0.977 (95% CI 0.977–0.978), 0.970 (95% CI 0.969–0.971), and 0.947 (95% CI 0.946–0.948), respectively. Also, the specificity, sensitivity, and negative predictive value were higher than 0.9 in all of the sets.

When comparing the performance between the model GRAIDS and the endoscopists, the expert endoscopist achieved the highest accuracy of 0.967 (95% CI 0.961–0.973). The accuracy of the competent endoscopist was 0.956 (95% CI 0.949–0.963), that of the trainee endoscopist was 0.886 (95% CI 0.875–0.897), and the accuracy of GRAIDS here was 0.928 (95% CI 0.919–0.937). Also, GRAIDS achieved a sensitivity of 0.942 (95% CI 0.924–0.957), very close to the expert endoscopist (0.945, 95% CI 0.927–0.959), and higher than that of the competent and trainee endoscopists (0.858 and 0.722, respectively). The positive predictive value (PPV) of GRAIDS was lower than that of the expert and competent endoscopists. Notably, GRAIDS could identify most of the cancer images that endoscopists misidentified, and GRAIDS was faster than any endoscopist (8 ms per image).

Based on the above results, researchers pointed out that GRAIDS could have two important roles in clinical applications. First, it could help endoscopists detect upper gastrointestinal cancers in real time. Second, it could reduce the incidence of undetected or misdetected malignancies. GRAIDS is now available online, which may provide some help to endoscopists and patients. Also, GRAIDS could play an important role in resource-limited regions or most developing countries.

However, this study still has some limitations. Firstly, only white-light images were used for the training and validation. Secondly, researchers strictly controlled the image quality, which may be doubtful in the applications in more complex situations. Finally, although the study included large amounts of endoscopy examination data and validated the model in many validation sets, future analysis in other populations is still needed.

3.1.3 **Breast cancer screening**

As one of the highest causes of death from cancer among women, breast cancer is a serious threat. Mammography is commonly used for breast cancer screening. However, the false-positive rate of mammography is very high. The use of CAD may help improve the problem to some extent. But few CAD tools have been proven to improve the diagnostic performance of mammography. Therefore, Wu et al. developed a novel CNN-based model for breast cancer screening [18].

There are at least four mammogram views for one mammography examination, including the right craniocaudal (R-CC), left craniocaudal (L-CC), right mediolateral oblique (R-MLO), and left mediolateral oblique (L-MLO). In Wu et al.'s study, a total of 1,001,093 images (229,426 digital mammography examinations) generated from 141,473 patients were included. The labels (benign or malignant) of the dataset were determined based on the pathology examinations after biopsy. As both benign and malignant findings may be present in some breasts, researchers applied a multi-task learning framework for the model building. Both the right and left breasts were tested for the benign and malignant findings, so there were four binary labels for one patient. Each image was cropped to a fixed size (CC views: 2677×1942 pixels; MLO views: 2974×1748 pixels).

Then, researchers trained four different deep multiview CNN screening models (view-wise model, image-wise model, breast-wise model, and joint model), all of which consisted of two parts: four view-specific columns based on ResNet-22 and two fully connected layers that mapped the hidden layer to the predicted probabilities. In this study, the training set was used to optimize the model parameters, and the validation set was only used for tuning the hyperparameters. The Adam optimization algorithm was used to train the single-view ResNet-22 on the breast level. The learning rate was set at 10^{-5}. The training was stopped when the AUC of the validation set no longer improved during 20 consecutive epochs, and the model with the highest AUC in the validation set was chosen as the optimal model. Additionally, an auxiliary patch-level classification model was also constructed based on the manual segmentation of clinicians. To get better model performance, the model ensemble technique was adopted to average the predicted values of the five different models above. This study found that when the predictive capabilities of the two inputs were unbalanced, the overall performance of the network was similar to that of a branch with better predictive performance. The CC view showed better predictive performance than the MLO view.

As the number of samples with benign or malignant labels was small, transfer learning based on a Breast Imaging-Reporting and Data System (BI-RADS) classification task was used to pre-train the screening models. The labels of BI-RADS included BI-RADS Category 0 ("incomplete"), BI-RADS Category 1 ("normal"), and BI-RADS Category 2 ("benign"). The architecture of the BI-RADS classification model was consistent with that of the screening model, except for the number of prediction values. The other training details were also consistent with the screening model. The results of the experiments showed that the performance of the screening model could be improved by using the transferring training weights of the BI-RADS classification model.

During the validation of the models, researchers conducted three cohorts, including the screening population, biopsied subpopulation, and reader study subpopulation, which had different population distributions. The AUC and precision-recall AUC (PRAUC) were calculated to assess the model performances. In the screening population cohort, the four models obtained high and similar AUCs. Finally, the ensemble of the four models obtained the best AUC of 0.778 (benign/not benign) and 0.899 (malignant/not malignant). In the biopsied subpopulation cohort, compared with the results of the screening population cohort, the AUCs of the models were significantly lower, indicating that the diagnosis of breast cancer remains a challenge in the biopsied subpopulation. The ensemble of image-and-heatmaps models achieved the highest predictive performance in biopsied subpopulation cohort, with an AUC of 0.850 in malignant/not malignant classification, and 0.696 in benign/not benign classification.

In this study, researchers also compared the diagnostic performance between the ensemble model and the radiologists on a test cohort including 1480 cases. The AUC of the ensemble model was 0.876, and the PRAUC was 0.318. The average AUC of the radiologists was 0.778 (range: 0.705−0.860), with a standard deviation of 0.0435. The average PRAUC of the radiologists was 0.364 (range: 0.244−0.453), with a standard deviation of 0.0496. The study also combined the predicted value of the ensemble model with the diagnosis of the radiologists by linear regression. The mean AUC of the combined model was 0.891, with a standard deviation of 0.0109. The average PRAUC of the combined model was 0.431, with a standard deviation of 0.0332. This indicated that the model had the potential to assist the radiologists in the interpretation of breast cancer screening examinations.

In summary, Wu et al.'s study built a deep multiview CNN model for the breast cancer screening [18]. The performance of the model exceeded that of the radiologists, and its combination with the radiologists achieved higher classification performance. Multitask learning has the potential to play a role in the modeling of imaging data with multiple modes. In addition, although a lot of images were used to train the model (1,001,093 images of four kinds), using pretraining weights can improve the performance of the constructed model. Therefore, in most complex medical image modeling tasks, pretraining is always necessary. The results of this study still require further clinical validation. Although the model's classification performance was better than that of the radiologists, more images of different modalities such as ultrasound and magnetic resonance imaging (MRI) are often needed to draw the conclusion in clinical diagnosis.

3.1.4 **Prostate cancer screening**

As one of the most common primary tumors, prostate cancer (PCa) causes 30,000 deaths in the United States every year [19]. In clinical practice, multiparametric MRI has been widely used to screen and stage PCa. Recently, Prostate Imaging Reporting and Data System (PI-RADS v2) has been used to interpret the results of prostate MRI due to its encouraging performance [20]. However, satisfactory performance relies on experienced radiologists, thereby affecting the clinical application of PI-RADS v2. Additionally, as PI-RADS v2 can only output five levels of conclusions, it is not conducive for the quantitative assessment of PCa. Radiomic methods can construct machine learning models by extracting and modeling many quantitative MRI features, which have the potential to improve the diagnostic performance in PCa. Therefore, Wang et al. evaluated whether radiomic features could enhance the diagnostic performance of PI-RADS v2 [21].

In this study, prostate images were obtained by multiparametric MRI using T1-weighted imaging (T1WI), T2-weighted imaging (T2WI), diffusion-weighted imaging (DWI), and dynamic contrast-enhanced (DCE) imaging. The diagnosis of tumor lesions on MRI was defined by an experienced radiologist and a genitourinary pathologist. The radiologist segmented the 3D tumor ROIs, including transitional zone (TZ) and/or peripheral zone (PZ), and the pathologist confirmed these ROIs histologically. Finally, 47 normal PZ ROIs, 54 tumor ROIs, and 48 normal TZ ROIs were included. The researchers then extracted eight first-order statistical (volumetric) radiomic features, including mean, median, 10th percentile, 90th percentile, entropy, kurtosis, skewness, and non-homogeneity. All of the features were normalized to the mean value of 0 and the variance value of 1. In this study, three feature sets were constructed, including a PI-RADS score set, a radiomic feature set, and a combined set (a combination of the above two feature sets).

Based on the SVM model with a radial basis function kernel, a model was constructed to diagnose PCa. Considering that the high-dimensional feature set may lead to overfitting, SVM and recursive feature elimination (SVM-RFE) were performed to eliminate the redundant radiomic features. Due to the small sample size of this study, the leave-one-out cross-validation (LOOCV) approach was performed to train and test the SVM model. Finally, the sigmoid function was used to convert the output of the model into the probability of PCa.

During the validation of the models, ROC analysis was applied to assess the prediction performance of SVM models developed from PI-RADS scores, radiomic features, and combined features. After calculating the AUCs for the three models, the Wilcoxon signed rank test was performed to measure the statistical difference.

The Youden index was used to calculate positive likelihood ratio (+LR), negative likelihood ratio (-LR), sensitivity, and specificity.

The results showed that the radiomic model trained by radiomic features performed better than PI-RADS scores in discriminating PCa from normal TZ + PZ (AUC: 0.952 versus 0.864) and PCa from normal TZ (AUC: 0.955 versus 0.878). However, there was no statistical difference in discriminating PCa from normal PZ (AUC: 0.972 versus 0.940).

In summary, compared with PI-RADS v2, the radiomic model achieved higher sensitivity but slightly lower specificity. The combined SVM model constructed by radiomic features and PI-RADS scores achieved better performance. The decision curve analysis (DCA) was used to visualize the net benefit of the three models. The net benefit of PI-RADS v2 was the lowest in discriminating PCa from normal prostate tissue (TZ + PZ, TZ, and PZ), with a statistically significant difference. Compared with the other two models in discriminating PCa from normal prostate tissue, the combined model showed a higher net benefit.

In the interpretation of prostate MRI, PI-RADS v2 has been playing a very critical role but still relies on experienced radiologists. Although PI-RADS v2 has been proven to have good diagnostic performance, its sensitivity is very low (60%−80% in previous reports [22]). In this study, the radiomic model built with machine learning algorithms outperformed PI-RADS v2 in many aspects. Also, the results showed that the diagnostic performance of PI-RADS v2 could be significantly improved by the radiomic model. The sensitivity increased from 0.790 to 0.944 in discrimination between PCa and normal PZ, 0.734 to 0.916 in discrimination between PCa and normal TZ, and the +LR also increased from 7.06 to 41.54 in discrimination between PCa and normal PZ. By feature analysis, these increases may be related to the radiomic features that can reflect increased vascularity, capillary permeability, and interstitial hypertension. Additionally, it is notable to point out that the performance of the combined model significantly exceeded that of PI-RADS v2 and the radiomic model. This may indicate that the combination of clinical experience and machine learning approaches deserves more attention.

Some limitations still exist, including the need for MRI-transrectal ultrasound fusion-guided in-bore biopsy, limited sample size, and lack of external validation. Therefore, it is necessary to conduct prospective multicenter studies in the future.

3.2 Application of radiomics in cancer staging

Accurate cancer staging determines decision-making in a cancer treatment strategy, and there are significant differences in the effectiveness of curative and palliative treatments for cancers in different stages. The tumor node metastasis (TNM) staging system proposed by the American Joint Committee on Cancer (AJCC) is one of the major cancer staging methods [16]. TNM staging system includes the evaluation of the primary tumor (T stage), regional mph node (N stage), and distant metastasis (M stage). Based on accurate TNM staging, patients can be free from overtreatment in the early stage and receive timely and effective treatment in the advanced stage, which can help develop individualized treatment strategies and achieve a rational allocation of medical resources [23].

The decision-making based on clinical cancer staging requires continuous progress and improvement in imaging techniques. For example, the liver is a common metastatic site of colorectal cancer, and the imaging features extracted from CT scans of the liver in patients with colorectal cancer can show abnormal texture, suggesting the possibility of liver metastasis. This can simplify the staging process and guide clinicians to conduct timely confirmatory tests on patients at risk, thereby minimizing treatment delays. In this section, we will mainly introduce the applications of radiomics in cancer staging.

3.2.1 Prediction of parametrial invasion in cervical cancer

Cervical cancer is the fourth most common female malignant tumor around the world [24]. The status of parametrial invasion (PMI) in patients with early-stage cervical cancer (ECC) is related to the recurrence and prognosis. However, the PMI status is not included in the current staging system of ECC. There are some pathological predictors, such as the depth of invasion, LNM, and lymphovascular invasion, that have been proven to be associated with PMI in ECC [25]. Previous studies have also reported some predictive models employing these indicators [26,27]. However, these pathological predictors can only be acquired during or after surgery, which is an invasive method.

Besides pathological predictors, MRI, especially T2WI and DWI, is valuable for the detection of PMI [28]. Nowadays, non-invasive radiomics has demonstrated great potential to help improve the diagnostic accuracy in cancer staging. The combination of radiomics and MRI may be helpful for the detection of PMI. Therefore, Wang et al. attempted to develop a radiomic model to predict the PMI status using T2WI and DWI images [29].

One hundred and thirty-seven ECC patients were retrospectively collected and enrolled (PMI: 43 cases, non-PMI: 94 cases). The primary and validation cohorts were created by a random partition of the cases at a ratio of 2:1. Consequently, the primary cohort included 95 cases, while the validation cohort had 42 cases. For both T2WI and DWI images, 1046 radiomic features of four kinds were extracted from the tumor ROIs, consisting of first-order statistical features, shape features, texture features, and wavelet-based features. To select the most effective ones from the high-dimensional features and avoid overfitting, the LASSO algorithm was adopted in the primary cohort. Thereafter, the radiomic signature, a linear combination of features, was obtained for the prediction of PMI. By integrating the signature and the clinicopathological characteristics, a radiomic model for PMI prediction was constructed via the SVM classifier in the primary cohort. To assess the predictive capability of the model, the discrimination and calibration performance was estimated and validated in the validation cohort, along with the radiomic nomogram being illustrated.

In both the primary and validation cohorts, significant differences were found for the radiomic signatures between PMI and non-PMI groups using independent sample t-test, which reflected the potential predictive value of the radiomic signatures in identifying PMI. Furthermore, the SVM model constructed by the combination of T2WI and DWI had good performance in discriminating PMI from non-PMI. The radiomic signature constructed from T2WI yielded AUCs of 0.797 and 0.780 in the primary and validation cohorts, respectively, while the radiomic signature constructed based on the union of T2WI and DWI got higher AUCs of 0.946 and 0.921. It can be concluded that the radiomic signature constructed from the combination of T2WI and DWI had much better performance than the radiomic signature from T2WI alone in identifying PMI status. By incorporating the radiomic signature from the combination of T2WI and DWI with age and pathological grade, a radiomic model was developed, based on which radiomic nomogram was built and achieved concordance index (C-index) values of 0.969 and 0.941 in the primary and validation cohorts, respectively.

According to the results, the model constructed by clinicopathological factors and the radiomic signature from the combination of T2WI and DWI had satisfactory performance in identifying the status of PMI for ECC patients. Previous studies have revealed the predictive value of radiomics in the precise cancer diagnosis and the following therapeutic effect [30]. Consistent with a previous study declaring that radiomic features extracted from multiparameter images may help improve the models' predictive performance [31], this study indicated that the radiomic signature from the combination of T2WI and DWI performed well. T2WI can provide detailed anatomical characteristics of tumor lesions. Additionally, DWI can measure the microscopic movement of water molecules in tissues and detect early pathological changes related to changes in the water content in tumor lesions. Therefore, DWI can play a complementary role to T2WI in PMI prediction. That's why the radiomic signature derived from the combination of T2WI and DWI can acquire a more precise diagnosis of PMI than a single of them.

Clinical cancer analysis and diagnosis by MRI greatly rely on the radiologists' subjective experience. In contrast, radiomic analysis is a more accurate and objective method, since it can explore the heterogeneity information of tumors by mining quantitative and high-dimensional features. This has also been proved in this study. For identifying PMI, radiologists got a lower accuracy than the radiomic method in MRI assessment.

A few limitations also need to be addressed in Wang et al.'s study [29]. Firstly, the data size was not large enough, especially the proportion of patients with PMI. More patients and samples should be involved to get a more persuasive result. Secondly, the data used in this study were from a single center, and the model was trusted to be validated in a multicenter scheme to evaluate its robustness.

3.2.2 Correlation between PET and CT features in lymph node metastasis

The accurate assessment of LNM before surgery is of great significance for the formulation of cancer treatment strategies. PET/CT is widely used for cancer staging as a non-invasive tool. For example, malignant melanoma and lung cancer can be estimated by 18F-FDG PET/CT, PCa can be evaluated by 68Ga-labeled prostate-specific membrane antigen (PSMA) PET/CT, and gastroenteropancreatic neuroendocrine tumors (GEP NETs) can be estimated by 68Ga-DOTATOC PET/CT. However, 18F-FDG PET/CT has a significant number of false-positive PET findings of LNM. For example, sometimes the LN inflammation caused by an infection in the head and neck or the lungs might be mistakenly detected as LNM [32]. To non-invasively and accurately capture the heterogeneity of LNs, Giesel et al. explored the correlation between maximum standardized uptake value (SUVmax) and CT radiomic analysis in PET/CT-based LN staging [33].

In this study, the metrics and parameters in the LNs of lung cancer, malignant melanoma, GEP NET, and PCa patients, including volumetric CT histogram, CT density, and SUVmax, were studied to explore the relationship between the components of functional PET and morphologic CT in PET/CT. The primary endpoint was CT density, and the secondary endpoints were SUVmax and short-axis diameter (SAD). Besides the CT density of LN in lung cancer patients, few studies have reported these available parameters for malignant melanoma, GEP NET, and PCa patients.

This study retrospectively enrolled and analyzed 1022 LNs from 148 patients (lung cancer: 40 patients with 327 LNs; malignant melanoma: 33 patients with 224 LNs; GEP NET: 35 patients with 217 LNs; PCa: 40 patients with 254 LNs) who had received PET/CT scans before surgery, biopsy, chemotherapy, or internal or external radiation therapy. SUVmax was analyzed 60 min after tracer injection, and volumetric CT histograms were analyzed in the unenhanced CT images of PET/CT scans. In this study, SUVmax was used to evaluate the 18F-FDG uptake, 68Ga-DOTATOC uptake, and 68Ga-PSMA uptake. Ignoring the tracer and type of tumor, PET-positive (PET+) was determined when SUVmax was more than 3 times that of the blood pool, PET-indeterminate (PET+/−) was defined when the SUVmax was 1−3 times that of the blood pool, and PET-negative (PET−) was determined otherwise. In the absence of any information about the patients, a 5-year experienced radiologist conducted the morphologic LN assessment and analyzed the volumetric CT histogram. Volumetric LN analysis was semiautomatically conducted using the software [34]. A dedicated software [35] for semiautomated LN segmentation was applied to analyze the CT density and SAD of the unenhanced CT scans of the PET/CT examinations. The analyses began with a seed point in the target LN, and the ROI was automatically determined by segmentation software. Thereafter, spatial parameters were extracted automatically by the software, and histograms were also analyzed. To validate the evaluative results of the semiautomated LN, the physician used the integrated multiplanar reconstruction 3D viewer to perform a visual inspection of each LN. The segmentation would be manually revised in all three dimensions, if necessary [33].

According to the results, the numbers of PET+, PET+/−, and PET− LNs for different cancers are shown in Table 3.2. Except for GEP NET patients, for whom SUVmax was either below the level of the mediastinal blood pool or more than triple the blood-pool level, PET+, PET+/−, and PET− LNs were found for all tumor types.

Table 3.2 Correlation between PET and CT data.

Tumor type	PET+	PET+/−	PET−	*P* Values + versus +/−	+ versus −	+/− versus −
Lung cancer						
No. of LNs	75	48	204			
CT density (HU)	31.3 (−10.4/ 39.2)	27.6 (−17.2/ 69.8)	−12.57 (−56.3/ 17.9)	.08	<.01	<.05
SAD (mm)	12.7 (4.1/ 32.1)	7.8 (3.1/ 17.3)	5.7 (1.9/ 14.2)	<.01	<.01	.12
Malignant melanoma						
No. of LNs	79	27	118			
CT density (HU)	27.9 (−16.7/ 66.4)	19.1 (−15/ 55.7)	−16.3 (−69/21.2)	.13	<.01	<.01
SAD (mm)	10 (4.1/ 35.8)	8.3 (3.1/ 20)	5 (2.1/8.1)	<.05	<.01	<.01
GEP NET						
No. of LNs	77	0	140			
CT density (HU)	33.7 (−10.6/ 69.5)	−	−11.6 (−64/19.4)	−	<.01	−
SAD (mm)	9.7 (3.1/ 36.8)	−	5.6 (2/12.3)	−	<.01	−
PCa						
No. of LNs	100	11	143			
CT density (HU)	19.2 (−44.2/ 47.1)	9.9 (−10.6/ 42.9)	−23.7 (−68.8/27)	.06	<.01	<.05
SAD (mm)	7.1 (3.1/ 22.7)	8.3 (5.5/ 12.6)	5.5 (1.9/ 9.9)	.78	<.01	.21

Data in parentheses represent the minimum and maximum. The number of LNs is according to PET status. P values are for two-sided t-tests between subgroups [33].

For patients with lung cancer, the CT density of PET+ LNs (31.3 HU) was significantly higher $(P < .01)$ than that of PET− LNs (−12.6 HU), and the SAD in PET+/− LNs (7.8 mm) and PET− LNs (5.7 mm) were significantly smaller $(P < .01)$ than that in PET+ LNs (12.7 mm). For patients with malignant melanoma, the CT density of PET+ LNs (27.9 HU) was significantly $(P < .01)$ higher than that of PET− LNs (−16.3 HU). The SAD in PET+/− LNs (8.3 mm, $P < .05$) and PET− LNs (5 mm, $P < .01$) was significantly lower than that in PET+ LNs (10 mm). For patients with GET NET, since PET-indeterminate LNs were not involved, only PET+ and PET− LNs could be correlated. The CT density of PET− LNs (−11.6 HU) was significantly lower $(P < .01)$) than that of PET+ LNs (33.7 HU), and the SAD in PET+ LNs (9.7 mm) was significantly higher than that of PET− LNs (5.6 mm, $P < .01$). For patients with PCa, the CT density of PET− LNs (−23.7 HU) was significantly lower $(P < .01)$ than that of PET+ LNs (19.2 HU). No significant $(P = .06)$ difference was found in the CT density between PET+ LNs (19.2 HU) and PET+/− LNs (9.9 HU). However, the CT density of PET+/− LNs was lower than that of PET+ LNs. There was a significant difference $(P < .01)$ in CT density between PET+/− and PET− LNs, and the SAD in PET− LNs (5.5 mm) was significantly larger $(P < .01)$ than that in PET+ LNs (7.1 mm). No statistically significant difference $(P = .78)$ was found in SAD either between PET+ and PET+/− LNs or between PET+/− and PET− LNs $(P = .21)$ (Table 3.2).

In patients with lung cancer, PET+ LNs with a CT density of more than 7.5 HU constituted 96%, while a CT density less than 7.5 HU accounted for 91% in PET− LNs, and all of the PET− LNs had a CT density lower than 20 HU. In patients with malignant melanoma, PET+ LNs with a CT density of more than 7.5 HU accounted for 91%, while those less than 7.5 HU constituted 90% in PET− LNs, and 99% of PET− LNs had a CT density lower than 20 HU. In patients with GEP NET, PET+ LNs with a CT density of more than 7.5 HU constituted 96%, while the CT density lower than 7.5 HU accounted for 89% in PET− LNs, and all of the PET− LNs had a CT density of less than 20 HU. In patients with PCa, the CT density of higher than 7.5 HU constituted 77% in PET+ LNs, while the CT density less than 7.5 HU accounted for 96% in PET− LNs, and 99% of PET− LNs had a CT density less than 20 HU. Despite the tumor type of LNs, PET+ LNs with a CT density higher than 7.5 HU accounted for 89%, while the CT density less than 7.5 HU constituted more than 92% in PET− LNs. More than 99% of PET− LNs were found to have a CT density lower than 20 HU. About 50% of the PET+/− LNs had a CT density of less than 20 HU, and 83% had a CT density higher than 7.5 HU.

In conclusion, the CT density measurements of LNs in lung cancer, malignant melanoma, GEP NET, and PCa patients were related to 18F-FDG uptake, 68Ga-DOTATOC uptake, and 68Ga-PSMA uptake, respectively. Thus, CT density had the potential to be used as an extra surrogate predictor in the diagnosis of LN. Specifically, it was available to differentiate the malignant and benign LN infiltration according to a CT density of 7.5 HU and to exclude the possibility of benign LN based on a CT density of 20 HU in clinical practice [33].

3.2.3 Prediction of lymph node metastasis in colorectal cancer

Colorectal cancer is one of the most common digestive tract cancer in the world. Accurately predicting the LNM status is of great significance in both prognosis monitoring and treatment planning for colorectal cancer patients. A few histopathologic findings (i.e., tumor differentiation and lymphatic invasion) are known as indicators of LNM; however, they are only available after surgery [36]. The preoperative prediction of the LNM status provides valuable information and support for treatment decision-making before adjuvant therapy and surgical resection [37]. A previous study reported the great potential of a combination of serum angiopoietin-like protein 2 and clinical factors in preoperatively predicting LNM for patients with colorectal cancer [38]. Alternatively, CT is commonly used preoperatively and plays a crucial role in the differentiation of colorectal cancer in clinical practice. However, the low accuracy of CT in identifying malignant nodes for colorectal cancer patients has limited its applications [39]. Radiomics has been developed and applied in many cancers to support clinical decision-making [40]. The combination of radiomics and CT will help predict the LNM in colorectal cancer.

Huang et al. attempted to construct and validate a radiomic nomogram that involved the clinicopathologic risk factors and radiomic signature for preoperative prediction of LNM in colorectal cancer [41]. A total of 326 colorectal cancer patients between January 2007 and April 2010 were retrospectively enrolled and used as the primary cohort. To evaluate the performance of the radiomic nomogram, an independent validation cohort of 200 patients was consecutively enrolled from 631 patients between May 2010 and December 2011. All patients had standard CT scans before the surgery. The LASSO regression method was utilized for selecting potential features, and constructing the radiomic signature. A total of 150 radiomic features extracted from CT images were reduced to 24 potential ones in the primary cohort, by which a radiomic signature (Rad-score) was constructed. Incorporating the radiomic signature, independent clinicopathologic risk factors, and LNM status reported by CT, a radiomic model was developed via multivariable logistic regression, and a radiomic nomogram was generated accordingly. Then, the radiomic nomogram's predictive performance was evaluated with regard to the calibration, discrimination, and clinical applicability [41].

A significant difference ($P < .001$) was found between LNM-positive and LNM-negative patients for the Rad-score in both the primary and validation cohorts (Table 3.3). Specifically, patients with LNM usually had higher Rad-scores than those without LNM in the primary cohort. The radiomic signature got a C-index of 0.718 (95% CI, 0.712−0.724) in the primary cohort, while in the validation cohort, it obtained a C-index of 0.773 (95% CI, 0.764−0.782). According to the subgroup analysis, the radiomic signature was also found to be significantly related to the LNM status.

The radiomic nomogram showed good calibration in predicting the LNM status in the validation cohort Fig. 3.3A and B. Non-significant statistical differences were found in the Hosmer-Lemeshow test ($P = .196$) and the radiomic nomogram got a C-index of 0.778 (95% CI, 0.769−0.787) in predicting the LNM status. A predictive

Table 3.3 Characteristics of patients in the primary and validation cohorts.

Characteristics	Primary cohort			Validation cohort		
	LNM (+)	LNM (−)	P	LNM (+)	LNM (−)	P
Age, mean ± SD, years	59.31 ± 13.90	63.19 ± 13.68	.008[a]	60.02 ± 13.45	64.88 ± 11.75	.007[a]
Gender, no. (%)			.720			.167
Male	110 (66.3)	103 (64.4)		61 (60.4)	67 (67.7)	
Female	56 (33.7)	57 (35.6)		40 (39.6)	32 (32.3)	
Primary site, no. (%)			.027[a]			.283
Cecum-ascending colon	44 (26.5)	23 (14.4)		26 (25.7)	13 (13.1)	
Transverse colon	5 (3.0)	3 (1.9)		3 (3.0)	7 (7.1)	
Descending colon	4 (2.4)	9 (5.6)		5 (5.0)	5 (5.1)	
Sigmoid colon	34 (20.5)	47 (29.4)		22 (21.8)	27 (27.3)	
Rectum	79 (47.6)	78 (48.8)		45 (44.6)	47 (47.5)	
CEA level, no. (%)			.006[a]			.456
Normal	94 (56.6)	114 (71.2)		57 (59.0)	61 (61.6)	
Abnormal	72 (43.4)	46 (28.7)		44 (41.0)	38 (38.4)	
Histologic grade, no. (%)			.001[a]			.017[a]
Well differentiated	2 (1.2)	4 (2.5)		0 (0)	5 (5.1)	
Moderately differentiated	137 (82.5)	147 (91.9)		86 (85.1)	90 (90.9)	
Poorly differentiated	27 (16.3)	9 (5.6)		15(14.9)	4 (4.0)	
CT-reported LNM status, no. (%)			.001[a]			<.001[a]
LNM (−)	60 (40.5)	88 (59.5)		43 (38.4)	69 (61.6)	
LNM (+)	106 (59.6)	72 (40.4)		58 (65.9)	30 (34.1)	
Rad-score, median (interquartile range)	0.211 (−0.075 to 0.480)	−0.101 (−0.387 to 0.101)	<.001[a]	0.136 (−0.009 to 0.435)	−0.093 (−0.312 to 0.116)	<.001[a]

LNM, lymph node metastasis; P value was derived from the univariable association analyses between each of the clinicopathologic variables and LNM status [41].
[a] P value <.05.

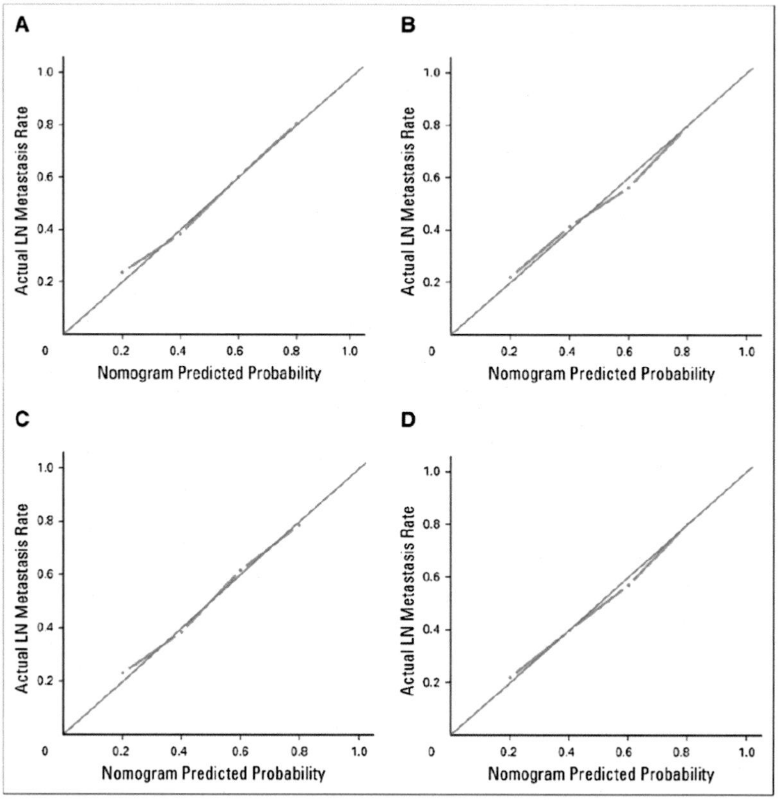

FIGURE 3.3

Calibration curves of the radiomic nomogram and the model with the addition of histologic grade in both cohorts. (A) Calibration curve of the radiomic nomogram in the primary cohort. (B) Calibration curve of the radiomic nomogram in the validation cohort. (C) Calibration curve of the model with the addition of histologic grade in the primary cohort. (D) Calibration curve of the model with the addition of histologic grade in the validation cohort [41].

model adding the histologic grade was also built. Good agreements between the predictions and observations of LNM were illustrated by the calibration curves in the primary and validation cohorts (Fig. 3.3C and D). Although the integration of the histologic grade to the model led to a slight improvement in the C-index in the validation cohort, no statistically significant increase in predictive performance was found (net reclassification index [NRI], 0.014; $P = .44$; event NRI, -0.70; non-event NRI, 0.72).

DCA was conducted for the radiomic nomogram and the model that integrated the radiomic signature and histologic grade (Fig. 3.4), showing that using the radiomic nomogram to predict LNM added more benefit than either the treat-all-patients

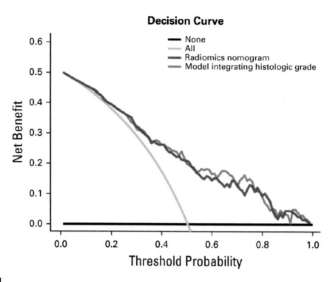

FIGURE 3.4

Decision curve analysis for the radiomic nomogram and the model with the addition of histologic grade [41].

as LNM or the treat-none-patients as the LNM scheme, when the threshold probability of a patient or a doctor was larger than 10%.

In this study, radiomics had a satisfactory performance in stratifying colorectal cancer patients according to their risk of LNM. To achieve the individualized preoperative diagnosis of LNM for colorectal cancer patients, a radiomic nomogram based on the radiomic signature, CEA status, and CT-reported LN status was generated and validated to facilitate treatment decision-making by doctors. Previous research investigated the LNM diagnostic performance of the preoperative tumor marker CEA and serum inflammatory markers for colorectal cancer patients, and their reported accuracy was less than 70% [38], which is lower than the C-index of the radiomic signature constructed in this study [41]. In conclusion, the non-invasive radiomic signature utilizing imaging information could work as a more convenient biomarker in predicting the LNM status for colorectal cancer patients.

3.2.4 Prediction of axillary lymph node status in breast cancer

Breast cancer is one of the most common cancers among women around the world. It is of great importance to accurately identify axillary lymph node (ALN) involvement in patients with breast cancer for prognosis and treatment decision-making [42]. Sentinel lymph node (SLN) is the first node draining primary cancer, whose dissection (SLND) is suggested to forecast the ALN status, especially for those with negative nodes [43]. Although SLND has fewer complications, there are still some obvious limitations, including the increase of considerable anesthesia time and expense, and side effects such as arm numbness or upper limb edema in 3.5%−10.9% of patients [44]. Besides, patients with early-stage breast cancer can be free from the SLN biopsy if the preoperative estimate of ALN status could be trusted since most of them have disease-free axilla.

Two-dimensional (2D) shear wave elastography (SWE) is a new ultrasound (US) technology that can estimate the stiffness of tissues, by which the B-mode image and a color-coded map showing the distribution of shear wave velocity are integrated [45]. Although 2D-SWE has promising potential in identifying malignant breast lesions from benign, its performance relies on the placement of ROIs and can only get an AUC of 0.759 in predicting ALN status [46]. Therefore, in the case of only SWE images of breast cancer, it may not be enough to accurately estimate the ALN status. In Zheng et al.'s study [47], a total of 584 female patients with 584 malignant breast lesions were enrolled for analysis (disease-free axilla [N0]: 337 cases; the low metastatic burden of axillary disease [N+(1−2)]: 150 cases; the heavy metastatic burden of axillary disease [N+(≥3)]: 97 cases). In their study, to preoperatively predict the ALN status in early-stage breast cancer patients, deep learning radiomics (DLR) based on conventional US and SWE was adopted.

Taking N0 as the negative reference standard, the lesions were randomly divided into the training and independent test cohorts (training: 466, test: 118). The characteristics included age, US size, BI-RADS category, tumor type, estrogen receptor (ER) status, progesterone receptor (PR) status, human epidermal growth factor receptor 2 (HER2), and Ki-67 proliferation index. There were no significant differences in the detailed characteristics between the training and test cohorts (t-test or Mann-Whitney U test, $P > .05$). The axillary US findings estimated by a radiologist with rich experience in oncology imaging yielded an accuracy of 0.635, an AUC of 0.735 with a sensitivity of 0.721 and a specificity of 0.573. In the training cohort, the best performance was obtained by the clinical parameter-combined DLR (AUC = 0.936). At the same time, DLR on images only got an AUC of 0.850, and classification by clinicopathologic data only acquired an AUC of 0.771. In the independent test cohort, AUCs of predicting ALN status decreased; however, these results were in agreement with those in the training cohort. Herein, the clinical parameter-combined DLR obtained the outmost predictive performance in the prediction of ALN status between N0 and any axillary metastasis N+(≥1) with an AUC of 0.902, which had significant improvement over the other methods, including axillary US findings (AUC: 0.735, $P < .001$), DLR on images only (AUC: 0.796, $P = .004$), and classification by clinicopathologic data (AUC: 0.727, $P = .002$). Quantitative metrics, including accuracy, sensitivity, specificity, PPV, and NPV of clinical parameter-combined DLR, were also generally higher than those of the other methods. Detailed statistical results are summarized in Table 3.4. Also, the prediction performance of DLR only on US or SWE images combined with clinical parameters was lower than the DLR on both US and SWE images combined with clinical parameters ($P = .006$ and $P = .002$, respectively).

Taking N+(1−2) as the negative reference standard, 197 and 50 lesions were used as the training and the independent test cohorts, respectively. In the training

Table 3.4 The results of predicting ALN status (N0 versus N+(≥1)).

Methods		AUC	Accuracy (%)	Sensitivity (%)	Specificity (%)	PPV (%)	NPV (%)
Axillary US		0.735 [0.694, 0.775]	63.5 [58.6, 70.4]	72.1 [76.1, 84.8]	57.3 [52.3, 64.9]	72.6 [67.9, 77.2]	57.3 [50.1, 61.2]
Classification by clinicopathologic data	Training	0.771 [0.719, 0.824]	73.6 [68.8, 78.0]	68.0 [59.8, 75.5]	79.6 [73.4, 84.9]	70.9 [62.7, 78.3]	77.3 [71.0, 82.8]
	Validation	0.755 [0.665, 0.845]	71.6 [63.3, 79.8]	63.3 [48.3, 76.6]	71.6 [59.3, 82.0]	62.0 [47.2, 75.3]	72.7 [60.3, 83.0]
	Independent test	0.727 [0.630, 0.825]	70.9 [62.1, 78.6]	62.0 [47.2, 75.3]	69.1 [56.7, 79.8]	59.6 [45.1, 73.0]	71.2 [58.7, 81.7]
DLR on images only	Training	0.850 [0.813, 0.887]	76.7 [72.1, 81.0]	71.6 [64.7, 77.8]	80.2 [74.0, 85.5]	77.9 [71.1, 83.7]	74.3 [68.0, 80.0]
	Validation	0.804 [0.717, 0.891]	72.4 [63.3, 79.8]	69.4 [54.6, 81.7]	79.1 [67.4, 88.1]	70.8 [55.9, 83.0]	77.9 [66.2, 87.1]
	Independent test	0.796 [0.708, 0.883]	71.6 [63.0, 79.4]	67.4 [52.5, 80.1]	79.1 [67.4, 88.1]	70.2 [55.1, 82.7]	76.8 [65.1, 86.1]
Clinical parameter combined DLR	Training	0.936 [0.910, 0.962]	85.7 [81.7, 89.1]	79.1 [71.6, 85.3]	93.6 [89.2, 96.5]	90.0 [83.5, 94.6]	85.9 [80.6, 90.2]
	Validation	0.904 [0.847, 0.961]	81.4 [73.9, 88.2]	74.0 [59.7, 85.5]	88.2 [78.1, 94.8]	82.2 [67.9, 92.0]	82.2 [71.5, 90.2]
	Independent test	0.902 [0.843, 0.961]	81.0 [73.4, 87.7]	81.6 [68.0, 91.2]	83.6 [72.5, 91.5]	78.4 [64.7, 88.7]	86.2 [75.2, 93.5]

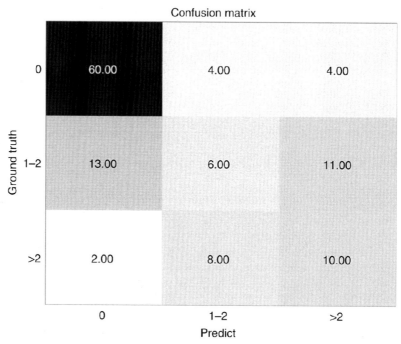

FIGURE 3.5

The confusion matrix of predicting metastasis among disease-free axilla, the low metastatic burden of axillary disease, and heavy metastatic burden of axillary disease [47].

cohort, DLR based on images only yielded an AUC of 0.874, and classification by clinicopathologic data got an AUC of 0.756. The predictive performance of the combination of DLR and clinical parameters improved greatly (AUC: 0.956) in the training cohort. Good performance was maintained in the test cohort with an AUC of 0.905, which showed significant improvement compared with the DLR based on images only (AUC: 0.777, $P = .04$) and the classification by clinicopathologic data (AUC: 0.686, $P = .03$). Three kinds of tasks in predicting the ALN status could be solved by this study. As the researchers depicted, N0 (337 lesions), N+(1−2) (150 lesions), and N+($\geq$3) (97 lesions) were three parts of the clinical endpoints. The study used conventional US and SWE images to construct models, and the overall accuracy of 0.805 was obtained in discriminating the three groups. Fig. 3.5 shows the confusion matrix. The model had good performance in distinguishing the N0 group but had lower results in distinguishing the other two groups.

To preoperatively predict ALN status of clinical T1 or T2 breast cancer patients, a clinical parameter-combined DLR method was developed and validated in this study [47]. It showed significantly better diagnostic performance in differentiating N0 and N+($\geq$1) patients than any single method. The model also had good performance in discriminating N+(1−2) from N+($\geq$3) patients. For the task of differentiating early-stage breast cancer, this model can serve as a non-invasive imaging biomarker, with a similar false-negative rate of SLND. In conclusion, the clinical parameter-combined DLR may assist breast clinicians in making suitable judgments for axillary treatment.

3.2.5 Prediction of lymph node metastases in gastric cancer

Locally advanced gastric cancer (LAGC) with wall invasion deeper than the submucosa is associated with poor clinical outcomes [48,49]. Approximately 70%−80% of patients with LAGC develop LNM, depending on the pathologic results of lymphadenectomy. The AJCC TNM staging system classifies the severity of LN involvement into four groups based on the number of LNMs: N0 (no LNM), N1 (1−2 LNMs), N2 (3−6 LNMs), N3a (7−15 LNMs), and N3b (>15 LNMs) [16]. Hence, the so-called N stage indicates the severity of LNM [50]. Accurate preoperative N staging is the basis of individual treatment of AGC [51]. Patients with N0 may not be eligible for lymphadenectomy, while patients with N1, N2, N3a, and N3b have a significantly different prognosis and may need a different extent of lymphadenectomy or neoadjuvant treatment [52,53]. Preoperative N staging using medical imaging is recommended by the European Society for Medical Oncology [54] and National Comprehensive Cancer Network (NCCN) [55] guidelines. By using enlarged and round-shaped LNs as an indicator of LNM, CT imaging plays an increasingly important role in preoperative N staging [56]. However, the predictability of CT is unsatisfactory for LNM in AGC.

Radiomic nomogram, a graphic representation of the model that combines the radiomic and clinical features, has also improved the prediction ability of LNM in many cancers. In addition, deep learning-driven radiomics showed excellent performance in cancer prognosis [57]. However, the application of deep learning radiomics in predicting N stages in LAGC remains to be investigated.

In order to accurately determine N stages (N0, N1, N2, N3a, and N3b) in LAGC, Dong et.al. developed a deep learning-driven radiomic nomogram (DLRN) to predict the number of LNM [58]. This study enrolled multicenter patients pathologically diagnosed as LAGC (pT2−4aNxM0), with the available CT scans less than 2 weeks before surgery. Patients treated by preoperative therapy or with previous abdominal diseases were excluded in the current study.

The researchers collected 679 LAGC patients from five centers in China, and divided them into four separate cohorts: a training cohort (PC, n = 225) and three validation cohorts (VC1, n = 178; VC2, n = 145; VC3, n = 131). They also collected an international validation cohort, dataset IVC, including 51 eligible patients from Italy. Chi-square test and t-test were used to check if there is a significant difference in gender or age between PC and VCs. Power calculation was performed to evaluate the minimum sample size of the PC and VCs.

The DLRN modeling pipeline is shown in Fig. 3.6. Three tumor ROIs were manually delineated on unenhanced and biphasic contrast-enhanced CT images by a radiologist (reader 1) with more than 10 years of experience. Only a 2D ROI

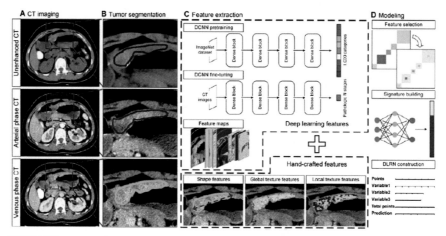

FIGURE 3.6

The DLRN modeling pipeline [58]. (A) CT imaging; (B) tumor segmentation; (C) feature segmentation; (D) modeling.

with the largest tumor region was delineated for each CT phase using ITK-SNAP software. Each ROI covered the highlighted tumor region and suspected degeneration region but excluded the adjacent visceral adipose tissues. The resegmentation datasets were used to assess intra-/inter-reader reproducibility of radiomic features. The DenseNet-201 architecture was adapted to develop the deep CNNs for deep learning feature extraction. The hand-crafted features consisted of shape, global texture, and local texture features. After the reproducibility assessment of radiomic features using the intra-/inter-class correlation coefficients and the coefficient of variation, the hierarchical clustering divided robust features into several clusters, in which the most representative features were reserved to construct predictive signatures using different methods, such as SVM and RF.

Experiments showed that SVM with a radial basis function kernel was the optimal choice for building three radiomic signatures, including unenhanced signature (7 features), venous signature (6 features), and arterial signature (6 features). The multivariable linear regression analysis in the primary cohort showed that arterial signature, venous signature, and clinical N stage were independent predictors for pathologic N stage (Fig. 3.7A). The NRI analysis revealed that the addition of an unenhanced signature into the DLRN did not show significantly better performance in the PC (NRI 0.0482; $P = .1870$). Fig. 3.7B exhibits a significant positive correlation between the DLRN score and pathologic N stage, and the Spearman correlation analysis also confirmed the significant positive correlation between them ($0.626-0.718$, $P < .0001$).

The DLRN showed good discrimination of N stages in all datasets (overall C-index: $0.777-0.821$). Moreover, in all the external validation cohorts, the overall C-index of DLRN was significantly better than clinical factors or clinical models ($P < .05$). In addition, the DLRN remains an excellent predictive mode regardless

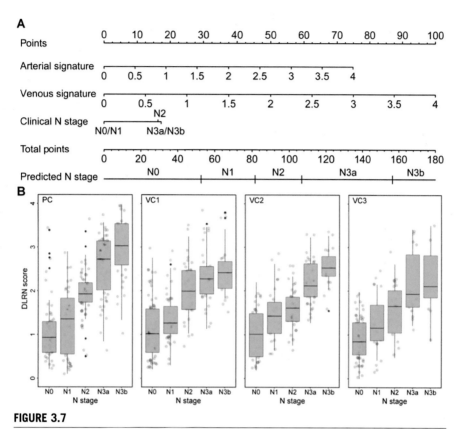

FIGURE 3.7

DLRN and its performance [58]. (A) DLRN constructed by two contrast-enhanced radiomic signatures and clinical N stage. (B) Box plots showing patterns of correlation between pathologic N stages and DLRN in PC, VC1, VC2, and VC3 cohorts.

of clinical factors, image thickness, and the version of CT system in the stratification analysis. By quantifying the net benefits, DCA was conducted to evaluate the clinical usefulness of the model in guiding lymphadenectomy, and demonstrated that additional benefit to patients could be obtained by the DLRN compared with other models or schemes. Furthermore, the calibration curves of the subgroup analysis (non-N0 versus N0, N2-3b versus N0-1, N3a-3b versus N0-2, and N3b versus N0-3a) showed good agreement between the DLRN predicted outcomes and the observed outcomes. The subgroup analysis showed that the DLRN could discriminate non-N0 from N0 groups in all cohorts (C-index: 0.777–0.821). Experimental results showed that 76/93 patients with false-negative LNM diagnosed by CT were correctly detected by the DLRN. In the non-Asian cohort IVC, the DLRN also showed a good predictive performance of pathologic N stage with a Spearman correlation coefficient of 0.727 and an overall C-index of 0.822, which further confirmed the generalization ability of DLRN. When evaluated in patients with follow-up, DLRN yielded a high predictive accuracy for OS (C-index, 0.646) and successfully divided patients into low- and high-risk groups (HR, 1.982).

In conclusion, DLRN showed a good predictive ability for N staging in AGC and reproducibility across different centers, which may serve as an easy-to-use tool for individualized diagnosis and treatment in LAGC.

3.2.6 Prediction of distant metastasis in lung adenocarcinoma

NSCLC is one of the most common types of lung cancer in the world, and the most common subtype of NSCLC is lung adenocarcinoma. As high as about 40% lung adenocarcinoma patients with stage II−III experienced distant metastasis after combined modality therapy in prospective trials [59]. The high risk of local recurrence and distant metastasis results in low overall survival (OS). Moreover, large randomized trials showed that the OS rate did not increase with the use of consolidation chemotherapy when patients received concurrent chemotherapy and radiation therapy [60] because of not selecting patients with a high risk of distant metastasis. Therefore, better biomarkers to predict patients with a high risk of distant metastasis are urgently needed for identifying subgroups that could benefit from systemic therapy, which are essential for improving prognosis.

Coroller et al. [61] explored the value of radiomics in predicting distant metastasis in locally advanced lung adenocarcinoma treated with chemoradiation (overall stage II−III). They excluded patients who received surgery or chemotherapy before the date of scheduled radiation therapy. A total of 182 patients received chemoradiation at their center from 2001 to 2013 and were enrolled for analysis. Before July 2009, 98 cases were treated, forming a training cohort, and 84 cases treated after July 2009 formed a validation cohort. The tumor ROI was manually segmented from CT images. Then radiomic features were extracted from the tumor ROIs. In the training cohort, researchers extracted 635 radiomic features for subsequent determination of the best feature subset for predicting distant metastasis and used the mRMR algorithm for feature selection. The mRMR algorithm adopted mutual information to measure the correlations between features and the status of distant metastasis. Under certain conditions, the mRMR algorithm obtained a set of features that had the greatest correlation with the status of distant metastasis, but with the smallest correlation between one another. A Cox regression model based on the selected radiomic features was trained on the training cohort to generate a radiomic signature. Clinical characteristic variables were selected using the log-rank test in the univariate analysis, and those with $P < .1$ were included in the multivariate clinical model. Finally, a combined model using radiomic signature and clinical characteristic variables was constructed. This study selected three key radiomic features to generate a radiomics signature. The radiomic signature had strong power for predicting distant metastasis in the training cohort (C-index = 0.61). In the training cohort, three significant clinical characteristic variables were overall stage (C-index = 0.63), gender (C-index = 0.63), and tumor grade (C-index = 0.61). The final clinical model contained overall stage and tumor grade. The C-index of the clinical model in the independent validation cohort was 0.57, while that of the model combining clinical factors and radiomic signature was 0.60. Adding radiomic signature to the clinical model resulted in a significant improvement of prediction performance in the validation dataset.

The difference in CT acquisition and reconstruction parameters is one deficiency of the current study. During the data collection period (from 2001 to 2013), some differences in CT acquisition between the training and validation cohorts appeared in some factors. However, radiomics can detect a strong signature to predict distant metastasis despite the variability in CT data. Besides, another deficiency of the research is that its clinical results were provided by a single-center, making it difficult to assess the generalizability of the results in other centers. Therefore, future work can involve independent validation cohorts from other centers. In summary, this study exhibited that the radiomic features were strongly correlated with distant metastasis in patients with locally advanced adenocarcinoma, and proposed an independently verified imaging biomarker for predicting distant metastasis. The proposed imaging biomarker identified early patients with a high risk of distant metastasis, which may help clinicians develop personalized treatment plans and improve the survival of NSCLC.

3.2.7 Prediction of distant metastasis in oropharyngeal cancer

More than 176,000 new cases of oropharyngeal cancers (OPCs) are diagnosed worldwide every year, and the 5-year survival rate of OPCs is as high as 88% [62]. Patients with OPCs generally receive surgical treatment, radiotherapy, or chemotherapy. However, chemotherapy places a heavy toxic burden on them. In addition, the quality of life of OPC patients is affected significantly by side effects, such as tissue fibrosis and xerostomia. In recent years, relevant research has focused on optimizing treatment plans for patients with human papillomavirus (HPV)-positive OPC to reduce the side effects after treatment and maintain the patient's normal quality of life, emphasizing the urgent development of accurate prognostic tools for clinical decision-making.

In clinical practice, the use of chemotherapy is often guided by the risk of distant metastasis. However, to date, few reliable predictors have been developed for distant metastasis, which is the leading cause of death in patients with HPV-positive OPCs. The existing risk factors of distant metastasis indicate that the shape features of tumor deposits (such as tumor size, LN size, boundary) are at a higher risk of distant metastasis.

Radiomics can objectively quantify the imaging phenotype of tumors with a potential prognostic value. Compared with other prognostic factors, the advantage of radiomics is that it can accurately quantify the size and 3D shape of the tumor and evaluate the tumor characteristics. For example, the TNM staging system only uses the 1D tumor measurement, and biopsy is limited by the sampled tissues. In contrast, radiomics could perform a comprehensive evaluation of the tumor volume. Overall, radiomics provides important information to assist clinical decision-making in a non-invasive and low-cost manner. Kwan et al. developed a radiomics-based biomarker to improve the predictive ability of distant metastasis in HPV-related OPC patients [63]. To enhance the predictivity of the clinical model, this study adopted some imaging features and signatures developed in head and neck cancer [40].

This study analyzed the CT images of 300 HPV-related OPC patients [63]. All patients underwent radiotherapy and CT scans for the head and neck. At the same time, 75% of the patients (225/300) received a contrast injection, and the primary tumor volume of each patient was manually delineated by a radiation oncologist. Multiparameter MRI images with appropriate sequences can better assess the degree of soft tissue disease (such as parapharyngeal extension, tongue base, etc.). When fused with CT of the gross tumor volumes (GTVs) level, multiparameter MRI may provide help for primary tumor segmentation. Generally, the final GTV was mainly based on the CT findings. This study extracted four types of radiomic features from the sketched primary tumor ROIs in the CT images. The four types of features were (1) shape features; (2) first-order statistical features; (3) texture features; and (4) wavelet-decomposed features. At the same time, the researchers included tumor diameter, tumor volume, and tumor stage in the model, and performed univariate and multivariate analyses together with the radiomic features. Bootstrap sampling (1000 times) was used to calculate the bias-corrected C-index of the model.

In the univariate analysis of distant metastasis-free survival (DMFS), the following features were significant: shape features: compactness (HR, 1.04; $P < .001$); first-order statistical characteristics: energy (hazard ratio [HR], 1.1; $P < .001$); texture features: GLRLM gray-level non-uniformity (GLN) (HR, 1.53; $P < .001$); wavelet-decomposed features: GLRLM GLN (HR, 1.19; $P < .001$); maximum tumor diameter (HR, 1.03; $P < .001$); GTV (HR, 1.23; $P < .001$); radiomic signature (HR, 1.53; $P < .001$), and stage III (HR, 3.32; $P < .001$). The C-index of the significant features for predicting DMFS were as follows: tumor volume (C-index, 0.674), stage III (C-index, 0.633), maximum diameter (C-index, 0.653), four discriminative radiomic features (C-index, 0.670−0.686), and the radiomic signature (C-index, 0.670). Integrating any of the four radiomic features and stage III was significantly higher than stage III alone (C-index, 0.701−0.714; all $P < .05$).

Subgroup analysis was performed to assess the increased predictivity of the radiomic signature and compactness (shape) within patients with high-risk distant metastasis in clinical practice. Compared with low-risk subgroups (such as stage I−II), the predictability of the radiomic signature and compactness (shape) in the high-risk subgroups was significantly improved, with a C-index of 0.663−0.779 (radiomic signature) and 0.680−0.796 (shape: compactness). These results indicated that adding radiomic features into clinical information had the strongest predictive power for distant metastasis in HPV-related OPC patients. Also, the four representative radiomic features and the radiomic signature used in this study were related to OS. For guiding treatment decisions, distant metastasis risk may be more relevant than OS. Therefore, the proposed imaging biomarkers could better identify patients with high-risk distant metastasis risk than the stage-based model used in clinical practice. In stage III, N2c, and N2b heavy smoker groups, the lower-risk subgroups were also identified by the proposed radiomic biomarkers.

The improvement of the radiomics-based model for predicting distant metastasis may be derived from the information extraction of early metastasis-related phenotypes in CT images of the primary tumor. In the study population, the median time to detect distant metastasis was about 1 year, and the earliest distant metastasis occurred less than 2 months after treatment. Angiogenesis, detachment, cell proliferation, and invasion are typical phenotypes for the sign of distant metastasis. The stage-based model for predicting distant metastasis is based on detachment, invasion, and tumor cell proliferation, but it ignores intratumoral heterogeneity associated with metastasis. Some important features, such as spatial differences in tumor cells, angiogenesis, and hypoxia, have not been captured. Radiomics can enhance the 3D assessment of total tumor growth for quantifying these macroscopic changes.

The stage-based distant metastasis model currently used in clinical practice has limitations, while the radiomics-based model has expanded the understanding of this disease subgroup and helped identify patients with a lower risk in these groups, who are presumed to have similar high distant metastasis risks. In addition, with the help of radiomics, biomarkers could stratify the distant metastasis risks in patients treated with radiation alone to enhance the subgroup of patients with DMFS that could benefit from other treatments. This study demonstrated that DMFS outcomes remained the same regardless of the treatment method for low-risk patients defined by imaging biomarkers, while for patients with a high risk defined by imaging biomarkers, DMFS outcomes were poor.

It is worth noting that the radiomic signature constructed by the four radiomic features performed better than stage III, but did not exceed single imaging features. This study also found that the radiomic signature provided better predictability of distant metastasis than OS, which indicates that the radiomic signature should be used as a biomarker for distant metastasis rather than OS.

3.2.8 Prediction of distant metastasis in nasopharyngeal carcinoma

Treatment failure in nasopharyngeal carcinoma is mainly concentrated in patients with distant metastasis, and they usually have a poor prognosis. At present, the clinical treatment decision-making of nasopharyngeal carcinoma is mainly based on the TNM staging system. Although patients with the same TNM stage received similar treatment, more than 20% of patients experienced distant metastasis and responded poorly to treatment [64]. The use of the TNM staging system, which only reflects the anatomical structure of tumor invasion but ignores the heterogeneity within the tumor, may be responsible for treatment failure. Past studies have indicated that the plasma Epstein-Barr virus DNA (EBV DNA) status can be used as an effective independent factor of distant metastasis for nasopharyngeal carcinoma. However, the results from the predictive models were unstable and non-specific, considering that most of them were built on the pretreatment detection of blood metabolism. Several molecular biomarkers are subjected to a small number of patients because of the complicated manipulation and high cost [65]. Therefore, an accurate and feasible tool is urgently needed for pretreatment risk assessment for distant metastasis.

Zhang et al. enrolled 176 patients with nasopharyngeal carcinoma and developed a radiomic model for predicting distant metastasis [66]. All the patients were randomly divided into a training cohort (n = 123) and an independent validation cohort (n = 53). The primary endpoint was measured from the date of the first MRI scan to the date of distant metastasis detection or the last follow-up. All patients underwent nasopharyngeal and neck MRI using a 1.5T or 3.0T device. Tumor segmentation was conducted on axial T2WI and contrast-enhanced T1WI images. Then, a total of 2803 radiomic features were extracted from the segmented tumor volumes. To screen out the most significant features for predicting distant metastasis, a combination of feature selection methods was utilized. Firstly, intra- and inter-class correlation coefficients (ICCs) were used to select robust radiomic features that were not influenced by variations in manual segmentation. Secondly, the discriminative features for distant metastasis were selected using univariate analysis with the Mann-Whitney U and χ2 tests. Thirdly, the features were ranked by the mRMR algorithm, and the top 10% were preserved for removing redundant features. Finally, the LASSO algorithm, together with backward elimination, was used to identify the key features. A distant metastasis MRI-based model (DMMM) was constructed using the logistic regression method in the training cohort. The workflow of this study is shown in Fig. 3.8.

The DMMM was based on seven key features and achieved an AUC of 0.827 in the training cohort and 0.792 in the validation cohort for predicting pretreatment

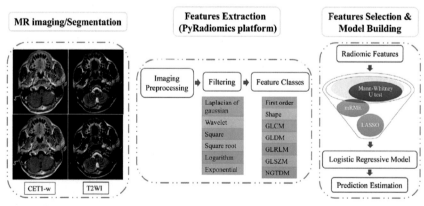

FIGURE 3.8

Workflow for prediction of distant metastasis in patients with nasopharyngeal carcinoma. The steps included (1) MRI acquisition and segmentation; (2) feature extraction; and (3) feature selection and development of models [66].

distant metastasis. An optimal cutoff value of 0.37 was identified and used to divide the patients into the high-risk group (n = 62) and the low-risk group (n = 114), between which a significant prognostic difference existed ($P < .001$). When performing a subgroup analysis for 5-year survival with early-stage and advanced-stage, this study did not find a significant difference between groups ($P = .39$). However, the high-risk group exhibited a shorter 5-year survival rate compared with the low-risk group ($P < .001$) in patients who received concurrent chemoradiotherapy.

In addition, the researchers built a clinical model using clinical variables. Plasma EBV DNA level and the N stage were identified as independent predictors of distant metastasis in the multivariate analysis. Compared to DMMM, the clinical model performed worse (training cohort: AUC, 0.652; validation cohort: AUC, 0.660). The current study also constructed a radiomic signature using the imaging features only. Five imaging features were identified to build the radiomic signature, which seemed to overfit the prediction of distant metastasis (training cohort: AUC, 0.816; validation cohort: AUC, 0.713).

In conclusion, Zhang et al.'s study used radiomics-relevant techniques to extract specific high-throughput radiomic features and constructed DMMM using clinical factors and radiomic features for the pre-treatment prediction of distant metastasis in nasopharyngeal carcinoma patients. Using DMMM, the current study divided the patients into high-risk and low-risk groups and found that the high-risk group had a poorer 5-year OS rate (12%) than the low-risk group (26%). Thus, DMMM may serve as a useful and non-invasive prognostic tool, aiding clinicians in identifying patients with high-risk distant metastasis and optimizing therapeutic strategies.

3.2.9 Prediction of occult peritoneal metastasis in gastric cancer

More than 50% of patients with distant metastatic gastric cancer have been diagnosed with peritoneal metastasis, which is recommended not to receive surgical treatment [67]. In clinical practice, CT is usually used to detect and diagnose peritoneal metastasis. The omental cake and obvious parietal peritoneum thickening on CT images are indicative of peritoneal metastasis, but most of these indications are usually found in late-stage peritoneal metastasis, thereby resulting in high specificity but low sensitivity for the CT detection of peritoneal metastasis [68]. This raises a thorny problem in clinical practice: about 10%−30% of advanced gastric cancer patients with CT-diagnosed negative peritoneal metastasis were confirmed as positive peritoneal metastasis during subsequent laparoscopies, namely occult peritoneal metastasis [69]. For patients with occult peritoneal metastasis, if peritoneal metastasis is detected during laparotomy, the surgical procedure should be aborted, otherwise improper surgical treatment would have a negative effect on the prognosis of the patient. Therefore, the early detection and diagnosis of peritoneal metastasis are vitally important for patients with gastric cancer to receive optimal treatment selection and avoid unnecessary surgical procedures.

According to NCCN guidelines, laparoscopy exploration (a category 2B recommendation) is recommended for patients with potentially resectable advanced gastric cancer [55]. However, in the United States, only 8% of gastric cancer patients underwent laparoscopy exploration before gastrectomy due to the invasive nature of laparoscopy [70]. Several clinical factors, such as Borrmann classification and TNM staging, were found to be significantly associated with the peritoneal metastasis status among gastric cancer patients, but no non-invasive and individualized model by far has been developed to predict occult peritoneal metastasis in clinical practice. Considering that both the synergies of the tumor cells and the peritoneal microenvironment are associated with peritoneal metastasis initiation, Dong et al. explored both the characteristics of primary tumors and peritoneum under CT images to develop a non-invasive tool for preoperative peritoneal metastasis detection [71].

This study enrolled 554 advanced gastric cancer patients with negative peritoneal metastasis by CT from four centers, and 122 patients were confirmed positive peritoneal metastasis by subsequent exploration laparoscopy [71]. The researchers divided patients from center 1 into one training cohort (n = 100) and one internal validation cohort (n = 226), and divided patients from center 2-4 into two external validation cohorts (Dataset-1 of 131 patients from center 2 and center 3; Dataset-2 of 97 patients from center 4). Within 2 weeks prior to laparoscopy, the enrolled patients underwent enhanced CT examination and diagnostic laparoscopy. The peritoneal metastasis status of any suspicious lesion discovered during laparoscopy was determined pathologically. Venous phase CT images were exported for manual segmentation. One radiologist (reader 1) with 10 years of experience in CT interpretation reviewed all slices of a patient and delineated the tumor on the slice with the largest tumor area and the peritoneal region on the slice with a peritoneal region (area>2 cm) nearest to the center of the primary tumor. In order to assess intra-reader agreement of radiomic features, 50 patients in the training cohort were randomly selected and resegmented by reader 1 at 3 months after initial segmentation. These cases were then segmented by another radiologist (reader 2) with 5 years of CT experience.

Two feature groups, with each group containing 133 features, were extracted from the two segmented regions. These features consisted of the histogram, shape, GLCM, and GLRLM. Meanwhile, the robustness of features from slices with different thicknesses was assessed on a simulated slice-thickness dataset from the 3D images of 30 patients. Slice-thickness agreement and feature inter-/intra-reader agreement were used to evaluate the robustness of radiomic features. Then top-N ranked features with mutual information were reserved. Finally, radiomic signatures were built using the best one among three state-of-the-art methods. Radiomic signatures for both primary tumors (RS1) and the peritoneum (RS2) were performed using the above process. The association between the clinical characteristics of patients and the peritoneal metastasis status was assessed by univariate analysis. Patient clusters with similar radiomic-expression patterns were explored using unsupervised clustering with the Euclidean distance metric shown by heatmaps.

Multivariable logistic regression with backward stepwise selection was adopted to build the clinical model based on the clinical characteristics, and the radio-clinical model based on the clinical characteristics and radiomic signatures. Akaike's information criterion was applied as the stopping rule. The radio-clinical model was visualized as a radiomic nomogram for clinical usefulness. The ROC curve, calibration curve, NRI, and DCA were used to evaluate the quality of all models. Moreover, a stratification analysis in different subgroups was performed to test the generalization ability of the radiomic nomogram.

Univariate analysis identified Borrmann type, tumor locations, mild CT-defined ascites, and Lauren type as significant predictors. Two features from the primary tumor and two features from the peritoneum were selected and integrated into RS1 and RS2, respectively. The two radiomic signatures yielded a significant variation between peritoneal metastasis-positive and peritoneal metastasis-negative groups (independent t-test, $P < .0001$ in all cases). The radio-clinical model identified the Lauren type and two radiomic signatures as significant predictors of peritoneal metastasis status using multivariable analysis. The radiomic nomogram was built based on the coefficients of the radio-clinical model (Fig. 3.9). There were no significant differences in the radiomic nomogram predicted values between peritoneal metastasis-positive and peritoneal metastasis-negative groups in each cohort (independent t-test, $P < .0001$). A model with only the two radiomic signatures was also built and validated on Dataset-2 because the Lauren type determined from the endoscopic biopsy tissue might lack in datasets from other centers. The radiomic nomogram revealed better discriminability than the clinical model in the internal validation cohort (NRI $= 0.460$, $P = .0008$) and Dataset-1. Using the bootstrapping validation, the radiomic nomogram also yielded high AUCs of 0.936, 0.925, and 0.917 in the internal validation cohort and two external validation cohorts, respectively. The Hosmer-Lemeshow test showed that the radiomic nomogram did not depart from a perfect fit in the calibration curve ($P > .05$). Performance of the radiomic nomogram was not affected by clinical factors and CT parameters (Delong test, $P > .05$) in the stratification analysis. In addition, the decision curves revealed that the radiomic nomogram had more net benefits than the all-laparoscopy and no-laparoscopy schemes in the validation cohorts when the threshold probability in the clinical decision was smaller than 30%.

Accurate staging is the basis of individualized treatment of malignant tumors. Recently, the eighth AJCC TNM staging system adopted a risk model for the individualized prediction of prognosis of gastric cancer for the first time [16]. The radiomic nomogram likewise provided an individualized risk prediction model for distant metastasis (M staging) in advanced gastric cancer. As a non-invasive staging method, the radiomic nomogram would play an important role in individualized treatment decision-making of gastric cancer. However, this study still has several limitations. The Lauren type in the radiomic nomogram was determined by the endoscopic biopsy specimen in the superficial mucosa of the tumor, but there may be minor discordance of Lauren classification between the biopsy and surgical specimens [72]. Although the Lauren type has a small weight in the radiomic

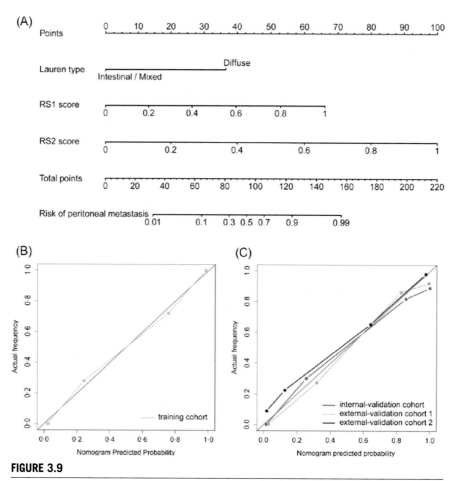

FIGURE 3.9

Development and performance of the radiomic nomogram [71]. (A) Nomogram based on radiomic signature scores and clinical factors. Calibration curves of the nomogram in the (B) training cohort and (C) three validation cohorts.

nomogram, this discordance should be studied in the future. Furthermore, this retrospective study did not include some clinical factors, such as CA125 and HER2, and the introduction of these factors may improve the performance of the radiomic nomogram.

3.3 Application of radiomics in histopathological diagnosis of cancer

Histopathological diagnosis based on biopsy or surgical tissues is an important part in the diagnosis of cancers. Although the histopathological diagnosis is often the golden standard of the diagnosis, it is invasive and sometimes it is a lagging indicator. How to get histopathological information using a non-invasive and preoperative manner is a great challenge. Radiomics provides a potential tool to non-invasively predict histopathological information based on preoperative medical images. Researchers have attempted to perform preoperative histopathological diagnosis in many cancers, such as prostate cancer, bladder cancer, cervical cancer, etc.

3.3.1 Prediction of Gleason score in prostate cancer

Prostate cancer is a leading cause of cancer death in American men [73]. Gleason grading is an important histological grading method for prostate cancer. Since the 1990s, the treatment guidelines for prostate cancer recommended by NCCN have pointed out that Gleason grade, the level of prostate-specific antigen (PSA), and tumor stage are important indicators to determine the treatment plan. The quantitative index of Gleason grading is Gleason score (GS). Compared with $GS \geq 7$, prostate cancer patients with $GS \leq 6$ had higher 5-year and 10-year survival rates and lower recurrence rates [74]. Studies have also shown that patients with prostate cancer with $GS = 7 \, (3 + 4)$ have better prognosis than those with $GS = 7 \, (4 + 3)$. GS combined with PSA level is widely used to evaluate the tumor invasiveness [75]. However, evaluating the invasiveness of prostate cancer by transrectal ultrasound-guided puncture and GS may cause discomfort to patients and also lead to misdiagnosis [76]. GS obtained by transrectal ultrasound-guided puncture is often different from that obtained by repeated puncture and prostatectomy. Therefore, it is necessary to find a non-invasive method for increasing patient comfort and providing accurate diagnosis results [77].

Although MRI is commonly used for detecting prostate cancer, there is no consensus that specific imaging biomarkers can be applied to evaluate the aggressiveness of prostate cancer. In addition to magnetic resonance spectroscopy and T2WI, the ADC obtained by DWI has also been proved to have a certain value in evaluating the invasiveness of prostate cancer [78].

Fehr et al. proposed a machine learning model for the automatic classification of prostate cancer invasion by combining the texture features of ADC and T2WI sequences [79]. For $GS = 6$ versus ≥ 7 and $GS = 7 \, (3 + 4)$ versus $7 \, (4 + 3)$, their model reached a fairly accurate classification. The experimental results showed that compared with measuring ADC means or T2 means, extracting quantitative texture features from conventional MRI could improve the ability of prostate cancer invasion classification and reduce the rate of misdiagnosis and overdiagnosis. In this study, 147 patients were included. When using the texture feature to distinguish prostate cancer $GS = 6 \, (3 + 3)$ and $GS = 7$, the accuracies were 93% for prostate cancer that occurred in both the PZ and TZ and 92% for prostate cancer that only occurred in the PZ, respectively. In order to balance the sample distribution, Gibbs sampling and synthetic minority over-sampling technique (SMOTE) were utilized to increase the number of samples to 200 in each group. The influence of two sampling methods on classification accuracy was analyzed.

When classifying cancer with GS = 6 (3 + 3) from ≥7, the comparison results of different augmentation methods and non-augmentation of each model are shown in Table 3.5. ROC analysis results showed that for patients with SMOTE sampling, RFE-SVM had the best prediction performance, while AdaBoost performed the worst (Fig. 3.10A). For patients with cancer occurring in PZ only, the performance of each model was similar (Fig. 3.10B).

The performance of the texture feature-based model in differentiating prostate cancer GS = 7(3 + 4) from GS = 7(4 + 3) was also investigated. This study showed that the texture features extracted by the ADC map and T2WI sequence were helpful in accurately classifying GS, and the data sampling could improve model stability.

3.3.2 Prediction of histopathological grade in bladder cancer

Bladder cancer is a common cancer in men. Cancer grade is an important prognostic factor for bladder cancer patients, and could affect the treatment plan, especially for non-muscle-invasive bladder cancer (NMIBC). For example, transurethral resection (TUR) is the standard treatment for low-grade NMIBC. However, the NCCN guidelines indicate that if a high grade of NMIBC is detected in the initial TUR, an additional TUR should be implemented to completely remove the lesion. For more malignant lesions, cystectomy is recommended. Therefore, accurate classification of bladder cancer grade is of great significance for the determination of prognosis and clinical decision-making.

Zhang et al. conducted a retrospective study, in which 61 patients with bladder cancer were included (high-grade group: 29; low-grade group: 32) [80]. A total of 102 radiomic features based on histogram or GLCM were calculated from DWI and ADC images to distinguish the low-/high-grade bladder cancer. This study utilized Mann-Whitney U-test to find the features with significant differences between low-grade and high-grade patients, and then the SVM method with RFE was applied to sort the features. Finally, 22 radiomic features remained through cross-validation to establish the classification model based on SVM (Fig. 3.11). The model's AUC and accuracy were 0.861 and 0.829, respectively. The results indicated that the radiomic features, especially ADC-based GLCM features, could reflect the difference between low-grade and high-grade bladder cancer.

3.3.3 Prediction of histopathological grade in cervical cancer

Cervical cancer is one of the most common cancers in women. At present, DWI has been widely used to evaluate the stage, histopathological characteristics, treatment response, and recurrence of cervical cancer. However, because of the heterogeneity of ADC value, there is no consensus on its application in the clinical characterization for cervical cancer lesions.

Liu et al. studied the value of radiomics on the ADC map to predict the histopathological grade of cervical cancer [81]. A total of 160 patients (mean age: 51 years; age range: 26–84 years) with pathologically confirmed cervical cancer were included.

Table 3.5 Results for GS 6(3 + 3) versus $\geq$7 classification with and without augmentation [79].

Methods	PZ and TZ sites			PZ sites only		
	34/159 samples Not augmented	34/159 samples Gibbs	34/159 samples SMOTE	34/159 samples Not augmented	34/159 samples Gibbs	34/159 samples SMOTE
SVM	0.83(0.06)	0.73(0.53)	0.82(0.65)	0.83(0.24)	0.70(0.46)	0.79(0.62)
RFE-SVM	0.83(0.03)	0.83(0.71)	0.93(0.91)	0.84(0.00)	0.89(0.83)	0.92(0.89)
AdaBoost	0.73(0.11)	0.69(0.38)	0.64(0.28)	0.79(0.34)	0.72(0.44)	0.72(0.44)
ADC-SVM	0.82(0.00)	0.57(0.22)	0.58(0.22)	0.84(0.00)	0.63(0.27)	0.59(0.23)
ADC & T2-SVM	0.82(0.00)	0.57(0.22)	0.64(0.38)	0.84(0.00)	0.63(0.29)	0.62(0.29)

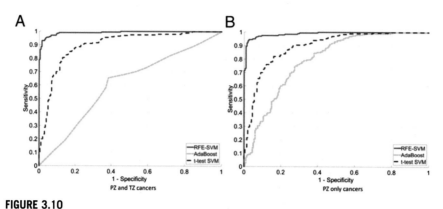

FIGURE 3.10

ROC curve analysis on models for GS $= 6$ and ≥ 7 occurring in PZ and TZ (A) and PZ only (B) [79].

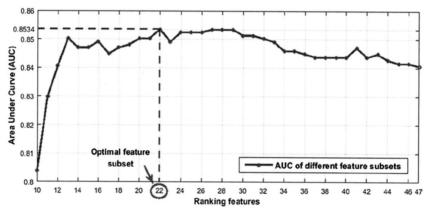

FIGURE 3.11

Classification performance of models based on different numbers of features [80].

International Federation of Gynecology and Obstetrics (FIGO) staging included IB ($n = 52$), II ($n = 94$), III ($n = 13$), and IV ($n = 1$). The histopathological grades included well-differentiated (G1, $n = 59$), moderately-differentiated (G2, $n = 51$), and poorly-differentiated (G3, $n = 43$) cases.

ADC maps were obtained from the isotropic DWI. On sagittal T2WI and DWI, radiologists manually outlined the tumor ROIs layer by layer, and the contours of ROIs were then copied to the corresponding positions on the ADC map. Subsequently, 208 radiomic features were extracted. The 3D radiomic features were obtained by averaging 2D radiomic feature values from all tumor slices. LASSO regression was used as the feature selection algorithm, and the histopathological grade of cervical cancer was used as the target to train classification models.

The best parameter lambda in LASSO was determined by 10-fold cross-validation with overall misclassification error (MCE) as the measurement index.

In Liu et al.'s experiments, 13 features from the ADC map of b800 and 12 features from ADC map of b1000 were retained [81]. A significant difference was found in the predictive performance of features from ADC of b800 and b1000 for tumor histopathological grading. Compared with ADC features of b800 (0.3758 $\pm$ 0.0118), the model of b1000 ADC features appeared to be slightly lower in overall misclassification error (0.3642 $\pm$ 0.0162) ($P = .0076$). In addition, the performance difference between 3D features and 2D center-slice features has also been studied. They found that 3D radiomic features had better performance than 2D center-slice features in stratifying the histopathological grade.

3.3.4 Identification of pathological subtype of lung ground-glass nodules

Lung cancer remains the leading cause of cancer-related deaths across the globe. Since adenocarcinomas occupy nearly 40% of all lung cancers, the radiomic studies of identification of lung adenocarcinoma have important clinical significance [82,83].

Most early lung cancers are adenocarcinomas, which usually manifest as ground-glass nodules (GGNs) on CT scans. Lung adenocarcinomas can be categorized into three subtypes: preinvasive adenocarcinoma, minimally invasive adenocarcinoma (MIA), and invasive adenocarcinoma (IAC), with very different disease-free survival rates and clinical management challenges. The 5-year disease-free survival rates of preinvasive adenocarcinoma and MIA are significantly higher than that of IAC. Limited surgical resection may be feasible for preinvasive adenocarcinomas or MIA patients. Thus, IAC is regarded as intermediate or high grade, whereas preinvasive adenocarcinoma and MIA are considered to be low grade due to their good prognosis. Follow-up CT is usually recommended for such patients until the nodule diameter is greater than 1.5 cm or the patient is over the age of 70 [84].

From the perspective of clinical significance and clinical management, preoperative non-invasive identification of preinvasive adenocarcinoma or MIA from IAC may provide significant guidance for clinicians. In previous studies, morphological features were most commonly used in the differential diagnosis of malignant GGNs [85]. However, GGNs have atypical features, thus, the quantitative parameters are variable. Under this circumstance, the radiomic technique with quantitative feature extraction and characterization algorithms may act as an important and effective tool.

Fan et al. [82] established a radiomic signature from CT scans to differentiate IAC from non-invasive lesions manifesting as GGNs. This study retrospectively included the patient population from three centers. The radiomic signature was built based on a primary cohort and evaluated based on three validation cohorts (one intra-cross-validation cohort and two external validation cohorts). In the primary cohort, 160 patients with 160 GGNs (77 non-invasive lesions and 83 IACs) were included. The three validation cohorts included 76 (36 non-invasive lesions and 40 IACs), 75 (30 non-invasive lesions and 45 IACs), and 84 (49 non-invasive lesions and 35 IACs) patients, respectively. A total of 355 3D radiomic features were extracted. Feature selection and radiomic signature building were performed using the LASSO regression based on the primary cohort. Two features were finally selected to build the radiomic signature, which demonstrated good discrimination ability. The radiomic signature achieved accuracies of 86.3%, 90.8%, 84.0%, and 88.1% in the four cohorts, respectively. Also, compared with clinical and CT characteristics (i.e., mean CT value, lobulation, pleural indentation, spiculation, air bronchogram, and spine like process), the radiomic signature was a better independent predictor for the identification of lung adenocarcinomas.

In terms of adenocarcinoma, the most common subtype of non-small cell lung cancer (NSCLC) and the most common true-positive finding in lung cancer screening, Beig et al. [83] conducted a study that aimed to differentiate adenocarcinoma from non-calcified granuloma, which is possibly the most prevalent and confounding false-positive finding in lung cancer screening. The two pathologic conditions usually have similar appearances on CT images. Similar to adenocarcinoma, most non-calcified granulomas tend to appear fluorodeoxyglucose avid on positron emission tomography (PET)/CT during the acute phase of infection. Previous studies focused more on distinguishing malignant and benign lung nodules. Therefore, little emphasis has been placed on the identification of adenocarcinomas from granulomas based on CT images. The attempt of this study may bring a standpoint from the perspective of radiomics for this challenge.

The final cohort enrolled 290 patients, later randomly allocated to a training cohort with 145 patients (73 adenocarcinomas and 72 granulomas) and a test cohort with 145 patients (72 adenocarcinomas and 73 granulomas). Researchers have hypothesized that the peritumoral regions hold potential information that could improve the efficacy of a single intranodular radiomic analysis. Thus, this study was designed to investigate whether radiomic features describing perinodular heterogeneity in a perinodular habitat could predict malignancy on CT images, and whether the combination of perinodular and intranodular radiomic features was more effective compared to intranodular features alone. The ROI was initially segmented manually across the nodule in an axial view, and then, based on the intranodular mask, a morphologic dilation was done to explore the perinodular regions up to a radial distance of 30 mm. Accordingly, the intranodular mask was then subtracted from the dilated mask to get a ring around the nodule. From the 30 mm perinodular region, rings of 5 mm were divided and features were extracted, including median, standard deviation, skewness, and kurtosis. Twelve nodule shape features were also extracted.

In the experimental part, the top 12 perinodular features that showed the best discriminative performance of adenocarcinomas from granulomas were first used to fit the linear discriminant analysis, quadratic discriminant analysis, SVM (linear and radial kernels), and RF classifiers. Next, quantitative radiomic features from intranodular and perinodular regions that showed the best discriminative performance of adenocarcinomas from granulomas were also used to fit the above classifiers. Then, the machine learning classifiers were independently validated and compared against a deep learning model trained by LeNet and the nodule assessments by two human readers.

In this study, features with the most outstanding predictive performance were found to be extracted from the spreading distance of 5 mm from the nodules. Higher expression of low-frequency Gabor features and higher filter responses of Laws energy were more frequently captured in the peritumoral regions. The top 12 radiomic features included three features from the spreading distance of 5 mm in the perinodular regions and nine features from the intranodular regions. Interestingly, none of the nodule shape features were used in the classifier development. The linear kernel SVM classifier achieved the highest AUC of 0.75 for the perinodular analysis and 0.80 for the combination of perinodular and intranodular analyses on the test set, which indicated the incremental value of perinodular information. The deep learning model-predicted probabilities obtained an AUC of 0.76, a sensitivity of 72%, and a specificity of 76%. As for the assessments by the two human readers, the AUCs on the test set were 0.61 and 0.60, respectively.

Thus, this study introduced a machine learning radiomic approach and successfully promoted the predictive performance in distinguishing adenocarcinomas from granulomas. The utility of combining the radiomic features from intranodular and perinodular regions on chest CT images provided more information, outperforming basic classifiers, the deep learning model, and human interpretations.

3.3.5 Identification of histologic subtype in non-small cell lung cancer

Lung cancer, as one of the most commonly diagnosed cancers in the world, has a very high incidence in China, European countries, and the United States. Among them, NSCLC takes up nearly 85% of all lung cancers. Lung adenocarcinoma and squamous cell carcinoma (SCC) are the two main histological subtypes of NSCLC. Their prognosis and recurrence rate are significantly different. In stage IA and IB patients, the prognosis of SCC is significantly worse than that of adenocarcinoma [86]. The prognosis of vascular invasion-positive adenocarcinoma is notably worse than that of vascular invasion-negative adenocarcinoma, while SCC has no significant distinction. Large vessel invasion has a higher incidence in SCC than that in adenocarcinoma. Accurate diagnosis not only improves the treatment effect but also avoids unnecessary side effects. Therefore, it is of great clinical value to distinguish lung adenocarcinoma from SCC before treatment.

Zhu et al. developed a CT-based radiomic method to classify lung adenocarcinoma and SCC [87]. The researchers retrospectively analyzed 441 lung cancer cases diagnosed between September 2010 and November 2013. The tumor ROI was manually segmented by a radiologist. To test the intraclass repeatability of features, the radiologist randomly selected 20 cases for secondary segmentation two weeks later. Besides, the other radiologist also segmented the 20 cases. ICCs were

Table 3.6 Selected features and performance [87].

Feature name	AUC	Sensitivity	Specificity
X3_fos_maximum	0.718	0.532	0.810
X0_GLCM_maximum_probability	0.845	0.660	0.929
X2_GLCM_cluster_tendency	0.872	0.766	0.905
X6_GLCM_variance	0.788	0.745	0.786
X1_GLRLM_RLN	0.787	0.574	0.857

used to evaluate the consistency of feature extraction, where ICC greater than 0.75 is considered to have a good consistency. Finally, researchers selected 485 features with ICCs higher than 0.75 for further analysis, which included tumor intensity, shape and size, texture, and wavelet features. Then, LASSO regression was used for feature selection, which finally reduced 485 features to five features in the training cohort. The AUC, sensitivity, and specificity based on the five features are shown in Table 3.6.

A radiomic signature, containing the five selected features, was established to classify lung adenocarcinoma and SCC. In the training cohort, the AUC of the radiomic signature was 0.905, with a sensitivity of 0.830 and a specificity of 0.929. In the validation cohort, the AUC was 0.893, with a sensitivity of 0.828 and a specificity of 0.900. These results showed that the radiomic signature was an effective prediction tool in both the training and validation cohorts.

Lung SCC is more sensitive to radiotherapy, indicating that the radiomic features proposed by Zhu et al. have potential clinical value and are low cost. Lung SCC patients can benefit from the radiomic features, because they can be used for selecting radiotherapy and chemotherapy before surgery to improve survival.

However, this study had some limitations. Only CT images were used in the study. The introduction of PET or other modalities may improve the performance of the radiomic signature. In addition, the dataset was small and from a single center, thereby limiting the scalability of radiomic features. A large multicenter cohort is expected to be built for verification. In summary, this study showed that radiomic features selected for constructing a radiomic signature could help to distinguish lung adenocarcinoma and SCC, thereby helping clinicians in diagnosis and treatment.

3.4 Application of radiomics in prediction of cancer gene mutation and molecular subtype

3.4.1 Prediction of somatic mutations in lung cancer

EGFR and KRAS mutations are the most frequent somatic mutations in lung cancer, and the prediction of these mutation is significant for targeted therapy. Velazquez et al. used quantitative CT radiomic features to predict somatic mutations in lung cancer patients [88]. Due to the difference in voxel spacing, researchers chose to use the cubic interpolation method to normalize the CT image, and then extract radiomic features, including (1) intensity features: first-order statistics calculated from the histograms of all voxel intensity values of the tumor; (2) texture features: texture features were used for quantitative tumor heterogeneity; (3) shape features: measurement of the shape and size of the tumor; (4) wavelet features: after applying a series of wavelet transformations to the CT images, the intensity and texture features were calculated. Wavelet transformations decomposed the original image into low-frequency and high-frequency information to focus the features on different frequency ranges of tumor voxels; and (5) Gaussian Laplace features: texture features extracted by using a Laplace Gaussian spatial band-pass filter to perform in-plane filtering and display different textures and anatomical patterns according to the spatial scale.

To ensure the robustness and repeatability of radiomic features, a repeatability test (n = 31) was performed to remove features with an ICC below 0.8. In addition, the method of principal component analysis was adopted to select the features with a Pearson coefficient greater than 0.9, and finally, 26 radiomic features were retained. Researchers found that Homogeneity and Inverse Variance were underrepresented relative to EGFR mutation, while Sum Entropy and Short Run Emphasis were overrepresented relative to EGFR mutation. The Sum Entropy was underrepresented relative to KRAS mutation. Total Energy was underrepresented relative to EGFR mutation but overrepresented in KRAS mutation.

A radiomic signature and a clinical signature were built using radiomic features and clinical features alone. Then a combined signature based on 20 radiomic features and 5 clinical features was built using RF algorithm. An overview of the method is shown in Fig. 3.12.

In order to develop and validate the predictive efficacy of radiomic and clinical features for gene mutations, the dataset (763 lung cancer patients, 183 EGFR mutation patients, and 215 KRAS mutation patients) was divided into the independent training and validation cohorts. The validation results of the predictive models are shown in Fig. 3.13 and Table 3.7. The combined signature had the highest AUCs in identifying EGFR+ versus EGFR−, KRAS+ versus KRAS−, and EGFR+ versus KRAS−.

In another study on lung adenocarcinoma [89], Wang et al. retrospectively collected preoperative CT images, EGFR mutation status, and clinical data of 844 patients with lung adenocarcinoma from two centers. Based on 14,926 CT images, a deep learning model was trained and constructed to predict the EGFR mutation status. Compared with previous studies which investigated hand-crafted radiomic features or clinical features, the performance of the proposed deep learning model was more significant ($P < .001$) in both the training set (n = 603; AUC = 0.85, 95% CI 0.83−0.88) and the validation set (n = 241; AUC = 0.81, 95% CI 0.79−0.83). The deep learning scores of EGFR+ and EGFR− tumors were significantly different ($P < .001$). Since CT is commonly applied in clinical diagnosis for

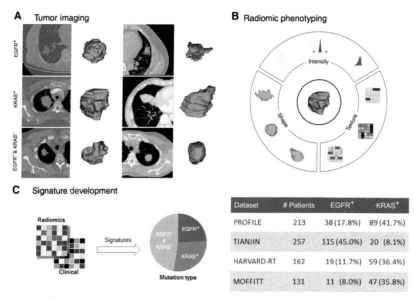

FIGURE 3.12

Workflow for predicting gene mutation [88]. (A) CT imaging (left) and 3D (right) segmentation of lung adenocarcinoma. (B) Quantification of tumors by extracting radiomic features. (C) Radiomic and clinical features were utilized to predict the EGFR and KRAS mutations in four separate datasets to observe the association between radiomic features and somatic gene mutations in lung adenocarcinoma.

lung cancer, this study concluded that the deep learning model could provide a potential method to predict the EGFR mutation status in a non-invasive way.

3.4.2 Prediction of gene mutations in gliomas

Gliomas are invasive tumors of the central nervous system, covering almost all age groups, and also the most common brain tumors in adults. According to the World Health Organization (WHO), lower-grade gliomas refer to grade II–III gliomas [90]. Radiogenomics for gliomas, as an emerging area of brain tumor research, aims to explore the relationship between radiomic features and genomic features. In the past 30 years, MRI technology has developed rapidly, from structural imaging to functional imaging, from qualitative to quantitative description, which has made MRI a crucial tool in clinical application of disease diagnosis and treatment, especially in neuroimaging. MRI, as the primary test method for gliomas, can detect the visual features of gliomas and visualize the quantification of these features, providing both temporal and spatial anatomical information. At the same time, with the rapid development of genetics, researchers have a deeper understanding of the complex molecular changes of gliomas. As defined by radiogenomics, most of the studies are trying to find the links between radiomic features and molecular

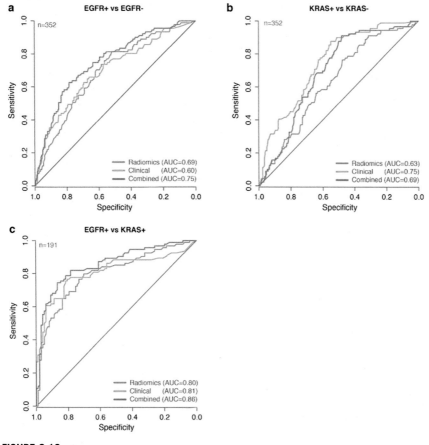

FIGURE 3.13

Prediction results using radiomic features, clinical features, and combined signature [88]. (A) EGFR+ versus EGFR−; (B) KRAS+ versus KRAS−; (C) EGFR+ versus KRAS+.

Table 3.7 Model performance of Radiomic, clinical and combined models [88].

	Signature	AUC	Specificity	Sensitivity	Accuracy	NPV	PPV
EGFR+ versus EGFR-	Radiomics	0.69	0.53	0.78	0.60	0.88	0.37
	Clinical	0.70	0.68	0.63	0.67	0.84	0.41
	Radiomics + clinical	0.75	0.62	0.75	0.65	0.988	0.41
KRAS+ versus KRAS-	Radiomics	0.63	0.54	0.64	0.57	0.82	0.32
	Clinical	0.75	0.65	0.71	0.66	0.87	0.41
	Radiomics + clinical	0.69	0.53	0.80	0.60	0.89	0.36
EGFR+ versus KRAS-	Radiomics	0.80	0.76	0.69	0.73	0.72	0.74
	Clinical	0.81	0.81	0.74	0.78	0.77	0.80
	Radiomics + clinical	0.86	0.88	0.69	0.79	0.75	0.84

AUC, *Areas under the ROC curves;* NPV, *Negative predictive value;* PPV, *Positive predictive value.*

features. Before the advent of radiogenomics, biogenetic tests were commonly used to assess tumors at the molecular level, whereas with the help of radiogenomics, these assessments could be accomplished by non-invasive image characterization. More importantly, the increasing availability of MRI and genetic data in clinical practice has accelerated the transformation of radiogenomics from hypothesis-driven research to data-driven analysis, which in turn brings the rapid development of mutual translation between radiomics and genomics.

Radiogenomics of gliomas is rapidly applied to a wide variety of studies. Based on the definition of molecular information, an increasing number of studies focusing on molecular expression have recently emerged; two representative aspects of which are (a) to use predefined molecular tags to assess the connections between imaging and genetics, and (b) to investigate the role of gene expression modules in functional sharing in genomes or clusters. A classical approach is to construct co-expressed gene modules from high-dimensional gene expression data via unsupervised algorithms such as hierarchical clustering. Identifying molecular factors with high accuracy is key to revealing highly expressed signaling pathways in gliomas. At the same time, accurate identification of molecular factors can help improve the understanding of the classification of gliomas subtypes. Studying the radiogenomics of glioblastoma begins with finding alternative radiomic features that can be used to predict classical molecular labels in gliomas [91].

To identify the relationship between low-grade gliomas and EGFR mutations, Li et al. used the data collected from Beijing Tiantan Hospital (MRI images and EGFR mutation information of 270 patients with low-grade gliomas collected from 2005 to 2012) and then extracted 431 radiomic features [92]. Then, researchers used logistic regression to select 41 features associated with EGFR expression among 431 features, which included 25 first-order statistical features, one morphological feature, and 15 texture features. To verify the efficacy of the selected features, all data were divided into a training cohort (n = 200) and a validation cohort (n = 70). The final AUC was 0.90 (sensitivity: 0.949 and specificity: 0.706) in the training cohort and 0.95 (sensitivity: 0.941 and specificity: 0.861) in the validation cohort. This study established the relationship between radiomic features and EGFR expression in low-grade gliomas, indicating that the use of non-invasive radiogenomics could facilitate the development of personalized therapy for patients with EGFR mutations [92].

Isocitrate dehydrogenase (IDH) mutations are of great diagnostic and prognostic significance for gliomas. Patients with IDH1 (or IDH2) mutated gliomas had a significant increase in OS time compared to patients with IDH1/2 wild-type tumors. Most low-grade IDH wild-type gliomas are similar to glioblastomas with poor prognosis in molecular and clinical manifestations. IDH mutant grade III gliomas have an even worse prognosis than IDH wild-type grade IV gliomas. Given the impact of IDH mutations on prognosis, IDH mutations were classified as an important diagnosis of glioma by the WHO in 2016. Pretreatment identification of IDH mutations can help in clinical decision-making. Firstly, imaging-determined IDH1 mutations in low-grade gliomas may allow physicians to take early action that is more effective than clinical observation; secondly, IDH mutant gliomas, due to the unusual epigenetic variation, are not sensitive to therapeutic interventions (e.g., temozolomide therapy or radiation/chemotherapy); finally, because the surgical resection of non-enhancing tumor areas can enhance the high-grade prognosis of IDH mutant gliomas, while wild-type gliomas do not benefit significantly from it, IDH mutation status of the early identification can guide the development of the surgical plan [93].

Chang et al. used a deep learning model to classify the IDH status in low- and high-grade gliomas based on preoperative MRI images [94]. Researchers retrospectively collected pathological data of glioma patients with a WHO grade II−IV from three centers, and the corresponding IDH mutation status was obtained from surgical or biopsy specimens. The composition of the dataset specifically included 201 patients from the Hospital of the University of Pennsylvania (HUP), 157 patients from Brigham and Women's Hospital (BWH), and 138 patients from the TCIA database. The researchers used manual or semiautomatic methods to obtain 3D tumor regions on T2-FLAIR MR images from three datasets, and the segmented regions were applied to the other MR sequences. Data from each center (HUP, BWH, and TCIA) were divided into training, validation, and test cohorts. The training and validation cohorts had similar distribution in mutation status and age. The residual neural network with 34 layers was applied to extract radiomic features from MRI. This study used three approaches to train the neural network: (1) Multi-modal multidirectional combinations of neural networks that train a neural network using all MR slices of each patient, (2) independently oriented neural network that trains a neural network for each dimension, and (3) an independent sequence neural network that trains a neural network for each MRI sequence.

Since the variation in IDH correlates with age, researchers combined the output of the network with age to construct a logistic regression model. The performance of the model was evaluated by the accuracy of the training, validation, and test cohorts. In addition, the network or logistic regression model was further evaluated by the AUC. This study selected the best modeling approach by evaluating the AUC of each model across all datasets, where only the age-established logistic regression models had AUCs of 0.88, 0.88, and 0.89 on the training, validation, and test cohorts, respectively. After 157 rounds of training on multimodal multidirectional combinations of neural networks, the AUCs were 0.93, 0.92, and 0.86 on the training, validation, and test cohorts, respectively. When combined with patient age, the AUCs were 0.95, 0.95, and 0.92.

Lu et al. also explored whether MRI could help to classify molecular subtypes in gliomas [95]. Data of 456 patients were collected from the Cancer Imaging Archive, which included preoperative MR images, survival data, histology, 1p/19q, and IDH status. Researchers developed a three-level model to classify glioma subtypes based on multimodal MR images. Another independent dataset ($n = 70$) was used to test the performance of the model. Experiments showed that the 1p/19q and IDH status could be distinguished by radiomics-based approaches. In the training cohort, AUCs were between 0.922 and 0.975 and accuracies were between 87.7% and 96.1%, while in the test cohort, the performance of the model was comparable to that of the training cohort, demonstrating the efficacy of the trained classifier. An accuracy of 81.8% was achieved in the classification of the five molecular subtypes based on the MR phenotype alone. With available histological data, higher accuracy of 89.2% can be achieved.

3.4.3 Prediction of KRAS/NRAS/BRAF mutations in colorectal cancer

The treatment of patients with colorectal cancer has made significant progress over the past decades. In recent years, radiomics-based studies have played a crucial role in the development of colorectal cancer treatment. Similarly, in the development of personalized medicine with the help of targeted therapy, radiomics is a powerful tool for improving the survival of patients and performing the genetic analysis of tumors [96]. NCCN guidelines recommend that patients with suspected or confirmed metastatic colorectal cancer should detect KRAS/NRAS/BRAF mutations, because the corresponding clinical treatment drugs for these mutation-negative patients are EGFR monoclonal antibodies cetuximab and panitumumab. Therefore, the prediction or identification of the KRAS/NRAS/BRAF mutation status is essential for predicting the treatment effect of colorectal cancer patients and formulating individualized treatment strategies. Pathological testing is the gold standard for detecting colorectal cancer gene mutations in clinical practice. However, biopsy specimens cannot fully reflect the genotype changes of tumors after biopsy, especially after multiple treatments; thus, the sampling of biopsy specimens may be limited by the heterogeneity of the tumor. Therefore, developing a non-invasive and repeatable method, which can reflect intratumoral heterogeneity and help identify the state of gene mutations, is of great significance for providing histologically assisted assessment. Circulating DNA analysis is a non-invasive method for genotype analysis of colorectal cancer [97]. However, insufficient tumor DNA in the blood circulation for genetic testing may be a disadvantage. Conversely, medical imaging examination has the advantage of displaying the entire tumor globally; thus, it has the potential to be used as a complementary method for genotype analysis.

Since CT is the primary choice as a clinical imaging method of colorectal cancer recommended by NCCN guidelines, Yang et al. explored the relationship between CT-based radiomic features and KRAS/NRAS/BRAF mutations [98]. Some previous studies used PET to assess the association between image features and genetic mutations in rectal cancer, colorectal cancer, and metastatic colorectal cancer [99], but the results were not consistent. In addition, previous studies only analyzed a few KRAS/NRAS/BRAF genes, and the results lacked verification. Moreover, the NCCN guidelines recommend that PET/CT should barely be used to evaluate ambiguous findings on CT. Therefore, this study used only CT images without

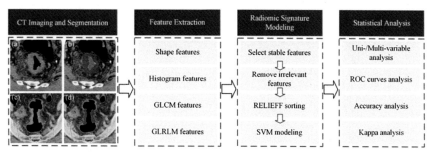

FIGURE 3.14

The workflow of data processing [98].

PET to predict gene mutation status. The workflow for predicting gene mutation in this study is shown in Fig. 3.14.

After evaluating the repeatability of features, 296 texture features with ICCs>0.8 were retained in the feature stability test. At the same time, 56 features showed predictive power in the initial univariate analysis. After establishing five feature sets, researchers used the RELIEFF algorithm to classify the features and selected the first three features for the SVM model. The results of feature selection and model performance are shown in Table 3.8.

This study selected the features with the best prediction performance and used SVM for training. Under the premise of ensuring the generalization of the model and the principle of the best prediction performance in the primary cohort, the optimal hyperplane was estimated. Three radiomic features were selected to form a 3D feature space. Then, patient data were projected into feature space as points, and the hyperplane of the SVM model was described with the optimal threshold. The diagram of the separation hyperplane and the visualization of patient information in the feature space is shown in Fig. 3.15.

At a given significance level ($P < .05$), the accuracy of verification was 0.996. The SVM model distinguished the mutant group from the wild-type group with an accuracy of 0.787 in the primary cohort and 0.750 in the validation cohort. Radiomic features were found to be significantly related to gene mutations. In the ROC analysis, the AUC of the radiomic features in the primary cohort was 0.869, and the AUC in the validation cohort was 0.829, as shown in Fig. 3.16.

To sum up, the radiomic model proposed in this study was related to KRAS/NRAS/BRAF mutations. It exhibited better AUC and specificity in predicting the mutations, but lower sensitivity, especially in the validation cohort. In addition, the results of this study showed that tumor stage and histological differentiation were not related to those mutations. Thus, CT-based radiomics can be used to predict KRAS/NRAS/BRAF in patients with colorectal cancer, thereby assisting the development of treatment strategies.

Table 3.8 Results of feature selection and model performance [98].

Feature categories	Feature name	Model performance (1000 times 10-fold cross-validation)			
		Accuracy (95% CI)	SEN	SPE	AUC (95% CI)
Shape	surface_area_to_volume_ratio maximum_radius Volume	0.706 (0.599–0.780)	0.685	0.734	0.760 (0.682–0.820)
Histogram	3_fos_mean_absulute_deviation 2_fos_range 1_fos_skewness	0.676 (0.580–0.766)	0.505	0.936	0.807 (0.716–0.894)
GLCM	4_GLCM_maximum_probability 6_GLCM_energy 1_GLCM_inverse_variance	0.752 (0.671–0.811)	0.679	0.872	0.842 (0.757–0.897)
GLRLM	3_GLRLM_LGLRE 1_GLRLM_RP 7_GLRLM_RP	0.746 (0.643–0.833)	0.669	0.854	0.834 (0.703–0.912)
Overall	4_GLCM_maximum_probability 6_GLCM_energy 8_GLCM_sum_average	0.766 (0.673–0.836)	0.701	0.858	0.860 (0.797–0.928)

(a)   (b)

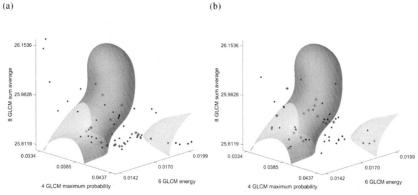

FIGURE 3.15

The separation hyperplane and the patients' features in the (A) primary cohort (B) validation cohort. The gray surface indicates a hyperplane. These points represent the patient (True negative, blue solid point; True positive, red solid point; False negative, red star point; False positive, blue star point) [98].

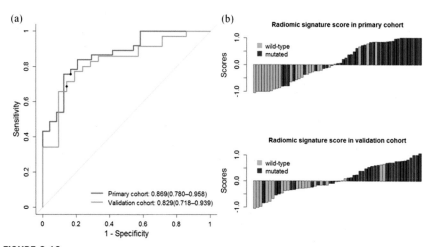

FIGURE 3.16

The performance of the radiomic signature in primary and validation cohorts. (A) ROC curve and AUC of the radiomic model. The red and blue lines represent the ROC curve in the primary cohort and the ROC curve in the validation cohort, respectively. The real point represents the optimal cut-off value (that is, the hyperplane of the SVM model). (B) The score of the radiomic feature of each patient in the primary cohort and validation cohort. Red marks indicate patients in the mutant group and green marks indicate patients in the wild-type group [98].

3.4.4 Prediction of molecular subtypes in breast cancer

Breast cancer is the most commonly diagnosed cancer among women. Depending on the receptor, breast cancer can be classified into different subtypes, including ER, PR, HER2, etc. The types of breast cancer include HER2 overexpression, luminal A, luminal B, and triple negative (TN, negative for all three receptors), etc. HER2-positive (HER2+) breast cancer is more aggressive and patients tend to have a worse prognosis than those who are HER2-negative (HER2−). ER-positive (ER+) and PR-positive (PR+) patients have lower mortality rates than ER-negative (ER−) or PR-negative (PR−) patients, while TN patients typically show more rapid recurrence [100]. With different molecular and receptor status, breast cancer subtypes have varied responses and prognoses to specific treatments [101].

Li et al. explored the application of radiomics in the classification of breast cancer subtypes [102]. They investigated the relationship between molecular subtypes, including the ER, PR, HER2, and TN fractions, and the MRI image phenotypes of invasive breast cancer samples, aiming to provide a radiomics-based quantitative label for assessing breast cancer prognosis, as well as supporting personalized medical strategies for patients with breast cancer. The study is based on MR images of 91 breast cancer patients with the same brand and field strength of scanning (GE, 1.5T).

This study used tumors on MRI images to predict breast cancer immunohistochemistry results (ER, PR, HER2, TN) [102]. Four classifiers were established for the phenotype: (1) estrogen (ER+ and ER−); (2) progesterone (PR+ and PR−); (3) HER2 (HER2+ and HER2−); and (4) TN (TN and others). ROC curves were used to evaluate the performance of each classifier and to test their statistical significance. The Mann-Whitney U-test was also used to test whether individual features were statistically significant across molecular subtype differences. Forward or backward stepwise selection was used to select the best set of features that were used as the inputs of the linear classifier. The results showed that ER-negative patients had larger tumor sizes, more irregular shapes, enhanced textural features, and exhibited more heterogeneity compared to ER-positive patients. Likewise, PR-negative patients exhibited a larger tumor size, more irregular shape, and more heterogeneity compared to PR-positive patients. TN patients also tended to be larger, more irregular in shape, and more heterogeneous than non-TN patients. The Mann-Whitney U-test showed that tumors of different molecular subtypes had a significant difference in the size and texture features of their MRI phenotypes.

This study showed that the tumor phenotype revealed by quantitative analysis of MR images can be used to predict tumor classification of invasive breast cancer. In the classification task of ER, PR, HER2, and TN, the corresponding AUCs were 0.89, 0.69, 0.69, and 0.69, respectively. The evaluation results showed that the computer-extracted tumor phenotypic features had significant ability in molecular classification. This study also revealed a statistically significant correlation between tumor phenotype and the status of each receptor, where tumors with a higher degree of malignancy are often larger and show more heterogeneity in contrast-enhanced images. After grouping tumors according to their size, the correlation between enhanced textural features and molecular fractions remained significant in different groups.

3.5 **Application of radiomics in other diseases**

Radiomics has been recently applied in clinical decision support for multiple diseases, including coronavirus disease 2019 (COVID-19), liver fibrosis, portal hypertension, and cardiovascular diseases. This chapter will introduce the utilization of radiomics in multiple diseases, respectively.

3.5.1 **Diagnosis of COVID-19**

COVID-19 has become a global concern and radiomics has proven to be effective in screening and diagnosis of COVID-19 [103]. As medical resources in many regions have become insufficient, it is important to quickly diagnose high risk COVID-19 patients with poor prognosis and to optimize medical resources early [104]. The effective method to control the disease is detecting COVID-19 correctly and rapidly. It is crucial to find patients with poor prognosis requiring special care.

In the early days of the outbreak of COVID-19, the lack of testing kits has prevented many infected people from being immediately quarantined. Therefore, it is important to find patients who may have a poor prognosis and to receive medical attention early to avoid spreading virus. It has been proven that CT can be used to diagnose COVID-19 and predict prognosis. The sensitivity of CT is much higher than RT-PCR to detect COVID-19 [105][106]. As a diagnostic tool, CT can be obtained quickly without much cost. Using CT images as a diagnostic tool can speed up the diagnostic process and identify potentially high-risk patients. Some studies have proven that deep learning can achieve hopeful results in assisting diagnosis of lung CT images by extracting features connecting the results [89,107]. The function of the deep learning model may therefore assist the diagnosis of COVID-19.

Wang et al. employed CT scans and constructed a deep learning model to diagnose and predict the prognosis of COVID-19 patients without human assistance [108]. The researchers retrospectively collected 5372 patients with CT scans from seven areas in China. First, 4106 patients with lung cancer were used for the pretraining of the deep learning system to learn lung characteristics. Thereafter, 1266 patients with COVID-19 or other pneumonia were recruited from six cities or provinces and used for training. Finally, the deep learning model was verified externally.

In the training set, the deep learning system obtained an $AUC = 0.90$, sensitivity $= 79\%$, and specificity $= 90\%$. $AUC = 0.87$ and 0.88, sensitivity $= 80\%$ and 79%, and specificity $= 77\%$ and 81% were obtained in two external validation sets. The deep learning score between the COVID-19 and other pneumonia groups was significantly different. The deep learning system has good universality in the diagnosis of COVID-19. It obtained good calibration curves in the two validation sets, indicating that it does not underestimate or overestimate the probability of COVID-19. The prediction results are shown in Fig. 3.17.

The researchers followed up 471 patients for more than 5 days. After that, the patients were successfully stratified by two groups according to median value of the deep learning features. This indicates that features produced by the deep learning model are hopeful to predict COVID-19.

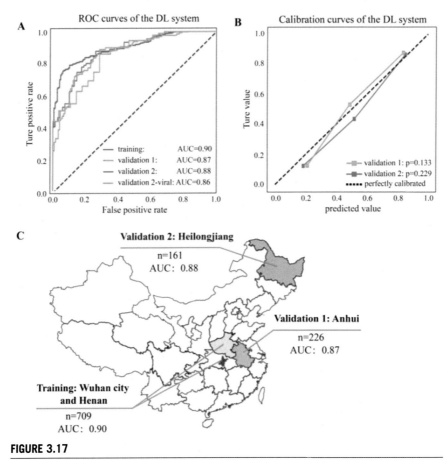

FIGURE 3.17

The prediction performance of the deep learning system [108]. (A) ROC curves of the deep learning system in the training set and the two external validation sets. (B) Calibration curves of the deep learning system in the two external validation sets. (C) AUC and distribution of the training set and the two external validation sets.

The visualization of the interested lung region produced by deep learning shows abnormal features found by the radiologist. Fig. 3.18 shows the suspicious lung area of eight patients with COVID-19. Although there are some non-lung tissues in the ROI entering the model, the target of the model is the lung area without interference from other tissues. Besides, the suspicious lung area highly overlaps the actual inflammation area. As shown in Fig. 3.18, the deep learning system automatically recognizes the ground-glass opacity (GGO) area. This is consistent with the radiologist's experience. In Fig. 3.18, the suspected lung area is distributed in both lungs, and is mainly concentrated in diffuse or mixed GGO. These suspicious lung areas are highly overlapping and consistent with actual abnormal lung areas.

The impressing result of the deep learning model indicates that it can help diagnose COVID-19. Suspected patients can undergo a full CT scan in just a few minutes.

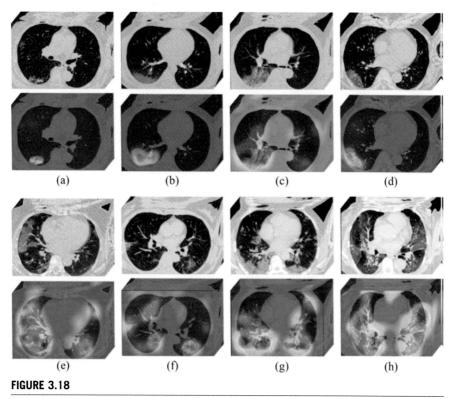

FIGURE 3.18

The abnormal areas identified by the deep learning system [108]. (a)-(h) are CT images of eight patients with COVID-19. The first and the third rows are CT images of the patients. The second and the fourth rows are heatmaps of the deep learning-discovered suspicious lung area. On the heatmaps, areas with red color are more important than blue areas.

The deep learning model can estimate the possibility of suffering from COVID-19. High-possibility patients who require emergency medical care can be found, thereby increasing its clinical value. The deep learning system can make prognosis and diagnosis predictions in less than 10 seconds. The deep learning system discovered important areas automatically. The suspicious lung area predicted by deep learning highly overlaps with the area used by the radiologist. Radiology characteristics, such as GGO, are very important for the diagnosis of COVID-19 [109].

Moreover, Fang et al. selected radiomic features to diagnose COVID-19 from CT images [110]. They evaluated the predictive power of features based on a univariate analysis. Twenty-three features between COVID-19 and other types of pneumonia were found to be significantly different. At the same time, the heatmap displayed a significant difference in expression between subgroups (Fig. 3.19), indicating an internal relationship between the CT phenotype of the lesion and the type of pneumonia.

In the clustering step, 17 different clusters were obtained and the main features were used to build the candidate feature set of the radiomic model. In order to control overfitting, the SVM model was constructed based on the four selected

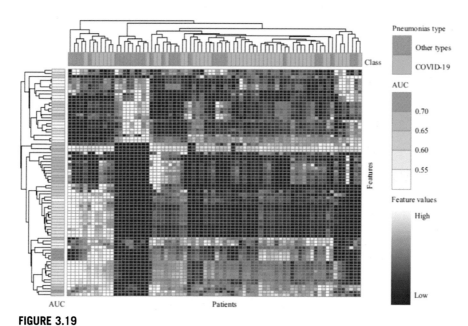

FIGURE 3.19

Radiomic heatmap on the overall set [110].

features, with an average accuracy of 0.820. The model showed strong predictive power in the training and test sets, with AUCs = 0.862 and 0.826, respectively. The Delong test revealed that there was no statistical difference in AUC between the two subgroups. The calibration curve showed that there was no difference between the predicted possibility and the actual possibility of COVID-19. The results of the Hosmer-Lemeshow test showed the calibration curve can fit the diagonal well, representing a good prediction. The experimental results showed that many radiological characteristics of pneumonia correlated highly with COVID-19 infection.

Besides above studies, Wu et al. also developed a deep learning model to diagnose COVID-19 pneumonia [111]. The inputs of the model are CT images of the largest lung area including three CT views. Images from multiple views provide more useful information without introducing redundancy. In order to distinguish different kinds of pneumonia, Wu et al. built a multiview fusion model using ResNet50 which took the three-view image set as input instead of typical RGB channels images usually used in ResNet50. The training set was consisted of 395 randomly selected three-view images, and the validation set was adopted to optimize hyperparameters. Throughout the training phase, the RMSprop optimizer was used to update the parameters of the model, where the learning rate of the model is 1×10^{-5} and the batch size is 4. The researchers first assessed the performance of the model using axial-view CT images. The AUC in the training, verification, and test sets were 0.767, 0.642, and 0.634, respectively. The accuracy of the verification and test set was 0.640 and 0.620, and the sensitivity was 0.676 and 0.622, respectively. The AUC of the training set was 0.905, the accuracy was 0.833, and the sensitivity was 0.825 in the multiview model. The AUCs of the multiview model in verification and test set were 0.732 and 0.819, the accuracies were 0.700 and 0.760, and the sensitivities were 0.730 and 0.811, respectively. As shown in Fig. 3.20, the multiview model acts better than the single-view model in classifying COVID-19.

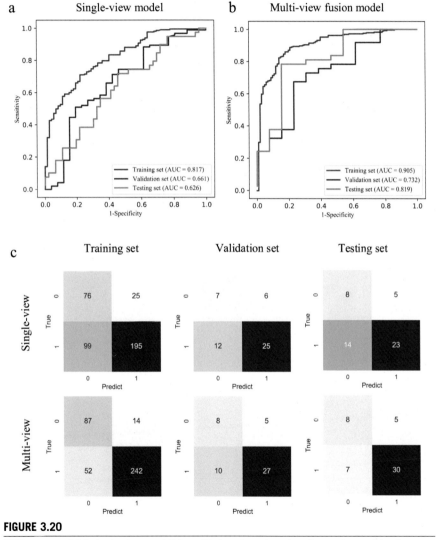

FIGURE 3.20

ROC curves of (a) single-view and (b) multi-view deep learning diagnosis models of COVID-19 pneumonia. (c) Confusion matrix of single-view and multi-view deep learning diagnosis models. 1 represents COVID-19 pneumonia, and 0 represents other pneumonia [111].

To visualize the diagnosis, Wu et al. provided three-view CT images of four patients in Fig. 3.21. GGO are clearly visible in the two COVID-19 patients (spotted by red arrows). The COVID-19 infection risk scores of the four patients were 0.801, 0.461, 0.946, and 0.315, respectively (ranging from 0 to 1). The critical value in this study was 0.653. It takes more than 10 minutes for a trained radiologist to examine a patient's CT image and identify the patient infected with COVID-19. In contrast, the multi-view deep learning model can take less than 5 seconds to obtain the screening

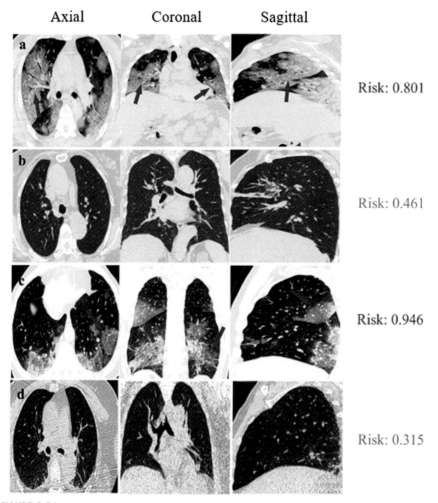

FIGURE 3.21

Representative examples of a pneumonia diagnosis [111]. (a) A 46-year-old male with COVID-19 pneumonia. (b) An 84-year-old female with bacterial pneumonia. (c) A 62-year-old male with COVID-19 pneumonia. (d) A 52-year-old female with bacterial pneumonia.

results in the identification of COVID-19 pneumonia, thereby reducing the radiologist's workload.

For radiologists, it is challenging to diagnose pneumonia quickly and accurately under a huge workload. The deep learning/radiomics methods provide potential tools for diagnosis and prognosis of COVID-19.

3.5.2 Staging of liver fibrosis

In China, the situation of hepatitis B virus infection is serious. Chronic hepatitis B (CHB) can progress to liver fibrosis. Assessing liver fibrosis is essential for monitoring and managing CHB patients. A biopsy is useful for staging liver fibrosis, but its disadvantages include invasiveness and the differences between inter-observers. Recently, many guidelines have recommended the use of non-invasive ultrasound imaging-based liver stiffness measurement to detect liver fibrosis.

Many studies have proven that the 2D-SWE can assess liver fibrosis well but is limited by many situations. The ROI and image quality standards are still unclear. Previous studies used to identify the critical values of cirrhosis in HBV-infected patients vary widely. The use of 2D-SWE value alone is not enough to accurately assess the stage of liver fibrosis. Radiomics can automatically extract quantitative features from medical images, making it possible to discover features that the human eye cannot recognize. Radiomics-based 2D-SWE analysis may provide better staging accuracy of liver fibrosis than 2D-SWE value alone.

Wang et al. used CNNs to analyze 2D-SWE images to realize the diagnosis of liver fibrosis stage [112]. They successfully collected 2D-SWE images of 398 patients from different centers and applied deep learning methods to assess liver fibrosis. A total of 1990 2D-SWE images were obtained from 12 hospitals and divided into training and validation cohorts. In the training cohort, deep learning radiomics of elastography (DLRE) showed the highest diagnostic accuracy (Fig. 3.22A and C). The AUC of DLRE reached an astonishing 1.00, 0.99, and 0.99 in the three stratifications of liver fibrosis stage (F4, $\geq$F3 and $\geq$F2). Sensitivity and specificity analysis also showed that DLRE was superior to other methods. In the validation cohort, the performance of DLRE had AUCs of 0.97 and 0.98 in diagnosis of F4 and $\geq$F3 (Fig. 3.22D and E).

This multicenter prospective research compared the accuracy of the three methods in the assessment of the liver fibrosis stage. DLRE can better assess liver cirrhosis and advanced fibrosis. For the DLRE, the AUC achieved 1.00 and 0.99 in the training cohort, and the AUC achieved 0.97 and 0.98 in the validation cohort. This shows that DLRE provides very accurate diagnostic performance. The diagnostic accuracy of 2D-SWE comes second. The AUCs in the training cohort were 0.87 and 0.81, while the AUCs in the validation cohort were 0.86 and 0.85. Subgroup analysis was conducted to find if different clinical indicators would affect the diagnostic accuracy between 2D-SWE and DLRE. The results presented that inflammation level would affect the accuracy of 2D-SWE performance, but not DLRE. These findings indicate that DLRE has the potential to assess liver fibrosis. It can provide

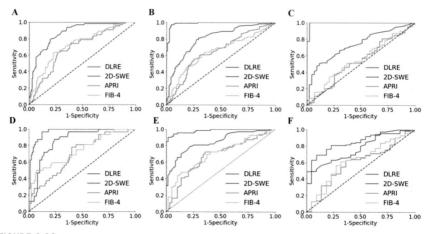

FIGURE 3.22

Comparison of ROC curves between DLRE, 2D-SWE, and biomarkers [112]. (A, D) F0-F3 versus F4 (F4) in the training and validation cohorts. (B, E) F0-F2 versus F3-F4 (≥F3) in the training and validation cohorts. (C, F) F0-F1 versus F2-F4 (≥F2) in the training and validation cohorts.

diagnostic accuracy similar to the reference standard. The diagnostic performance of DLRE is higher than 2D-SWE. DLRE can overcome the influence of inflammation when assessing liver cirrhosis. Compared with the 2D-SWE value, DLRE provides a more comprehensive assessment. It significantly improves the accuracy of cirrhosis and advanced fibrosis assessment. The current DLRE model can still be further improved. In this research, participants with F0–F1 were less than other participants. This may be due to the seriousness of the patients included. Further expansion of the sample size in future research will improve the accuracy of DLRE. The study also found that DLRE was highly dependent on the amount of data. The increase of 2D-SWE slice number may improve the diagnostic accuracy.

3.5.3 Diagnosis of portal hypertension

Portal hypertension in liver cirrhosis often occurs due to the high dynamic circulation and severe clinical symptoms, such as varicose vein bleeding and renal insufficiency [113]. Classification of portal hypertension based on portal venous pressure helps to distinguish patients with a high risk of poor condition from others. The appliance of measuring portal pressure is helpful in predicting progression of disease and determining treatment method. Assessing portal pressure for chronic liver patients should be through hepatic venous catheterization (through the transcervical, transfemoral, or transbrachial approach) to measure the hepatic venous pressure gradient (HVPG). Subclinical portal hypertension is defined as HVPG >5 mm Hg but <10 mm Hg and clinically significant portal hypertension (CSPH) is the HVPG ≥10 mm Hg. Severe portal hypertension often results in many complications (varicose veins occur and high possibility of liver decompensation). Non-invasive examinations were recommended compared to endoscopy examinations at the Baveno VI consensus meeting [113]. The meeting recommended to combining patients with liver stiffness less than 20 kPa and platelet count more than 150,000/μL to exclude livers with high-risk varicose veins or varicose veins in need of treatment, sclerosis, and safe evasion of an esophagogastric duodenoscope. Whether non-invasive methods can reliably identify patients with portal hypertension and whether hepatic venous catheters and esophagogastric duodenoscopy can be avoided in some patients requires in-depth research.

Qi et al. intend to develop a virtual HVPG model, based on CT angiography images, to diagnose CSPH [114]. This virtual HVPG model can be used to predict HVPG in patients with cirrhosis. The researchers verified the performance of this model to identify portal hypertension in patients with liver cirrhosis. As expected, virtual HVPG showed good identity and prediction performance in both training and validation sets, with AUCs of 0.83 and 0.89, respectively, and it had significant consistency with invasive HVPG. This study further evaluated the performance of transient elastography in the diagnosis of portal hypertension. According to the results, transient elastography measurement performed well in predicting the diagnosis of liver stiffness. Due to the high correlation between extrahepatic factors and the development of portal hypertension, researchers cannot reliably estimate HVPG by liver stiffness [115]. Therefore, researchers use virtual HVPG as a supplementary parameter for liver stiffness, particularly in patients with obesity, hepatic necrotizing inflammation, or severe ascites. As a non-invasive method, virtual HVPG integrates individual anatomical features and hepatic portal hemodynamic changes. It can achieve the invasiveness that serum markers cannot, and can be repeatedly calculated, facilitating repeated application in standard clinical practice. Virtual HVPG can quickly diagnose and determine whether further treatment is needed or if invasive methods can be avoided for patients. It can also be used to evaluate drug treatment effects and intervention results.

Liu et al. proposed a radiomic tool capable of identifying CSPH [116]. They developed a radiomic model for hepatic venous pressure gradient (rHVPG), which supplies a non-invasive tool for the accurate detection of CSPH.

The study included 385 patients with cirrhosis from five centers. Among them, 163 patients from four centers (Beijing Shijitan Hospital, Beijing Youan Hospital, Xingtai People's Hospital, and the Third Xiangya Hospital) were regarded as validation sets. The study obtained 20,648 radiomic features from portal venous phase CT images, and then used LASSO regression analysis to select 11 potential predictors. These predictors included seven features from the liver and four features from the spleen. The rHVPG model was established using these 11 radiological predictors. There was no statistical difference between the classification based on rHVPG and the classification based on HVPG. The ICC values for inter-observer and intra-observer consistency assessments were between 0.92−0.99 and 0.97−0.99, respectively. These results indicate that rHVPG has robust reliability and repeatability.

In the training set, rHVPG had a good diagnostic performance for liver cirrhosis CSPH. The C-index, sensitivity, specificity, positive predictive value, and negative predictive value were 0.849, 78.7%, 76.9%, 94.1%, and 43.5%, respectively. Using HVPG as a reference, 77.9% of cases were correctly diagnosed. Compared with non-invasive imaging-based and serum-based models, the rHVPG model showed the highest diagnostic performance. The AUCs of rHVPG and other models were 0.849, 0.778, 0.549, 0.505, 0.473, 0.558, and 0.483, respectively. In forward-looking verification, the rHVPG model achieved satisfactory performance on four external independent validation sets, with C-indices of 0.889, 0.800, 0.917, and 0.827, respectively. The sensitivity and specificity results of each validation set were 69.3% and 100%, 85.7% and 80.0%, 83.3% and 100%, and 63.6% and 100%, respectively.

Assessing liver stiffness is the most effective alternative measurement of HVPG, which can identify CSPH in cirrhosis. Liu et al. found that FibroScan performed better than the serum-based model, which is different compared to other researches. However, the diagnostic accuracy of FibroScan for CSPH is not satisfactory. Acute exacerbations are more frequent in HBV patients, whereas FibroScan's exaggerated liver stiffness is related to the degree of necrotizing inflammation. It should also be noted that obese patients are related to the inaccurate liver stiffness by FibroScan. In addition, severe portal hypertension may affect liver stiffness measurement because of extrahepatic factors which are increasingly associated with disease progression. Liu et al. proposed that the rHVPG could act as a supplementary parameter [116]. However, there still require more researches to investigate how much the necrotizing inflammation and obesity can influence the effectiveness of rHVPG to identify CSPH in cirrhosis. Meanwhile, rHVPG models are very safe and repeatable. Because HVPG measurement is subject to invasive limitations, it is not suitable for dynamic monitoring. Clinicians can diagnose the patient's CSPH on CT images using rHVPG models, which will contribute to clinical decision-making.

3.5.4 Diagnosis of cardiovascular plaques

Fractional flow reserve (FFR) is the gold standard for assessing coronary artery lesions. However, clinical FFR examinations require pressure guide wires, which makes such examinations very expensive and can cause damage to patients. Coronary computed tomography angiography (CCTA) is very important for interventional decision-making on myocardial ischemic diseases [117]. Although CCTA can display the structure of the coronary artery, it cannot reflect the physiological and pathological features of coronary artery disease. Moreover, the specificity of CCTA for identifying functional myocardial ischemia is not good, so it is difficult for CCTA to identify obvious functional stenosis in severe patients. Therefore, distinguishing ischemic lesions from non-ischemic lesions requires obtaining more information from CCTA and adopting more accurate methods to advance the diagnosis. FFRCT is an emerging method that can identify lesions with hemodynamic changes. However, FFRCT takes a lot of time and money. To address the above issues,

Hu et al. conducted a study using radiomics to detect high-risk plaques [118]. This study used radiomics to analyze CCTA, diagnose myocardial ischemia, and predict major adverse cardiovascular events (MACEs). A total of 119 patients with CCTA and FFR measurements were enrolled and divided into a training set ($n = 88$) and a validation set ($n = 31$). The conventional CCTA parameters in the training set do not show significant variation compared to validation set. Training set has a higher degree of stenosis compared to validation set. In this research, the researchers selected 1409 radiomic features from the cardiovascular ROI. Analysis within and between observers showed that there were 1359 features with ICC>0.75. LASSO regression selected three wavelet features from 1359 features. Pseudocolor images are shown in Fig. 3.23. Robust testing showed that the effectiveness of radiological features was affected by a slice gap instead of the direction of slice and filter settings.

The researchers used the three radiomic features to establish a radiomic model. In addition, a conventional model based on four conventional CCTA features was also developed. Compared with the conventional model, the radiomic model performed better in distinguishing ischemic and non-ischemic lesions in the training set. But in the validation set, these radiomic features were not better than conventional parameters. One reason may be that MACEs are influenced by many factors and a single variable cannot provide enough information. The inconsistency of CT equipments may also influence the results. Equipment and reconstruction algorithms may adversely affect the robustness and stability of radiomic features. The inconsistency of the CT scanners in different sets may cause large differences in the characteristics of radiomics. In this research, all selected features were based on wavelet transformed GLCM features. GLCM shows the correlation between voxels in a specified direction. This research showed that ischemic lesions exhibited greater local gray-scale similarity and greater texture changes. The results show that digging into image features can help distinguish ischemic lesions.

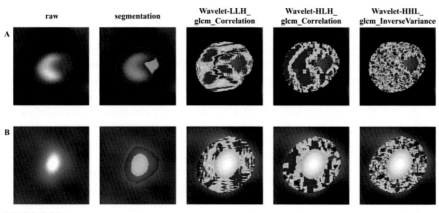

FIGURE 3.23

Radiomic features of two patients. The raw imaging, segmentation, and wavelet feature maps for two patients are displayed in (A) and (B) [118].

3.5.5 Identification of coronary plaques with napkin-ring sign

Major adverse cardiovascular events are usually associated with four distinct plaque characteristics in coronary CT angiography. Among them, high-risk plaque features usually present spotty calcification, positive remodeling, and low attenuation. As a feature of high-risk coronary artery atherosclerotic plaque on a CT coronary angiogram, the napkin-ring sign (NRS) represents a cross section of a coronary artery showing luminal narrowing by a low attenuating eccentric structure. However, in clinical practice, the identification of the NRS is challenging due to inter-reader variability. Therefore, Kolossváry et al. explored the role of radiomic features in identifying the NRS plaque [119].

From 2674 consecutive coronary CT angiography examinations, 39 patients with NRS plaque were screened out. After two radiologists reviewed the results and evaluated the image quality, a total of 30 patients were included. By matching the plaque characteristics, researchers constructed a non-NRS group that was very similar to the NRS group. The researchers performed automatic image segmentation and extracted eight conventional quantitative features, including the remodeling index, minimal plaque attenuation, maximal plaque attenuation, lesion length, area stenosis, mean plaque attenuation, mean plaque burden, and lesion volume. In addition, 4440 radiomic features were extracted, including 44 first-order statistical features, 3585 gray-level co-occurrence matrix (GLCM)-based features, 55 gray-level run length matrix (GLRLM)-based features, and 756 geometry-based statistical features. The 3D image arrays were transformed into a one-dimensional (1D) vector in the calculation of first-order statistical features.

In the assessment of traditional plaque characteristics, researchers graded all plaques into minimal, mild, moderate, and severe, according to the degree of lumen stenosis, and also into calcified, partially calcified, and non-calcified, according to the degree of calcification. They classified the low attenuation plaques based on the threshold of 30 HU, and the spotty calcification plaques based on the visible 3-mm calcified plaque component. A permutation test was performed to compare features between non-NRS and NRS groups. ROC curve analysis was conducted, and the corresponding AUCs were calculated. The PPVs, negative predictive values (NPVs), sensitivity, and specificity were also calculated based on the Youden index. A linear regression analysis was performed to evaluate the potential clusters among 4440 radiomic features. The optimal number of clusters was determined by using the average silhouette method. For further validation, the top three radiomic features and the top three conventional quantitative features were included for stratified five-fold cross-validation. All models were trained on the training cohort and validated on an independent test cohort. It should be noted that a high-dimensional radiomic feature set was used in this study; however, the sample size was very small. This may result in higher family-wise error rates in statistical tests. In this study, Bonferroni correction was used to control the above problem. Bonferroni correction requires that all features are independent of each other; therefore, the researchers adopted a principal component analysis to calculate the number of informative parameters. Forty-two principal components were finally identified. After the Bonferroni correction, the threshold of the P value was less than .0012 (0.05/42).

The results showed that the patient characteristics, scan parameters, image quality parameters, and qualitative plaque characteristics had no significant differences between the non-NRS and NRS groups, which indicated that the matching of the non-NRS group was successful. For the eight conventional quantitative features, there were no statistical differences between the non-NRS and NRS groups, and a single-feature AUC was generally low (less than 0.8). For 4440 radiomic features, about 20% (916) showed statistical differences between the non-NRS and NRS groups. Specifically, there were 25% (11) first-order statistical features, 20.7% (742) GLCM-based features, 54.5% (30) GLRLM-based features, and 17.6% (133) geometry-based features with statistical differences between the NRS and non-NRS group. In the ROC curve analysis, about 10% (440) of the radiomic features had an AUC greater than 0.8. Specifically, there were 18.2% (8) first-order statistical features, 9.7% (348) GLCM-based features, 54.5% (30) GLRLM-based features, and 7.1% (54) geometry-based features having an AUC greater than 0.8. The radiomic features obtaining higher AUCs were "short-run low gray-level emphasis", "long-run low gray-level emphasis", "surface ratio of component 2", "long run emphasis", and "surface ratio of component 7", which obtained the AUC values of 0.918, 0.894, 0.890, 0.888, and 0.888, respectively. In the cluster analysis of radiomic features, the number of clusters was determined to be 44 by using linear regression analysis.

In the performance comparison between radiomic features and conventional quantitative features, three radiomic features obtained higher AUCs indicated by the five-fold cross-validated ROC curves, which represented the better performance of the radiomic features in identifying NRS plaques than the conventional quantitative features. Despite the relatively small sample size of coronary plaques and the small number of voxels they contained in coronary CT angiography, this study still proved that radiomic features could identify NRS in coronary plaques, and that radiomic features were more effective than conventional quantitative features. Among all of the radiomic features, those describing the spatial distribution of voxels showed better diagnostic performance than the first-order statistical features. Notably, several radiomic features with NRS recognition function had no corresponding imaging findings in previous studies, implying that the radiomic features may be able to identify new image markers related to the NRS that are still unknown. This study also has some limitations: (1) All of the images were generated from the same scanner; (2) The sample size was still small; and (3) The conclusions of this study need to be further validated on independent external datasets.

References

[1] Lambin P, Rios-Velazquez E, Leijenaar R, et al. Radiomics: extracting more information from medical images using advanced feature analysis. Euro J Cancer 2012;48(4): 441−6.
[2] Tian J, Dong D, Liu Z, et al. Radiomics in Medical Imaging—Detection, Extraction and Segmentation. Artificial Intelligence in Decision Support Systems for Diagnosis in Medical Imaging. Springer; 2018.

[3] Gillies RJ, Kinahan PE, Hricak H. Radiomics: images are more than pictures, they are data. Radiology 2016;278(2):563−77.

[4] Hawkins S, Wang H, Liu Y, et al. Predicting malignant nodules from screening CT scans. J Thorac Oncol 2016;11(12):2120−8.

[5] Peikert T, Duan F, Rajagopalan S, et al. Novel high-resolution computed tomography-based radiomic classifier for screen-identified pulmonary nodules in the National Lung Screening Trial. PloS One 2018;13(5):e0196910.

[6] Ardila D, Kiraly AP, Bharadwaj S, et al. End-to-end lung cancer screening with three-dimensional deep learning on low-dose chest computed tomography. Nat Med 2019; 25(6):954−61.

[7] National Lung Screening Trial Research Team. Reduced lung-cancer mortality with low-dose computed tomographic screening. N Engl J Med 2011;365(5):395−409.

[8] Kumar D, Chung AG, Shaifee MJ, et al. Discovery radiomics for pathologically-proven computed tomography lung cancer prediction//International Conference Image Analysis and Recognition. Cham: Springer; 2017. p. 54−62.

[9] Tanoue LT, Tanner NT, Gould MK, et al. Lung cancer screening. Am J Respir Crit Care Med 2015;191(1):19−33.

[10] Hall M, Frank E, Holmes G, et al. The WEKA data mining software: an update. ACM SIGKDD explorations newsletter 2009;11(1):10−8.

[11] Cohen WW. Fast effective rule induction//Machine learning proceedings 1995. Morgan Kaufmann; 1995. p. 115−23.

[12] Balagurunathan Y, Kumar V, Gu Y, et al. Test−retest reproducibility analysis of lung CT image features. J Digit Imaging 2014;27(6):805−23.

[13] McWilliams A, Tammemagi MC, Mayo JR, et al. Probability of cancer in pulmonary nodules detected on first screening CT. N Engl J Med 2013;369(10):910−9.

[14] Alonzo TA. Clinical prediction models: a practical approach to development, validation, and updating: by Ewout W. Steyerberg 2009:528. 528.

[15] Luo H, Xu G, Li C, et al. Real-time artificial intelligence for detection of upper gastrointestinal cancer by endoscopy: a multicentre, case-control, diagnostic study. Lancet Oncol 2019;20(12):1645−54.

[16] Amin MB, Greene FL, Edge SB, et al. The eighth edition AJCC cancer staging manual: continuing to build a bridge from a population-based to a more "personalized" approach to cancer staging. CA: A Canc J Clin 2017;67(2):93−9.

[17] Pohlen T, Hermans A, Mathias M, et al. Full-resolution residual networks for semantic segmentation in street scenes//Proceedings of the IEEE Conference on Computer Vision and Pattern Recognition. 2017. p. 4151−60.

[18] Wu N, Phang J, Park J, et al. Deep neural networks improve radiologists' performance in breast cancer screening. IEEE Trans Med Imaging 2019;39(4):1184−94.

[19] Siegel RL, Miller kd, Jemal A. Cancer statistics, 2016. CA Cancer J Clin 2016;66(1): 7−30. 2016.

[20] Park SY, Oh YT, Jung DC, et al. Prediction of biochemical recurrence after radical prostatectomy with PI-RADS version 2 in prostate cancers: initial results. Eur Radiol 2016;26(8):2502−9.

[21] Wang J, Wu CJ, Bao ML, et al. Machine learning-based analysis of MR radiomics can help to improve the diagnostic performance of PI-RADS v2 in clinically relevant prostate cancer. Eur Radiol 2017;27(10):4082−90.

[22] Roethke MC, Kuru TH, Schultze S, et al. Evaluation of the ESUR PI-RADS scoring system for multiparametric MRI of the prostate with targeted MR/TRUS fusion-guided biopsy at 3.0 Tesla. Eur Radiol 2014;24(2):344−52.

[23] Glastonbury CM, Bhosale PR, Choyke PL, et al. Do radiologists have stage fright? Tumor staging and how we can add value to the care of patients with cancer. Radiology 2016;278(1):11.

[24] Cohen PA, Jhingran A, Oaknin A, et al. Cervical cancer. Lancet 2019;393(10167): 169−82.

[25] Ma C, Zhang Y, Li R, et al. Risk of parametrial invasion in women with early stage cervical cancer: a meta-analysis. Arch Gynecol Obstet 2018;297(3):573−80.

[26] Baiocchi G, de Brot L, Faloppa CC, et al. Is parametrectomy always necessary in early-stage cervical cancer? Gynecol Oncol 2017;146(1):16−9.

[27] Dabi Y, Willecocq C, Ballester M, et al. Identification of a low risk population for parametrial invasion in patients with early-stage cervical cancer. J Transl Med 2018;16(1): 163.

[28] Qu JR, Qin L, Li X, et al. Predicting parametrial invasion in cervical carcinoma (stages IB1, IB2, and IIA): diagnostic accuracy of T2-weighted imaging combined with DWI at 3 T. Am J Roentgenol 2018;210(3):677−84.

[29] Wang T, Gao T, Guo H, et al. Preoperative prediction of parametrial invasion in early-stage cervical cancer with MRI-based radiomics nomogram. Eur Radiol 2020:1−9.

[30] Liu Z, Wang S, Di D, J.W., et al. The applications of radiomics in precision diagnosis and treatment of oncology: opportunities and challenges. Theranostics 2019;9(5): 1303.

[31] Napel S, Mu W, Jardim-Perassi BV, et al. Quantitative imaging of cancer in the postgenomic era: radio (geno) mics, deep learning, and habitats. Cancer 2018;124(24): 4633−49.

[32] Pfluger T, Melzer HI, Schneider V, et al. PET/CT in malignant melanoma: contrast-enhanced CT versus plain low-dose CT. Eur J Nucl Med Mol Imaging 2011;38(5): 822−31.

[33] Giesel FL, Schneider F, Kratochwil C, et al. Correlation between SUVmax and CT radiomic analysis using lymph node density in PET/CT-based lymph node staging. J Nucl Med 2017;58(2):282−7.

[34] Moltz JH, Bornemann L, Kuhnigk JM, et al. Advanced segmentation techniques for lung nodules, liver metastases, and enlarged lymph nodes in CT scans. IEEE J Select Top Signal Process 2009;3(1):122−34.

[35] Flechsig P, Kratochwil C, Schwartz LH, et al. Quantitative volumetric CT-histogram analysis in N-staging of 18F-FDG−Equivocal patients with lung cancer. J Nucl Med 2014;55(4):559−64.

[36] Glasgow SC, Bleier JIS, Burgart LJ, et al. Meta-analysis of histopathological features of primary colorectal cancers that predict lymph node metastases. J Gastrointest Surg 2012;16(5):1019−28.

[37] Smith AJ, Driman DK, Spithoff K, et al. Guideline for optimization of colorectal cancer surgery and pathology. J Surg Oncol 2010;101(1):5−12.

[38] Toiyama Y, Inoue Y, Shimura T, et al. Serum angiopoietin-like protein 2 improves preoperative detection of lymph node metastasis in colorectal cancer. Antican Res 2015; 35(5):2849−56.

[39] Dighe S, Purkayastha S, Swift I, et al. Diagnostic precision of CT in local staging of colon cancers: a meta-analysis. Clin Radiol 2010;65(9):708−19.

[40] Aerts HJWL, Velazquez ER, Leijenaar RTH, et al. Decoding tumour phenotype by noninvasive imaging using a quantitative radiomics approach. Nat Commun 2014; 5(1):1−9.

[41] Huang Y, Liang C, He L, et al. Development and validation of a radiomics nomogram for preoperative prediction of lymph node metastasis in colorectal cancer. J Clin Oncol 2016;34(18):2157−64.

[42] Ahmed M, Purushotham AD, Douek M. Novel techniques for sentinel lymph node biopsy in breast cancer: a systematic review. Lancet Oncol 2014;15(8):e351−62.

[43] Lyman GH, Somerfield MR, Bosserman LD, et al. Sentinel lymph node biopsy for patients with early-stage breast cancer: American Society of Clinical Oncology clinical practice guideline update. J Clin Oncol 2017;35(5):561−4.

[44] Boughey JC, Moriarty JP, Degnim AC, et al. Cost modeling of preoperative axillary ultrasound and fine-needle aspiration to guide surgery for invasive breast cancer. Ann Surg Oncol 2010;17(4):953−8.

[45] Shiina T, Nightingale KR, Palmeri ML, et al. WFUMB guidelines and recommendations for clinical use of ultrasound elastography: Part 1: basic principles and terminology. Ultrasound Med Biol 2015;41(5):1126−47.

[46] Berg WA, Cosgrove DO, Doré CJ, et al. Shear-wave elastography improves the specificity of breast US: the BE1 multinational study of 939 masses. Radiology 2012; 262(2):435−49.

[47] Zheng X, Yao Z, Huang Y, et al. Deep learning radiomics can predict axillary lymph node status in early-stage breast cancer. Nat Commun 2020;11(1):1−9.

[48] Wang S, Feng C, Dong D, et al. Preoperative computed tomography-guided disease-free survival prediction in gastric cancer: a multicenter radiomics study. Med Phys 2020. https://doi.org/10.1002/mp.14350. In press.

[49] Sun R, Fang M, Tang L, et al. CT-based deep learning radiomics analysis for evaluation of serosa invasion in advanced gastric cancer. Eur J Radiol 2020;132:109277.

[50] Chen W, Wang S, Dong D, et al. Evaluation of lymph node metastasis in advanced gastric cancer using magnetic resonance imaging-based radiomics. Front Oncol 2019;9:1265.

[51] Li J, Dong D, Fang M, et al. Dual-energy CT−based deep learning radiomics can improve lymph node metastasis risk prediction for gastric cancer. Eur Radiol 2020; 30(4):2324−33.

[52] Zhang L, Dong D, Zhang W, et al. A Deep Learning Risk Prediction Model for Overall Survival in Patients with Gastric Cancer: A Multicenter Study. Radiother Oncol 2020; 150:73−80.

[53] Zhang W, Fang M, Dong D, et al. Development and validation of a CT-based radiomic nomogram for preoperative prediction of early recurrence in advanced gastric cancer. Radiother Oncol 2020;145:13−20.

[54] Smyth EC, Verheij M, Allum W, et al. Gastric cancer: ESMO Clinical Practice Guidelines for diagnosis, treatment and follow-up. Ann Oncol 2016;27(Suppl. l_5):v38−49.

[55] Ajani JA, D'Amico TA, Almhanna K, et al. Gastric cancer, version 3.2016, NCCN clinical practice guidelines in oncology. J Natl Compr Canc Netw 2016;14(10): 1286−312.

[56] Meng L, Dong D, Chen X, et al. 2D and 3D CT Radiomic Features Performance Comparison in Characterization of Gastric Cancer: A Multi-center Study. IEEE J Biomed Health Inform 2020. https://doi.org/10.1109/JBHI.2020.3002805. In press.

[57] Peng H, Dong D, Fang MJ, et al. Prognostic value of deep learning PET/CT-based radiomics: potential role for future individual induction chemotherapy in advanced nasopharyngeal carcinoma. Clin Cancer Res 2019;25(14):4271−9.

[58] Dong D, Fang MJ, Tang L, et al. Deep learning radiomic nomogram can predict the number of lymph node metastasis in locally advanced gastric cancer: an international multi-center study. Ann Oncol 2020;31(7):912−20.

[59] Albain KS, Swann RS, Rusch VW, et al. Radiotherapy plus chemotherapy with or without surgical resection for stage III non-small-cell lung cancer: a phase III randomised controlled trial. Lancet 2009;374(9687):379−86.

[60] Hanna N, Neubauer M, Yiannoutsos C, et al. Phase III study of cisplatin, etoposide, and concurrent chest radiation with or without consolidation docetaxel in patients with inoperable stage III non−small-cell lung cancer: the Hoosier Oncology Group and US Oncology. J Clin Oncol 2008;26(35):5755−60.

[61] Coroller TP, Grossmann P, Hou Y, et al. CT-based radiomic signature predicts distant metastasis in lung adenocarcinoma. Radiother Oncol 2015;114(3):345−50.

[62] Ferlay J, Soerjomataram I, Dikshit R, et al. Cancer incidence and mortality worldwide: sources, methods and major patterns in GLOBOCAN 2012. Int J Cancer 2015;136(5): E359−86.

[63] Kwan JYY, Su J, Huang SH, et al. Radiomic biomarkers to refine risk models for distant metastasis in HPV-related oropharyngeal carcinoma. Int J Radiat Oncol Biol Phys 2018;102(4):1107−16.

[64] Zhang L, Huang Y, Hong S, et al. Gemcitabine plus cisplatin versus fluorouracil plus cisplatin in recurrent or metastatic nasopharyngeal carcinoma: a multicentre, randomised, open-label, phase 3 trial. Lancet 2016;388(10054):1883−92.

[65] Ren X, Yang X, Cheng B, et al. HOPX hypermethylation promotes metastasis via activating SNAIL transcription in nasopharyngeal carcinoma. Nat Commun 2017;8(1): 1−18.

[66] Zhang L, Dong D, Li H, et al. Development and validation of a magnetic resonance imaging-based model for the prediction of distant metastasis before initial treatment of nasopharyngeal carcinoma: a retrospective cohort study. EBioMedicine 2019;40: 327−35.

[67] Fujitani K, Yang HK, Mizusawa J, et al. Gastrectomy plus chemotherapy versus chemotherapy alone for advanced gastric cancer with a single non-curable factor (REGATTA): a phase 3, randomised controlled trial. Lancet Oncol 2016;17(3): 309−18.

[68] Burbidge S, Mahady K, Naik K. The role of CT and staging laparoscopy in the staging of gastric cancerresearcher. Clin Radiol 2013;68(3):251−5.

[69] Sarela AI, Lefkowitz R, Brennan MF, et al. Selection of patients with gastric adenocarcinoma for laparoscopic staging. Am J Surg 2006;191(1):134−8.

[70] Karanicolas PJ, Elkin EB, Jacks LM, et al. Staging laparoscopy in the management of gastric cancer: a population-based analysis. J Am Coll Surg 2011;213(5):644−51. e1.

[71] Dong D, Tang L, Li ZY, et al. Development and validation of an individualized nomogram to identify occult peritoneal metastasis in patients with advanced gastric cancer. Ann Oncol 2019;30(3):431−8.

[72] Wang X, Ding Y, Wang S, et al. Intratumoral and peritumoral radiomics analysis for preoperative Lauren classification in gastric cancer. Cancer Imaging 2020;20:83.

[73] Siegel RL, Miller KD, Jemal A. Cancer statistics. CA: A Can J Clin 2015;65(1):5. 2015.

[74] Wright JL, Salinas CA, Lin DW, et al. Prostate cancer specific mortality and Gleason 7 disease differences in prostate cancer outcomes between cases with Gleason 4+ 3 and Gleason 3+ 4 tumors in a population based cohort. J Urol 2009;182(6):2702−7.

[75] Ahmed HU, Akin O, Coleman JA, et al. Transatlantic Consensus Group on active surveillance and focal therapy for prostate cancer. BJU Int 2012;109(11):1636−47.

[76] Epstein JI, Feng Z, Trock BJ, et al. Upgrading and downgrading of prostate cancer from biopsy to radical prostatectomy: incidence and predictive factors using the modified Gleason grading system and factoring in tertiary grades. Eur Urol 2012;61(5): 1019−24.

[77] Gong L, Xu M, Fang M, et al. Noninvasive prediction of high-grade prostate cancer via biparametric MRI radiomics. J Magn Reson Imaging 2020;52(4):1102−9.

[78] Berglund RK, Masterson TA, Vora KC, et al. Pathological upgrading and up staging with immediate repeat biopsy in patients eligible for active surveillance. J Urol 2008;180(5):1964−8.

[79] Fehr D, Veeraraghavan H, Wibmer A, et al. Automatic classification of prostate cancer Gleason scores from multiparametric magnetic resonance images. Proc Natl Acad Sci Unit States Am 2015;112(46):E6265−73.

[80] Zhang X, Xu X, Tian Q, et al. Radiomics assessment of bladder cancer grade using texture features from diffusion-weighted imaging. J Magn Reson Imaging 2017; 46(5):1281−8.

[81] Liu Y, Zhang Y, Cheng R, et al. Radiomics analysis of apparent diffusion coefficient in cervical cancer: a preliminary study on histological grade evaluation. J Magn Reson Imaging 2019;49(1):280−90.

[82] Fan L, Fang MJ, Li ZB, et al. Radiomics signature: a biomarker for the preoperative discrimination of lung invasive adenocarcinoma manifesting as a ground-glass nodule. Eur Radiol 2019;29(2):889−97.

[83] Beig N, Khorrami M, Alilou M, et al. Perinodular and intranodular radiomic features on lung CT images distinguish adenocarcinomas from granulomas. Radiology 2019; 290(3):783−92.

[84] Lee HY, Choi YL, Lee KS, et al. Pure ground-glass opacity neoplastic lung nodules: histopathology, imaging, and management. Am J Roentgenol 2014;202(3):W224−33.

[85] Fan L, Liu SY, Li QC, et al. Multidetector CT features of pulmonary focal ground-glass opacity: differences between benign and malignant. Br J Radiol 2012; 85(1015):897−904.

[86] Bodendorf MO, Haas, et al. Prognostic value and therapeutic conse-quences of vascular invasion in non-small cell lung carcinoma. Lung Cancer 2009;64(1):71−8.

[87] Zhu X, Dong D, Chen Z, et al. Radiomic signature as a diagnostic factor for histologic subtype classification of non-small cell lung cancer. Eur Radiol 2018;28(7):2772−8.

[88] Velazquez ER, Parmar C, Liu Y, et al. Somatic mutations drive distinct imaging phenotypes in lung cancer. Cancer Res 2017;77(14):3922−30.

[89] Wang S, Shi J, Ye Z, et al. Predicting EGFR mutation status in lung adenocarcinoma on computed tomography image using deep learning. Eur Respir J 2019;53(3):1800986.

[90] Chen B, Liang T, Yang P, et al. Classifying lower grade glioma cases according to whole genome gene expression. Oncotarget 2016;7(45):74031−42.

[91] Bai HX, Lee AM, Yang L, et al. Imaging genomics in cancer research: limitations and promises. Br J Radiol 2016;89(1061):20151030.

[92] Li Y, Liu X, Xu K, et al. MRI features can predict EGFR expression in lower grade gliomas: a voxel-based radiomic analysis. Eur Radiol 2018;28(1):356−62.

[93] Parsons DW, Jones S, Zhang, et al. An integrated genomic analysis of human glioblastoma multiforme. Science 2008;321(5897):1807—12.

[94] Chang K, Bai HX, Zhou H, et al. Residual convolutional neural network for the determination of IDH status in low-and high-grade gliomas from MR imaging. Clin Cancer Res 2018;24(5):1073—81.

[95] Lu CF, Hsu FT, Hsieh KLC, et al. Machine learning—based radiomics for molecular subtyping of gliomas. Clin Cancer Res 2018;24(18):4429—36.

[96] Van de Velde CJ, Boelens, et al. EURECCA colorectal: multidisciplinary management: European consensus conference colon & rectum. Euro J Cancer 2014;50(1): 1—e1.

[97] Tabernero J, Lenz HJ, Siena S, et al. Analysis of circulating DNA and protein biomarkers to predict the clinical activity of re-gorafenib and assess prognosis in patients with metastatic colorectal cancer: a retrospective, exploratory analysis of the COR-RECT trial. Lancet Oncol 2015;16(8):937—48.

[98] Yang L, Dong D, Fang M, et al. Can CT-based radiomics signature predict KRAS/NRAS/BRAF mutations in colorectal cancer? Eur Radiol 2018;28(5):2058—67.

[99] Lovinfosse P, Koopmansch B, Lambert F, et al. 18F-FDG PET/CT imaging in rectal cancer: relationship with the RAS mutational status. Br J radiol 2016;89(1063): 20160212.

[100] Carey LA, Perou CM, Livasy, et al. Race, breast cancer subtypes, and survival in the Carolina Breast cancer study. J Am Med Assoc 2006;295(21):2492—502.

[101] Bagaria SP, Ray, et al. Personalizing breast cancer staging by the inclusion of ER, PR, and HER2. JAMA Surg 2014;149(2):125—9.

[102] Li H, Zhu Y, Burnside ES, et al. Quantitative MRI radiomics in the prediction of molecular classifications of breast cancer subtypes in the TCGA/TCIA data set. NPJ Breast Cancer 2016;2(1). 1-0.

[103] Meng L, Dong D, Li L, et al. A Deep Learning Prognosis Model Help Alert for COVID-19 Patients at High-Risk of Death: A Multi-center Study. IEEE J Biomed Health Inform 2020;24(12):3576—84.

[104] Li C, Dong D, Li L, et al. Classification of Severe and Critical COVID-19 Using Deep Learning and Radiomics. IEEE J Biomed Health Inform 2020;24(12):3585—94.

[105] Xie X, Zhong Z, Zhao W, et al. Chest CT for typical 2019-nCoV pneumonia: relationship to negative RT-PCR testing. Radiology 2020:200343.

[106] Dong D, Tang Z, Wang S, et al. The role of imaging in the detection and management of COVID-19: a review. IEEE Rev Biomed Eng 2020;14:16—29.

[107] Song J, Shi J, Dong D, et al. A new approach to predict progression-free survival in stage IV EGFR-mutant NSCLC patients with EGFR-TKI therapy. Clin Cancer Res 2018;24(15):3583—92.

[108] Wang S, Zha Y, Li W, et al. A fully automatic deep learning system for COVID-19 diagnostic and prognostic analysis. Eur Respir J 2020;56:2000775.

[109] Zhang S, Li H, Huang S, et al. High-resolution computed tomography features of 17 cases of coronavirus disease 2019 in Sichuan province, China. Eur Respir J 2020; 55(4).

[110] Fang M, He B, Li L, et al. CT radiomics can help screen the coronavirus disease 2019 (COVID-19): a preliminary study. Sci China Inf Sci 2020;63:172103.

[111] Wu X, Hui H, Niu M, et al. Deep learning-based multi-view fusion model for screening 2019 novel coronavirus pneumonia: a multicentre study. Eur J Radiol 2020:109041.

[112] Wang K, Lu X, Zhou H, et al. Deep learning Radiomics of shear wave elastography significantly improved diagnostic performance for assessing liver fibrosis in chronic hepatitis B: a prospective multicentre study. Gut 2019;68(4):729–41.

[113] Qi X, Berzigotti A, Cardenas A, et al. Emerging non-invasive approaches for diagnosis and monitoring of portal hypertension. Lancet Gastroenterol Hepatol 2018;3(10): 708–19.

[114] Qi X, An W, Liu F, et al. Virtual Hepatic Venous Pressure Gradient with CT Angiography (CHESS 1601): A Prospective Multicenter Study for the Noninvasive Diagnosis of Portal Hypertension. Radiology 2019;290(2):370–7.

[115] Berzigotti A. Non-invasive evaluation of portal hypertension using ultrasound elastography. J Hepatol 2017;67(2):399–411.

[116] Liu F, Ning Z, Liu Y, et al. Development and validation of a radiomics signature for clinically significant portal hypertension in cirrhosis (CHESS1701): a prospective multicenter study. Ebiomedicine 2018;36:151–8.

[117] Shaw LJ, Hausleiter J, Achenbach S, et al. Coronary computed tomographic angiography as a gatekeeper to invasive diagnostic and surgical procedures: results from the multicenter CONFIRM (Coronary CT Angiography Evaluation for Clinical Outcomes: an International Multicenter) registry. J Am Coll Cardiol 2012;60(20):2103–14.

[118] Hu W, Wu X, Dong D, et al. Novel radiomics features from CCTA images for the functional evaluation of significant ischaemic lesions based on the coronary fractional flow reserve score. Int J Cardiovasc Imaging 2020;36:2039–50. https://doi.org/10.1007/s10554-020-01896-4.

[119] Kolossváry M, Karády J, Szilveszter B, et al. Radiomic features are superior to conventional quantitative computed tomographic metrics to identify coronary plaques with napkin-ring sign. Circul: Cardiovas Imag 2017;10(12):e006843.

Treatment evaluation and prognosis prediction using radiomics in clinical practice

Chapter outline

Radiomics and its Clinical Application. https://doi.org/10.1016/B978-0-12-818101-0.00002-1

Treatment evaluation and prognosis prediction of cancers using radiological data currently depends on doctor's experience, and requires pathological or serological tests. However, radiological assessment would be affected by the subjective observation of the radiologists. While radiomics could preoperatively capture the histopathological alterations of the lesion via extracting high-throughput quantitative features. The capture of the radiological subtle changes would correlate with the postoperative prognosis and assist personalized medicine. Quantification of medical imaging using radiomics has the potential to realize treatment evaluation and prognosis prediction of cancers with improved accuracy.

4.1 Radiomics and its application in treatment evaluation

4.1.1 Evaluation of radiotherapy

The heterogeneity of tumors refers to the interpersonal difference with the same kind of malignancy, or different genetic phenotypes of tumor cells within one tumor lesion. The interpersonal difference heterogeneity may be caused by different genetic milieu, such as number and characteristics of a chromosome, histopathological type, clinical grading, differentiating, and cell evolution. Intrapersonal tumor may also present with different spectra of mutation and biological characteristics, which reflects the high complexity and variety in the process of malignancy tumor evolution. Because there are various subtypes of tumor cells in tumor tissue, the tumor presents with various immunological characteristics, growth rate, invasion of normal tissue, etc. Such interpersonal and intrapersonal tumor differences could be summarized as tumor heterogeneity. The heterogeneity of the tumor may cause its different sensitivities to radiotherapy. Radiomics could construct a radiological signature which correlates with tumor heterogeneity, thus realizing treatment evaluation of radiotherapy.

There are five main reasons for the difference of the radiotherapy curative effect in a clinical setting, which are as follows: (a) the account of stem cells in a tumor lesion, (b) the substantial radiotherapy sensitivity of stem cells, (c) hemorrhage, (d) reoxygenation in the tissue adjacent to the tumor, and (e) regeneration capacity of particles during radiotherapy. The substantial sensitivity of tumor cells correlates with the common origin of tumor cells or the histopathological type [1−3]. Currently, the quantification of radiosensitivity requires measurement of survival rate of the in vitro tumor and unmatched DNA double-strand breakage. Previous studies proved that radiosensitivity of the tumor is the independent key factor for survival prediction of radiotherapy [4−8]. But these studies have limitations of low planting efficiency of tumor cells, and the long time of preparing the in vitro tumor and measurement of DNA. Thus, using radiomics/radiogenomics to evaluate radiosensitivity is still unrevealed. Besides, dose limitation of nonbenign tissue is also an important factor for radiation therapy and curative effect. Radiological dose, co-occurrence probability ratio of tumor and nonbenign tissue, as well as economic factors, should be fully considered in the process of radiotherapy effect evaluation.

4.1.1.1 Application 1 of radiomics for radiotherapy effect evaluation: association of radiomic data extracted from static respiratory–gated CT scans with disease recurrence in lung cancer patients treated with SBRT

Personalized treatment nowadays requires a more comprehensive understanding of tumor heterogeneity. It aims to make appropriate treatment decision-making based on different cancer types as well as conditions of each patient to achieve an improved treatment effect and prognosis. However, lack of an effective method for treatment effect evaluation is the main barrier for the promotion of precision medicine [9].

The most commonly used cancer treatments include surgical resection, chemotherapy, and radiotherapy. For non−small cell lung cancer (NSCLC), resection remains the most effective treatment, but some patients have to accept stereotactic body radiation therapy (SBRT) as the standard treatment because of potential complications [10]. Unlike traditional radiotherapy, SBRT requires a higher radiation dose in a specific region, which significantly improves the overall postoperative survival. It presents a better effect for the control of a local lesion, which makes it an alternative to surgical resection. However, although SRBT exhibits a satisfactory effect, some patients will still have distal metastases (13%−23%) and local recurrence (4%−14%). Besides, patients at the early stage, especially the ones who have larger size tumors (grade IB-IIA), should accept neoadjuvant chemotherapy. Thus, SRBT is not a universal treatment regime. It is clinically important to select suitable patients to perform SRBT. Prediction of recurrence will assist treatment decision-making.

Radiomics, as a noninvasive method, could figure out the correlation between the imaging features and the clinical target [11−13]. It extracted radiomic features from the lesions to depict tumor phenotypes, which could be provided as a prognostic factor with strong reproducibility [14−16].

Computed tomography (CT) is widely used in radiotherapy planning, and is important for postoperative follow-up and prognosis evaluation. CT-based radiomics has great potential value for prognosis prediction of SBRT in NSCLC. Although CT was proven to be effective for lung cancer disease and treatment decision-making, using CT for SBRT effect evaluation is still unexplored [17]. CT value and textural features were predictive factors for prognosis of SBRT; however, this lacked reproducibility and stability [18−21]. Thus, Huynh et al. utilized CT-based radiomics to perform a preoperative effect evaluation of SBRT in NSCLC.

Huynh et al. enrolled 113 cases of NSCLS patients (grade I−II) who accepted SBRT treatment, and extracted 1605 CT radiomic imaging features, including shape and size, statistics, and textural features (MATLAB 2013). Discretization was conducted on original images to reduce noise, and normalization was performed on the region of interest (ROI) to ensure comparability among patients. Interpolation was performed on CT voxels to resize them to 1 mm^3. Traditional radiomic features extracted in this study included tumor size, maximum two-dimensional diameter and three-dimensional diameter. The clinical factors included age, sex, performance status, and grading, which were treated as predictors. Feature stability analysis was conducted using a reference image database to evaluate the therapy response dataset to calculate the interclass correlation coefficient (ICC). Features with ICC larger than 0.8 were reserved as qualified features. The number of features was reduced to 855 from 1605 after the stability analysis. Then, principal component analysis (PCA) was used to perform feature reduction. Twelve features were selected after PCA analysis.

Distal metastasis or local recurrence was utilized as the endpoint. Bilateral Wilcoxon rank sum test was conducted to reveal the correlation between the radiomic features and endpoints. Significant difference was defined with a P-value less than .1. Concordance index (C-index) was then used to assess the ability of the features for prognosis prediction. The result manifested that the selected features were effective for the treatment effect prediction of SBRT. Feature with a C-index larger than 0.5 manifested its efficiency for SBRT prognosis prediction. With a higher value of the feature, it was more likely to have distal metastasis or local recurrence. Otherwise, a lower value of the feature manifested in decreased possibility of distal metastasis or local recurrence. The C-indices of traditional radiological factors, radiomic features, as well as clinical factors are shown in Fig. 4.1.

The result showed that traditional radiological factors (tumor size and diameter) and radiomic features (LoG 3D run low gray-level short run emphasis, and stats median) all correlated with overall survival. Radiomic feature Wavelet LLH stats range was predictive of dismal metastasis.

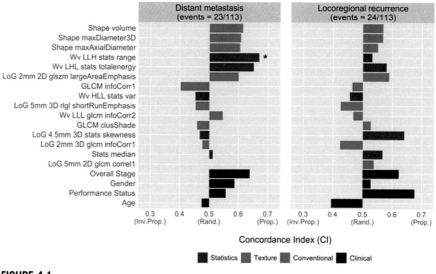

FIGURE 4.1

The ability of radiomic features for prediction of distal metastasis and local recurrence. Color red represents the statistical features. Color blue represents the textural features. Color black represents the clinical factors. *represents the *P*-value < .1.

4.1.1.2 Application 2 of radiomics for radiotherapy effect evaluation: comparison between radiological experts and radiomics for prediction of early recurrence in lung cancer following stereotactic ablative radiation therapy

For lung cancer patients at the early stage who cannot accept surgical resection, stereotactic ablative radiation therapy (SABR) is the recommended therapy by the guidelines [22,23]. The 3-year survival rate of SABR could compete for the 90% of surgical resection for local region control [24]. However, malignant lung injury would occur in some patients who accepted SABR, which was similar to recurrence. When resecting this part of the lesion, it showed that it was only fibrosarcoma. For these patients, resection is unnecessary, which would cause more pain for the patients. Thus, if preoperative prediction of local recurrence could be realized using CT, it would be of great clinical significance for treatment decision-making of salvage resection in patients with a high risk of recurrence.

The median local recurrence time of SABR was approximately 15 months. Some patients would have local recurrence in 5 years [25]. Qualitative CT radiological factors for prediction of local recurrence included an enlarged opaque region, a larger lesion after 1 year, an enlarged border, elimination of the linear border, etc [26–28]. However, these qualitative predictors present variability among observers and depended on the subjective assessment of doctors. Furthermore, some of the predictive factors required more than 1 year to acquire, thus this could not predict the recurrence in a timely manner.

Mattonen et al. assumed that radiomics could increase the accuracy of prediction on local recurrence via identifying subtle radiological changes on radiological images. Thus, Mattonen et al. collected 182 CT images from 45 cases who accepted SABR (15: local recurrence, 30: nonlocal recurrence). Radiological experts predicted the local recurrence of 45 enrolled cases using traditional qualitative radiological factors. At the same time, they extracted 22 histogram features and 22 gray level co-occurrence matrix (GLCM) features, and used a support vector machine (SVM) to construct the radiomics signature to predict local recurrence. The radiomics signature achieved area under the receiver operating characteristic curve (AUC) of 0.85, misclassification rate of 24%, false-positive rate of 24%, and false-negative rate of 23%, which were in accordance with assessment results of radiological experts. The radiomics signature could also identify an early nontypical recurrence lesion that was difficult to recognize by clinicians within 6 months after the resection.

4.1.1.3 Application 3 of radiomics for radiotherapy effect evaluation: texture analysis on parametric maps derived from dynamic contrast-enhanced magnetic resonance imaging in head and neck cancer

Dynamic contrast-enhanced magnetic resonance imaging (DCE-MRI) has become an important tool for assessment of tumor-related vasculature. A series of tumor biomarkers could be acquired via constructing a pharmacokinetic model on a T1-weighted image, such as volume transfer rate (K^{trans}) and volume fraction of extravascular extracellular space (V_e) [29,30]. For advanced head and neck squamous cell carcinoma (HNSCC) patients, DCE-MRI has great potential for therapy response assessment and prognosis prediction [31−33]. Specifically, indicators derived from DCE-MRI such as K^{trans} and V_e could provide additional important information for prognosis prediction with neck nodal metastases. Because of the complicated tumor vasculature, HNSCC presents with strong heterogeneity [34,35]. Tumor heterogeneity was correlated with tumor malignancy. For example, tumor heterogeneity of the blood supply may underlie treatment resistance as it prevents therapeutic efficacy. Thus, assessment of tumor heterogeneity would indirectly evaluate the malignancy of the tumor and perform prediction of the treatment effect. A great deal of published studies proved that mean, median, and standard variance of pixel values on the lesion could be used to describe the holistic characteristics of the tumor. However, these commonly used factors could not comprehensively depict the morphological characteristics of the tumor. Radiomics imaging biomarker provided a new solution to reflect tumor heterogeneity to assist assessment in the treatment of HNSCC.

Texture analysis is the main method to assess tumor heterogeneity. Unlike the abovementioned median and standard variance, radiomics could quantify the images via extracting textural features correlated with tumor heterogeneity. For example, GLCM is a commonly used algorithm for texture analysis. Texture analysis of the image presented excellent efficacy on tumor differentiation and treatment response prediction [36−38]. Karahaliou et al. verified the availability of texture analysis for assessment of tumor heterogeneity to classify benign and malignant tumors in breast cancer. El Naqa et al. utilized PET images to extract texture features, and performed treatment assessment in cervical cancer [39]. Alic et al. revealed that with a higher value of the radiomic textural features, patients were more likely to acquire better treatment responses with limb sarcoma [40]. However, the texture analysis of DCE-MRI pharmacokinetic maps has not been investigated in head and neck cancers for predicting treatment response yet.

Hence, Jasen et al. retrospectively collected 19 cases of HNSCC, all of whom accepted radio/chemotherapy. Patients underwent examination with MRI before and 10−14 days after the commencement of chemoradiotherapy. MRI was performed on a 1.5 T scanner. According to pharmacokinetic modeling, K^{trans} and V_e were calculated. On the image of K^{trans} and V_e, Jasen et al. conducted a texture analysis. Firstly, they used the Ostu algorithm to perform noise reduction. Then, GLCM was obtained to further calculate two main textural features: Energy and Homogeneity. The formulas for these two features are as follows:

$$\text{Energy}(E) = \sum_{i,j} p(i,j)^2 \tag{4.1}$$

$$\text{Homogeneity}(H) = \sum_{i,j} \frac{p(i,j)}{1 + |i - j|} \tag{4.2}$$

The result showed that there were no significant differences found for the common summarizing measures (mean and standard deviation) for K^{trans} and V_e ($P > .05$). However, textural feature energy extracted based on the image of V_e presented a significantly higher value in intratreatment scans than in pretreatment scans. It manifested that texture analysis based on parametric maps derived from DCE-MRI could provide a radiological indicator to depict tumor heterogeneity; meanwhile, chemoradiotherapy could significantly decrease tumor heterogeneity.

4.1.2 Evaluation of response to targeted therapy

Cancer cells share common characteristics with their normal hosts, which leads to the lack of unique molecular targets. Therefore, anticancer chemotherapeutic agents cannot achieve the high level of selective toxicity like bacterial or viral chemotherapeutic agents. The selectivity of most cancer chemotherapeutic drugs (including vincristine, doxorubicin, topotecan, cyclophosphamide, and paclitaxel) for cancer cells is low, which may lead to increased toxicity to normal tissues with strong proliferation rate, such as gastrointestinal tract, bone marrow, and hair follicles. Due to the side effects caused by toxicity to normal tissues, anticancer chemotherapy is usually administered at a suboptimal dose, which often leads to failure of the final treatment and greatly limits the use of cytotoxic chemotherapy [41]. However, targeted therapy can increase the exposure of cancer cells, improve the selectivity of treatment on cancer cells, and reduce the influence of treatment on normal cells by coupling therapeutic agents to kinds of antibodies within cancer cells or other ligands which could recognize tumor-related antigens [41]. Although targeted therapy has achieved amazing results, it is limited to a few patients. Therefore, biomarkers with a predictive value of treatment response are vital to introduce targeted therapy into clinical practice. Erlotinib and gefitinib are successfully introduced into clinical practice, which largely depends on finding predictive biomarkers (i.e., epidermal growth factor receptor (EGFR) mutation status). Other targeted drugs, such as cetuximab in the treatment of NSCLC, have not been used in clinics, to a large extent, because they lack the predictive biomarkers associated with the treatment response. Medical imaging can be used to evaluate the efficacy of targeted drugs so it can visualize and quantify individual disease progression invasively [42].

4.1.2.1 Application 1 of radiomics on the evaluation of the response to targeted therapy: evaluation of the treatment response of gefitinib in early nonsmall cell lung cancer with EGFR mutation

Tumor volume measured on medical images has always been one of the most traditional biomarkers for drug discovery and clinical routine. Two-dimensional measurement of RECIST criteria defined by the World Health Organization was used to measure the tumor burden to evaluate the drug treatment by using some substitutes such as single dimensional measurement. Previous study showed that the change in tumor burden during treatment has potential as biomarkers [43].

However, in addition to volume measurement, medical imaging could provide much more information to characterize cancer phenotypes. Intuitively, medical imaging is highly likely to be used for prediction of treatment response because it can visualize and quantify the process of disease progression of individual patients in a noninvasive way. There are more and more studies on the exploration of quantitative imaging characteristics that reflect tumor phenotypes and tumor biology. Recent studies have shown that radiomic signatures based on quantitative CT images can be used to predict prognosis and distant metastasis (DM) of lung cancer successfully [14,44]. In addition, studies have confirmed that the volume percentage of ground glass opacity in patients with missense mutations in exon 21 of EGFR is higher compared with those in tumors with other mutations significantly [45]. This might be caused by the fact that missense mutations in exon 21 are more common in squamous cell carcinoma. Although a large number of studies on the correlation among quantitative imaging features, tumor phenotypes, and mutation status are still under exploration, preliminary evidence suggests that these features may be associated with clinical outcomes and potential genomic signature of lung cancer.

In the clinical trial by Aerts and his colleagues, they explored the value of quantitative CT-based features to predict allergenic EGFR mutations associated with treatment response of gefitinib [42]. To investigate the association between radiomic signature and treatment response of gefitinib and EGFR mutation status, Aerts et al. extracted 183 imaging CT-based features from 47 NSCLC patients before and after treatment. The difference value between the imaging features before and after treatment was defined as Delta dataset. First, the top 15 features with the largest coefficient of variation are chosen. After removing the features with a high correlation (Spearman correlation coefficient >0.95), 11 independent imaging features were obtained. Finally, 13 features were obtained after including volume and maximum diameter features. Radiomics analysis was used to quantify these differences and the process is shown in Fig. 4.2.

Receiver operating characteristic (ROC) curve and area under the ROC curve (AUC) were used to assess the association between imaging features and EGFR mutation status. Fig. 4.3 shows the AUC values of pretreatment, posttreatment, and delta imaging features. Volume and maximum diameter features in delta dataset were identified as the strongest predictors, the AUC values of which were 0.91 and 0.78. In addition, Gabor_Energy_dir135_w3, an imaging feature, was significantly associated with EGFR mutation status with an AUC value of 0.74. These results demonstrated that radiomic features which quantified tumor phenotypes have predictive value for EGFR mutation.

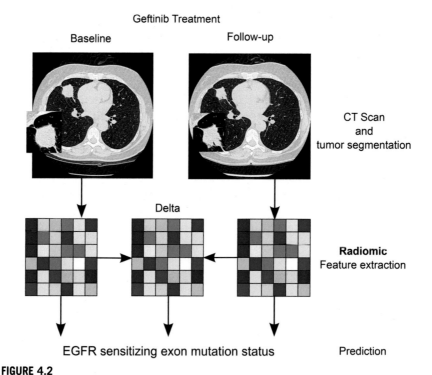

FIGURE 4.2

Study design. Patients with Gefitinib treatment were included. Tumor segmentation and radiomic feature extraction was conducted on baseline and the first follow-up CT scans. Features from baseline, follow-up CT scans, and the delta datasets were used to predict the EGFR mutation status.

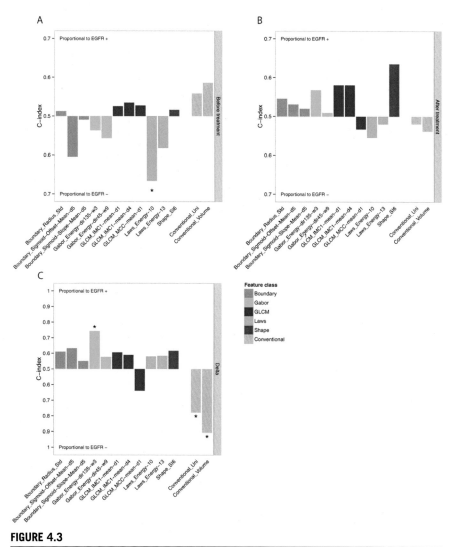

FIGURE 4.3

VPredict value of radiomic features extracted from (A) before treatment scan, (B) posttreatment scan, and (C) delta dataset for the prediction of EGFR mutation status.

This study suggested that radiomic features could quantify the treatment response of gefitinib and discriminate the EGFR mutation status using a noninvasive approach. The radiomics-based tool to predict the treatment response can be used to improve risk stratification between drug-sensitive and drug-resistant patients in NSCLC patients. Furthermore, since medical imaging is often used in clinical practice, it may provide an alternative opportunity to aid decision support making at a lower additional cost.

4.1.2.2 Application 2 of radiomics in the evaluation of the response to targeted therapy: CT-based radiomics analysis for the evaluation of treatment response of immunosuppressive therapy in lung cancer patients

In the United States, lung cancer has been the leading cause of cancer death over decades. Although overall survival has improved, the mortality of lung cancer has not significantly decreased, which might be caused by the early metastasis, late diagnosis, and resistance to conventional and targeted therapy. Therefore, human beings have tried to apply different treatment methods to treat lung cancer. Among these methods, immunotherapy has had a profound treatment response to many other cancers. In 2016, after the successful clinical trials of nivolumab and pembrolizumab, the United States approved immunotherapy as the first-line treatment for some NSCLC patients [46]. Unfortunately, responders to immunotherapy may lead to drug resistance for melanoma, even long-term ones.

As a kind of monoclonal antibody, immune checkpoint inhibitors could improve the immunotherapy response to cancer through the block of inhibitory signals. PD-1/PD-L1 pathway is a specific one that immune checkpoint inhibitors could target, which acts as a switch of immune activity and can enhance the immunotherapy response through the disruption of the interaction among T-cell surface proteins. Thus, the expression of PD-1 and PD-L1 in tumor infiltrating T cells (or T cells) was associated with the response to immune checkpoint inhibitors. Some clinical trials did not even consider the significant threshold value of PD-L1 expression [47].

Besides intratumoral heterogeneity, microenvironment factors might lead to the failure of treatment. Heterogeneous and inefficient vascular system could result in hypoxia and acidosis. Conversely, hypoxia and acidosis could block the activation of T cells and induce severe disability.

Radiomics attempts to automatically extract quantitative imaging features from medical images and analyze the association between these features with therapeutic response. These features have been regarded as covariates in machine learning models for the prediction of the outcome of individual patients, and have been used in many cases for the prediction of treatment response [48]. Statistical-based imaging models can infer the correlation between quantitative features and treatment response, but they cannot provide a mechanistic explanation for the success or failure of treatment. However, this began to transform as a recent work has linked the imaging signature to upregulation of the inflammatory gene set. This benefits from the mathematical modeling of biological knowledge, which enables us to explore the causal mechanism of the therapeutic response.

Daryoush Saeed-Vafa et al. extracted histogram, shape and size, and textural features from the CT images of 51 patients with metastatic lung adenocarcinoma. These patients were treated with a part of three different immune checkpoints [49]. Sparse partial least squares (PLS) discriminant analysis was used to analyze the association between the imaging features and the response to treatment. According to RECIST version 1.1, complete or partial response was defined as good response and stable or

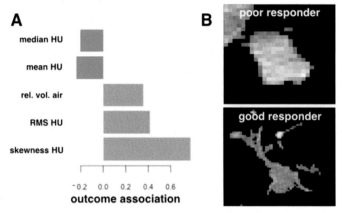

FIGURE 4.4

Radiomic analysis. (A) The top 5 variables with highest predictive value to predict treatment response. (B) Example of CT images for lung tumor.

progressive disease was defined as poor response. Fig. 4.4 shows the five most relevant imaging features of the treatment response. Among them, the skewness of the HU histogram (measuring the asymmetry of distribution) was found with the strongest association with treatment response and the following strongest associated features were root mean square of HU distribution, relative volume of air in the segmented tumor, and average and median value of HU distribution.

In addition, Daryoush Saeed-Vafa et al. found that the response of lung tumors to immunotherapy was negatively correlated with tumor convexity, and the response was positively correlated with the margin core size ratio. The image example in Fig. 4.4B shows that one is a typical tumor layer with poor response to immunotherapy, and the other is a typical tumor layer with good response.

Although previous studies have shown that higher convexity (roundness) in lung tumors is associated with better survival [48], this study found that invasive tumors with more concavity had better response to immunotherapy. The reason is unclear, but one possible explanation is that tumors that respond less to conventional therapy and are more aggressive, are more susceptible to immunotherapy. A recent study showed that patients with faster tumor growth before immunotherapy responded better to immunotherapy [50].

4.1.2.3 Application 3 of radiomics on the evaluation of the response to targeted therapy: PET/MRI-based radiomics analysis on the evaluation of treatment response to immune checkpoint inhibitor therapy in renal cell carcinoma

The key to defining individualized treatment decision and follow-up strategy is early identification of changes in tumor structure and function. Currently, the assessment of treatment response is conducted in the late phase of the treatment procedure.

This might lead to overtreatment for a variety of patients: (1) those who are resisted to treatment; and (2) those who occurred metastasis inhibition response.

Fluorothymidine positron emission tomography (FLT-PET) has been used to illustrate cell proliferation in clinical practice. Murakami et al. showed that uptake levels of FLT in xenotransplantation models of renal cell carcinoma began to decrease after 7 days of cell growth inhibition therapy [51]. Bao et al. applied sunitinib, a cell growth inhibitor, into the treatment of glioblastoma (GBM) xenograft models. A decrease in FLT uptake was also observed after only 7 days [52]. Therefore, FLT uptake might be a promising marker to visualize early therapeutic effects in the treatment of cell inhibitors.

MRI could provide high-contrast structural and functional information and is widely used in the examination before and after treatment. T2-weighted MR images could show the difference of water content in the internal structure of the lesions. Diffusion weighted imaging (DWI) images of MRI capture the cellular structure changes of tissues according to the difference of water molecule movement in different tissues. Obtained from DWI, apparent diffusion coefficient (ADC) maps have shown great potential as imaging biomarkers for the therapeutic response. Therefore, both T2WI and ADC maps can capture the in vivo changes in tumor angiogenesis (e.g., cell growth inhibition therapy) and tissue anatomy.

In addition, the combination of multimodal imaging has great potential in clinical applications. MRI provides anatomic localization and attenuation correction maps for quantification of PET data, which is due to simultaneous acquisition in the same reference frame, which can overlay the independent in vivo structural, functional, and metabolic characteristics of the tumor response.

Currently, radiomics analysis was applied in the assessment of the response to treatment in metastatic RCC patients (poor prognosis, 5-year survival rate was 12.3%) [53]. Tyrosine kinase inhibitor (TKI) has been introduced as cell inhibitors for advanced RCC and studies have shown that it can prolong the progression-free survival (PFS) of metastatic RCC patients [54]. Preclinical studies have shown that the early therapeutic response of sunitinib is a combination of antiangiogenesis and tumor proliferation inhibition, which means that FLT-PET and MRI could be used to visualize and capture the changes associated with targeted therapy.

Antunes et al. [55] performed radiomic analysis to identify independent or combined features of FLT-PET/MRI images related to voxel changes in metastatic RCC patients during targeted therapy. This study attempted to improve the characterization of the response to targeted therapy in a single imaging sequence by analyzing the features of ADC, T2WI, and FLT-PET images.

In their study, image preprocessing included alignment of the internal acquisition space, bias field correction of T2WI image, interacquisition coregistration, and T2WI intensity standardization. The alignment of internal acquisition space enabled the volume of T2WI, PET, and ADC images in each collection set to align in space, so as to solve the difference of image size and voxel size specific to the protocol; bias field correction of T2WI was conducted by using Gaussian low pass filter to convolute the image to avoid artifacts by the radio frequency nonuniformity or static field nonuniformity of the imaging instrument. Image registration is the spatial registration of images collected at different time points to avoid the impact of organ and patient movement when collecting images at different time points; T2WI intensity standardization generates a standardized map by calculating the intensity of the same healthy tissue region collected on T2WI images, and then applies it to the whole T2WI to avoid the difference of image intensity between different acquisitions in the same tissue region.

Based on PET and T2WI images, Antunes et al. extracted 66 imaging features. All these features were ranked according to the ratio of the Bhattacharyya distance between the RCC regional features before and after treatment and between the tested and retested normal regional features. The study found that SUV and ADC Haralick features ranked relatively high in these two patients, indicating low variability between test and retest. Most of the T2WI imaging features ranked relatively low, which suggested high variability between test and retest. Previous studies have shown that ADC texture features are more stable than T2WI features in feature reliability comparison [56]. In addition, it was found that there were uptake differences across the whole tumor region. However, the change area captured by SUV was homogeneous, which reflected that the significant changes due to treatment were captured by molecular imaging. It was also found that the regions of variation observed on the difference maps of the original ADC and T2WI images were visually more heterogeneous (significant difference in a small neighborhood of voxels), which meant that the changes of different modal images at the anatomical or structural level were captured at the voxel level. Different kinds of medical images might be able to acquire different information about early treatment responses, and fusion of different imaging modalities seems to capture the complementary information to characterize the response of TKI treatment comprehensively.

4.1.2.4 Application 4 of radiomics on the evaluation of response to targeted therapy: radiomics analysis on the prediction of progression-free survival in EGFR-mutation NSCLC with EGFR-TKI therapy

NSCLC is the main cause of cancer death, and its prevalence is increasing worldwide. In advanced NSCLC, EGFR mutation was usually occurred. Previous randomized trials found that EGFR TKIs could improve the prognosis in different subgroups of NSCLC compared with conventional chemotherapy [57]. The National Comprehensive Cancer Network (NCCN) recommended it as the first-line treatment; however, a variety of patients develop resistance to EGFR-TKI within 1 year after treatment. Recent studies have shown that TKI treatment could prolong the survival time. However, how to evaluate individual response to EGFR-TKI treatment is still very challenging. Early identification of rapid-progression patients in EGFR-TKI treatment plays an important role in treatment strategy making and clinical outcomes.

A common assumption to predict the benefits of TKI is that progression is influenced by the type of mutation and clinical characteristics (e.g., smoking status).

However, recent studies have shown noninvasive images provide a new method for risk stratification of EGFR TKI, so as to predict different treatment outcomes for individual patients. O'Connor et al. investigated quantitative imaging biomarkers through various strategies in targeted therapy, and revealed the effectiveness and necessity of these strategies to predict clinical outcomes early [58]. In the study of O'Connor et al. no multicenter validation was performed.

Song and his colleagues [59] proposed a method to assess the efficacy of the recommended EGFR-TKI treatment for individual patients. The whole experimental scheme was shown in Fig. 4.5, including patient registration, development of CT-based phenotype signature, signature verification based on two independent sets, and PFS comparison between patients receiving TKI treatment and patients receiving chemotherapy, establishment of individualized survival progress prediction model and multicenter validation.

They extracted 1032 CT-based features automatically for each patient. Twelve key CT features for prognosis prediction were selected and radiomic signature was developed in the training set using the least absolute shrinkage and selection operator (LASSO) (the left parts of Fig. 4.6A–C, represent the training set, validation set 1, and validation set 2, respectively). Results on these three sets showed that patients with slow progression were more than patients with rapid progression. The proportion of patients with rapid progression in each group was 36%, 35%, and 33%, respectively. Significant differences in PFS existed between rapid-progression and slow-progression subgroups in all sets (the middle parts of Fig. 4.6A–C, and P values $< .001$ for all sets). The AUC values of time-dependent ROC curve (the right parts of Figs. 4.6A, 4.9B and C) were 0.711–0.738 for 10 months and 0.701–0.822 for 1 year.

The Kaplan–Meier (K-M) survival curve (Fig. 4.7) showed that the PFSs of rapid-progression subgroup (median PFS: 5.6 months) and chemotherapy subgroup (median PFS: 4.5 months) were of no statistical significance. However, significant differences existed in PFS between these two subgroups and the slow-progression subgroup (median PFS: 10.7 months, $P < .0001$).

According to NCCN guidelines, disease progression is a common cause of discontinuation of EGFR-TKI treatment; however, how to assess the individualized patient progress is very challenging. Addressing this, Song et al. proposed a noninvasive approach. The prognosis strategy proposed in this study could achieve effective stratification in NSCLC patients treated with EGFR-TKI.

4.1.2.5 Application 5 of radiomics on the evaluation of response to targeted therapy: radiomics analysis on the prediction of treatment response to targeted therapy in patient with HER2 (ERBB2)-positive breast cancer

Human epidermal growth factor receptor 2 (HER2)-positive breast cancer is heterogeneous in morphology and genetics. No more than 35% of patients might respond to trastuzumab. The molecular profiling such as PAM50 could divide HER2 positive tumors into intrinsic molecular subtypes related to response and provided insight

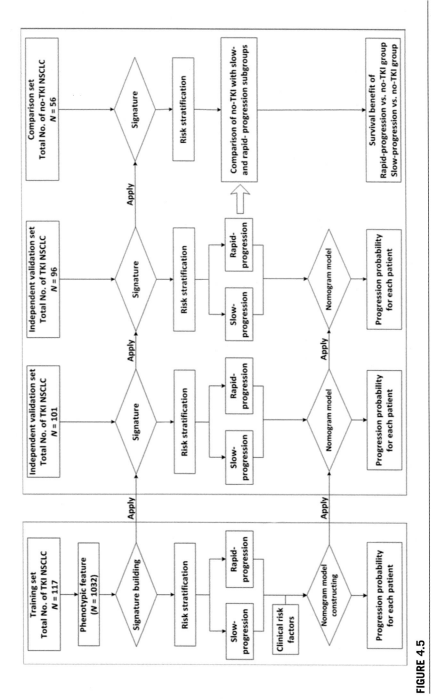

FIGURE 4.5

The flowchart of this study.

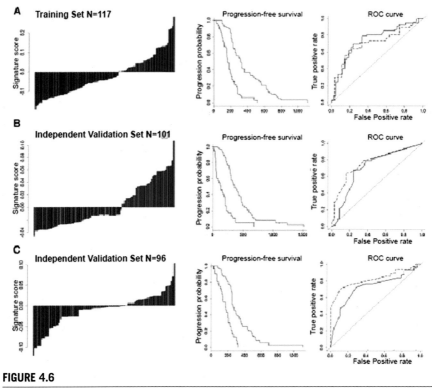

FIGURE 4.6

The distribution of signature score (left), Kaplan–Meier survival (middle), and ROC curves (right). (A) The training cohort. (B) Validation 1. (C) Validation 2.

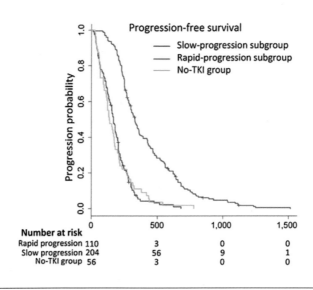

Number at risk			
Rapid progression	110	3	0	0
Slow progression	204	56	9	1
No-TKI group	56	3	0	0

FIGURE 4.7

Progression probability of different subgroups.

into treatment response [60]. HER2-enriched subtype accounted for 40%−50% of HER2-positive breast cancers. Because of their high rate of response to HER2 targeted therapy, they have special therapeutic value. Although breast cancer with positive HER2 gains biological significance, biomarkers are not available for the prediction of the efficacy of anti-HER2 therapy. Therefore, it is necessary to develop new methods to evaluate the clinical effect of HER2-targeted therapy.

In breast cancer, the imaging features extracted from MRI images can quantify tissue phenotype, and have been proved to be sensitive to many aspects of cancer biological factors. Although some recent studies [61] have explored a radiomics approach to evaluate the treatment response based on pretreatment and interim MRI, the method is usually not easy to understand and its relationship with tumor biological behaviors is not clear. Although a few studies involving breast radiogenomics have explored the relationship between image and biology, few works have put these findings in the context of therapeutic response results [61,62]. Therefore, the relationship between the radiogenomic signature and the response to targeted therapy is still unclear. Similarly, almost all radiogenomic methods focused on the correlation between molecular and genomic features and imaging features, without explicitly considering the correlation between radiomic features and histopathological features. The radiogenomics method uses the radiomic signatures with a known morphological basis and response-related molecular subtypes to evaluate treatment response, which can provide biological explanation and provide information for treatment decisions.

Braman N et al. [63] evaluated subtypes related to therapeutic response of HER2-positive breast cancer using imaging characteristics from regions of tumor and peritumoral microenvironment. In addition, they examined the possible association between radiogenomic signature of HER2-enriched breast cancer patients and targeted neoadjuvant chemotherapy for HER2 in two independent validation datasets. A total of 209 patients were enrolled in this study (average age: 51.1 years, standard deviation: 11.7 years).

Firstly, the gray value of the image was scaled in the standard intensity range from the maximum to minimum intensity values. Multiple radiologist experts provided labels on three adjacent slices of DCE-MRI scans. These labels were derived from five rings, each of which was 3 mm (excluding skin, air, or chest muscle). This process was consistent with previous studies on tumor microenvironment [62]. In this study, each annular region and all annular regions were analyzed by radiomic analysis. This study found that the average AUC was 0.76 (95% CI: 0.69−0.84) to distinguish the response-associated HER2-enriched subtypes and nonenriched HER2-positive tumors based on the radiomic signature of intratumoral features. In addition, the discrimination performance of peritumoral features was better than that of intratumoral features with AUC values in cross-validation of 0.85 (95% CI: 0.79−0.90). The radiomic signature that incorporating imaging features with both intratumoral and peritumoral region performed best with cross-validation AUC of 0.89 (95% CI: 0.84−0.93), which was significantly better than that constructed only by intratumoral features ($P = .04$). In two pathological response datasets (PRC1 and PRC2), this study found that HER2-enriched radiomic signature is of acceptable performance for prediction of pathologic complete response. In the PRC1 dataset, the classifier combined with peritumoral and intratumoral features was significantly correlated with treatment response (AUC = 0.80; $P = .003$). The ability of the classifier to predict treatment response was further validated in PRC2 dataset, and the AUC of distinguishing pathological complete response from nonpathological complete response was 0.69 (95% CI: 0.53−0.84).

In this study, a radiogenomic signature was identified from intratumoral region and tumor microenvironment. This signature could characterize HER2-enriched molecular subtypes related to treatment response, and could be used to evaluate the efficacy of neoadjuvant chemotherapy against HER2.

4.1.3 Application of radiogenomics in efficacy evaluation

With the development of medical imaging technology and the advancement of precision medicine, radiogenomics play an important role in precision oncology. The key difficulty of precise treatment of a tumor is heterogeneity. Tumor cells can be all kinds of cells with different microenvironments, which include not only the difference of tumor external morphology but also the difference of tumor internal tissue structure. This means that the difference or heterogeneity of the tumor should be fully considered in the process of diagnosis and treatment. Otherwise, it may lead to wrong treatment. In a broad sense, precision medicine uses modern genetic technology, molecular imaging technology, and biological information technology, combined with the living environment and clinical characteristics of patients, to diagnose and classify the disease accurately. Its major goals are to develop personalized disease prevention and treatment programs, including accurate risk prediction, disease diagnosis, disease classification, drug application, efficacy evaluation, etc. If early risk assessment and testing can be carried out, interventions or preventive treatment can be implemented. It not only avoids the occurrence of diseases but also greatly reduces the medical cost, which is also the key content of precision medicine to help improve the survival rate and reduce the medical cost.

Two kinds of information, genomics and imaging, can be used for precise treatment. The advantage of genomic information lies in its big individual differences, but the cost is high and it has limitations in the changes of inter/intratumor. Though images have good repeatability, its specificity is poor, which is complementary to genomics. Therefore, genomics and images can be potentially combined. Radiogenomics relates to the imaging features of diseases to gene phenotypes, gene mutations, and gene characteristics (including individual gene expression and the detection of special gene subtype expression).

Radiogenomics is associated with two closely related but different scientific issues: one is the relationship between genotype variations and clinical variability observed in response to radiotherapy; and the other is the relationship between specific imaging patterns and specific gene expression patterns that reveal the underlying pathophysiology of cells. In radiobiology, a general assumption is that a certain proportion of differences in the phenotypes of interest can be attributed to genotype variation. In clinical, this hypothesis is concretized that it may have serious treatment-related toxicity risk for some patients, but it has potential efficacy for most patients. We hypothesize that the overall goal of radiogenomics is to isolate alleles and potential radiomic features associated with genetic differences in phenotypes. Gene expression in various human tissues enriches our understanding of cellular pathways and numerous pathological conditions. The investigation of different cancer tissues related to healthy tissue samples has clarified the process of tumorigenesis and helped to enhance staging and subclassification of various malignant tumors. Each gene expression feature contains ten to hundreds of genes, which can significantly improve the diagnosis, prognosis, and prediction of treatment response [64,65]. Radiogenomics studies the relationship between the radiomic features and gene expression patterns of cancer patients [15,66]. A study used public gene expression data and survival data of patients with NSCLC enabling the identification of prognostic imaging biomarkers [67]. This strategy for identifying imaging biomarkers may be able to evaluate new imaging patterns more quickly, thereby facilitating the process of personalized therapies. Another study used a neural network to compare clinician-defined features extracted from contrast-enhanced CT (CECT) images of patients with hepatocellular carcinoma (HCC) and gene expression patterns [68]. A total of 78% gene expression profiles related to cell proliferation, liver synthesis, and prognosis can be reconstructed by the combination of the 28 reported features. In another study, features extracted from MR images were used to predict the global gene expression pattern of patients with GBM, revealing that a permeable phenotype was associated with a significant reduction in survival [66]. However, gene expression analysis relies on sampled tissue specimens from surgery, with multiple risks and potential complications, so it is not feasible for many patients with cancer. In contrast to genetic profiling studies, radiomic features capture the heterogeneity of the tumor in a noninvasive three-dimensional way, which has the potential to be used in routine clinical care [15,66].

Radiogenomic features provide valuable biomarkers for a clinical decision-making system [69], including prognostic and predictive factors [70], such as response to treatment and tolerance of nonmalignant tissues. Although there are many advantages, radiogenomics biomarkers are easily affected by experiments and the inconsistency of images. Therefore, standardization of image acquisition, segmentation, study design, and analysis methods are essential for tumor diagnosis, prognosis, and prediction in oncology [71].

4.1.3.1 Application 1 of radiogenomics in efficacy evaluation: non–small cell lung cancer radiogenomics map identifies relationships between molecular and imaging phenotypes with prognostic implications

NSCLC is one of the most common types of lung cancer. It is composed of tumors with obvious molecular heterogeneity, which is caused by the difference of intrinsic oncogenic signaling pathways [72]. Molecular characteristics of NSCLC form the basis of clinical diagnosis and treatment [73]. Recently, the molecular properties of NSCLC are characterized by quantitative image features [74]. The development of RNA sequencing technology has brought new opportunities to characterize the molecular pathway of NSCLC [75]. Therefore, the emergence of radiogenomics can identify noninvasive biomarkers, which reflects the cellular and molecular characteristics of NSCLC. This noninvasive image biomarker can be used as an alternative to molecularly defined features and enable noninvasive precision medicine.

RNA sequence of patients with NSCLC has specific gene expression characteristics. To evaluate the relationship between the recognition gene expression profiles and the prognostic imaging phenotype, Mu Zhou et al. constructed the radiogenomics map to connect the CT imaging phenotype and gene expression characteristics based on 113 NSCLC patients. The study included patients with NSCLC undergoing surgery from two medical centers. All patients underwent chest CT before surgery and had tumor samples that were cryopreserved at $-80°C$ after surgery for RNA sequencing. An open-source platform—ePAD—for quantitative image annotation was used to develop a lung annotation template for selecting semantic image features, and 87 semantic image features were extracted. These features reflects the nodule shape, boundary, texture, and overall lung characteristics. The features with low frequency were deleted, and 35 semantic features with a frequency of more than 10% were retained for analysis. The RNA components in tumor tissues were isolated and sequenced. A total of 60,498 genes were identified, and RNA transcription information was obtained. There were at least five explanations for these transcriptions in 70% of the samples. The highly expressed genes were studied and consistent gene clusters were established. In this study, the top 10 gene clusters with the highest homogeneity score were selected. Functional enrichment analysis was used to annotate these 10 gene clusters, which were named as transposable genes [76]. A tool—PRECOG (https://precog.stanford.edu/ [77])—was used to link the genes with prognosis, so as to evaluate the relationship between these 10 gene clusters and survival in adenocarcinoma and squamous cell carcinoma. In addition, univariate Cox proportional risk regression was used to evaluate the relationship between gene clusters and overall survival. The z score was calculated to evaluate the correlation of each metagene with overall survival (positive value indicated poor prognosis, negative value indicated good prognosis). Then, a global meta-z score was obtained by using the Stouffer method (a z score greater than 2 and less than 2 was statistically significant). Then, t-test (P value is less than .05) and Spearman correlation analysis with multiple tests obtained 32 semantic features that were significantly related to gene clusters, and an image genomics map was established to link the semantic features and transposed genes. For example, the relationship between gene cluster 19 and imaging features is a typical example in radiogenomic maps. In addition, fuzzy nodule density and boundary are related to late cell cycle genes, and transposition genes related to EGF pathway are related to ground glass shadow, irregular nodule, and nodule with fuzzy boundary. This study showed that radiogenomics can characterize the molecular pathways of NSCLC, so as to analyze the molecular characteristics of NSCLC noninvasively.

Compared with previous studies, this study had several advantages [73−78]. Firstly, 87 semantic features defined by the controlled vocabulary were extracted from each patient to reflect the radiologic characteristics of pulmonary nodules (such as location of nodal, tumor shape and texture, and the features generated from the macroscopic environment of the lesion such as emphysema and fibrosis). Secondly, RNA sequences were used to characterize the transcription profile of each tumor. This study summarized these data by using gene clusters as a group of coexpressed genes and gene-enrichment analysis was used to annotate these gene clusters with different molecular pathways. In addition, it shows the prognostic association of each gene cluster in two important NSCLC histological structures (adenocarcinoma and squamous cell carcinoma) by measuring the prognostic significance of molecules in an overall survival study from public data. In this study, the image genomics map was constructed, which can link the CT imaging features with specific gene expression features in RNA sequences of patients with NSCLC.

4.1.3.2 Application 2 of radiogenomics in efficacy evaluation: magnetic resonance perfusion image features uncover an angiogenic subgroup of glioblastoma patients with poor survival and better response to antiangiogenic treatment

MRI has become an indispensable detection method in the field of neuroimaging. As the main detection method of GBM, MRI can monitor the visual features of GBM, quantify these features, and provide anatomical information from time and space dimensions. Meanwhile, with the development of gene tagging, a deeper understanding of complex molecular events of GBM has been constructed. For example, a previous study showed a strong correlation between methylation of the MGMT gene promoter and temozolomide, indicating that the MGMT gene can be used as an independent factor for the evaluation of the prognosis of GBM patients [79].

Liu et al. used preoperative perfusion weighted imaging (PWI) MRI features to identify GBM patients who had different tumor image characteristics and molecular activities, which could benefit from antiangiogenic therapy. A total of 117 patients undergoing PWI MRI before surgery were collected from The Cancer Genome Atlas (TCGA, $n = 48$) and Stanford University Medical Center (SUMC, $n = 69$), including gene expression subtype information, clinical chemotherapy information, and overall survival.

In this study, the heterogeneity of the whole tumor was quantitatively considered. A total of 46 quantitative nonparametric features were extracted from each GBM tumor's contrast-enhanced area of PWI, including 6 statistical features describing tumor volume, 40 histogram features quantitating regional differences and describing the internal heterogeneity of a PWI voxel value.

The PWI features are normalized, and the GBM classification based on PWI features is clustered unsupervised in each dataset. Two clustering results are obtained in TCGA and SUMC datasets. Normalized PWI features and clustered GBM are based on PWI features in each set through the unsupervised clustering method. Two clustering results were obtained both in TCGA and SUMC sets. In order to verify the reproducibility of clustering, a random forest model was constructed using the TCGA set to predict the results of SUMC, and the results were compared with the above results of unsupervised clustering. Similarly, SUMC set was also used to build a model to predict the clustering of TCGA and compare this with the above results. The K-M survival analysis was carried out based on different variables (age > 60 years, gender, number of lesions, gene expression types, and cluster group of PWI features) with a log-rank test. Furthermore, the Cox survival regression model was constructed to evaluate the association between the cluster of PWI features and overall survival. The results showed that the survival rate of cluster II was lower than that of cluster I both in TCGA and SUMC, and this difference was also significant in other variables, which suggested that the PWI features could be used to describe inter/intratumoral heterogeneity and assist in identifying clinically relevant subcategories. In addition, to verify PWI features that can be used as biomarkers of the antiangiogenic therapy response, K-M survival analysis was used to evaluate the prognostic value of clustering. Antiangiogenic therapy did not improve overall survival when combining all patients together, which was consistent with a previous study [78]. However, the survival of patients receiving antiangiogenic therapy was significantly longer than that of patients without antiangiogenic therapy in cluster II ($P = .022$, log-rank test). Finally, enrichment analysis was used to identify the difference in molecular activity among clusters of PWI features. A total of 13 gene sets, including angiogenesis signal pathway, vascular system development, and tissue hypoxia, were significantly related to cluster II. The shared genes lead to the core enrichment of the angiogenesis signal pathway and hypoxia signal composed of ANG and VEGF-A, and transformation of growth factor beta 2 (TGFB2, was also known as malignant glioma−derived T-cell inhibitor). The negative transcriptional regulation of the angiogenesis pathway in cluster II suggested the efficacy of antiangiogenic therapy.

The results showed that quantitative features based on PWI can be used to identify and predict GBM in future clinical trials. The patients with angiogenic subtypes may benefit from antiangiogenic therapy.

4.1.3.3 Application 3 of radiogenomics in efficacy evaluation: relationships between computer-extracted mammographic texture pattern features and BRCA1/2 mutation status: a cross-sectional study

Epidemiology shows that the increased intensity of mammography is an independent risk factor for sporadic breast cancer [80]. Although breast mammographic density has a strong heritable component, it is still debated whether breast mammographic density is related to the risk of hereditary breast cancer. More than half of hereditary breast cancer cases are associated with BRCA1 and BRCA2 mutations [81]. Nearly 50% are likely to develop breast cancer at the age of 50 years among women with BRCA1/2 mutations [81]. It is of great clinical significance for breast cancer screening and prevention to identify high-risk patients by analyzing mammographic images.

By extracting quantitative texture features from mammographic images, Gierach et al. evaluated the relationship between these texture features and BRCA1/2 gene mutations in breast cancer patients, and the machine learning method was used to screen BRCA1/2 gene mutations. About 137 BRCA1/2 mutation patients (carriers) and 100 nonmutation patients (noncarriers) were included from the NIH Clinical Center with Strict inclusion criteria (Fig. 4.8). The 137 carriers were divided into 5 groups according to their age, and 6 people (30 people in total) were randomly selected from each group to comprise the test set; 30 noncarriers were selected in the same way to be put into the test set, forming the final test set together with 30 carriers; and the remaining 177 participants (107 carriers and 70 noncarriers) formed the final training set. The results showed that there was no difference in the age distribution of noncarriers between the training set and the test set ($P = .44$), and the age distribution of carriers between two sets was also similar ($P = .95$).

All mammographic images were digitized with a pixel size of 0.095 mm (267 dots per inch) and 8-bit quantization in grayscale. The interactive computer threshold method developed by the NIH Clinical Center was used to standardize and quantify the percent mammographic density (PMD) by an experienced breast specialist. The intraobserver consistency coefficient was 0.89 by measuring 100 participants again. Selection of 256 * 256 pixels in the central breast area behind the nipple were manually selected as the ROI by the same researcher (Fig. 4.9). In this study, 9 gray intensity features and 29 texture features were extracted from the ROI, and 91 participants were randomly selected for the redelineation of the ROI to evaluate the intraobserver consistency of features (0.79−0.99). The best features were selected step by step according to Wilks' lambda feature selection criteria with leave one method in the training set (Fig. 4.10). Finally, three gray intensity features, M1: AVE, M2: MinCDF, and M3: Balance, and two texture features, T1: Energy and T2: MAXF (COOC), were retained to construct the classification model. Bayes artificial neural network (BANN) algorithm was used to distinguish BRCA1/2 mutation carriers and noncarriers based on selected quantitative features, and ROC curve with AUC was used to evaluate the identification ability of the BANN classifier. The BANN classifier (AUC was 0.68) showed better performance than that of PMD alone (AUC was 0.59), but there was no significant statistical difference ($P = .52$). To evaluate the influence of mammographic density, a classifier was constructed by combining PMD with the selected quantitative texture features, and the final AUC was 0.72. Spearman correlation coefficient was used to evaluate the correlation between selected quantitative texture features and PMD, age, etc. The carriers showed a lower value of the gray intensity feature and more inconsistent texture features. For three selected features, gray intensity feature M1 was positively correlated with PMD ($P < .001$), while M2 and M3 were weakly negatively correlated with PMD ($P = .04$). Texture features T1 and T2 were negatively correlated with PMD, and positively correlated with age. All selected gray features had a strong correlation, while only M2 had a strong positive correlation with the two texture

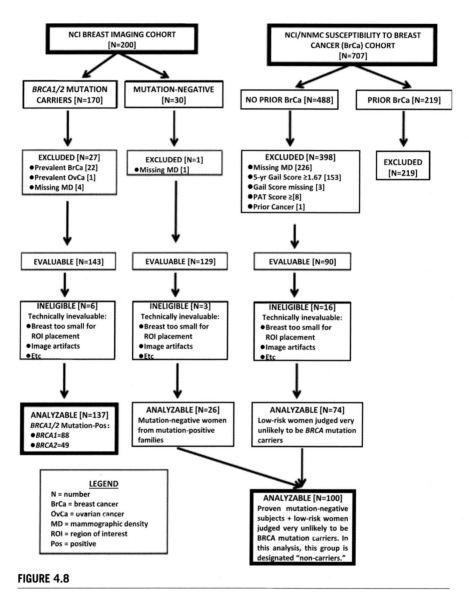

FIGURE 4.8

Inclusion criteria [82].

features, and the two texture features had a strong positive correlation ($P < .001$). Since the average age of carriers is about 10 years younger than that of noncarriers, the study also conducted an age matching sensitivity analysis on the test set. First, the BRCA1/2 mutation carriers and noncarriers were matched according to age (age difference ± 3 years), and Wilcoxon rank sum test was used to verify the mean pairing difference of the Bann probability score between carriers and

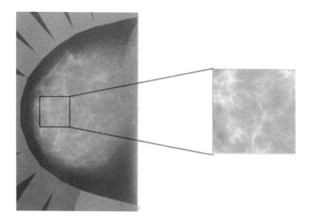

FIGURE 4.9

Selection of ROI [82].

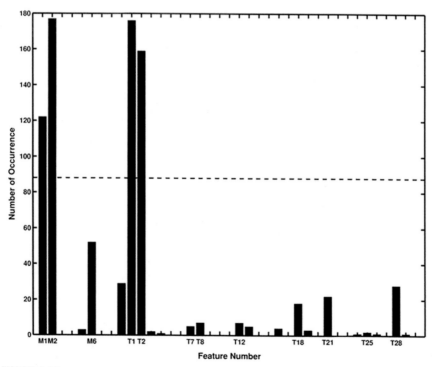

FIGURE 4.10

Times that each feature was selected in the step-by-step feature selection method [82].

noncarriers in the age matching set. In addition, the prediction probability of the BANN classifier was also analyzed by a similar pairing difference according to the selected features and PMD. The mean pairing difference of the prediction probability of the classifier constructed by the selected features and the classifier constructed only by PMD was statistically significantly greater than zero ($P = .02$). Finally, participants older than 55 years were deleted and the remaining participants were analyzed. In this set, the value of T1 was lower in carriers, that is, the image was more nonuniform and thick (Fig. 4.11). The mean pairing difference of the probability scores of the BANN classifier based on the quantitative features was of critical statistical significance ($P = .055$). However, the performance of identifying BRCA1/2 mutation carriers and noncarriers was not significantly changed when PMD was added into the BANN classifier ($P = .06$).

This study showed that the quantitative features were related to BRCA1/2 mutation. The classifier based on quantitative features had the potential to improve the interpretation of breast images through real-time risk stratification of women who were allowed to be screened.

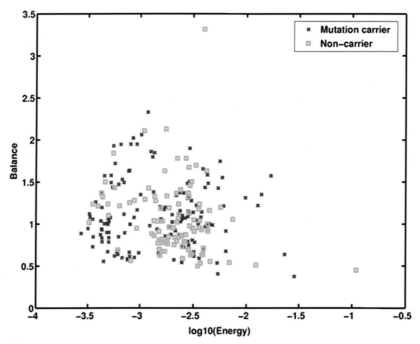

FIGURE 4.11

Scatterplot of the computer-extracted parenchymal features of T1: energy and M3: balance for BRCA1/2 mutation carriers and noncarriers [82].

4.1.3.4 Application 4 of radiogenomics in efficacy evaluation: a radiogenomics signature for predicting the clinical outcome of bladder urothelial carcinoma

Bladder cancer is the most common malignant tumor of the urinary system in the world [83]. As the most common subtype of bladder cancer, bladder urothelial carcinoma (BLCA) accounts for more than 90% of all bladder cancers [84,85]. BLCA is complex and difficult to treat disease with high mortality and high incidence rate if the optimal treatment is not carried out. Therefore, detailed long-term monitoring is needed [86]. Unfortunately, although BLCA is common, monitoring management often goes wrong. The traditional clinical staging system cannot accurately predict the prognosis of or guide the treatment plan for BLCA [87]. Therefore, identification of specific noninvasive biomarkers is helpful in monitoring prognosis, and developing appropriate clinical management for each patient is an urgent clinical need.

Lin P et al. constructed a nomogram to predict the prognosis of BLCA patients using CECT images, genomic characteristics, and clinical parameters. A total of 62 BLCA patients (with median age of 67.5 years) were included from the TCGA database, and CECT images and RNA sequence data were also collected [88]. The tumor with the largest diameter was selected as the ROI and was manually sketched by a radiologist with 10 years of experience. Texture features were extracted by Ultrosomics software (GE Healthcare). Finally, 1076 texture features were extracted from the ROI of each patient, including GLCM, wavelet transform, local binary pattern, and co-occurrence of local anisotropic gradient direction. Progression-free interval (PFI) was the endpoint. The median follow-up was 484.5 days, and the median of the event was 649 days. According to the univariable Cox proportional risk regression analysis, 28 texture features were significantly correlated with PFI of BLCA patients ($P < .05$) and were retained for further analysis; 1014 gene features were significantly correlated with PFI of BLCA patients ($P < .05$), and the features with $P < .001$ were retained for further analysis. Optimal features were selected through LASSO-Cox regression with 10-fold cross validation to construct the radiomics prognostic signature and transcriptomics prognostic signature. Finally, 7 texture features were reserved to construct the radiomics signature, including CoLIAGe2D_WindowSize9_firstorder_Minimum, wavelet-HHH_lbp-3D-k_firstorder_Median, wavelet-HHL_lbp-3D-m1_firstorder_Kurtosis, wavelet-HLH_lbp-3D-k_firstorder_Maximum, wavelet-HLH_lbp-3D-m1_firstorder_Median, wavelet-LHH_lbp-3D-k_firstorder_Kurtosis, and wavelet-LLH_lbp-3D-m1_firstorder_InterquartileRange; 10 genes were reserved to construct the radiomics signature, including ARHGDIB, DENND2D, DRAM1, GBP2, HSH2D, ICAM2, KRT8, LUZP6, NDUFAF3, and RPL41. Patients were divided into a high-/low-risk group based on the median values of radiomics and transcriptomics signature. K-M survival analysis with a log-rank test was used to show the survival status of high-risk and low-risk patients. K-M analysis showed that BLCA patients with high risk (higher radiomics signature) had shorter PFI than patients with low risk (lower radiomics signature), and the same result was obtained for the transcriptomics signature. ROC curve and AUC were used to evaluate the prediction performance of the selected features, and C-index was calculated to evaluate the performance of the survival prediction model [89,90]. The AUC of the radiomics model was 0.956, and sensitivity and specificity were 0.928 and 0.896, respectively; AUC of the transcriptomics model was 0.948, and sensitivity and specificity were 1 and 0.676, respectively. The C-indices of the two models were 0.791 and 0.799, respectively. The result indicated that these two risk scores had good predictive performance for prognosis of BLCA patients. In order to provide a simple and easy-to-use clinical application tool to predict the clinical results, the nomogram integrating radiomics signature, transcriptomics signature, and clinical parameters was constructed. In order to evaluate the potential molecular significance of the radiomics signature, the weighted correlation network analysis (WGCNA) was used to assess the relationship between radiomics signature and molecular function [91]. According to variance analysis, the top 50% genes in variability were used for WGCNA. The features that had the highest correlation with the radiomics signature were used in the enrichment analysis. The results showed that these genes were significantly enriched in the PI3K-AKT signaling pathway.

This study evaluated the clinical application of radiomics and transcriptomics. Radiomics signature could accurately stratify the risk of patients in some cases. The performance could be improved by integrating radiomics signature, transcriptomics signature, and clinical parameters. In addition, the results emphasized the need for understanding the radiomics signature, which was essential for cancer research and treatment.

4.2 Radiomics-based prognosis analysis

The prognosis is used for predicting the development of the disease and could help oncologists to evaluate treatment options and decide suitable treatments. It refers to the possible outcomes of a disease, such as death, recurrence, and chance of recovery. A better prognosis is usually related to a larger probability of treatment success.

Usually, some survival statistics are used to estimate a patient's prognosis. The most commonly used is overall survival (i.e., OS), the duration of the patient being alive from the time of diagnosis or the start of the treatment. The corresponding overall survival rate is the percentage of patients who will be alive at a certain time after diagnosis or treatment initiation. Measuring the overall survival is one way to see how well a new treatment works in a clinical trial.

Besides, disease-free survival (DFS) and PFS are more specific and are often used to evaluate the prognosis of cancer treatments. The DFS, also called relapse-free survival (i.e., RFS), is defined as the interval between date of remission and date of recurrence, and the corresponding DFS rate is the percentage of patients in complete remission after finishing treatment. There are different types of recurrence, including local recurrence, regional recurrence, and distant recurrence (also called metastasis), which mean the cancer is in the same place as the original cancer or very close to it. The tumor has then grown into lymph nodes or tissues near the original cancer, and the cancer has spread to organs or tissues far from the original cancer, respectively. PFS represents the duration that a patient lives with the disease but it does not get worse since the start of the treatment, while the PFS rate means the percentage of patients who did not have new tumor growth or cancer spread during this time. Compared to DFS, PFS is used under the condition that cancer is still there but not growing or spreading.

Therefore, the evaluation of the prognosis usually includes the estimation of recurrence, metastasis, DFS, PFS, and OS. The prediction of recurrence/metastasis is one of the main aims of current studies, which is usually evaluated with area under the receiver operating characteristic curve (AUC), accuracy, specificity, and sensitivity, and further related to survival prediction. The other main direction of current studies is the DFS/PFS and OS prediction directly, which are usually evaluated by the C-index.

Before, the commonly used prognostic factors included demographic factors (i.e., age, sex), behavioral factors (e.g., alcohol consumption, smoking history), tumor stage, histology, and molecular biomarkers (i.e., EGFR, ALK, ROS1, HER2). With the rapid development of radiomics, radiomics-based prognostic factors play more and more important role in prognosis evaluation. Currently, cancer is usually divided into two main types: solid tumor cancers and cancers in the blood. The most commonly investigated solid tumor cancers include lung (details are shown in Tables 4.1 and 4.2), breast(details are shown in Table 4.3), prostate (details are shown in Table 4.4), colorectal (details are shown in Table 4.5), esophageal cancer and gastric cancer (details are shown in Table 4.6), liver cancer (details are shown in Table 4.7), pancreatic cancer (details are shown in Table 4.8), cervical cancer (details are shown in Table 4.9), and central nervous system (CNS) cancers (details are shown in Table 4.10). Other solid tumor cancers were also studied (details are shown in Table 4.11). Cancers that are not considered solid cancers are often lumped together in the category of blood cancers: lymphoma, leukemia, and myeloma (details are shown in Table 4.12). Due to different treatment and diagnosis methods of different types of cancer, the radiomics-based prognostic analysis was usually performed on a certain type of cancer treated with a certain treatment. Given the large amount of literature, only the representative studies, such as different methods, different features, different modalities, and different metrics, are listed.

4.2.1 **Lung cancer**

Worldwide, the leading cause of cancer-related death is lung cancer [218], with NSCLC as the most commonly diagnosed histologic subtype [219]. During the past 30 years, the 5-year survival rate of patients with metastatic disease has remained at 5% [220]. Additionally, due to its contrast in medical images, the number of radiomics studies on lung cancer is significantly higher than other sites. According to NCCN Guideline Version 2.2020 for treatment of NSCLC [221], treatments for lung cancer include surgery, radiation therapy, chemotherapy,

Table 4.1 Description of studies using different features in the radiomics analysis to relate to recurrence/metastasis in lung cancer.

Author, year	Modality	Study population	Clinical outcome	C-index/AUC, P value, HR Test/validation	N	External validation	Treatment
Coroller et al. [92]	CT	Stage II–III NSCLC	Distant metastasis (DM)	C-index = 0.60	98 + 64	No	ChemoRT
Timmeren et al. [93]	CT	Stage I–IV NSCLC	Locoregional recurrence (LRR), OS	Average C-index of 0.63 for OS	141 + 94 + 61 + 41	Yes	(Chemo)-radiotherapy
Huynh et al. [94]	CT	Stage I–II NSCLC	DM	C-index = 0.67	113	No	Stereotactic body radiation therapy (SBRT)
Huynh et al. [95]	CT	Stage IA–IIA NSCLC	DM	Median C-index = 0.667	112	No	Stereotactic ablative radiotherapy (SABR)
Lafata et al. [96]	CT	Stage I NSCLC	Recurrence, local recurrence (LR), and nonlocal recurrence	AUC = 0.72, 0.83, and 0.60 for the recurrence, local recurrence, and nonlocal recurrence	70	No	SBRT
Mattonen et al. [97]	CT	Stage I–IIA NSCLC	Early prediction of recurrence within <6 months	AUC = 0.85, classification error of 24%, FPR of 24%, and FNR of 23%	45	No	SABR
Dou et al. [92]	CT	Stage II–III NSCLC	DM	C-index = 0.65 (P-value $< 7.57 \times 10^{-6}$)	200	No	Radiation
Khorrami et al. [98]	CT	Stage IA–IIA NSCLC	Recurrence	AUC = 0.74–0.76 HR = 1.66–1.74	350 + 80 + 195	Yes	Surgery

Study	Modality	Stage	Outcome	Results	N	Independent validation	Treatment
D'Antonoli et al. [99]	CT	Stage IA–IIB NSCLC	LR, DM, and total recurrence (TR)	$AUC_{TR} = 0.760$; $AUC_{DM} = 0.759$; $AUC_{LR} = 0.750$	124	No	Surgery
Vaidya et al. [100]	CT	Stage IA–IIA NSCLC	5-year recurrence	$AUC = 0.78$; $P < .005$	50 + 43	Yes	Surgery and adjuvant chemotherapy
Hao et al. [101]	PET	Stage IA–IB NSCLC	DM	$AUC = 0.82 \pm 0.3$	48	No	SBRT
Oikonomou et al. [102]	PET/CT	Stage I–II NSCLC	Local control (LC), lobar control, regional control (RC), distant control (DC), recurrence free progression (RFP)	RC: [PC4-R:0.38, $P = .02$], DC: [PC4-HR: 0.51, $P = .02$ and PC1-HR: 1.12, $P = .01$], RFP: [PC1-HR: 1.08, $P = .04$], DSS: [PC2-HR: 1.34, $P = .03$ and PC3-HR: 0.64, $P = .02$]; OS: PC4-HR: 0.45, $P = .004$ and PC3-HR: 0.74, $P = .02$	150	No	SBRT

Table 4.2 Description of studies using different features in the radiomics analysis to relate to survival in lung cancer.

Author, year	Modality	Study population	Clinical outcome	C-index/AUC, P value, HR Test/validation	N	External validation	Treatment
Huang et al. [103]	CT	Stage IA–IIB NSCLC	DFS	C-index = 0.72	282	No	Surgery
Wang et al. [104]	CT	Stage I NSCLC	RFS	C-index = 0.829, $P < .001$	378	No	Surgery
Yu et al. [105]	CT	Stage I NSCLC	OS, DM, regional recurrence (RR)	OS: HR = 1.02, $P = .0438$ DM: HR = 1.04, $P = .0402$ RR: HR = 1.04, $P = .0617$	147 + 295	Yes	Surgery SABR
Tunali et al. [106]	CT	Stage I–IV NSCLC	OS	HR = 0.40; $P = .042$	61 + 47	Yes	Surgery
Grossmann et al. [107]	CT	Stage I–IV NSCLC	Survival	C-index = 0.73, $P < 10^{-9}$	262 + 89	Yes	Surgery
Kirienko et al. [108]	PET/CT	Stage I–IV NSCLC	DFS	CT C-index = 0.61 PET C-index = 0.64 PET+CT C-index = 0.65	295	No	Surgery
Hosny et al. [109]	CT	Stage I–IIIb NSCLC	2-year OS	AUC = 0.71 for surgery AUC = 0.70 for radiotherapy	1194 (7 cohorts)	Yes	Surgery radiotherapy
Aerts et al. [110]	CT	Stage I–IV NSCLC; stage I–IV H&N	OS	Lung: C-index = 0.65, $P < .001$ H&N1: C-index = 0.69, $P < .001$ H&N2: C-index = 0.69, $P < .001$	422 + 225 + 136 + 95 + 89	Yes	Radiotherapy/ chemoradiotherapy

Study	Modality	Stage	Endpoint	Results	N		Treatment
Li et al. [111]	CT	Early (IA, IB, IIA) stage NSCLC	OS RFS LR-RFS	OS:C-index = 0.81 RFS: C-index = 0.80 LR-RFS: C-index = 0.80	59	No	SBRT
Ramella et al. [112]	CT	Stage III	Adaptive/nonadaptive	AUC = 0.82	91	No	Chemotherapy
Xu et al. [113]	CT	Stage III NSCLC	OS; Progression; DM; locoregional recurrence	6-month OS: AUC = 0.74 OS: HR = 6.16, $P < .001$ DM: HR = 3.99, $P = .0004$ Progression: HR: 3.20, $P = .02$ locoregional recurrence: HR = 2.74, $P = .02$	179 + 89	Yes	Chemotherapy
Li et al. [114]	CT	Stage I–IIA NSCLC	Survival nodal failure	Survival: C-index = 0.640 ± 0.029 Nodal failure: C-index = 0.664 ± 0.063	100	No	SBRT
Nitin Ohri	PET/CT	Locally advanced NSCLC	OS	Log-rank $P < .001$	201	No	Chemotherapy
Arshad et al. [115]	PET/CT	Stage I–III NSCLC	OS	Validation: HR = 1.61, $P = .00465$	133 + 204 + 21	Yes	Radiotherapy/chemoradiotherapy
[116]	PET/CT	Stage III NSCLC	OS	AUC = 0.95	30	No	Chemotherapy
Kim et al. [117]	CT	Stage IIIB–IV EGFR-mutant adenocarcinoma	PFS	C-index = 0.77	48	No	EGFR TKI
Ravanelli et al. [118]	CT	Stage IV adenocarcinoma	6-Mon progression 1-year progression	6-Mon progression: AUC = 0.8 1-year progression: AUC = 0.76	50	No	EGFR TKI

Continued

Table 4.2 Description of studies using different features in the radiomics analysis to relate to survival in lung cancer.—*cont'd*

Author, year	Modality	Study population	Clinical outcome	C-index/AUC, P value, HR Test/validation	N	External validation	Treatment
Song et al. [119]	CT	Stage IV NSCLC	PFS	Validation1: HR = 3.77, C-index = 0.72, Validation 2: HR = 3.67, C-index = 0.72	117 + 101 + 96 + 56	Yes	EGFR TKI
Li et al. [120]	CT	Stage IV (ALK)-positive NSCLC	PFS	C-index, 0.717; time-dependent AUC, 0.824	63 + 105	Yes	TKI Crizotinib
Park et al. [121]	PET/CT	EGFR-mutant NSCLC	PFS	HR: 3.80, P = .02	161 + 212	Yes	EGFR TKI
Sun et al. [122]	CT	Different types of cancer	OS	HR = 0·58, P = .0081	134 + 119 + 100 + 137	Yes	Immunotherapy
Tunali et al. [123]	CT	Advanced-stage NSCLC	Hyperprogressive disease (TTP<2Mon)	AUC = 0.804 to 0.865	228	No	Immunotherapy
Tunali et al. [124]	CT	NSCLC	PFS OS	6-month OS: AUC = 0.784 24-month OS: AUC = 0.716	180 + 90 + 62	Yes	Immunotherapy
Trebeschi et al. [125]	CT	NSCLC	1-year OS	AUC = 0.76	203 + 39 + 262	Yes	Immunotherapy
Khorrami et al. [126]	CT	NSCLC	Response OS	Response: AUC = 0.85/0.81 OS: C-index = 0.72	50 + 62 + 27	Yes	Immunotherapy
Mu et al. [127]	PET/CT	Stage III–IV NSCLC	Durable clinical benefit (DCB); PFS; OS	DCB: AUC = 0.83/0.81 PFS: C-index = 0.74/0.77 OS: C-index = 0.83/0.80	146 + 48	Yes	Immunotherapy

Table 4.3 Description of studies using different features in the radiomics analysis to relate to prognosis in breast cancer.

Author, year	Modality	Study population	Clinical outcome	C-index/AUC, P value, HR Test/validation	N	External validation	Treatment
Chan et al. [128]	DCE-MRI	Early-stage breast cancer	OS (yes/no)	Leave one out cross validation: AUC = 0.77 Bootstrap: AUC = 0.73	563	No	Breast conserving therapy
Li et al. [129]	MR	TCGA breast cancer	Good prognosis versus bad prognosis	AUC = 0.88, 0.76, 0.68, and 0.55 for MammaPrint, Oncotype DX, PAM50 risk of relapse based on subtype, and PAM50 risk of relapse based on subtype and proliferation	84	No	NaN
Park et al. [130]	MRI	Invasive breast cancer	DFS	C-index = 0.76	294	No	Neoadjuvant chemotherapy
Drukker et al. [131]	MRI	Breast cancers measuring 3 cm or greater	RFS	C-index = 0.72	162	No	Chemotherapy
Yoon et al. [132]	DWI-MRI FDG-PET/ CT	Locally advanced breast cancer	Pathologic response Recurrence PFS	NaN	83	No	Neoadjuvant chemotherapy

Continued

Table 4.3 Description of studies using different features in the radiomics analysis to relate to prognosis in breast cancer.—*cont'd*

Author, year	Modality	Study population	Clinical outcome	C-index/AUC, P value, HR Test/validation	N	External validation	Treatment
Molina-Garcia et al. [133]	PET/CT	Locally advanced breast cancer	Recurrence DFS OS	DFS: HR: 0.89, $P = .05$ OS: HR: 0.76, $P = .006$	68	No	Neoadjuvant chemotherapy
Groheux et al. [134]	FDG-PET/CT	Stage II–III ER+/HER2- breast cancer	Event-free survival (EFS)	NaN	143	No	Neoadjuvant chemotherapy
Yoon et al. [132]	DWI-MRI FDG-PET/CT	Locally advanced breast cancer	Pathologic response Recurrence PFS	NaN	83	No	Neoadjuvant chemotherapy
Huang et al. [135]	DWI-MRI FDG-PET/CT	Invasive breast cancer	RFS	3-year RFS: AUC = 0.75 2-year RFS: AUC = 0.68	113	No	Surgery, radiation, and/or chemotherapy

Table 4.4 Description of studies using different features in the radiomics analysis to relate to prognosis in prostate cancer.

Author, year	Modality	Study population	Clinical outcome	C-index/AUC, P value, HR Test/ validation	N	External validation	Treatment
Ginsburg et al. [136]	T2w MRI	PCa	Biochemical recurrence (BCR)	AUC = 0.83	16	No	Radiotherapy
Gnep et al. [137]	T2w MRI	Localized prostate adenocarcinoma	BCR	C-index = 0.90	74	No	Radiotherapy
Shiradkar et al. [138]	Biparametric MRI	Pca	BCR	AUC = 0.73	70 + 50	Yes	Radical prostatectomy/ radiotherapy/hormone therapy

Table 4.5 Description of studies using different features in the radiomics analysis to relate to prognosis in colorectal cancer.

Author, year	Modality	Study population	Clinical outcome	C-index/AUC, P value, HR Test/validation	N	External validation	Treatment
Liu et al. [139]	MRI	Rectal cancer	Synchronous metastases	AUC = 0.827	177	No	TME, without neoadjuvant treatment, chemotherapy, or chemoradiotherapy
Jalil et al. [140]	MRI	Locally advanced rectal cancer (LARC)	OS DFS RFS	Texture features were associated with long-term survival	56	No	Long-course chemoradiotherapy
Meng et al. [141]	MRI	LARC	DFS	DFS: C-index = 0.788 3-year DFS: AUC = 0.837	108	No	Neoadjuvant chemoradiotherapy (NACRT) followed by total mesorectal excision (TME)
Lovinfosse et al. [142]	PET/CT	LARC	Survival	Coarseness was associated with DFS and DSS	86	No	NACRT
Helden et al. [143]	PET/CT	Metastatic colorectal cancer	PFS OS	Some radiomic features correlates with survival	99	No	First-/third-line standard systemic treatment
Badic et al. [144]	CT	Rectal and colon adenocarcinoma	OS	Some radiomic feature correlates with survival	61	No	Surgery
Badic et al. [145]	CT	Stage I–IV colon cancer	OS PFS	OS: HR = 8.4, P = .005 PFS: HR = 22.8, P < .0001	64	No	Surgery
Dai et al. [146]	CT	Stage I–III colon cancer	OS RFS	OS: AUC = 0.768; RFS: AUC = 0.744	701	No	Radical surgery

Study	Imaging	Cancer type	Outcome	Results	Sample	Multi-center	Treatment
Jeon et al. [147]	T2-MRI	LARC	Local recurrence (LR), distant metastasis (DM), and DFS	LR: C-index = 0.951 ± 0.026 DM:C-index = 0.894 ± 0.048 DFS: C-index = 0.897 ± 0.046	101	No	Preoperative chemoradiotherapy (CCRT) and TME
Dercle et al. [148]	CT	Liver metastatic colorectal cancer	Treatment sensitive or insensitive OS	Treatment sensitive: CRC-FC^{HQ}: AUC = 0.80 CRC-FC^{SD}: AUC = 0.72 CRC-F^{HQ}: AUC = 0.59 CRC-F^{SD}: AUC = 0.55 OS: CRC-FC^{HQ}: HR = 44.3, $P = .0001$ CRC-FC^{SD}: HR = 6.5, $P = .005$ CRC-F^{HQ}: HR = 1.9, $P = .43$ CRC-F^{SD}: HR = 0.96, $P = .96$	667 (CRC-FC^{HQ}, CRC-FC^{SD}, CRC-F^{HQ}, CRC-F^{SD})	No	EGFR-targeted therapies

Table 4.6 Description of studies using different features in the radiomics analysis to relate to prognosis in esophageal and gastric cancers.

Author, year	Modality	Study population	Clinical outcome	C-index/AUC, P value, HR Test/validation	N	External validation	Treatment
Ganeshan et al. [149]	CT	Esophageal cancer	OS	Uniformity: OR = 4.45; P = .039	21	No	NaN
Yip et al. [150]	CT	Stage T2 or greater esophageal cancer	OS	Entropy + maximal wall thickness: AUC = 0.0767 uniformity+maximal wall thickness: AUC = 0.802	36	No	Neoadjuvant chemoradiotherapy
Piazzese et al. [151]	CT	Esophageal cancer	OS	Zone distance variance$_{GLDZM}$ was identified as the only stable CT radiomic feature statistically correlated with OS	213	No	Chemoradiotherapy with and without cetuximab
Xie et al. [152]	CT	Esophageal squamous cell carcinoma	OS	C-index = 0.705 3-year survival: AUC = 0.805	87 + 46	Yes	Definitive concurrent chemoradiotherapy
Nakajo et al. [153]	PET/CT	Esophageal cancer	Response PFS OS	Texture features can predict tumor response, but all of them have limited value in prediction of prognosis of patients	52	No	Chemoradiotherapy
Paul et al. [154]	PET/CT	Locally advanced esophageal cancer	Response 3-year OS	Response: AUC = 0.823 ± 0.032 3-year OS: AUC = 0.750 ± 0.108	64	No	Chemoradiotherapy
Foley et al. [155]	PET/CT	Esophageal cancer; gastroesophageal junctional	OS	AIC: 2238.007 X^2 20.621, P < .001	403	No	Surgery, neoadjuvant chemotherapy (NACT) or neoadjuvant chemoradiotherapy (NACRT), definitive chemo-radiotherapy (dCRT) or palliative therapy

Study	Modality	Cancer type	Endpoint	Results	N		Treatment
Foley et al. [156]	PET/CT	Esophageal cancer; gastroesophageal junctional	OS	No statistically significant difference in OS between patient quartiles was demonstrated in prognostic models incorporating PET image features	302 + 101 + 46	Yes	Surgery, neoadjuvant chemotherapy (NACT) or neoadjuvant chemoradiotherapy (NACRT), definitive chemo-radiotherapy (dCRT) or palliative therapy
Chen et al. [157]	PET/CT	Esophageal squamous cell carcinoma	Pathological remission OS DFS	OS: HRs: 3.58 for score 2, and 15.19 for score 3, $P < .001$; DFS: HRs: 1.39 for score 2 and 6.04 for score 3, $P = .001$	44	No	Neoadjuvant chemoradiotherapy followed by esophagectomy
Yoon et al. [158]	CT	(HER2)-positive advanced gastric cancer	Binarized OS with cutoff of 12 months	AUC > 0.7	26	No	Trastuzumab-based chemotherapy
Giganti et al. [159]	CT	Gastric cancer	OS	AIC: 40.85	56	No	Surgery
Li et al. [160]	CT	Gastric cancer	OS	C-index = 0.82	181	No	Radical resection
Jiang et al. [161]	CT	Stage I–IV gastric cancer	DFS OS	Internal cohort: OS: HR = 0.148, $P < .001$; DFS: HR = 0.176, $P < .001$ External cohort: OS: HR = 0.394, $P < .001$; DFS: HR = 0.412, $P < .001$ Training:DFS: C-index = 0.850; OS: C-index = 0.860	228 + 186 + 1177	Yes	Postoperative adjuvant chemotherapy
Jiang [162]	PET/CT	Stage I–IV gastric cancer	DFS OS	DFS: C-index = 0.794 OS: C-index = 0.789	214	No	Radical gastrectomy

Table 4.7 Description of studies using different features in the radiomics analysis to relate to prognosis in Liver cancer.

Author, year	Modality	Study population	Clinical outcome	C-index/AUC, P value, HR Test/validation	N	External validation	Treatment
Zhou et al. [163]	CT	Hepatocellular carcinoma (HCC)	Early recurrence (≤ 1 year)	AUC = 0.836	215	No	Partial hepatectomy
Zheng et al. [164]	CT	HCC	Time to Recurrence (TTR); OS	TTR: C-index = 0.587 OS: C-index = 0.710	212 + 107	No	Hepatectomy
Kim et al. [165]	Gadoxetic acid–enhanced MRI	Single HCC 2 –5 cm in diameter	Early DFS versus late DFS	C-index = 0.716	167	No	Hepatectomy
Chen et al. [166]	CT	HCC	OS and DFS	Textural features were associated with DFS and OS	61	No	Hepatectomy
Cozzi et al. [167]	CT	Stage A to C Barcelona Clinic Liver Cancer (BCLC)	Local control (LC) OS	LC: 5-feature: AUC = 0.660 3-feature: AUC = 0.640 OS: AUC = 0.801	138	No	Volumetric modulated arc therapy
Akai et al. [168]	CT	Resectable HCC	DFS OS	Log-rank: DFS; $P = 1.1 \times 10^{-4}$ OS: $P = 4.8 \times 10^{-7}$ OS: HR = 1.06, $P = 8.4 \times 10^{-8}$	127	No	Initial hepatectomy
Li et al. [169]	CT	Single large HCC (>5 cm)	OS	Hepatectomy: HR = 0.836, $P = .047$ TACE: HR: 1.209, $P = .024$	130	No	Hepatectomy or transcatheter arterial chemoembolization (TACE)
Xia et al. [170]	CT	HCC	OS with interpretable biological meaning	Volume fraction: C-index = 0.72 cluster prominence: C-index = 0.65	371 + 38	No	Hepatectomy or LT

Study	Modality	Cancer type	Endpoints	Results	Sample size		Treatment
Fu et al. [171]	CT	Intermediate-advanced HCC	TTP OS	TTP: F1: HR(−/+) = 0.802/ 2.184 P = .002 F2: HR(−/+) = 0.455/ 1.298 P = .004 F3: HR(−/+) = 0.665/ 1.503 P = .008 F4: HR(−/+) = 0.663/ 1.486 P = .007 OS F5: HR(−/+) = 0.759/ 2.115 P = .005	261	No	TACE or TACE plus sorafenib
Park et al. [172]	PET/CT	HCC	OS DFS	DFS: PET positive: HR = 2.896, P = .005 OS: PET positive: HR = 4.164, P = .051	92	No	Hepatectomy
Blanc-Durand et al. [173]	PET/CT	Unresectable hepatocellular carcinoma (uHCC)	OS PFS	PFS-pPET-RadScore: HR = 120; P = .006 OS-pPET-RadScore: HR = 16.1; P = .001	47	No	Transarterial radioembolization using Yttrium-90 (90Y-TARE)

Table 4.8 Description of studies using different features in the radiomics analysis to relate to prognosis in pancreatic cancer.

Author, year	Modality	Study population	Clinical outcome	C-index/AUC, P value, HR Test/validation	N	External validation	Treatment
Tang et al. [174]	MRI	Resectable pancreatic cancer	Recurrence	Internal validation: AUC = 0.876 External validation: AUC = 0.846	177 + 126	Yes	Surgery
Kim et al. [175]	PET/CT	Pancreatic ductal adenocarcinoma (PDAC)	Recurrence	Heterogeneity index: HR = 1.702, P = .027	93	No	Surgery
Zhou et al. [176]	CT	Unresectable pancreatic cancer with malignant biliary obstruction	Restenosis-free survival	C-index = 0.779	106	No	Irradiation stent placement
Zhang et al. [177]	CT	NSCLC PDAC	OS	C-index = 0.651	422 + 68	No	Surgery
Cui et al. [178]	PET/CT	Locally advanced pancreatic cancer (LDPC)	OS	Radiomics signature: HR = 3.72, P = .037	139	No	Stereotactic body radiation therapy (SBRT)
Yue et al. [179]	PET/CT	Pancreatic adenocarcinoma (PA)	OS	Δμ (homogeneity): HR = 0.033, P = .065 Δμ (variance): HR = 0.731, P = .078 Δμ(cluster tendency): HR = 1.087, P = .081	26	No	Radiotherapy
Kim et al. [175]	PET/CT	Pancreatic ductal adenocarcinoma (PDAC)	Recurrence	Heterogeneity index: HR = 1.702, P = .027	93	No	Surgery
Hyun et al. [180]	PET/CT	PDAC	OS	Entropy: HR = 5.59, P = .028 2-year OS: AUC = 0.720	137	No	Curative surgery Chemoradiotherapy Chemotherapy supportive care

Table 4.9 Description of studies using different features in the radiomics analysis to relate to prognosis in cervical cancers.

Author, year	Modality	Study population	Clinical outcome	C-index/AUC, P value, HR Test/validation	N	External validation	Treatment
Altazi et al. [181]	PET/CT	Cervical cancer	Locolregional recurrence (LRR) Distant metastasis (DM)	LRR: AUC = 0.92 DM: AUC = 0.92	80	No	Chemoradiotherapy (CRT)
Reuzé et al. [182]	PET/CT	Locally advanced cervical cancer (LACC)	Local recurrence (LR)	AUC = 0.76	118	No	Concurrent chemoradiation followed by brachytherapy
Meng et al. [183]	MRI	LACC	Recurrence	Recurrence at 4 weeks after chemoradiotherapy initiated: T2WI: AUC = 0.61 ADC:AUC = 0.74 T2WI + ADC: AUC = 0.73	34	No	Concurrent chemoradiotherapy (CCRT)
Wormald et al. [184]	MRI	Stage I–II cervical cancer	Recurrence	AUC = 0.916, P = .006	125	No	Trachelectomy or hysterectomy
Lucia et al. [185]	PET/CT and MRI	LACC	Locoregional control (LRC) Recurrence	Recurrence: accuracy = 94% LRC: accuracy = 100%	102	No	CRT
Ho et al. [186]	PET/CT	LACC	Response OS	Response: AUC = 0.75–0.81 OS: HR = 4.70, P = .009	44	No	External-beam radiotherapy followed by intensity-modulated radiotherapy (IMRT)

Continued

Table 4.9 Description of studies using different features in the radiomics analysis to relate to prognosis in cervical cancers.—*cont'd*

Author, year	Modality	Study population	Clinical outcome	C-index/AUC, P value, HR Test/validation	N	External validation	Treatment
Chen et al. [187]	PET/CT	Cervical cancer	OS;PFS; distant metastasis-free survival (DMFS); pelvic relapse-free survival (PRFS)	OS: HGRE: HR = 4.34, $P < .0001$ PFS: HGRE: HR = 2.86, $P < .0001$ PPFS: HGRE: HR = 4.69, $P < .0001$	142	No	CCRT and intracavitary brachytherapy
Ho et al. [188]	DWI-MRI	Cervical cancer	OS;DFS; Central recurrence-free survival; local recurrence-free survival;	DFS: ADC: HR = 0.36, $P = .02$	69	No	CCRT followed by brachytherapy
Fang et al. [189]	MRI	Stage IB-IIA cervical cancer	DFS	C-index = 0.753	248	No	Radical hysterectomy
Lucia et al. [190]	MRI PET/CT	LACC	DFS locoregional control (LRC)	DFS: AUC = 0.95/ 0.93 LRC: AUC = 0.93/ 0.92	112 + 50 + 28	Yes	External-beam radiotherapy followed by brachytherapy

Table 4.10 Description of studies using different features in the radiomics analysis to relate to prognosis in central nervous system cancers.

Author, year	Modality	Cancer sites	Clinical outcome	C-index/AUC, P value, HR Test/validation	N	External validation	Treatment
Zhang et al. [191]	MRI	Skull base meningiomas	Progression/recurrence (P/R)	Accuracy: 90%	60	No	Incomplete resection
Nie et al. [192]	MRI	High-grade gliomas (HGG)	OS	Accuracy: 90.66%	68 + 25	Yes	Resection, concurrent high conformal radiation therapy, and chemotherapy
Sanghani et al. [193]	MRI	Glioblastoma multiforme	OS	Short/long: accuracy: 98.7% Short/medium/long: accuracy: 88.95%	163 BraTS 2017 dataset	No	NaN
Liu et al. [194]	MRI	HGG	OS bad or good with cutoff of 650 days	Accuracy: 75%	68	No	NaN
Wu et al. [195]	MRI	HGG	OS	Two modality: Accuracy: 92.31%	135 + 86	Yes	NaN
Liu et al. [196]	MRI	Low-grade gliomas (LGG)	PFS	C-index = 0.823	216 + 84	Yes	NaN
Prasanna et al. [197]	MRI	Treatment-navie gliomas	OS	C-index = 0.735	65	No	NaN
Zhang et al. [198]	MRI	Gliomas	OS	C-index = 0.974	105	No	NaN
Chen et al. [199]	MRI	Glioblastoma multiforme	OS	12-month accuracy: 0.851	127	No	NaN
Tan et al. [200]	MRI	HGG	OS	C-index = 0.758	112 + 35	Yes	NaN
Papp et al. [201]	(^{11}C-MET) PET	Treatment-navie gliomas	36-mo survival	AUC = 0.90–0.91	70	No	NaN
Li et al. [202]	PET/CT	Glioma	OS	Log-rank $P < .05$	127	No	NaN

Table 4.11 Description of studies using different features in the radiomics analysis to relate to prognosis in other solid cancers.

Author, year	Modality	Cancer sites	Clinical outcome	C-index/AUC, P value, HR Test/validation	N	External validation	Treatment
Leijenaar et al. [203]	CT	Oropharyngeal squamous cell carcinoma	DFS OS	Validation1:C-index = 0.628 (P = 2.72e-9) Validation2: C-index = 0.634 (P = 2.7e-6) Validation3: C-index = 0.647 (P = 5.35e-6)	542	Yes	Radical gastrectomy
Wang et al. [204]	CT	Ovarian cancer	Recurrence	C-index = 0.713/ 0.694	151 + 49 + 45	Yes	Debulking surgery
Bogowicz et al. [205]	CT	Head and neck cancer	2-Year survival HPV status	2-Year survival: AUC = 0.61–1 HPV status: AUC = 0.69–0.82	1174	Yes	NaN

Table 4.12 Description of studies using different features in the radiomics analysis to relate to prognosis in lymphoma.

Author, year	Modality	Cancer sites	Clinical outcome	C-index/AUC, P value, HR Test/validation	N	External validation	Treatment
Zhou et al. [206]	PET/CT	Primary gastric DLBCL		PET: PFS: HR = 14.642, P = .002 OS: HR = 28.685, P = .012 CT: PFS: HR = 11.504, P = .007 OS: HR = 11.791, P = .016	35	No	
Aide et al. [207]	PET/CT	Diffuse large B-cell lymphoma (DLBCL)	PFS OS	PFS: HR = 3.17, P = .032 OS: HR = 3.78, P = .02	82	No	NaN
Tatsumi et al. [208]	PET before and after treatment	Follicular lymphoma (FL)	PFS	Therapy response: AUC = 0.720; PFS: NS	45	No	Chemotherapy
Lue et al. [209]	PET/CT	HL	PFS OS	PFS: HR = 6.640, P = .026 OS: HR = 14.54, P = .012	42	No	Chemotherapy
Lue et al. [210]	PET/CT	HL		PET: Therapy response: OR = 36.4, P = .014 PFS: HR = 9.286, P = .023 OS: HR = 41.02, P = .001 CT: Therapy response: OR = 30.4, P = .014 PFS: HR = 18.480, P = .012	35	No	Chemotherapy

Continued

Table 4.12 Description of studies using different features in the radiomics analysis to relate to prognosis in lymphoma.—*cont'd*

Author, year	Modality	Cancer sites	Clinical outcome	C-index/AUC, *P* value, HR Test/validation	N	External validation	Treatment
Wang et al. [211]	PET/CT	Renal/adrenal lymphoma	OS	OS: HR = 9.016, *P* = .046	19	No	NaN
Parvez et al. [212]	PET/CT	NHL	DFS OS	DFS: *P* = .013; OS: *P* = .035	82	No	Standard immune-chemotherapy
Wang et al. [213]	PET/CT	Nasal-type extranodal natural killer/T-cell lymphoma (ENKTL)	PFS OS	PFS: C-index = 0.588 OS: C-index = 0.628	110	No	Chemotherapy with LVP and concurrent radiotherapy
Mayerhoefer et al. [214]	PET/CT	Mantle cell lymphoma (MCL)	2-Year PFS	AUC = 0.83	107	No	CD20 antibody-based immune-(chemo)therapy
Chen et al. [215]	MRI	Primary central nervous system lymphoma (PCNSL)	OS	OS: HR = 3.075; *P* = .021	52	No	Chemotherapy
Ganeshan et al. [216]	CT	Hodgkin's lymphoma (HL) and high-grade non-Hodgkin's lymphoma (NHL)	PFS	PFS: HR = 25.5, *P* < .001	29	No	Chemotherapy
Morvan et al. [217]	PET	Multiple myeloma	PFS	Prediction error: 0.36 ± 0.015	66	No	NaN

targeted therapy, and immunotherapy for different stages and gene expression. In clinics, CT and PET/CT are the recommended technique in cancer diagnosis and treatment evaluation. Therefore, most of the radiomics studies in lung cancer focus on the analysis of CT or PET/CT images.

4.2.1.1 Prediction of recurrence/metastasis
4.2.1.1.1 CT imaging

To predict the recurrence or DM, the study population mainly focused on early-stage patients (stage I−II) treated with surgery or SABR/SBRT. Therefore, CT is the most commonly used imaging modality. The main pipeline includes radiomics signature generation with LASSO, linear discriminant analysis (LDA), or multivariable logistic regression method, followed by multivariable logistic regression analysis with clinical variables incorporated for the final prediction model.

A radiomics signature of four features based on a Laplacian of Gaussian (LoG) filter consisting of wavelet HHL skewness, GLCM cluster shade, and LoG 2D skewness, combined with stage and grade, could be used for DM prediction with AUC of 0.60 for patients with locally advanced NSCLC (stage II−III) treated with chemoradiotherapy [92]. For the same treatment, Timmeren et al. [93] constructed a six-feature-based radiomics signature for predicting locoregional recurrence (LRR) in patients with stage I−IV, but failed in the external validation cohort. More studies built recurrence/DM models for patients with early-stage NSCLC and treated with SABR/SBRT. Huynh et al. [94,95] trained and compared radiomics models utilizing CT images under different conditions—average intensity projection (AIP) and free breathing (FB)—and found that the AIP radiomics model outperformed the FB radiomics model with average AUC of 0.67 in DM prediction for early-stage NSCLC patients (stage I−II). Additionally, 2-radiomics-based signatures were also found to be meaningful in predicting recurrence, local recurrence, and nonlocal recurrence with AUC values of 0.72, 0.83, and 0.60, respectively [96]. The early prediction of recurrence within 6 months since the start of SABR was also achieved with high AUC of 0.85 using 5 radiomic features also for early-stage NSCLC patients [97], which outperformed physician performance.

Recently, peritumoral space around the tumor attracted the attention of investigators and it plays an important role. Given the hypothesis that more invasive tumors may have different morphologic patterns in the tumor periphery because of the presence of microscopic disease, the peritumoral space around the tumor, which was the region extending radially from the nodule boundary up to roughly 3−9 mm, can provide valuable distant failure-related information [222,223]. Khorram et al. [98] constructed a radiomics signature with peritumoral features and tumoral features; together with the tumor stage, the AUC could achieve 0.74−0.76 in recurrence prediction after surgery in two different external test cohorts. D'Antonoli's work [99] also used the tumor features and peritumoral lung parenchyma features to construct a radiomics signature to predict local recurrence (LR), DM, and total recurrence (TR) at follow-up for stage IA−IIB NSCLC patients treated with surgery, and also obtained satisfactory results with AUCs of 0.750, 0.759, and 0.760, respectively.

Similarly, the tumor features and peripheral region features were also used to predict DM for locally advanced NSCLC (stage II—III) patients treated with radiation therapy, and achieve an AUC of 0.65.

Furthermore, pathology features were also incorporated into the CT-based radiomics analysis, which could achieve a significantly higher AUC of 0.78 in predicting 5-year recurrence-free survival in the external validation cohort treated with surgical resection followed by adjuvant chemotherapy [100], which provided another direction named RaPtomics.

4.2.1.1.2 PET/CT imaging

Besides CT imaging, several studies are also based on PET/CT images with significantly fewer cases. Using the tumor periphery PET features, DM could be accurately predicted with a high AUC of 0.83 in stage IA—IB NSCLC patients treated with SBRT [101], which could also be applied in local advanced cervical cancer. Given most of the previous studies used the LASSO method to select meaningful features, Oikonomou et al. used the principal components (PCs) analysis on 43 CT- and PET-derived features, which were significantly correlated with local control (LC), lobar control, regional control (RC), distant control (DC), RFS, OS, and disease-specific survival (DSS) of SBRT treatment [102].

4.2.1.2 Prediction of survival

Most of the lung cancer radiomics studies tried to provide prognostic signatures through the combination of different radiomic features which were capable of predicting survival or stratifying patients based on expected survival. Relevant studies cover nearly all of the treatments on patients with all stages based on CT imaging analysis and PET/CT analysis. The analysis method includes conventional radiomics analysis and deep learning—based analysis.

4.2.1.3 Surgery

A 5-CT-feature—based radiomics signature together with clinical stage, histologic grade, gender, and age were used to build a DFS prediction nomogram model with a C-index of 0.720, which was significantly higher than the clinical nomogram model and AJCC 7th staging system [103] in patients with stage IA—IIB NSCLC treated with surgery. Later, a radiomic signature consisted of more CT-based features ($n = 8$, shape, histogram, and textural features), combined with tumor stage, that could be used to predict RFS with a high C-index of 0.829 for patients with stage I NSCLC treated with surgery [104].

Unlike using the LASSO method or multivariable cox/logistic regression method to construct the radiomics signature using commonly used radiomics features, a mortality risk index was generated using the random survival forests (RSFs) method, which consisted of 2 textural features and was an independent predictor of OS, DM, and regional recurrence in both surgery and SABR cohorts [105]. Additionally, a series of new features from radial deviation and radial gradient maps was also proved to be associated with lung cancer survival after surgery [106].

Further, Grossmann et al. [107] presented novel and consistent associations between radiomics, molecular pathways, and clinical factors using the Iterative Signature Algorithm, and demonstrated that radiomics can predict molecular pathway status and thus improve the prognostic performance of clinical and gene signatures with a C-index of 0.73 in survival prediction.

Besides CT imaging, Kirienko et al. [108] combined PET-based features (three textural features + SUVmean), CT-based features (one textural feature), and clinical stage to construct a DFS prediction model with a higher AUC of 0.65.

With the rapid development of deep learning, a deep learning model was applied successfully in prognosis evaluation. Hosny et al. [109] developed a 3D deep learning network for 2-year OS prediction in stage I—III patients treated with radiotherapy and achieved an AUC of 0.70. When they transferred this network to predict the 2-year OS of patients who received surgery, a high AUC of 0.71 could also be obtained. The high intraclass correlation coefficient of 0.91 further validates its robustness. This work provided the possibility of using the currently developed model for different medical applications after tuning the corresponding dataset.

4.2.1.4 Radiation therapy/chemotherapy/concurrent chemoradiotherapy
4.2.1.4.1 CT imaging
As one of the early successful radiomics studies, Aerts et al. [110] described a combination of CT-based features (size, shape, texture, and wavelets) that could predict outcome in lung cancer patients treated with radiotherapy/chemoradiotherapy, and could be further utilized in patients with head and neck cancers who received similar treatment directly. Then, a series of studies using different features and machine learning methods were used to predict the prognosis of patients treated with radiation therapy/chemotherapy/concurrent chemoradiotherapy. This work showed that the prognostic factors learned from medical images may be similar for different cancers treated with different treatments due to some consistent nature of the tumor.

Later, the sematic features attracted the investigator's attention, and proved an improved prediction performance with the incorporation of radiomic features. Li et al. [111] combined manually scored radiological features (semantics), radiomic features, and ECOG to obtain the OS, RFS, and LR-RFS prediction models with high average C-indices of 0.81, 0.80, and 0.80, respectively, in patients treated with SBRT. Similar studies were performed on stage III patients treated with concurrent chemoradiation, and reveal radiomic signature mixing semantic and image-based features demonstrates promising results for personalized adaptive radiotherapy in NSCLC with AUC of 0.82 [112].

Furthermore, unsupervised two-way clustering method was also used in clustering the radiomic features, and the subclusters were significantly correlated with the survival and nodal failure with C-indices of 0.640 ± 0.029 and 0.664 ± 0.063, respectively [114], which are better than PCA-based metafeatures and LASSO-based signatures.

Transfer learning, an approach that tunes a pretrained networks with images from other domains on a new dataset, can solve the issue of a limited sample size.

Time series CT scans were also investigated using transfer learning of the popular ResNet convolutional neural network (CNN) model, which showed significant capability in predicting survival (OS) and cancer-specific outcomes (progression, DM, and local-regional recurrence) [113]. In the work of Rahul et al. a decision tree classifier model with the input of the combination of the features learned by a pretrained deep learning network, radiomics features, and traditional quantitative features could achieve an accuracy of 90% for prediction of survival in adenocarcinoma patients [224].

4.2.1.4.2 PET/CT imaging

Although less frequently investigated due to the less PET data, PET-based radiomic features have also shown prognostic value for patients with lung cancer. One textural feature calculated from the GLCM in pretreatment PET identified using the LASSO procedure was an independent predictor of overall survival [225]. Similarly, a 2-feature based radiomic signature from PET images was also proved to be significantly correlated with OS in patients treated with radiotherapy/chemoradiotherapy [115]. A novel quantitative feature set describing intratumor heterogeneity by partitioning PET and CT images into several concentric regions was proposed, and outperformed the commonly used radiomic features for predicting OS status after 2 years with a high AUC of 0.95 [116].

4.2.1.5 Targeted therapy
4.2.1.5.1 CT imaging

Targeted therapies have changed the landscape of treatments for NSCLC. Several targeted therapies have been approved for patients with NSCLC harboring genetic alterations in several oncogenes, including EGFR, anaplastic lymphoma kinase (ALK), ROS1, RET6, NTRK1, and NRG1 fusions, oncogenic somatic mutations in BRAF (V600E and non-V600E), intragenic insertions in ERBB2, and exon 14 skipping mutations in the MET proto-oncogene1 [226,227]. However, not all patients with mutated genes would benefit from the corresponding inhibitors of mutant oncoproteins. Therefore, radiomics analysis provides a good way to select beneficial patients through the predicted prognosis. Currently, EGFR TKI is the most widely used targeted therapy in clinical practice due to the high EGFR mutation rate.

Using a conventional radiomics analysis, a PFS prediction model consisted of one shape feature, one textural feature, age, baseline tumor diameter, and treatment response that could achieve a C-index of 0.77 for patients treated with first-line EGFR TKIs [117]. Ravanelli et al. [118] trained a radiomics signature with 5 histogram features, which could be used to predict a 6-month progression and 1-year progression with an AUC of 0.80 and 0.76, respectively. Both of the above studies were only investigated in around 50 cases; Song et al. [119] curated more data from different institutions, and generated a 12-CT-feature—based radiomics signature, together with N stage and smoke status, which could predict PFS with a high C-index of 0.72 in two different external TKI-treated validation cohorts. The generated signature was not correlated in patients treated with chemotherapy.

For other kinds of TKI, Li et al. [120] investigated the prognostic value of the radiomics signature in ALK-positive stage IV NSCLC patients treated with TKI targeting ALK-rearrangement. The 3-CT-feature-based radiomics signature can capture valuable information related to the tumor phenotype, and has high prognostic value in stage IV ALK-mutated nonsynchronous nodules in NSCLC patients treated with TKI Crizotinib.

4.2.1.5.2 PET/CT imaging
So far, the PET/CT imaging—based radiomics analysis for prognosis evaluation of TKI is limited. Park et al. [121] investigated the predictive value of PET-based heterogeneity textural parameters for PFS of EGFR TKI in EGFR-mutated NSCLC patients, which could be used to identify a subpopulation at increased risk of early EGFR TKI failure.

4.2.1.6 Immunotherapy
4.2.1.6.1 CT imaging
Immunotherapy, a new therapeutic option to treat cancer by enhancing the patient's immune system, has become one of the main promising treatment modalities recently. Among the many immunotherapeutic strategies, immune checkpoints blockade agents, targeting the immunosuppressive molecules such as cytotoxic T-lymphocyte—associated protein 4 (CTLA-4), programmed cell protein (PD-1), and its ligand PD-L1, have shown significant clinical benefit in the treatment of NSCLC [228—230]. Anti-PD-1 inhibitors, nivolumab and pembrolizumab, have been granted approval for the treatment of patients with advanced NSCLC by the US Food and Drug Administration and European Medicines Agency. Therefore, most of the studies focused on anti-PD-1 inhibitors.

The corresponding studies were first performed on CT images. Sun et al. [122] first developed an 8-CT-feature—based radiomics signature of CD8 cells, which is proved to be associated with improved overall survival in univariate (hazard ratio 0.58, $P = .0081$) and multivariate analyses (0.52, $P = .0022$) in immunotherapy. More directly, Tunali et al. built economical classifier models with pretreatment CT radiomic features combined with clinical covariates to predict hypeprogression and progressive disease phenotypes with AUCs of 0.80—0.87 [123], which were also highly correlated with PFS and OS of immunotherapy [124]. The significant correlation between the signature and hypoxia further reveals the potential biological meaning of the signature. Trebeschi et al. [125] developed a CT-based radiomic signature that significantly discriminated progressive disease from stable and responsive disease (AUC $= 0.83$) among NSCLC patients treated with immunotherapy, which could also be used for the 1-year OS prediction with an AUC of 0.76. Through further correlation analysis with cell cycle progression and mitosis, a link between high tumor proliferation and improved response to immunotherapy was found. Recently, Khorrami et al. [126] retrospectively analyzed data acquired from 139 NSCLC patients at two institutions, and extracted the changes of intranodular and perinodular texture descriptors from CT images between baseline and the posttherapy scans("delta"). Using an LDA classifier trained with 8 delta radiomic features, the responders could be distinguished with AUCs of 0.81 and 0.85 in two different validation cohorts. This model was associated with OS with a C-index of 0.72. Moreover, some perinodular features were associated with the density of TILs on diagnostic biopsy samples, which demonstrated the utility of perinodular regions in characterizing the tumor microenvironment.

4.2.1.6.2 PET/CT imaging

For PET/CT studies, Mu et al. [127] first developed PET/CT-based immunotherapy-related radiomic signatures for durable clinical benefit, PFS and OS prediction in advanced stage NSCLC patients, and the good results in both retrospective and prospective cohorts showed improved predictive ability compared to PET or CT features alone.

4.2.2 Breast cancer

In women worldwide, breast cancer is the most common cancer with the highest incidence. Early response and prognosis to treatment prediction are clinical and research hotspots in breast cancer. Therefore, radiomics is also used widely in breast cancer research. MRI is widely applied in screening high risk women, staging, recurrence monitoring, and providing complementary information for uncertain findings on mammography and ultrasonography, therefore most of the radiomics analyses were performed on MRI images. Additionally, as other commonly used medical images, PET/CT was also performed in breast cancer diagnosis and treatment evaluation. However, given the limited number of patients who received PET/CT, most PET/CT radiomics investigations in breast cancer is at the feasibility level [231]. So far, most of the studies focus on the response prediction of different treatments for breast cancer; only a few studies investigated the prognostic value of radiomics in predicting survival. Details are shown in Table 4.3.

4.2.2.1 Prediction of survival
4.2.2.1.1 MRI

Some studies categorized the survival with different cutoffs to give binarized prediction using radiomics. Chan et al. [128] developed a fully automatic method to predict breast conserving therapy failure in patients with early-stage breast cancer from a single pretreatment MRI scan. Li et al. [129] distinguished the good and poor prognosis through the investigation of the relationships between breast MR—based image phenotypes (CEIPs) with gene expression assays of MammaPrint, Oncotype DX, and PAM50, which showed the promise for image-based phenotyping in predicting the recurrence risk of breast cancer.

A 4-T2-feature—based radiomics signature was trained and used for the DFS prediction of neoadjuvant chemotherapy in patients who underwent surgery for invasive breast cancer, and achieved a high C-index of 0.76 with the incorporation of N-stage and molecular subtype [130]. Drukker et al. [131] investigated the automatically calculated most enhancing tumor volume (METV) from DCE-MRI images, and found it was significantly associated with DFS (published C-statistic 0.72 [0.60; 0.84]).

4.2.2.1.2 PET/CT imaging

Molina-Garcia et al. [133] reported that parameters derived from 18F-FDG PET were associated with a neoadjuvant chemotherapy response, recurrence, and PFS in locally advanced breast cancer (LABC). On the contrary, Groheux et al.'s [134] textural analysis of PET images could not add the prognostic value compared to the based PET parameter, i.e., metabolically active tumor volume in patients with stage II–III ER+/HER2-breast cancer treated with neoadjuvant chemotherapy. Later, some studies investigated the supplementary information by combining PET/CT and MRI images. Yoon et al. [132] demonstrated that texture-based analysis of tumor heterogeneity on FDG PET/CT and MR can predict NAC response and disease recurrence in LABC. Specifically, higher metabolic heterogeneity on PET images was significantly predictive in unfavorable chemotherapy response and worse disease prognosis. Huang et al. [135] performed an unsupervised clustering of 113 patients with breast cancer based on 18F-FDG PET- and MRI-derived parameters and identified three tumor clusters significantly correlated with RFS.

4.2.3 Prostate cancer

For men in Western countries, prostate cancer (PCa) is the most common cancer. Due to the advantage of high soft tissue contrast, multiparametric MRI (mp-MRI) plays an important role in diagnosis and treatment of PCa. Diagnosis and aggressiveness of prostate cancer in mp-MRI data are the main focus of current prostate radiomics studies [232], and only limited studies focused on the recurrence prediction for different treatments. Details are shown in Table 4.4.

4.2.3.1 Prediction of recurrence

Currently, radiomic features derived from pretreatment mp-MRI have been successfully utilized to predict biochemical recurrence (BCR) of PCa after radical prostatectomy, radical radiotherapy, or external beam radiotherapy.

Ginsburg et al. [136] identified prognostic radiomics features by implementing the PLS method to embed the MRI-based features in a low dimensional space, and using the variable importance in the projections method to quantify the contributions of individual features for classification of the PLS embedding. Finally, a logistic regression classifier with the input of the three identified Gabor wavelet features yielded an AUC of 0.83 for predicting the risk of BCR following RT. However, the application of this model was limited in the small cohort of 16 patients. With a larger dataset, Gnep et al. [137] also investigated the association between radiomics features and BCR following RT. This study enrolled a retrospective cohort of 74 patients who underwent pretreatment mp-MRI, and found 28 T2w-based GLCOM-related statistical features and four morphological features (tumor diameter, perimeter, area, and volume) were significantly associated with BCR

($P < .05$). The most relevant features, T2w contrast, T2w difference variance, ADC median, tumor volume, and tumor area, could achieve Harrell's concordance index (C-index) from 0.76 to 0.82 ($P < .05$). By the combination of these most features in a RSF model, the C-index could be improved to 0.90. Furthermore, Shiradkar et al. [138] trained a machine learning classifier with a larger cohort of 70 patients using radiomic features from bpMRI (T2WI and ADC maps), which resulted in an AUC of 0.73 in the independent validation cohort in predicting BCR after adjuvant therapy [138].

4.2.4 Colorectal cancer

Currently, colorectal cancer is a common and fatal type of cancer in the worldwide with increasing incidence and mortality every year. Once diagnosed with metastatic colon cancer, the patients would have extremely poor prognosis. Predictive factors to identify patients with high possibility of getting benefit from more aggressive treatment are urgently needed. Due to the successful application of radiomics biomarkers in lung cancer, many researchers tried to investigate the prognostic value of the radiomics analysis in colorectal cancer. Details are shown in Table 4.5.

4.2.4.1 Prediction of recurrence/metastasis

The signature generated with the combination of six MRI-radiomic features and four clinical characteristics could be used to predict synchronous distant metastasis (SDM) in patients with rectal cancer treated with different treatments with a high AUC of 0.827 and accuracy of 87% in the validation cohort, which could aid in tailoring treatment strategies [139].

4.2.4.2 Prediction of survival
4.2.4.2.1 MRI

In the early studies, Jalil et al. [140] utilized 56 patients to investigate the prognostic value of textural features from MRI images in locally advanced rectal cancer (LARC) patients treated with long-course chemoradiotherapy, and found some textural features could predict OS and DFS independently. Further studies with more cases were performed. Later, based on 108 LARC patients treated with total mesorectal excision (TME), Meng et al. [141] developed a Cox model with the combination of an MRI-based radiomics signature and clinical features, which achieved a C-index of 0.788 in PFS estimation, and an AUC of 0.837 in 3-year time-dependent AUC.

4.2.4.2.2 PET/CT imaging

PET/CT radiomics also plays an important role in predicting prognosis of colorectal cancer. Eighty-six patients with LARC were enrolled to investigate the relationship between radiomic features and DSS, DFS and OS. Compared to intensity- and volume-based parameters, textural analysis of baseline 18F-FDG PET/CT provided strong independent predictors of survival with better predictive power in patients with LARC [142]. Using a radiomics analysis, Helden et al. [143] demonstrated a significant association between improved prognosis and baseline low tumor volume and heterogeneity as well as high sphericity on FDG PET.

4.2.4.2.3 CT imaging

Additionally, CT images were also investigated using radiomics analysis in colorectal cancer. Badic et al. [144] also investigated the potential complementary value of noncontrast and contrast-enhanced CT radiomics in colorectal cancer, and found that some survival associated radiomic features had moderate correlations between nonenhanced and enhanced CT images, which suggested that complementary prognostic value may be extracted from both modalities when available. Their further study showed that the combination of enhanced CT radiomics, gene expression, and histopathological examination of primary colorectal cancer could achieve significantly higher prognostic stratification power [145]. Using more CT data from stage I–III, 701 colon cancer patients, Dai et al. [146] successfully developed death- and relapse-specific radiomics signatures to predict OS and RFS of radical surgery with high accuracy.

Compared to the above single-time point radiomics analysis, Jeon et al. [147] first developed delta-radiomics signatures using MRI images for rectal cancer patients treated with chemoradiotherapy (CCRT) followed by TME, and achieved high C-indices of 0.951 ± 0.026, 0.894 ± 0.048, and 0.897 ± 0.046 for local recurrence, DM and DFS, respectively.

Besides the common treatment, prognosis of new treatments was also predicted with radiomics analysis. Dercle et al. [148] used 4 different metastatic colorectal cancer cohorts that received different EGFR targeted therapies to generate a sensitive biomarker consisted of temporal decrease in tumor spatial heterogeneity plus boundary infiltration, which succeeded and outperformed existing biomarkers (KRAS-mutational status and tumor shrinkage by RECIST 1.1) in predicting sensitivity to anti-EGFR therapy with AUCs of 0.80 and 0.72 but failed in predicting chemotherapy response with AUCs of 0.59 and 0.55. Additionally, this signature was significantly associated with OS (two-sided $P < .005$).

4.2.5 **Esophageal and gastric cancers**

Esophageal (or esophago-gastric) cancer and gastric cancer are leading causes of cancer-related deaths worldwide with annual 456,000 and 952,000 new cases, respectively [233]. In this part, we will provide a critical review of radiomic findings related to the survival analysis in esophageal and gastric cancers. Details are shown in Table 4.6.

4.2.5.1 Esophageal/esophago-gastric cancer
4.2.5.1.1 CT imaging

At early stages with small-number investigations using CT images, Ganeshan et al. indicate that lower unenhanced CT-based histogram uniformity before the initiation of treatment was an independent predictor for poorer OS [149]. Based on the analysis of pretreatment and posttreatment contrast-enhanced images of 36 patients, Yip et al. found the histogram entropy and the uniformity between the two time points had a significant decrease and increase, respectively. Compared to morphologic assessment alone, survival models that included a combination of pretreatment entropy and uniformity with maximal wall thickness assessment had better performance [150].

Later studies were investigated with more data. Piazzese et al. [151] performed radiomic analysis of contrast- and noncontrast-enhanced planning CT images in terms of stability, dimensionality, and contrast agent dependency based on 213 patients with esophageal cancer (OC) from multicenters, and identified zone distance variance$_{GLDZM}$ as the only stable CT-based OS-correlated radiomic feature, independent of dimensionality and contrast administration.

Besides the tumoral region features, more studies focus on the subregions of the tumor. Xie et al. [152] curated independent patient cohorts with esophageal squamous cell carcinoma from two hospitals, and extracted features from subregions clustered from patients' tumor regions using the K-means method. The model combined with seven subregional radiomic features could achieve a C-index of 0.705 (0.628−0.782, 95% CI) in the validation cohorts for OS prediction of definitive concurrent chemoradiotherapy.

4.2.5.1.2 PET/CT imaging

The early stage of PET/CT radiomics analysis in esophageal/esophago-gastric cancer was usually investigated with small number of cases and was at the feasibility level. In a 52 patient-based study, PET/CT-based GLSZM intensity variability, GLSZM size-zone variability, as well as standard volumetric parameters, such as metabolic tumor volume (MTV) and total lesion glycolysis (TLG), were predictors of tumor response but not progression-free or overall survival to chemoradiotherapy in patients with esophageal squamous cancer [153]. On the contrary, in a study of 65 patients with local advanced-staged esophageal cancer, Paul et al. found that models incorporating 9 features and 8 features were predictors of response (with an AUROC value of 0.823) and survival (with an AUC of 0.750), respectively, using a genetic algorithm for the feature selection also for chemoradiotherapy [154].

Later PET/CT studies were investigated with larger cohorts. In a 403 patient-based study, TLG, histogram energy, and kurtosis were found independently associated with OS regardless of the treatment [155]. However, their further study [156], which incorporated PET image features in prognostic models, showed that there was no significant difference in OS between patient quartiles in the external validation cohort, and also indicated that PET harmonization did not significantly change the results of model validation. The opposite conclusion means more work is needed on standardizing the PET features.

Besides the above commonly used treatment, Chen et al. [157] investigated the role of PET/CT radiomic features in predicting the outcome of the trimodality treatment (neoadjuvant chemoradiotherapy and surgery), and found primary tumor histogram entropy, SUVmax reduction ratio, and tumor code similarity were independently associated with surgical pathological response, OS, and DFS.

4.2.5.2 Gastric cancer
4.2.5.2.1 CT imaging
For CT-based analysis, Yoon et al. investigated 26 patients with gastric cancer who were HER2 positive before the start of trastuzumab treatment. In this study, GLCM contrast, variance, correlation, and angular second moment (also known as energy or uniformity) were found significantly associated with OS [158]. In another study, Giganti et al. showed that the first-order energy, entropy, and skewness were significantly associated with prognosis, and could increase the performance of a multivariate prognostic model for risk stratification in 56 gastric cancer patients treated with surgery [159]. With more data ($N = 181$), Li et al. [160] trained and validated a radiomics nomogram including 9-feature-based radiomics signature, T stage, N stage, and differentiation, which exhibited significant prognostic superiority over the clinical nomogram and R-signature alone with a C-index of 0.82 in predicting OS of gastric cancer patients treated with radical resection. Recently, the first radiomics study in predicting OS and PFS of chemotherapy in patients with gastric cancer was performed in CT images, and a 19-CT-feature-based radiomics signature was generated to add incremental value to the TNM staging system and clinical-pathologic risk factors for individual survival estimation in thousands of external validation patients [161].

4.2.5.2.2 PET/CT imaging
Among the PET-based researches, the studies of radiomics are very limited. Jiang [162] used 3 PET-based radiomic features to construct a rad-score, together with clinical variables including location, CA199, depth of invasion, and metastasis stage, while DFS and OS models were developed and achieved high C-indices of 0.794 and 0.789 in DFS and OS prediction for radical gastrectomy in the validation cohort with gastric cancer. Moreover, the radiomics signature could predict which patients could benefit from postsurgical chemotherapy. The PET/CT radiomics studies for gastric cancer is still preliminary, there is a great need of standardization for different multicenter data before including PET/CT radiomics in the clinical routine for gastric cancer.

4.2.6 Liver cancer
Liver cancer is one of the most common cancers worldwide, and is increasing rapidly with the increase rate of 2%−3% annually during 2007 through 2016, although the speed has slowed from recent years [220]. The diagnostic protocol for liver cancer is increasingly refined with the maturity of different clinical imaging modalities, such as CT, PET, and MRI, but the prognosis of liver cancers remains unsatisfactory [234]. Moreover, it is highlighted that different biological behavior

of liver cancers affects the survival and the patients, and the tumoral heterogeneity can also be an important indicator in determining the possibility of a clinical response to treatment [235,236]. Thus, radiomics, which could find significant biological and genomic characteristics of the tumors, was also widely investigated in helping make treatment plan for liver cancer by predicting the prognosis of different treatments. As the most common type of primary liver cancer, HCC is the main focus of the current studies. Details are shown in Table 4.7.

4.2.6.1 Prediction of recurrence/metastasis
4.2.6.1.1 CT imaging
Zhou et al. proved the prognostic value of radiomic signatures for early recurrence of HCC patients treated with partial hepatectomy [163]. By incorporating the 23-feature radiomics signature generated with the LASSO method, age, internal arteries, radiologic evidence of necrosis, and Barcelona clinical liver cancer stage into the multivariable logistic regression model, the predictive ability could be significantly improved with an AUC of 0.836 compared to clinical predictors.

Zheng et al. [164] developed a 6-radiomic-feature–based radiomics score from baseline CT images, which was valuable in predicting prognosis of HCC patients treated with liver resection, and might be served as complementary to the current staging system to help stratify solitary HCC patients for individualized treatments. Together with the capsule, vascular invasion, and γ-Glutamyl transferase, the radiomic nomogram could be used to predict the time to recurrence and OS with C-indices of 0.587 and 0.710 in the validation cohort.

4.2.6.1.2 MRI
Only few reports have investigated the prognostic performance of preoperative MRI-based features in predicting early recurrence of HCC. Kim et al. [165] evaluated the predictive ability of the radiomics model in early (2 years) and late (>2 years) recurrence prediction after curative resection in cases with a single HCC 2–5 cm in diameter using preoperative gadoxetic acid–enhanced MRI. The developed prediction model with features from 3-mm border extension showed comparable performance with that of the postoperative clinicopathologic model for predicting early recurrence.

4.2.6.2 Prediction of survival
4.2.6.2.1 CT imaging
Chen et al. [166] did some preliminary work showing textural features of Gabor and Wavelet transformation, especially the varying Dif., potentially providing prognostic information beyond traditional indicators such as those of the Barcelona Clinic Liver Cancer (BCLC). Cozzi et al. found capacity and BCLC stage could be used as a robust biomarker for local control and OS prediction [167]. Furthermore, Akai et al. proved the DFS and OS predictive value of the random forest–based radiomic analysis for HCC patients treated with hepatectomy [168]. All of the above studies indicated the potential value of the radiomic signatures in prognosis prediction in liver cancer research.

Unlike the above studies which focused on one treatment, Li et al. [169] investigated 130 patients with single HCC (>5 cm) in BCLC stage B or C who underwent either liver resection or transcatheter arterial chemoembolization (TACE) by CT, and found that wavelet features were correlated with OS. Based on these features, the patients were stratified into four groups, and found if patients with positive liver resection marings were treated with TACE, they would have severe compromises in OS. In contrast, TACE− patients would get better therapeutic outcomes by undergoing liver resection and similarly TACE is beneficial to LR− and TACE+ patients. Thus, such radiomic parameters have the potential to help in selecting the correct therapeutic plans for each individual.

Other research has focused on whether HCC patients who have undergone TACE should receive sorafenib simultaneously in order to control the level of vascular endothelial growth factor [171]. Radiomic features from 197 patients who had received TACE therapy were extracted. The results showed that Gabor-1−90 (filter 0) and wavelet-3-D (filter 1.0) were highly correlated with time to progression (TTP) and OS, respectively. Particular patients with Gabor-1-90 (filter 0) ≤ 3.8190 or wavelet-2-D (filter 1.5) ≤ 6.7515 appeared to be most likely to obtain survival benefit from the combination therapy.

While most of the current studies try to construct a connection between the radiomic features and clinical outcome, Xia et al. [170] selected the radiomic features according to their association with gene modules. The imaging features describing the volume fraction and textural heterogeneity in subregions, which were significantly correlated with prognostic gene modules, have the potential to predict OS with interpretable biological meaning.

4.2.6.2.2 PET/CT imaging
There are limited studies that performed radiomics analysis using PET/CT data in liver cancer. Park et al. [172] showed the prognostic value of PET positive in HCC patients treated with hepatectomy. Blanc-Durand et al. [173] reported that a radiomics signature derived from pretreatment whole-liver 18F-FDG PET imaging could predict PFS and overall survival (OS) in patients with advanced HCC treated with transarterial radioembolization using Yttrium-90. Unlike the common pipeline of tumor region−based radiomics analysis, this study uses an integrative whole-liver approach and underlines the importance of the incorporation of adjacent liver parenchyma to explore the tumor environment.

4.2.7 **Pancreatic cancer**
Pancreatic adenocarcinoma is one of the most aggressive cancers with poor prognosis. For the patients with pancreatic adenocarcinoma, surgical resection is the only curative treatment, but only a small portion of them are candidates for surgical resection and the 5-year survival rate after surgery is only approximately 10% [237]. Most of these patients would receive palliative chemoradiotherapy [238]. Details are shown in Table 4.8.

4.2.7.1 Prediction of recurrence/metastasis

Tang et al. [174] developed an MRI-based radiomics signature and the corresponding nomogram to stratify patients with resectable pancreatic adenocarcinoma into early recurrence (DFS $\leq$ 12 months) and non-early recurrence groups. The incorporation of serum carbohydrate antigen 19–9 and stage into the radiomics signature resulted in an improved AUC of 0.85–0.88. The cohort of 303 patients from two medical centers in this study represents one of the largest studies in this area.

4.2.7.2 Prediction of survival
4.2.7.2.1 CT imaging

For CT radiomics studies, Zhou et al. [176] developed an 8-radiomic-feature-based model using 620 features extracted from the arterial and venous phases, which could perform well in restenosis-free survival prediction in patients with unresectable pancreatic cancer with malignant biliary obstruction who received an irradiation stent, and identify the patients with slow progression who should consider undergoing irradiation stent placement for a longer restenosis-free survival.

Deep learning was also applied in pancreatic cancer. Using transfer learning, a CNN-based survival model was built and tested with preoperative CT images of patients with resectable pancreatic ductal adenocarcinoma (PDAC). The proposed CNN-based survival model outperforms Cox proportional hazard model-based radiomics pipeline in PDAC prognosis. This method also offers a better fit for OS patterns with a C-index of 0.651 and overcomes the limitations of conventional survival models [177].

4.2.7.2.2 PET/CT imaging

For PET/CT studies to investigate the prognosis of radiotherapy, a retrospective study, which enrolled 139 locally advanced pancreatic cancer patients treated with SBRT, identified a 7-feature-based radiomics signature from pretreatment scans, which was the only significant predictor of OS [178]. Comparatively, Yue et al. analyzed both preradiation and postradiation FDG PET/CT images of 26 patients with pancreatic adenocarcinoma who had been treated with radiotherapy. In this work, the changes in homogeneity, variance, and cluster tendency between preradiation and postradiation PET/CT images were significantly associated with OS [179]. To predict the prognosis of surgery, Kim et al. [175] evaluated the prognostic value of the heterogeneity in 93 patients with pancreatic adenocarcinoma who underwent surgical resection, and patients with lower heterogeneity factor (that is, more heterogeneous) were significantly correlated with recurrence. Hyun et al. [180] investigated the prognostic value of textural features in pancreatic adenocarcinoma patients treated with diverse treatment modalities including curative surgery, concurrent chemoradiotherapy, chemotherapy, and supportive care. For time-dependent ROC curve analysis for 2-year survival prediction, entropy showed the highest AUC of 0.720 among textural parameters and conventional PET/CT parameters such as TLG (AUC = 0.697) and MTV (AUV = 0.692). Patients with higher entropy would have worse survival. The further multivariate analysis identified clinical stage, tumor size, serum carbohydrate antigen 19—9 level, and entropy as independently significant OS predictor, while TLG was excluded due to the insignificance.

4.2.8 **Cervix cancer**

Cervical cancer is one of the most common cancers of the female reproductive system and ranks as the third deadliest disease among women worldwide [239]. The 5-year overall survival (OS) rate is still low for advanced stage patients (57% for stage II, 35% for stage III, and 16% for stage IV) [240—242]. The treatment plan for cervical cancer is usually made based on the clinical stage. For early stage, surgical resection is the standard treatment, while concurrent chemoradiotherapy is performed on locally advanced cancer [243]. Many clinical parameters, such as stage, histology, and lymph node status, have been regarded as prognostic factors in clinic for cervical cancer patients. Recent developments of radiomics have shown the potential added value in prognostic evaluation of cervical cancer, compared to clinical and histopathological variables [244]. Due to the superior sensitivity in the pretherapeutic evaluation, MRI and PET are the two main applied functional imaging modalities in the diagnosis of cervical cancer. Therefore, most radiomics studies in cervical cancer are based on PET and MRI images. Details are shown in Table 4.9.

4.2.8.1 Prediction of recurrence/metastasis

Despite the increased local control rates recently in cervical cancer, DM is still the main reason of treatment failure, and at least 20% developed DM after the completion of therapy [245,246]. In patients with positive para-aortic involvement, the DM rate is more than 40% [247]. Reliable tools or biomarkers that can identify the patients with high risk of recurrence and distant failure at early time are urgently needed to help clinicians optimize the treatment plan in advance.

4.2.8.1.1 PET/CT imaging

Regarding recurrence, Altazi et al. [181] extracted and selected 12 PET-based radiomic features to construct six multiple logistic regression models. Among these models, four models were significantly associated with recurrence in cervical cancer patients treated with chemotherapy, and achieved higher accuracy compared to univariate-radiomic feature and SUV in terms of recurrence and DM prediction. In another recent retrospective study, which enrolled 118 locally advanced cervical cancer (LACC) patients treated with chemoradiation, a radiomics signature that consisted of SUVpeak, homogeneity, low gray-level zone emphasis, and high gray-level zone emphasis was derived from PET images. This signature could achieve AUC of 0.86 in differentiating patients with and without recurrence, which was significantly higher than that for maximum SUV alone (0.67) in local recurrence prediction [182].

Besides the conventional texture features, shell feature, which can also be used to represent the heterogeneity of tumor periphery, was proposed and proved to have better DM prediction ability compared to other features such as intensity, geometry,

GLCM texture, and neighborhood gray tone difference matrix—based texture in patients with cervical cancer treated with concurrent chemoradiation followed with high-dose rate intracavitary brachytherapy [101].

4.2.8.1.2 MRI

Recently, the run length nonuniformity (RLN) derived from T2-weighted images and the energy derived from ADC maps were proved to high recurrence prediction ability, and their combination could achieve the highest accuracy in predicting recurrence with an AUC of 0.885 for patients with LACC [183]. Wormald et al. [185] performed a radiomics analysis in stratified groups based on the tumor volume, and found that textural features from ADC maps and T2-W images were different between high- and low-volume tumors. Moreover, the combination of ADC-based radiomic features and clinic-pathological features could improve prediction of recurrence with an AUC of 0.916 compared to the clinic-pathological model.

4.2.8.1.3 Combined PET/CT imaging and MRI

In a study at the feasibility level, radiomic features of ADC $Entropy_{GLCM}$ and PET GLU_{NGLRLM}, which were extracted from functional DWI-MRI and PET images, respectively, were proved to be associated with recurrence and distance metastasis for LACC patients treated with chemoradiotherapy. The results also demonstrated that tumors with lower ADC $Entropy_{GLCM}$ or lower PET GLU_{NGLRLM} may have a better locoregional control probability [184].

4.2.8.2 Prediction of survival
4.2.8.2.1 PET/CT imaging

During early studies with small number of cases, Ho et al. [186] retrospectively reviewed 44 patients with bulky ($\geq$4 cm) cervical cancer treated with concurrent chemoradiotherapy (CCRT), and analyzed both pretreatment and intratreatment (2 weeks) PET scans. A textural feature from baseline images and the change in TLG were found to be significantly correlated with OS. Lately, in a study with 142 patients included, stages (IIIA—IIIB) and a high gray-level run emphasis derived from PET-based GLRLM were proved to be prognostic factors for worse OS in patients with cervical cancer (stage IB—IIIB) who underwent CCRT followed by intracavitary brachytherapy (ICBT) [187].

4.2.8.2.2 MRI

For the studies analyzed based on MRI images, Ho et al. [188] found the mean ADC value extracted from the primary tumor in pretreatment MRI was significantly associated with DFS and OS in cervical cancer patients treated with CRT. In a recent study, which curated 248 patients with early-stage cervical cancer from two institutions, 18 MRI-radiomic features were selected for building a radiomic score, which was significantly correlated with DFS. Together with two clinical features (lymph node metastasis and lymph-vascular invasion), a multivariable Cox model was trained for DFS prediction for patients with early-stage cervical cancer who had undergone radical hysterectomy [189].

4.2.8.3 Combined PET/CT imaging and MRI

Some studies also investigated the added value of combining MRI images and PET/CT images in predicting survival. In the study referred above [184], ADC Entropy$_{GLCM}$, ADC Entropy$_{GLCM}$, and CE-MRI RLVAR$_{GLRLM}$ derived from pretreatment MRI were significantly correlated with the DFS. Moreover, they also developed a radiomics DFS prediction model with combined features from PET and MRI images, which achieved an accuracy of 90% (sensitivity 92%−93%, specificity 87%−89%) in predicting DFS for patients with LACC in external validation cohorts from different medical centers (two French and one Canadian) [190].

4.2.9 Central nervous system cancers

Due to the complexity, diversity, and dismal prognosis, CNS diseases are among the leading causes of disability and death. Therefore, accurate prognosis prediction of CNS diseases, especially for CNS tumors, is of crucial importance to improve the clinical decision-making capacity and precise treatment [248]. According to findings from recent research, radiomics also plays an important role in prognosis evaluation in CNS diseases. Details are shown in Table 4.10.

4.2.9.1 Prediction of recurrence/metastasis

Zhang et al. [191] retrospectively analyzed 60 patients diagnosed with skull base meningiomas treated with incomplete resection, and found that T1 maximum probability, T1 cluster shade, and ADC correlation are the most significant parameters using the random forest method. Moreover, the trained prediction model could achieve an AUC of 0.88 in differentiation of progression/recurrence.

4.2.9.2 Prediction of survival

4.2.9.2.1 MRI

As a commonly used supervised machine learning model, SVM is also frequently applied in outcome prediction. The whole-tumor rCBV histogram-based SVM model has been used for 6-month and 1-, 2-, and 3-year survival prediction of glioma, and achieved AUCs of 0.7−0.8 in the independent patient [249]. SVM has also been used to predict 2-class (short and long OS) and 3-class (short, medium, and long OS) using multichannel MR images-based radiomic features [193], and the combination of anatomic (DTI) and functional (rs-fMRI) data could predict good outcomes (>650-day survival) vs. poor outcomes (<650-day) in high-grade glioma with an accuracy of 75% [194].

Another commonly used radiomics pipeline in prognosis analysis in glioma is segmentation-feature extraction-feature selection (e.g., LASSO)-classification (e.g., logistic regression)/prognosis (e.g., Cox hazard regression). Liu et al. [196] developed a 9-feature−based radiomics signature, which was used to predict the PFS of low grade glioma with clinic-pathologic risk factors involved in the multivariable cox regression model. Moreover, this signature was associated with the immune response, programmed cell death, cell proliferation, and vasculature development. Prasanna et al. [197] leveraged a radiomics analysis to evaluate the efficacy of peritumoral brain zone features from preoperative MRI in predicting long- (>18 months) versus short-term (<7 months) survival in GBM, and found a subset of ten radiomic "peritumoral" MRI features, suggestive of intensity heterogeneity and textural patterns, which was found to be predictive of survival ($P = 1.47 \times 10^{-5}$) as compared to features from an enhancing tumor, necrotic regions, and known clinical factors. Similar studies using this pipeline were also applied successfully in Refs. [198–200].

Taking advantage of a scale invariant feature transform (SIFT) feature in image characterizing, Wu et al. [195] developed a sparse representation-based method to convert a local SIFT descriptor into a global tumor feature, proposed a locality preserving projection and sparse representation-combined feature selection method, and employed a multifeature collaborative sparse representation classification to combine the information of multimodal MRI images to classify OS time.

A research study was carried out to compare the accuracy of different machine learning methods in predating the OS (short-term, mid-term, and long-term) for glioma patients using Brats 2017 dataset samples that consisted of 163 samples of brain MRIs. In this work, various types of features including intensity and statistical texture, volumetric, and deep features were used for the training of various machine learning (ML) methods. Different ML methods that included SVM, i.e., LDA, logistic regression and K-nearest neighbors (KNNs), were employed and compared based on accuracy. The best model with the highest prediction accuracy is the LDA model with the input of deep learning features extracted by a pretrained CNN [250].

With the further development of deep learning, Lao et al. [251] developed a CNN to predict the survival rate of GBM patients, which achieved index of 0.71, and was improved with the inclusion of the clinical data. Nie et al. [192] have developed a two-stage learning-based method to predict OS of high-grade gliomas patient. A multimodule and multichannel 3D CNN-based deep learning network was developed using T1 postcontrast, DTI, and resting state functional MRI images in the first stage, which extracted high-level predictive features. These features together with tumor-related features including age, tumor size, and histology were fed into an SVM in the second stage, and generate the final prediction result (long OS vs. short OS) with an accuracy of 90.66%. Not only predicting prognosis, Hao et al. proposed a Pathway-Associated Sparse Deep Neural Network that can also describe complex biological processes regarding biological pathways for prognosis by leveraging prior biological knowledge of pathway databases and by taking hierarchical nonlinear relationships of biological processes into account. This model outperformed other common used models including logistic LASSO, SVM, and NN to predict the outcome (short-term vs. long-term survival) of GBM with an AUC of 0.66 [252].

4.2.9.2.2 PET/CT imaging

Though MRI is widely used in gliomas, the high sensitivity and specificity of PET is considered as a promising diagnostic and longitudinal therapeutic monitoring.

Papp et al. [201] established machine learning-driven survival models for glioma built on in vivo ^{11}C-MET PET characteristics, ex vivo characteristics, and patient characteristics, which achieved an AUC of 0.90—0.91 in predicting 36-month survival. Li et al. [202] developed an isocitrate dehydrogenase (IDH) genotype prediction model using ^{18}F-FDG-PET/CT images, which could be also used to predict OS.

4.2.10 Other solid cancers

In this section, some studies that used different methods in the radiomics analysis but are not referred in the above sections are listed here. Details are shown in Table 4.11.

CT artifacts are a big challenge in radiomics studies. For oropharyngeal squamous cell carcinoma, Leijenaar et al. [203] developed a radiomics signature using 4-CT features which were less affected by the CT artifacts, and achieved C-indices higher than 0.628 in three different external cohorts. Additionally, although CT artifacts were shown to be of influence, the signature had significant prognostic power regardless if patients with CT artifacts were included.

Combination of the deep learning network and the Cox hazard regression model is a new direction in prognosis prediction using radiomics analysis. Wang et al. [204] proposed a deep learning model that could extract effective CT-based prognostic biomarkers for high-grade serous ovarian cancer (HGSOC), and provided a preoperative and noninvasive model for individualized recurrence prediction in HGSOC with C-indices of 0.713 and 0.694 in the independent validation cohorts.

Assembling data from multiple centers is one of the major challenges in radiomics. It is almost impractical to share data between hospitals due to the restriction of legal and ethical regulations. Therefore, distributed learning, which could enable training models on multicenter data without data leaving the hospitals, attracts investigator's attention. Bogowicz et al. [205] tested the feasibility of distributed learning of radiomics data for 2-year OS and HPV status prediction in patients with head and neck cancer. The radiomics distributed learning solution DistriM, which consists of a master script and a site script, was used. The site script is executed at each medical institution, where the data are located, and waits for a learning call from the master script. The master script is run by the researcher and initiates the distributed learning procedure. This script also mediates the transmission of the model coefficients to and from the sites. When model learning is complete, the master script outputs the model coefficients of the learned model. The results showed both feature selection and classification are feasible in a distributed manner using radiomics data, which provides new possibility for training more reliable radiomics models with multicenter data.

4.2.10.1 Blood cancers
4.2.10.1.1 Lymphoma
For blood cancer, nearly all of the radiomics prognostic studies are focused on lymphoma. Because of the complex heterogeneity, lymphoma presents serious challenges for diagnosis and treatment. Given the diverse types of lymphoma, both

the intertumoral and intratumoral heterogeneity of lymphoma are common [253,254], and the intratumoral heterogeneity is related to disease progression and poor prognosis [206]. In this sense, exploration of the heterogeneity of lymphoma is essential to identify the highly invasive lymphoma for treatment selection. As a useful measure of heterogeneity, radiomics is a good try. A few studies have explored its prognostic role in lymphoma, and PET/CT was the most common modality.

4.2.10.1.2 PET/CT imaging

Currently PET/CT is recommended for initial staging, and is also the standard imaging technique to assess the treatment at the end of treatment for patients with Hodgkin's lymphoma (HL) and diffuse large B-cell lymphoma (DLBCL), and is also recommended for initial staging, thus most of the radiomics studies were focused on PET/CT imaging.

For these studies, the recommended 41% SUVmax threshold (or a fixed threshold) is widely used for semiautomatically delineating the ROI. For the lesion with low ^{18}F-FDG uptake relative to the surrounding tissues, coregistered CT was used to aid manual lesion delineation.

For studies regarding DLBCL, Zhou et al. [206] extracted features from the same tumor region delineated from PET and CT images, and multivariate analysis identified kurtosis, metabolic tumor volume (MTV), and gray-level nonuniformity (GLNU) in PET and sphericity, kurtosis, gray-level nonuniformity (GLNU) and high gray-level zone emphasis (HGZE) in CT as independent prognostic factors in OS and PFS estimation. However, PET-based feature and CT-based feature were not combined for further analysis. Unlike most studies that regard the tumor region as the ROI, another study by Aide et al. [207] evaluated the diagnostic and prognostic value of skeletal textural features on baseline FDG PET in DLBCL patients. This study extracted features from the volume of interest encompassing the axial skeleton and the pelvis and selected the features correlated with bone marrow involvement, and found skewness demonstrated better discriminative power over bone marrow biopsy and PET visual analysis for patient stratification for OS and PFS.

Tatsumi et al. [208] analyzed pretreatment and posttreatment FDG PET examinations in 45 patients with follicular lymphoma (FL) and demonstrated that quantitative SUV-related or volumetric FDG PET parameters were applicable to evaluate treatment response in FL. Texture analysis showed promise in predicting treatment response. Although post-treatment and the change of PET parameters were considered as the predictors of PFS in the univariate Cox regression analysis, all of them proved to have limited value in predicting recurrence after chemotherapy since none of them was the predictor in the multivariate analysis.

For the studies regarding HL, Lue et al. [209] extracted 450 PET-based radiomic features from 42 patients and found that intensity nonuniformity extracted from a gray-level run-length matrix, kurtosis, and the Ann Arbor stage were independently associated with PFS and OS, respectively. Moreover, a prognostic scoring system was devised and improved the risk stratification of the current staging classification. They further calculated the CT-based radiomic features besides the PET features, and found HIR_GLRM$_{PET}$ and RLNU_GLRM$_{CT}$ in high-frequency wavelets served as independent predictive factors for treatment response. ZSNU_GLSZM$_{PET}$, INU_GLRM$_{PET}$, and wavelet SRE_GLRM$_{CT}$ served as independent prognostic factors for survival outcomes. Therefore, a prognostic stratification model based on integration with clinical and PET/CT imaging prognostic factors was constructed and could be allowed to identify the four risk groups for survival outcomes in HL patients [210].

For other types of lymphoma, Wang et al. [211] explored the relationship between PET radiomic features and OS in 19 patients with primary renal (PRL)/adrenal lymphoma (PAL), and found the texture analysis of PET images could potentially serve as a noninvasive strategy to predict the OS of patients with PRL and PAL. Parvez et al. [212] explored the relationship between PET radiomic features and DFS/OS in 82 patients with aggressive B-cell lymphoma, and found although several features correlated with DFS and OS, they could not predict therapy response. In this sense, a larger cohort should be validated to confirm the clinical prognostication. Tatsumi et al. [208] analyzed pretreatment and posttreatment FDG PET examinations in 45 FL patients and demonstrated that quantitative SUV-related or volumetric FDG PET parameters were applicable to evaluate treatment response in FL. Texture analysis showed promise in predicting treatment response. Although posttreatment and the change of PET parameters were the candidates, all of them proved to have limited value in predicting recurrence after chemotherapy. This was the only study reporting that texture features were not significant predictors of PFS in FL.

Currently, only a few studies constructed the prediction model with internal and/or external validation. Based on 110 patients with nasal-type extranodal natural killer/T cell lymphoma (ENKTL), Wang et al. [213] developed a 4-radiomic-feature-based and 3-radiomic-feature-based signatures for PFS and OS estimation. Together with clinical variables (International Prognostic Index, Eastern Cooperative Oncology Group performance status), a PFS and OS nomogram could be constructed, which achieved high C-indices of 0.811 and 0.818 in the training cohort, but lower C-indices of 0.588 and 0.628 in the validation cohort for PFS and OS prediction, respectively. This suggested that the stability of the models should be considered with caution. After analysis on 107 treatment-naive MCL patients scheduled to receive CD20 antibody-based immuno(chemo)therapy, Mayerhoefer et al. [214] found SUVmean and entropy were significantly predictive of 2-year PFS, and their combination could predict 2-year PFS with an AUC of 0.83 with the addition of clinical/laboratory/biological data. Moreover, they also identified high SUVmean and high entropy as high "metabolic risk," which was associated with a poorer prognosis.

4.2.10.1.3 MRI

There are also several studies utilizing MRI. Chen et al. [215] used multivariate Cox regression analyses to investigate the radiomic features of the lesions manually contoured from contrast-enhanced MRI of primary central nervous system lymphoma (PCNSL) patients treated with chemotherapy, and demonstrated statistically significant association between radiomics on contrast-enhanced MRI and prognosis of PCNSL patients at the first time.

4.2.10.1.4 CT imaging

As we introduced above, PET/CT imaging is the most widely investigated modality, and the use of CT in lymphoma has been limited. Ganeshan et al. [216] investigated the ability of a CT-based radiomics analysis in providing additional prognostic information in patients with HL and high-grade non-Hodgkin's lymphoma (NHL), and found kurtosis in CT images was a significant predictor of PFS, which means CT can potentially provide prognostic information complementary to PET for patients with HL and aggressive NHL.

From the above literature, we can see the trend of prognostic radiomics analysis has larger data, external validation, reproducible features, and novel stable models.

4.2.10.1.5 Myeloma

Multiple myeloma (MM) accounts for about 10%−15% of hematological malignancies, and is characterized by the clonal proliferation of malignant plasma cells in the bone marrow. Because of the high sensitivity and whole-body imaging characteristics, 18F-FDG PET is widely used in initial staging and therapeutic monitoring in MM. Due to limited cases, there were limited radiomics studies in myeloma. Morvan et al. [217] proposed a two-stage method with RFS and variable importance (VIMP) for both feature selection and prediction. The results confirmed the prognostic value of radiomic features for MM patients and demonstrated that quantitative/heterogeneity image-based features could reduce the error of the predicted progression. This is the first work using RFS on PET images for the progression prediction of MM patients.

According to the above literature, radiomics is useful for treatment evaluation and prognosis in cancer patients with different treatments. The studies were focused on a large range of cancer research using multimodality image, omics, and clinical data. We also noticed that there were limited studies focused on blood cancer due to limited cases and difficulty of ROI selection. With the development of radiomics, the main trends include large-scale data collection, reproducible and quantitative image features, automated analytics methods, and interpretability of radiomics.

References

[1] Menegakis A, et al. Residual γH2AX foci after ex vivo irradiation of patient samples with known tumourtype specific differences in radio-responsiveness. Radiother Oncol 2015;116:480−5.

[2] Menegakis A, et al. γH2AX assay in ex vivo irradiated tumour specimens: a novel method to determine tumour radiation sensitivity in patient-derived material. Radiother Oncol 2015;116:473−9.

[3] Slonina D, et al. Intrinsic radiosensitivity of healthy donors and cancer patients as determined by the lymphocyte micronucleus assay. Int J Radiat Biol 1997;72:693−701.

[4] Bjork-Eriksson T, et al. Tumor radiosensitivity (SF2) is a prognostic factor for local control in head and neck cancers. Int J Radiat Oncol Biol Phys 2000;46:13−9. 2000.

[5] Chitnis MM, et al. IGF 1R inhibition enhances radiosensitivity and delays double-strand break repair by both non-homologous end-joining and homologous recombination. Oncogene 2014;33:5262−73.

[6] Du S, et al. Attenuation of the DNA damage response by transforming growth factor-beta inhibitors enhances radiation sensitivity of non-small-cell lung cancer cells in vitro and in vivo. Int J Radiat Oncol Biol Phys 2015;91:91−9.

[7] Kahn J, et al. The mTORC1/mTORC2 inhibitor AZD2014 enhances the radiosensitivity of glioblastoma stem-like cells. Neuro Oncol 2014;16:29−37.

[8] West CM, et al. The independence of intrinsic radiosensitivity as a prognostic factor for patient response to radiotherapy of carcinoma of the cervix. Br J Cancer 1997;76:1184−90.

[9] Lambin P, et al. Predicting outcomes in radiation oncology−multifactorial decision support systems. Nat Rev Clin Oncol 2013;10:27−40.

[10] Potters L, et al. American Society for Therapeutic Radiology and Oncology (ASTRO) and American College of Radiology (ACR) practice guideline for the performance of stereotactic body radiation therapy. Int J Radiat Oncol Biol Phys 2010;76:326−32.

[11] Leijenaar RT, et al. Stability of FDG-PET Radiomics features: an integrated analysis of testretest and inter-observer variability. Acta Oncol 2013;52:1391−7.

[12] Parmar C, et al. Robust radiomics feature quantification using semiautomatic volumetric segmentation. PLoS One 2014;9:e102107.

[13] Rios Velazquez E, et al. A semiautomatic CT-based ensemble segmentation of lung tumors: comparison with oncologists' delineations and with the surgical specimen. Radiother Oncol 2012;105:167−73.

[14] Aerts HJ, et al. Decoding tumour phenotype by noninvasive imaging using a quantitative radiomics approach. Nat Commun 2014;5:4006.

[15] Segal E, et al. Decoding global gene expression programs in liver cancer by noninvasive imaging. Nat Biotechnol 2007;25:675−80.

[16] Zinn PO, et al. Radiogenomic mapping of edema/cellular invasion MRI-phenotypes in glioblastoma multiforme. PLoS One 2011;6:e25451.

[17] Kim H, et al. Quantitative computed tomography imaging biomarkers in the diagnosis and management of lung cancer. Invest Radiol 2015;50:571−83.

[18] De Ruysscher D, et al. Quantification of radiation-induced lung damage with CT scans: the possible benefit for radiogenomics. Acta Oncol 2013;52:1405−10.

[19] Palma DA, et al. Lung density changes after stereotactic radiotherapy: a quantitative analysis in 50 patients. Int J Radiat Oncol Biol Phys 2011;81:974–8.

[20] Kyas I, et al. Prediction of radiation-induced changes in the lung after stereotactic body radiation therapy of non-small-cell lung cancer. Int J Radiat Oncol Biol Phys 2007;67:768–74.

[21] Defraene G, et al. CT characteristics allow identification of patient-specific susceptibility for radiation-induced lung damage. Radiother Oncol 2015;117(1):29–35.

[22] Ettinger DS, et al. Non-small cell lung cancer, version 1.2015. J Natl Compr Cancer Netw 2014;12:1738–61.

[23] Vansteenkiste J, et al. Early and locally advanced non-small-cell lung cancer (NSCLC): ESMO clinical practice guidelines for diagnosis, treatment and follow-up. Ann Oncol 2013;24(Suppl. 6):vi89–98.

[24] Chang JY, et al. Stereotactic ablative radiotherapy versus lobectomy for operable stage I non-small-cell lung cancer: a pooled analysis of two randomised trials. Lancet Oncol 2015;16:630–7.

[25] Senthi S, et al. Patterns of disease recurrence after stereotactic ablative radiotherapy for early stage nonsmall cell lung cancer: a retrospective analysis. Lancet Oncol 2012;13:802–9.

[26] Huang K, et al. Radiographic changes after lung stereotactic ablative radiotherapy (SABR): can we distinguish recurrence from fibrosis? A systematic review of the literature. Radiother Oncol 2012;102:335–42.

[27] Huang K, et al. High-risk CT features for detection of local recurrence after stereotactic ablative radiotherapy for lung cancer. Radiother Oncol 2013;109:51–7.

[28] Peulen H, et al. Validation of high risk features on CT for detection of local recurrence after SBRT for stage I NSCLC. J Thorac Oncol 2015;10:S2.

[29] Padhani AR, Husband JE. Dynamic contrast-enhanced MRI studies in oncology with an emphasis on quantification, validation and human studies. Clin Radiol 2001;56:607–20.

[30] Padhani AR, Khan AA. Diffusion-weighted (DW) and dynamic contrast-enhanced (DCE) magnetic resonance imaging (MRI) for monitoring anticancer therapy. Targeted Oncol 2010;5:39–52.

[31] Asaumi J, et al. Application of dynamic contrast-enhanced MRI to differentiate malignant lymphoma from squamous cell carcinoma in the head and neck. Oral Oncol 2004;40:579–84.

[32] Shukla-Dave A, et al. Dynamic contrast-enhanced magnetic resonance imaging as a predictor of outcome in head-and neck squamous cell carcinoma patients with nodal metastases. Int J Radiat Oncol Biol Phys 2012;82:1837–44.

[33] Chawla S, et al. Pretreatment diffusion-weighted and dynamic contrast enhanced MRI for prediction of local treatment response in squamous cell carcinomas of the head and neck. AJR Am J Roentgenol 2013;200:35–43.

[34] Jackson A, et al. Imaging tumor vascular heterogeneity and angiogenesis using dynamic contrast enhanced magnetic resonance imaging. Clin Cancer Res 2007;13:3449–59.

[35] Jansen JF, Koutcher JA, Shukla-Dave A. Non-invasive imaging of angiogenesis in head and neck squamous cell carcinoma. Angiogenesis 2010;13:149–60.

[36] Just N. Improving tumour heterogeneity MRI assessment with histograms. Br J Cancer 2014;111:2205–13.

[37] Karahaliou A, et al. Assessing heterogeneity of lesion enhancement kinetics in dynamic contrast-enhanced MRI for breast cancer diagnosis. Br J Radiol 2010;83: 296—309.

[38] Yang X, Knopp MV. Quantifying tumor vascular heterogeneity with dynamic contrast-enhanced magnetic resonance imaging: a review. BioMed Res Int 2014;2011(1): 732848.

[39] El Naqa I, et al. Exploring feature-based approaches in PET images for predicting cancer treatment outcomes. Pattern Recogn 2009;42:1162—71.

[40] Alic L, et al. Heterogeneity in DCE-MRI parametric maps: a biomarker for treatment response? Phys Med Biol 2011;56:1601—16.

[41] Theresa P, et al. New guidelines to evaluate the response to treatment in solid tumors. J Natl Cancer Inst 2000;92:205—16.

[42] Aerts H, et al. Defining a radiomic response phenotype: a pilot study using targeted therapy in NSCLC. Sci Rep 2016;6:33860.

[43] Zhao B, et al. A pilot study of volume measurement as a method of tumor response evaluation to aid biomarker development. Clin Cancer Res 2010;16:4647—53.

[44] Huang Y, et al. Radiomics signature: a potential biomarker for the prediction of disease-free survival in early-stage (I or II) non—small cell lung cancer. Radiology 2016;281:947—57.

[45] Yang Y, et al. EGFR L858R mutation is associated with lung adenocarcinoma patients with dominant ground-glass opacity. Lung Cancer 2015;87:272—7.

[46] Thungappa S, et al. Immune checkpoint inhibitors in lung cancer: the holy grail has not yet been found. ESMO Open 2017;2:e000162.

[47] Grigg C, Rizvi NA. PD-L1 biomarker testing for nonsmall cell lung cancer: truth or fiction? J Immunother Cancer 2016;4:48.

[48] Grove, et al. Quantitative computed tomographic descriptors associate tumor shape complexity and intratumor heterogeneity with prognosis in lung adenocarcinoma. PLoS One 2015;10:e0118261.

[49] Saeed-Vafa D, et al. Combining radiomics and mathematical modeling to elucidate mechanisms of resistance to immune checkpoint blockade in non-small cell lung cancer. bioRxiv 2017. https://doi.org/10.1101/190561.

[50] Champiat S, et al. Hyperprogressive disease is a new pattern of progression in cancer patients treated by anti-PD-1/PD-L1. Clin Cancer Res 2017;23:1920—8.

[51] Murakami M, et al. Increased intratumoral fluorothymidine uptake levels following multikinase inhibitor sorafenib treatment in a human renal cell carcinoma xenograft model. Oncol Lett 2013;6:667—72.

[52] Bao X, et al. Early monitoring antiangiogenesis treatment response of sunitinib in U87MG tumor xenograft by 18F-FLT MicroPET/CT Imaging. BioMed Res Int 2014;2014:218578.

[53] Motzer RJ, et al. Activity of SU11248, a multitargeted inhibitor of vascular endothelial growth factor receptor and platelet-derived growth factor receptor, in patients with metastatic renal cell carcinoma. J Clin Oncol 2006;24:16—24.

[54] Motzer RJ, et al. Sunitinib versus interferon alfa in metastatic renal-cell carcinoma. N Engl J Med 2007;356:115—24.

[55] Jacob A, et al. Radiomics analysis on FLT-PET/MRI for characterization of early treatment response in renal cell carcinoma: a proof-of-concept study. Transl Oncol 2016;9: 155—62. 2016.

[56] Viswanath S, et al. Identifying quantitative in vivo multi-parametric MRI features for treatment related changes after laster interstitial thermal therapy of prostate cancer. Neurocomputing 2014;144:13−23.

[57] Lee SM, et al. Randomized trial of erlotinib plus whole-brain radiotherapy for NSCLC patients with multiple brain metastases. J Natl Cancer Inst 2014;106.

[58] O'Connor J, et al. Imaging biomarker roadmap for cancer studies. Nat Rev Clin Oncol 2017;14:169−86.

[59] Song JD, et al. A new approach to predict progression-free survival in stage IV EGFR-mutant NSCLC patients with EGFR-TKI therapy. Clin Cancer Res 2018;24(15): 3583−92. https://doi.org/10.1158/1078-0432.CCR-17-2507.

[60] Prat A, et al. Research-based PAM50 subtype predictor identifies higher responses and improved survival outcomes in HER2-positive breast cancer in the NOAH study. Clin Cancer Res 2014;20:511−21.

[61] Waugh SA, et al. Magnetic resonance imaging texture analysis classification of primary breast cancer. Eur Radiol 2016;26(2):322−30.

[62] Wu J, et al. Heterogeneous enhancement patterns of tumor-adjacent parenchyma at MR imaging are associated with dysregulated signaling pathways and poor survival in breast cancer. Radiology 2017;285(2):401−13.

[63] Braman N, et al. Association of peritumoral radiomics with tumor biology and pathologic response to preoperative targeted therapy for HER2 (ERBB2)-positive breast cancer. JAMA Netw Open 2019;2:e192561.

[64] Chang HY, et al. Robustness, scalability, and integration of a wound-response gene expression signature in predicting breast cancer survival. Proc Natl Acad Sci USA 2005;102:3738−43.

[65] Chen X, et al. Gene expression patterns in human liver cancers. Mol Biol Cell 2002;13: 1929−39.

[66] Diehn M, et al. Identification of noninvasive imaging surrogates for brain tumor gene-expression modules. Proc Natl Acad Sci USA 2008;105:5213−8.

[67] Gao X, et al. The method and efficacy of support vector machine classifiers based on texture features and multi-resolution histogram from 18F-FDG PET-CT images for the evaluation of mediastinal lymph nodes in patients with lung cancer. Eur J Radiol 2015; 84:312−7.

[68] Harry VN, et al. Use of new imaging techniques to predict tumour response to therapy. Lancet Oncol 2010;11:92−102.

[69] Buettner R, Wolf J, Thomas RK. Lessons learned from lung cancer genomics: the emerging concept of individualized diagnostics and treatment. J Clin Oncol 2013; 31:1858−65.

[70] Yaromina A, Krause M, Baumann M. Individualization of cancer treatment from radiotherapy perspective. Mol Oncol 2012;6:211−21.

[71] Dancey JE, et al. Guidelines for the development and incorporation of biomarker studies in early clinical trials of novel agents. Clin Cancer Res 2010;16:1745−55.

[72] Travis WD, et al. The 2015 World Health Organization classification of lung tumors: impact of genetic, clinical and radiologic advances since the 2004 classification. J Thorac Oncol 2015;10(9):1243−60.

[73] Cancer Genome Atlas Research Network. Comprehensive molecular profiling of lung adenocarcinoma. Nature 2014;511(7511):543−50.

[74] Lee HJ, et al. Epidermal growth factor receptor mutation in lung adenocarcinomas: relationship with CT characteristics and histologic subtypes. Radiology 2013; 268(1):254–64.

[75] Byron SA, et al. Translating RNA sequencing into clinical diagnostics: opportunities and challenges. Nat Rev Genet 2016;17(5):257–71.

[76] Gevaert O, et al. Nonsmall cell lung cancer: identifying prognostic imaging biomarkers by leveraging public gene expression microarray data–methods and preliminary results. Radiology 2012;264(2):387–96.

[77] Gentles AJ, Newman AM, Liu CL, et al. The prognostic landscape of genes and infiltrating immune cells across human cancers. Nat Med 2015;21(8):938–45.

[78] Gilbert MR, et al. A randomized trial of bevacizumab for newly diagnosed glioblastoma. N Engl J Med 2014;370(8):699–708.

[79] Hegi ME, Diserens AC, Gorlia T, Hamou MF, de Tribolet N, Weller M, et al. MGMT gene silencing and benefit from temozolomide in glioblastoma. N Engl J Med 2005; 352(10):997–1003. https://doi.org/10.1056/NEJMoa043331.

[80] Boyd NF, et al. Mammographic densities and breast cancer risk. Cancer Epidemiol Biomarkers Prev 1998;7:1133–44.

[81] Clark AS, Domchek SM. Clinical management of hereditary breast cancer syndromes. J Mammary Gland Biol Neoplasia 2011;16:17–25. https://doi.org/10.1007/s10911-011-9200-x.

[82] Gierach GL, et al. Relationships between computer-extracted mammographic texture pattern features andBRCA1/2mutation status: a cross-sectional study. Breast Cancer Res 2014;16(4):424.

[83] Bray F, et al. Global cancer statistics 2018: GLOBOCAN estimates of incidence and mortality worldwide for 36 cancers in 185 countries. CA Cancer J Clin 2018;68: 394–424. https://doi.org/10.3322/caac.21492.

[84] Cumberbatch MGK, Jubber I, Black PC, Esperto F, Figueroa JD, Kamat AM, et al. Epidemiology of bladder cancer: a systematic review and contemporary update of risk factors in 2018. Eur Urol 2018;74(6):784–95. https://doi.org/10.1016/j.eururo.2018.09.001.

[85] Matuszewski M, et al. Preliminary evaluation of the diagnostic usefulness of Uroplakin 2 with an assessment of the antioxidant potential of patients with bladder cancer. BioMed Res Int 2018:8693297.

[86] Peng C, et al. A colorimetric immunosensor based on self-linkable dual-nanozyme for ultrasensitive bladder cancer diagnosis and prognosis monitoring. Biosens Bioelectron 2019;126:581–9.

[87] Van Kessel KEM, et al. Molecular markers increase precision of the European Association of Urology non-muscle-invasive bladder cancer progression risk groups. Clin Cancer Res 2018;24:1586–93.

[88] Liu J, et al. An integrated TCGA pan-cancer clinical data resource to drive high-quality survival outcome analytics. Cell 2018;173:400–416 e411.

[89] Heagerty PJ, Zheng Y. Survival model predictive accuracy and ROC curves. Biometrics 2005;61:92–105.

[90] Schroder MS, et al. survcomp: an R/Bioconductor package for performance assessment and comparison of survival models. Bioinformatics 2011;27:3206–8.

[91] Langfelder P, Horvath S. WGCNA: an R package for weighted correlation network analysis. BMC Bioinf 2008;9:559.

[92] Coroller TP, Grossmann P, Hou Y, Velazquez ER, Leijenaar RT, Hermann G, et al. CT-based radiomic signature predicts distant metastasis in lung adenocarcinoma. Radiother Oncol 2015;114(3):345−50.

[93] van Timmeren JE, van Elmpt W, Leijenaar RTH, Reymen B, Monshouwer R, Bussink J, et al. Longitudinal radiomics of cone-beam CT images from non-small cell lung cancer patients: evaluation of the added prognostic value for overall survival and locoregional recurrence. Radiother Oncol 2019;136:78−85.

[94] Huynh E, Coroller TP, Narayan V, Agrawal V, Hou Y, Romano J, et al. CT-based radiomic analysis of stereotactic body radiation therapy patients with lung cancer. Radiother Oncol 2016;120(2):258−66.

[95] Huynh E, Coroller TP, Narayan V, Agrawal V, Romano J, Franco I, et al. Associations of radiomic data extracted from static and respiratory-gated CT scans with disease recurrence in lung cancer patients treated with SBRT. PLoS One 2017;12(1): e0169172.

[96] Lafata KJ, Hong JC, Geng R, Ackerson BG, Liu J-G, Zhou Z, et al. Association of pretreatment radiomic features with lung cancer recurrence following stereotactic body radiation therapy. Phys Med Biol 2019;64(2):025007.

[97] Mattonen SA, Palma DA, Johnson C, Louie AV, Landis M, Rodrigues G, et al. Detection of local cancer recurrence after stereotactic ablative radiation therapy for lung cancer: physician performance versus radiomic assessment. Int J Radiat Oncol Biol Phys 2016;94(5):1121−8.

[98] Khorrami M, Bera K, Leo P, Vaidya P, Patil P, Thawani R, et al. Stable and discriminating radiomic predictor of recurrence in early stage non-small cell lung cancer: multi-site study. Lung Cancer 2020;142:90−7.

[99] Akinci D'Antonoli T, Farchione A, Lenkowicz J, Chiappetta M, Cicchetti G, Martino A, et al. CT radiomics signature of tumor and peritumoral lung parenchyma to predict nonsmall cell lung cancer postsurgical recurrence risk. Acad Radiol 2020; 27(4):497−507.

[100] Vaidya P, Wang X, Bera K, Khunger A, Choi H, Patil P, et al. RaPtomics: Integrating Radiomic and Pathomic Features for Predicting Recurrence in Early Stage Lung Cancer. SPIE; 2018.

[101] Hao H, Zhou Z, Li S, Maquilan G, Folkert MR, Iyengar P, et al. Shell feature: a new radiomics descriptor for predicting distant failure after radiotherapy in non-small cell lung cancer and cervix cancer. Phys Med Biol 2018;63(9):095007.

[102] Oikonomou A, Khalvati F, Tyrrell PN, Haider MA, Tarique U, Jimenez-Juan L, et al. Radiomics analysis at PET/CT contributes to prognosis of recurrence and survival in lung cancer treated with stereotactic body radiotherapy. Sci Rep 2018;8(1):4003.

[103] Huang Y, Liu Z, He L, Chen X, Pan D, Ma Z, et al. Radiomics signature: a potential biomarker for the prediction of disease-free survival in early-stage (I or II) non−small cell lung cancer. Radiology 2016;281(3):947−57.

[104] Wang T, Deng J, She Y, Zhang L, Wang B, Ren Y, et al. Radiomics signature predicts the recurrence-free survival in stage I non-small cell lung cancer. Ann Thorac Surg 2020;109(6):1741−9.

[105] Yu W, Tang C, Hobbs BP, Li X, Koay EJ, Wistuba II, et al. Development and validation of a predictive radiomics model for clinical outcomes in stage I non-small cell lung cancer. Int J Radiat Oncol Biol Phys 2018;102(4):1090−7.

[106] Tunali I, Stringfield O, Guvenis A, Wang H, Liu Y, Balagurunathan Y, et al. Radial gradient and radial deviation radiomic features from pre-surgical CT scans are associated with survival among lung adenocarcinoma patients. Oncotarget 2017;8(56): 96013−26.

[107] Grossmann P, Stringfield O, El-Hachem N, Bui MM, Velazquez ER, Parmar C, et al. Defining the biological basis of radiomic phenotypes in lung cancer. Elife 2017;6: e23421.

[108] Kirienko M, Cozzi L, Antunovic L, Lozza L, Fogliata A, Voulaz E, et al. Prediction of disease-free survival by the PET/CT radiomic signature in non-small cell lung cancer patients undergoing surgery. Eur J Nucl Med Mol Imag 2018;45(2):207−17.

[109] Hosny A, Parmar C, Coroller TP, Grossmann P, Zeleznik R, Kumar A, et al. Deep learning for lung cancer prognostication: a retrospective multi-cohort radiomics study. PLoS Med 2018;15(11):e1002711.

[110] Aerts HJ, Velazquez ER, Leijenaar RT, Parmar C, Grossmann P, Carvalho S, et al. Decoding tumour phenotype by noninvasive imaging using a quantitative radiomics approach. Nat Commun 2014;5(1):1−9.

[111] Li Q, Kim J, Balagurunathan Y, Qi J, Liu Y, Latifi K, et al. CT imaging features associated with recurrence in non-small cell lung cancer patients after stereotactic body radiotherapy. Radiat Oncol 2017;12(1):158.

[112] Ramella S, Fiore M, Greco C, Cordelli E, Sicilia R, Merone M, et al. A radiomic approach for adaptive radiotherapy in non-small cell lung cancer patients. PLoS One 2018;13(11):e0207455.

[113] Xu Y, Hosny A, Zeleznik R, Parmar C, Coroller T, Franco I, et al. Deep learning predicts lung cancer treatment response from serial medical imaging. Clin Cancer Res 2019;25(11):3266−75.

[114] Li H, Galperin-Aizenberg M, Pryma D, Simone CB, Fan Y. Unsupervised machine learning of radiomic features for predicting treatment response and overall survival of early stage non-small cell lung cancer patients treated with stereotactic body radiation therapy. Radiother Oncol 2018;129(2):218−26.

[115] Arshad MA, Thornton A, Lu H, Tam H, Wallitt K, Rodgers N, et al. Discovery of pre-therapy 2-deoxy-2-18F-fluoro-D-glucose positron emission tomography-based radiomics classifiers of survival outcome in non-small-cell lung cancer patients. Eur J Nucl Med Mol Imag 2019;46(2):455−66.

[116] Astaraki M, Wang C, Buizza G, Toma-Dasu I, Lazzeroni M, Smedby Ö. Early survival prediction in non-small cell lung cancer from PET/CT images using an intra-tumor partitioning method. Phys Med 2019;60:58−65.

[117] Kim H, Park CM, Keam B, Park SJ, Kim M, Kim TM, et al. The prognostic value of CT radiomic features for patients with pulmonary adenocarcinoma treated with EGFR tyrosine kinase inhibitors. PLoS One 2017;12(11):e0187500.

[118] Ravanelli M, Agazzi GM, Ganeshan B, Roca E, Tononcelli E, Bettoni V, et al. CT texture analysis as predictive factor in metastatic lung adenocarcinoma treated with tyrosine kinase inhibitors (TKIs). Eur J Radiol 2018;109:130−5.

[119] Song J, Shi J, Dong D, Fang M, Zhong W, Wang K, et al. A new approach to predict progression-free survival in stage IV EGFR-mutant NSCLC patients with EGFR-TKI therapy. Clin Cancer Res 2018;24(15):3583−92.

[120] Li H, Zhang R, Wang S, Fang M, Zhu Y, Hu Z, et al. CT-based radiomic signature as a prognostic factor in stage IV ALK-positive non-small-cell lung cancer treated with TKI Crizotinib: a proof-of-concept study. Front Oncol 2020;10(57).

[121] Park S, Ha S, Lee S-H, Paeng JC, Keam B, Kim TM, et al. Intratumoral heterogeneity characterized by pretreatment PET in non-small cell lung cancer patients predicts progression-free survival on EGFR tyrosine kinase inhibitor. PLoS One 2018;13(1): e0189766.

[122] Sun R, Limkin EJ, Vakalopoulou M, Dercle L, Champiat S, Han SR, et al. A radiomics approach to assess tumour-infiltrating CD8 cells and response to anti-PD-1 or anti-PD-L1 immunotherapy: an imaging biomarker, retrospective multicohort study. Lancet Oncol 2018;19(9):1180—91.

[123] Tunali I, Gray JE, Qi J, Abdalah M, Jeong DK, Guvenis A, et al. Novel clinical and radiomic predictors of rapid disease progression phenotypes among lung cancer patients treated with immunotherapy: an early report. Lung Cancer 2019;129:75—9.

[124] Tunali I, Tan Y, Gray JE, Katsoulakis E, Eschrich SA, Saller J, et al. Hypoxia-related radiomics predict immunotherapy response: a multi-cohort study of NSCLC. bioRxiv 2020. 2020.04.02.020859, https://doi.org/10.1101/2020.04.02.020859.

[125] Trebeschi S, Drago SG, Birkbak NJ, Kurilova I, Calin AM, Pizzi AD, et al. Predicting response to cancer immunotherapy using non-invasive radiomic biomarkers. Ann Oncol 2019;30(4).

[126] Khorrami M, Prasanna P, Gupta A, Patil P, Velu PD, Thawani R, et al. Changes in CT radiomic features associated with lymphocyte distribution predict overall survival and response to immunotherapy in non—small cell lung cancer. Cancer Immunol Res 2020;8(1):108—19.

[127] Mu W, Tunali I, Gray JE, Qi J, Schabath MB, Gillies RJ. Radiomics of 18 F-FDG PET/ CT images predicts clinical benefit of advanced NSCLC patients to checkpoint blockade immunotherapy. Eur J Nucl Med Mol Imag 2019:1—15.

[128] Chan H, van der Velden BH, Loo CE, Gilhuijs KG. Eigentumors for prediction of treatment failure in patients with early-stage breast cancer using dynamic contrast-enhanced MRI: a feasibility study. Phys Med Biol 2017;62(16):6467.

[129] Li H, Zhu Y, Burnside ES, Drukker K, Hoadley KA, Fan C, et al. MR imaging radiomics signatures for predicting the risk of breast cancer recurrence as given by research versions of MammaPrint, Oncotype DX, and PAM50 gene assays. Radiology 2016; 281(2):382 91.

[130] Park H, Lim Y, Ko ES, Cho H-h, Lee JE, Han B-K, et al. Radiomics signature on magnetic resonance imaging: association with disease-free survival in patients with invasive breast cancer. Clin Cancer Res 2018;24(19):4705—14.

[131] Drukker K, Li H, Antropova N, Edwards A, Papaioannou J, Giger ML. Most-enhancing tumor volume by MRI radiomics predicts recurrence-free survival "early on" in neoadjuvant treatment of breast cancer. Cancer Imag 2018;18(1):12.

[132] Yoon HJ, Kim Y, Chung J, Kim BS. Predicting neo-adjuvant chemotherapy response and progression-free survival of locally advanced breast cancer using textural features of intratumoral heterogeneity on F-18 FDG PET/CT and diffusion-weighted MR imaging. Breast J 2019;25(3):373—80.

[133] Molina-García D, García-Vicente AM, Pérez-Beteta J, Amo-Salas M, Martínez-González A, Tello-Galán MJ, et al. Intratumoral heterogeneity in 18 F-FDG PET/ CT by textural analysis in breast cancer as a predictive and prognostic subrogate. Ann Nucl Med 2018;32(6):379—88.

[134] Groheux D, Martineau A, Teixeira L, Espié M, de Cremoux P, Bertheau P, et al. 18 FDG-PET/CT for predicting the outcome in ER+/HER2-breast cancer patients: comparison of clinicopathological parameters and PET image-derived indices including tumor texture analysis. Breast Cancer Res 2017;19(1):3.

[135] Huang S-y, Franc BL, Harnish RJ, Liu G, Mitra D, Copeland TP, et al. Exploration of PET and MRI radiomic features for decoding breast cancer phenotypes and prognosis. NPJ Breast Cancer 2018;4(1):1–13.

[136] Ginsburg SB, Rusu M, Kurhanewicz J, Madabhushi A, editors. Computer Extracted Texture Features on T2w MRI to Predict Biochemical Recurrence Following Radiation Therapy for Prostate Cancer. Medical Imaging 2014: Computer-Aided Diagnosis. International Society for Optics and Photonics; 2014.

[137] Gnep K, Fargeas A, Gutiérrez-Carvajal RE, Commandeur F, Mathieu R, Ospina JD, et al. Haralick textural features on T2-weighted MRI are associated with biochemical recurrence following radiotherapy for peripheral zone prostate cancer. J Magn Reson Imag 2017;45(1):103–17.

[138] Shiradkar R, Ghose S, Jambor I, Taimen P, Ettala O, Purysko AS, et al. Radiomic features from pretreatment biparametric MRI predict prostate cancer biochemical recurrence: preliminary findings. J Magn Reson Imag 2018;48(6):1626–36.

[139] Liu H, Zhang C, Wang L, Luo R, Li J, Zheng H, et al. MRI radiomics analysis for predicting preoperative synchronous distant metastasis in patients with rectal cancer. Eur Radiol 2019;29(8):4418–26.

[140] Jalil O, Afaq A, Ganeshan B, Patel U, Boone D, Endozo R, et al. Magnetic resonance based texture parameters as potential imaging biomarkers for predicting long-term survival in locally advanced rectal cancer treated by chemoradiotherapy. Colorectal Dis 2017;19(4):349–62.

[141] Meng Y, Zhang Y, Dong D, Li C, Liang X, Zhang C, et al. Novel radiomic signature as a prognostic biomarker for locally advanced rectal cancer. J Magn Reson Imag 2018; 48(3):605–14.

[142] Lovinfosse P, Polus M, Van Daele D, Martinive P, Daenen F, Hatt M, et al. FDG PET/CT radiomics for predicting the outcome of locally advanced rectal cancer. Eur J Nucl Med Mol Imag 2018;45(3):365–75.

[143] van Helden EJ, Vacher YJL, van Wieringen WN, van Velden FHP, Verheul HMW, Hoekstra OS, et al. Radiomics analysis of pre-treatment [18F]FDG PET/CT for patients with metastatic colorectal cancer undergoing palliative systemic treatment. Eur J Nucl Med Mol Imag 2018;45(13):2307–17.

[144] Badic B, Desseroit MC, Hatt M, Visvikis D. Potential complementary value of non-contrast and contrast enhanced CT radiomics in colorectal cancers. Acad Radiol 2019;26(4):469–79.

[145] Badic B, Hatt M, Durand S, Jossic-Corcos CL, Simon B, Visvikis D, et al. Radiogenomics-based cancer prognosis in colorectal cancer. Sci Rep 2019;9(1):9743.

[146] Dai W, Mo S, Han L, Xiang W, Li M, Wang R, et al. Prognostic and predictive value of radiomics signatures in stage I-III colon cancer. Clin Transl Med 2020;10(1):288–93.

[147] Jeon SH, Song C, Chie EK, Kim B, Kim YH, Chang W, et al. Delta-radiomics signature predicts treatment outcomes after preoperative chemoradiotherapy and surgery in rectal cancer. Radiat Oncol 2019;14(1):43.

[148] Dercle L, Lu L, Schwartz LH, Qian M, Tejpar S, Eggleton P, et al. Radiomics response signature for identification of metastatic colorectal cancer sensitive to therapies targeting EGFR pathway. J Natl Cancer Inst 2020;112(12).

[149] Ganeshan B, Skogen K, Pressney I, Coutroubis D, Miles K. Tumour heterogeneity in oesophageal cancer assessed by CT texture analysis: preliminary evidence of an association with tumour metabolism, stage, and survival. Clin Radiol 2012;67(2):157−64.

[150] Yip C, Landau D, Kozarski R, Ganeshan B, Thomas R, Michaelidou A, et al. Primary esophageal cancer: heterogeneity as potential prognostic biomarker in patients treated with definitive chemotherapy and radiation therapy. Radiology 2014;270(1):141−8.

[151] Piazzese C, Foley K, Whybra P, Hurt C, Crosby T, Spezi E. Discovery of stable and prognostic CT-based radiomic features independent of contrast administration and dimensionality in oesophageal cancer. PLoS One 2019;14(11).

[152] Xie C, Yang P, Zhang X, Xu L, Wang X, Li X, et al. Sub-region based radiomics analysis for survival prediction in oesophageal tumours treated by definitive concurrent chemoradiotherapy. EBioMedicine 2019;44:289−97.

[153] Nakajo M, Jinguji M, Nakabeppu Y, Nakajo M, Higashi R, Fukukura Y, et al. Texture analysis of 18F-FDG PET/CT to predict tumour response and prognosis of patients with esophageal cancer treated by chemoradiotherapy. Eur J Nucl Med Mol Imag 2017;44(2):206−14.

[154] Paul D, Su R, Romain M, Sébastien V, Pierre V, Isabelle G. Feature selection for outcome prediction in oesophageal cancer using genetic algorithm and random forest classifier. Comput Med Imag Graph 2017;60:42−9.

[155] Foley KG, Hills RK, Berthon B, Marshall C, Parkinson C, Lewis WG, et al. Development and validation of a prognostic model incorporating texture analysis derived from standardised segmentation of PET in patients with oesophageal cancer. Eur Radiol 2018;28(1):428−36.

[156] Foley KG, Shi Z, Whybra P, Kalendralis P, Larue R, Berbee M, et al. External validation of a prognostic model incorporating quantitative PET image features in oesophageal cancer. Radiother Oncol 2019;133:205−12.

[157] Chen Y-H, Lue K-H, Chu S-C, Chang B-S, Wang L-Y, Liu D-W, et al. Combining the radiomic features and traditional parameters of 18F-FDG PET with clinical profiles to improve prognostic stratification in patients with esophageal squamous cell carcinoma treated with neoadjuvant chemoradiotherapy and surgery. Ann Nucl Med 2019;33(9):657−70.

[158] Yoon SH, Kim YH, Lee YJ, Park J, Kim JW, Lee HS, et al. Tumor heterogeneity in human epidermal growth factor receptor 2 (HER2)-positive advanced gastric cancer assessed by CT texture analysis: association with survival after trastuzumab treatment. PLoS One 2016;11(8).

[159] Giganti F, Antunes S, Salerno A, Ambrosi A, Marra P, Nicoletti R, et al. Gastric cancer: texture analysis from multidetector computed tomography as a potential preoperative prognostic biomarker. Eur Radiol 2017;27(5):1831−9.

[160] Li W, Zhang L, Tian C, Song H, Fang M, Hu C, et al. Prognostic value of computed tomography radiomics features in patients with gastric cancer following curative resection. Eur Radiol 2019;29(6):3079−89.

[161] Jiang Y, Chen C, Xie J, Wang W, Zha X, Lv W, et al. Radiomics signature of computed tomography imaging for prediction of survival and chemotherapeutic benefits in gastric cancer. EBioMedicine 2018;36:171−82.

[162] Jiang Y, Yuan Q, Lv W, Xi S, Huang W, Sun Z, et al. Radiomic signature of (18)F fluorodeoxyglucose PET/CT for prediction of gastric cancer survival and chemotherapeutic benefits. Theranostics 2018;8(21):5915−28.

[163] Zhou Y, He L, Huang Y, Chen S, Wu P, Ye W, et al. CT-based radiomics signature: a potential biomarker for preoperative prediction of early recurrence in hepatocellular carcinoma. Abdom Radiol 2017;42(6):1695−704.

[164] Zheng B-H, Liu L-Z, Zhang Z-Z, Shi J-Y, Dong L-Q, Tian L-Y, et al. Radiomics score: a potential prognostic imaging feature for postoperative survival of solitary HCC patients. BMC Cancer 2018;18(1):1148.

[165] Kim S, Shin J, Kim D-Y, Choi GH, Kim M-J, Choi J-Y. Radiomics on gadoxetic acid−enhanced magnetic resonance imaging for prediction of postoperative early and late recurrence of single hepatocellular carcinoma. Clin Cancer Res 2019;25(13):3847−55.

[166] Chen S, Zhu Y, Liu Z, Liang C. Texture analysis of baseline multiphasic hepatic computed tomography images for the prognosis of single hepatocellular carcinoma after hepatectomy: a retrospective pilot study. Eur J Radiol 2017;90:198−204.

[167] Cozzi L, Dinapoli N, Fogliata A, Hsu W-C, Reggiori G, Lobefalo F, et al. Radiomics based analysis to predict local control and survival in hepatocellular carcinoma patients treated with volumetric modulated arc therapy. BMC Cancer 2017;17(1):829.

[168] Akai H, Yasaka K, Kunimatsu A, Nojima M, Kokudo T, Kokudo N, et al. Predicting prognosis of resected hepatocellular carcinoma by radiomics analysis with random survival forest. Diagn Interv Imaging 2018;99(10):643−51.

[169] Li M, Fu S, Zhu Y, Liu Z, Chen S, Lu L, et al. Computed tomography texture analysis to facilitate therapeutic decision making in hepatocellular carcinoma. Oncotarget 2016;7(11):13248.

[170] Xia W, Chen Y, Zhang R, Yan Z, Zhou X, Zhang B, et al. Radiogenomics of hepatocellular carcinoma: multiregion analysis-based identification of prognostic imaging biomarkers by integrating gene data—a preliminary study. Phys Med Biol 2018;63(3):035044.

[171] Fu S, Chen S, Liang C, Liu Z, Zhu Y, Li Y, et al. Texture analysis of intermediate-advanced hepatocellular carcinoma: prognosis and patients' selection of transcatheter arterial chemoembolization and sorafenib. Oncotarget 2017;8(23):37855−65.

[172] Park JH, Kim DH, Kim SH, Kim MY, Baik SK, Hong IS. The clinical implications of liver resection margin size in patients with hepatocellular carcinoma in terms of positron emission tomography positivity. World J Surg 2018;42(5):1514−22.

[173] Blanc-Durand P, Van Der Gucht A, Jreige M, Nicod-Lalonde M, Silva-Monteiro M, Prior JO, et al. Signature of survival: a 18F-FDG PET based whole-liver radiomic analysis predicts survival after 90Y-TARE for hepatocellular carcinoma. Oncotarget 2018;9(4):4549.

[174] Tang TY, Li X, Zhang Q, Guo CX, Zhang XZ, Lao MY, et al. Development of a novel multiparametric MRI radiomic nomogram for preoperative evaluation of early recurrence in resectable pancreatic cancer. J Magn Reson Imag 2020;52:231−45.

[175] Kim Y-i, Kim YJ, Paeng JC, Cheon GJ, Lee DS, Chung J-K, et al. Heterogeneity index evaluated by slope of linear regression on 18 F-FDG PET/CT as a prognostic marker for predicting tumor recurrence in pancreatic ductal adenocarcinoma. Eur J Nucl Med Mol Imag 2017;44(12):1995−2003.

[176] Zhou H-F, Han Y-Q, Lu J, Wei J-W, Guo J-H, Zhu H-D, et al. Radiomics facilitates candidate selection for irradiation stents among patients with unresectable pancreatic cancer. Front Oncol 2019;9(973).

[177] Zhang Y, Lobo-Mueller EM, Karanicolas P, Gallinger S, Haider MA, Khalvati F. CNN-based survival model for pancreatic ductal adenocarcinoma in medical imaging. BMC Med Imag 2020;20(1):11.

[178] Cui Y, Song J, Pollom E, Alagappan M, Shirato H, Chang DT, et al. Quantitative analysis of 18F-Fluorodeoxyglucose positron emission tomography identifies novel prognostic imaging biomarkers in locally advanced pancreatic cancer patients treated with stereotactic body radiation therapy. Int J Radiat Oncol Biol Phys 2016;96(1):102—9.

[179] Yue Y, Osipov A, Fraass B, Sandler H, Zhang X, Nissen N, et al. Identifying prognostic intratumor heterogeneity using pre- and post-radiotherapy 18F-FDG PET images for pancreatic cancer patients. J Gastrointest Oncol 2017;8(1):127—38.

[180] Hyun SH, Kim HS, Choi SH, Choi DW, Lee JK, Lee KH, et al. Intratumoral heterogeneity of 18 F-FDG uptake predicts survival in patients with pancreatic ductal adenocarcinoma. Eur J Nucl Med Mol Imag 2016;43(8):1461—8.

[181] Altazi BA, Fernandez DC, Zhang GG, Hawkins S, Naqvi SM, Kim Y, et al. Investigating multi-radiomic models for enhancing prediction power of cervical cancer treatment outcomes. Phys Med 2018;46:180—8.

[182] Reuzé S, Orlhac F, Chargari C, Nioche C, Limkin E, Riet F, et al. Prediction of cervical cancer recurrence using textural features extracted from 18F-FDG PET images acquired with different scanners. Oncotarget 2017;8(26):43169.

[183] Meng J, Liu S, Zhu L, Zhu L, Wang H, Xie L, et al. Texture Analysis as Imaging Biomarker for recurrence in advanced cervical cancer treated with CCRT. Sci Rep 2018;8(1):1—9.

[184] Wormald BW, Doran SJ, Ind TEJ, D'Arcy J, Petts J, deSouza NM. Radiomic features of cervical cancer on T2-and diffusion-weighted MRI: prognostic value in low-volume tumors suitable for trachelectomy. Gynecol Oncol 2020;156(1):107—14.

[185] Lucia F, Visvikis D, Desseroit M-C, Miranda O, Malhaire J-P, Robin P, et al. Prediction of outcome using pretreatment 18 F-FDG PET/CT and MRI radiomics in locally advanced cervical cancer treated with chemoradiotherapy. Eur J Nucl Med Mol Imag 2018;45(5):768—86.

[186] Ho K-C, Fang Y-HD, Chung H-W, Yen T-C, Ho T-Y, Chou H-H, et al. A preliminary investigation into textural features of intratumoral metabolic heterogeneity in 18F-FDG PET for overall survival prognosis in patients with bulky cervical cancer treated with definitive concurrent chemoradiotherapy. Am J Nuclear Med Mol Imaging 2016; 6(3):166.

[187] Chen S-W, Shen W-C, Hsieh T-C, Liang J-A, Hung Y-C, Yeh L-S, et al. Textural features of cervical cancers on FDG-PET/CT associate with survival and local relapse in patients treated with definitive chemoradiotherapy. Sci Rep 2018;8(1):1—11.

[188] Ho JC, Allen PK, Bhosale PR, Rauch GM, Fuller CD, Mohamed AS, et al. Diffusion-weighted magnetic resonance imaging as a predictor of outcome in cervical cancer after chemoradiation. Int J Radiat Oncol Biol Phys 2017;97(3):546—53.

[189] Fang J, Zhang B, Wang S, Jin Y, Wang F, Ding Y, et al. Association of MRI-derived radiomic biomarker with disease-free survival in patients with early-stage cervical cancer. Theranostics 2020;10(5):2284—92.

[190] Lucia F, Visvikis D, Vallières M, Desseroit M-C, Miranda O, Robin P, et al. External validation of a combined PET and MRI radiomics model for prediction of recurrence in cervical cancer patients treated with chemoradiotherapy. Eur J Nucl Med Mol Imag 2019;46(4):864—77.

[191] Zhang Y, Chen J-H, Chen T-Y, Lim S-W, Wu T-C, Kuo Y-T, et al. Radiomics approach for prediction of recurrence in skull base meningiomas. Neuroradiology 2019;61(12): 1355−64.

[192] Nie D, Lu J, Zhang H, Adeli E, Wang J, Yu Z, et al. Multi-channel 3D deep feature learning for survival time prediction of brain tumor patients using multi-modal neuroimages. Sci Rep 2019;9(1):1103.

[193] Sanghani P, Ang BT, King NKK, Ren H. Overall survival prediction in glioblastoma multiforme patients from volumetric, shape and texture features using machine learning. Surg Oncol 2018;27(4):709−14.

[194] Outcome prediction for patient with high-grade gliomas from brain functional and structural networks. In: Liu L, Zhang H, Rekik I, Chen X, Wang Q, Shen D, editors. International Conference on Medical Image Computing and Computer-Assisted Intervention. Springer; 2016.

[195] Wu G, Shi Z, Chen Y, Wang Y, Yu J, Lv X, et al. A sparse representation-based radiomics for outcome prediction of higher grade gliomas. Med Phys 2019;46(1):250−61.

[196] Liu X, Li Y, Qian Z, Sun Z, Xu K, Wang K, et al. A radiomic signature as a non-invasive predictor of progression-free survival in patients with lower-grade gliomas. Neuroimage 2018;20:1070−7.

[197] Prasanna P, Patel J, Partovi S, Madabhushi A, Tiwari P. Radiomic features from the peritumoral brain parenchyma on treatment-naive multi-parametric MR imaging predict long versus short-term survival in glioblastoma multiforme: preliminary findings. Eur Radiol 2017;27(10):4188−97.

[198] Zhang X, Lu H, Tian Q, Feng N, Yin L, Xu X, et al. A radiomics nomogram based on multiparametric MRI might stratify glioblastoma patients according to survival. Eur Radiol 2019;29(10):5528−38.

[199] Chen X, Fang M, Dong D, Liu L, Xu X, Wei X, et al. Development and validation of a MRI-based radiomics prognostic classifier in patients with primary glioblastoma multiforme. Acad Radiol 2019;26(10):1292−300.

[200] Tan Y, Mu W, Wang X-C, Yang G-Q, Gillies RJ, Zhang H. Improving survival prediction of high-grade glioma via machine learning techniques based on MRI radiomic, genetic and clinical risk factors. Eur J Radiol 2019;120:108609.

[201] Papp L, Pötsch N, Grahovac M, Schmidbauer V, Woehrer A, Preusser M, et al. Glioma survival prediction with combined analysis of in vivo 11C-MET PET features, ex vivo features, and patient features by supervised machine learning. J Nucl Med 2018;59(6): 892−9.

[202] Li L, Mu W, LIU Z, Liu Z, Wang Y, Ma W, et al. A non-invasive radiomic method using 18F-FDG PET predicts isocitrate dehydrogenase genotype and prognosis in patients with glioma. Front Oncol 2019;9:1183.

[203] Leijenaar RT, Carvalho S, Hoebers FJ, Aerts HJ, Van Elmpt WJ, Huang SH, et al. External validation of a prognostic CT-based radiomic signature in oropharyngeal squamous cell carcinoma. Acta Oncol 2015;54(9):1423−9.

[204] Wang S, Liu Z, Rong Y, Zhou B, Bai Y, Wei W, et al. Deep learning provides a new computed tomography-based prognostic biomarker for recurrence prediction in high-grade serous ovarian cancer. Radiother Oncol 2019;132:171−7.

[205] Bogowicz M, Jochems A, Deist TM, Tanadini-Lang S, Huang SH, Chan B, et al. Privacy-preserving distributed learning of radiomics to predict overall survival and HPV status in head and neck cancer. Sci Rep 2020;10(1):1−10.

[206] Zhou Y, Ma X-L, Pu L-T, Zhou R-F, Ou X-J, Tian R. Prediction of overall survival and progression-free survival by the 18F-FDG PET/CT radiomic features in patients with primary gastric diffuse large b-cell lymphoma. Contrast Media Mol Imaging 2019; 2019.

[207] Aide N, Talbot M, Fruchart C, Damaj G, Lasnon C. Diagnostic and prognostic value of baseline FDG PET/CT skeletal textural features in diffuse large B cell lymphoma. Eur J Nucl Med Mol Imag 2018;45(5):699−711.

[208] Tatsumi M, Isohashi K, Matsunaga K, Watabe T, Kato H, Kanakura Y, et al. Volumetric and texture analysis on FDG PET in evaluating and predicting treatment response and recurrence after chemotherapy in follicular lymphoma. Int J Clin Oncol 2019;24(10):1292−300.

[209] Lue K-H, Wu Y-F, Liu S-H, Hsieh T-C, Chuang K-S, Lin H-H, et al. Prognostic value of pretreatment radiomic features of 18F-FDG PET in patients with hodgkin lymphoma. Clin Nucl Med 2019;44(10):e559−65.

[210] Lue K-H, Wu Y-F, Liu S-H, Hsieh T-C, Chuang K-S, Lin H-H, et al. Intratumor heterogeneity assessed by 18F-FDG PET/CT predicts treatment response and survival outcomes in patients with Hodgkin lymphoma. Acad Radiol 2019.

[211] Wang M, Xu H, Xiao L, Song W, Zhu S, Ma X. Prognostic value of functional parameters of 18F-FDG-PET images in patients with primary renal/adrenal lymphoma. Contrast Media Mol Imaging 2019;2019.

[212] Parvez A, Tau N, Hussey D, Maganti M, Metser U. 18F-FDG PET/CT metabolic tumor parameters and radiomics features in aggressive non-Hodgkin's lymphoma as predictors of treatment outcome and survival. Ann Nucl Med 2018;32(6):410−6.

[213] Wang H, Zhao S, Li L, Tian R. Development and validation of an 18 F-FDG PET radiomic model for prognosis prediction in patients with nasal-type extranodal natural killer/T cell lymphoma. Eur Radiol 2020.

[214] Mayerhoefer ME, Riedl CC, Kumar A, Gibbs P, Weber M, Tal I, et al. Radiomic features of glucose metabolism enable prediction of outcome in mantle cell lymphoma. Eur J Nucl Med Mol Imag 2019;46(13):2760−9.

[215] Chen C, Zhuo H, Wei X, Ma X. Contrast-enhanced mri texture parameters as potential prognostic factors for primary central nervous system lymphoma patients receiving high-dose methotrexate-based chemotherapy. Contrast Media Mol Imaging 2019; 2019.

[216] Ganeshan B, Miles K, Babikir S, Shortman R, Afaq A, Ardeshna K, et al. CT-based texture analysis potentially provides prognostic information complementary to interim fdg-pet for patients with hodgkin's and aggressive non-hodgkin's lymphomas. Eur Radiol 2017;27(3):1012−20.

[217] Morvan L, Carlier T, Jamet B, Bailly C, Bodet-Milin C, Moreau P, et al. Leveraging RSF and PET images for prognosis of multiple myeloma at diagnosis. Int J Comp Assist Radiol Surg 2020;15(1):129−39.

[218] Torre LA, Siegel RL, Jemal A. Lung Cancer Statistics. Lung Cancer and Personalized Medicine. Springer; 2016. p. 1−19.

[219] Jamal-Hanjani M, Wilson GA, McGranahan N, Birkbak NJ, Watkins TB, Veeriah S, et al. Tracking the evolution of non−small-cell lung cancer. N Engl J Med 2017; 376(22):2109−21.

[220] Siegel RL, Miller KD, Jemal A. Cancer statistics, 2020. CA Cancer J Clin 2020;70(1): 7−30.

[221] (NCCN). NCCN. NCCN Clinical Practice Guidelines in Oncology. Non-small Cell Lung Cancer Version 2. 2020 [cited 2019. Available from: https://www.nccn.org/professionals/physician_gls/pdf/nscl.pdf.

[222] Dou TH, Coroller TP, van Griethuysen JJ, Mak RH, Aerts HJ. Peritumoral radiomics features predict distant metastasis in locally advanced NSCLC. PLoS One 2018; 13(11).

[223] Avanzo M, Stancanello J, Pirrone G, Sartor G. Radiomics and deep learning in lung cancer. Strahlenther Onkol 2020:1–9.

[224] Paul R, Hawkins SH, Balagurunathan Y, Schabath MB, Gillies RJ, Hall LO, et al. Deep feature transfer learning in combination with traditional features predicts survival among patients with lung adenocarcinoma. Tomography 2016;2(4):388.

[225] Ohri N, Duan F, Snyder BS, Wei B, Machtay M, Alavi A, et al. Pretreatment 18F-FDG PET textural features in locally advanced non–small cell lung cancer: secondary analysis of ACRIN 6668/RTOG 0235. J Nucl Med 2016;57(6):842–8.

[226] Yoda S, Dagogo-Jack I, Hata AN. Targeting oncogenic drivers in lung cancer: recent progress, current challenges and future opportunities. Pharmacol Therapeut 2019;193: 20–30.

[227] Skoulidis F, Heymach JV. Co-occurring genomic alterations in non-small-cell lung cancer biology and therapy. Nat Rev Cancer 2019;19(9):495–509.

[228] Rizvi NA, Mazières J, Planchard D, Stinchcombe TE, Dy GK, Antonia SJ, et al. Activity and safety of nivolumab, an anti-PD-1 immune checkpoint inhibitor, for patients with advanced, refractory squamous non-small-cell lung cancer (CheckMate 063): a phase 2, single-arm trial. Lancet Oncol 2015;16(3):257–65.

[229] Reck M, Rodríguez-Abreu D, Robinson AG, Hui R, Csőszi T, Fülöp A, et al. Pembrolizumab versus chemotherapy for PD-L1–positive non–small-cell lung cancer. N Engl J Med 2016;375(19):1823–33.

[230] Brahmer J, Reckamp KL, Baas P, Crinò L, Eberhardt WEE, Poddubskaya E, et al. Nivolumab versus docetaxel in advanced squamous-cell non–small-cell lung cancer. N Engl J Med 2015;373(2):123–35.

[231] Sollini M, Cozzi L, Ninatti G, Antunovic L, Cavinato L, Chiti A, et al. PET/CT radiomics in breast cancer: mind the step. Methods 2020;S1046-2023(19):30263–4.

[232] Sun Y, Reynolds HM, Parameswaran B, Wraith D, Finnegan ME, Williams S, et al. Multiparametric MRI and radiomics in prostate cancer: a review. Australas Phys Eng Sci Med 2019;42(1):3–25.

[233] Sah B-R, Owczarczyk K, Siddique M, Cook GJR, Goh V. Radiomics in esophageal and gastric cancer. Abdom Radiol 2019;44(6):2048–58.

[234] Jeong WK, Jamshidi N, Felker ER, Raman SS, Lu DS. Radiomics and radiogenomics of primary liver cancers. Clin Mol Hepatol 2019;25(1):21.

[235] Lin D-C, Mayakonda A, Dinh HQ, Huang P, Lin L, Liu X, et al. Genomic and epigenomic heterogeneity of hepatocellular carcinoma. Cancer Res 2017;77(9):2255–65.

[236] Lu L-C, Hsu C-H, Hsu C, Cheng A-L. Tumor heterogeneity in hepatocellular carcinoma: facing the challenges. Liver Cancer 2016;5(2):128–38.

[237] Conlon KC, Klimstra DS, Brennan MF. Long-term survival after curative resection for pancreatic ductal adenocarcinoma. Clinicopathologic analysis of 5-year survivors. Ann Surg 1996;223(3):273.

[238] Lee JW, Lee SM. Radiomics in oncological PET/CT: clinical applications. Nucl Med Mol Imaging 2018;52(3):170–89.

[239] Tefera B, Kerbo AA, Gonfa DB, Haile MT. Knowledge of cervical cancer and its associated factors among reproductive age women at Robe and Goba Towns, Bale zone, Southeast Ethiopia. Glob J Med Res 2016;16(1).

[240] Siegel RL, Miller KD, Ahmedin J. Cancer statistics. CA Cancer J Clin 2018;68(1): 7−30. 2018.

[241] McGuire S. World cancer report 2014. Geneva, Switzerland: World Health Organization, International agency for research on cancer, WHO press, 2015. Adv Nutr 2016; 7(2):418−9.

[242] Tewari KS, Sill MW, Long HJI, Penson RT, Huang H, Ramondetta LM, et al. Improved survival with bevacizumab in advanced cervical cancer. N Engl J Med 2014;370(8): 734−43.

[243] Bhatla N, Aoki D, Sharma DN, Sankaranarayanan R. Cancer of the cervix uteri. Int J Gynecol Obstet 2018;143:22−36.

[244] Ai Y, Zhu H, Xie C, Jin X. Radiomics in cervical cancer: current applications and future potential. Crit Rev Oncol Hematol 2020;152:102985.

[245] Mackay HJ, Wenzel L, Mileshkin L. Nonsurgical management of cervical cancer: locally advanced, recurrent, and metastatic disease, survivorship, and beyond. Am Soc Clin Oncol Educ Book 2015;35(1):e299−309.

[246] Whitney CW, Sause W, Bundy BN, Malfetano JH, Hannigan EV, Fowler J, Wesley C, et al. Randomized comparison of fluorouracil plus cisplatin versus hydroxyurea as an adjunct to radiation therapy in stage IIB-IVA carcinoma of the cervix with negative para-aortic lymph nodes: a Gynecologic Oncology Group and Southwest Oncology Group study. J Clin Oncol 1999;17(5):1339.

[247] Schmid M, Franckena M, Kirchheiner K, Sturdza A, Georg P, Dörr W, et al. Distant metastasis in patients with cervical cancer after primary radiotherapy with or without chemotherapy and image guided adaptive brachytherapy. Gynecol Oncol 2014;133(2): 256−62.

[248] Fan Y, Feng M, Wang R. Application of radiomics in central nervous system diseases: a systematic literature review. Clin Neurol Neurosurg 2019:105565.

[249] Emblem KE, Pinho MC, Zöllner FG, Due-Tonnessen P, Hald JK, Schad LR, et al. A generic support vector machine model for preoperative glioma survival associations. Radiology 2015;275(1):228−34.

[250] Machine learning and deep learning techniques to predict overall survival of brain tumor patients using MRI images. In: Chato L, Latifi S, editors. 2017 IEEE 17th International Conference on Bioinformatics and Bioengineering (BIBE); 2017. 23-25 Oct. 2017.

[251] Lao J, Chen Y, Li Z-C, Li Q, Zhang J, Liu J, et al. A deep learning-based radiomics model for prediction of survival in glioblastoma multiforme. Sci Rep 2017;7(1):1−8.

[252] Hao J, Kim Y, Kim T-K, Kang M. PASNet: pathway-associated sparse deep neural network for prognosis prediction from high-throughput data. BMC Bioinform 2018; 19(1):1−13.

[253] Swerdlow SH, Campo E, Pileri SA, Harris NL, Stein H, Siebert R, et al. The 2016 revision of the World Health Organization classification of lymphoid neoplasms. Blood 2016;127(20):2375−90.

[254] Schürch CM, Federmann B, Quintanilla-Martinez L, Fend F. Tumor heterogeneity in lymphomas: a different breed. Pathobiology 2018;85(1−2):130−45.

Summary and prospects

Chapter outline

5.1 Summary

Massive volumes of medical records are generated rapidly in healthcare centers due to the growing demand for medical services. It becomes increasingly important to optimize clinical workflows, not only to reduce labor costs but also to provide patients with more efficient and accurate medical services. Medical imaging technology, the most common method in clinical diagnosis and therapy, is expected to address this challenge as patients have shown unprecedented demand for noninvasive imaging. Imaging is an important technology in medicine and helps with decision-making [1]. Despite improvements in auxiliary diagnostic techniques, the diagnosis and assessment of cancer are still challenging. Imaging assessment of disease often relies on a visual assessment from human experts. However, the role of

Radiomics and its Clinical Application. https://doi.org/10.1016/B978-0-12-818101-0.00001-X

medical imaging is rapidly evolving from being viewed as initial diagnostic tools to having a core role in personalized precision medicine. After the concept of radiomics was proposed [2,3], medical images that preserve information about the pathology and physiology of the tumor were converted into high-dimensional data. The information can be leveraged through a quantitative image analysis and clinical decision support systems to improve medical decision-making [4]. Radiomics is based on decades of computer-aided diagnosis, prognosis, and therapeutic research [5]. Widespread use of technologies such as computed tomography (CT) and magnetic resonance imaging (MRI) provide rich data resources for radiomics analysis. The processing of radiomics includes identification of a large number of quantitative features in digital images, as well as data mining for knowledge extraction and application. It can extract quantitative features from medical images such as CT, MR, and/or positron emission tomography using high-throughput computing, automate the interpretation process of images, and is expected to change the clinical workflow of imaging research.

Radiomics objectively and quantitatively describes tumor phenotypes by extracting high-throughput quantitative radiomic features from medical imaging [1,2]. Radiomic features are extracted from medical images by mathematical algorithms to discover tumor characteristics that may not be directly detected by the human eye. Therefore, radiomics can help to capture important phenotypic information to provide valuable information for personalized treatment [6]. Radiomic features can reflect information about the cancer phenotype as well as the tumor microenvironment [7]. Besides, radiomics data combined with other relevant bioinformatics data can help to make more accurate and reliable clinical decisions [8]. The potential of radiomics to improve clinical decision-making is unquestionable, and the field is growing rapidly [9]. Now, the main challenge is to collect and integrate optimally multimodal data sources in a quantitative manner so that clinical predictions and outcomes can be predicted accurately and reliably [10].

The automatic extraction of quantitative features in medical imaging data represents the latest development direction of radiomics. There is a clear trend where researchers intend to introduce more deep learning approaches into radiomics due to its advance of learning disease-specific features from medical images. However, the major bottleneck remains for developing robust deep learning models as scalable training cohorts are strongly required.

Radiomics can identify complex information in medical images, transform qualitative and subjective image analysis into quantitative assessments, and even quantify image information that is unrecognizable by humans to complement clinical decision-making. Current challenges include clinical utility and model reproducibility across clinical centers. Only when radiomic findings are well validated and applied across hospitals will we maximize the clinical value of radiomics research.

5.2 Prospect

Radiomics is designed to provide an efficient way to reduce healthcare costs and improve the diagnosis and treatment. First, the cost of radiomics is relatively low, given that most patients with tumors already have medical images available [11]. Second, radiomics can potentially reduce the number of biopsies required. A biopsy is an invasive examination that is associated with high risks and costs [12]. Third, it also has the advantage of identifying early treatment response [13]. Therefore, radiomics analysis has a good clinical application prospect for multiple healthcare tasks.

5.2.1 **Prospective clinical application of radiomics**

5.2.1.1 Radiogenomics

There are two core scientific issues in radiogenomics:

(1) Relationship between the gene phenotype and radiotherapy outcomes

There is a scientific hypothesis in the field of radiobiology that some pathological phenotypes are highly correlated with some genetic phenotypes. This hypothesis prompted many studies on the association of radiotherapy toxicity (pathological phenotypes) and gene subtypes [14]. The goal of radiogenomics is to establish the relationship between radiomics, gene subtypes, and pathological phenotypes.

(2) Relationship between radiomics and specific gene expression patterns

The gene expression profiles of different tissues have deepened our understanding of cellular pathways and different pathological conditions. Differential analysis of tumors and normal tissue using radiogenomics will also help us understand the characteristics of tumor gene expression [15]. Another goal of radiogenomics is to find the statistical connection between radiomics and gene expression patterns.

5.2.1.2 Immunotherapy

In the field of oncology, many studies have been conducted on biomarkers, since immunological and imaging biomarkers are two important research topics [16]. For a normal and stable immune response, antigen-specific T cells with memory effects are essential [17]. Antigens on tumor cells that are specifically recognized by the immune system are called tumor antigens. The properties of these antigens are derived from protein mutations in tumor cells. If a tumor cell can be located by the immune system, the tumor antigen will be recognized by the antigen-presenting cells or dendritic cells, and then "notify" ordinary T cells to become T cells with tumor antigen-specific characteristics. Immunotherapy is based on T cells with tumor antigen specificity [18−21].

There are many ways in which tumor cells can evade attacks by cytotoxic T cells, such as mutations that interfere with some immune levels, like PD-L1 (a protein with potential markers). Tumor cells with more mutations produce more tumor antigens and are therefore more sensitive to immunotherapy, making anti-PD-1 immunotherapy possible. If such variant tumors can be identified by radiomics, it will help guide the immunotherapy method and prognosis prediction.

5.2.1.3 Virtual biopsy

Due to the cancer heterogeneity, different parts of the tumor have different molecular characteristics. In clinical practise, it is not possible to perform biopsies on all parts of the tumor, and therefore, biopsy samples cannot express the whole information of the tumor [8]. In this respect, radiomics has the potential to perform virtual biopsy using medical imaging.

5.2.1.4 Delta radiomics

The existing research mainly focuses on imaging data, which are acquired at a single time point and mainly before the start of treatment. Delta radiomics contains quantitative features acquired during treatment that reflect changes in the tumor, so it will improve the ability for diagnosis and prognostic prediction [22,23].

5.2.2 Formulate the research norms

It is important to use a unified and standardized quality score for evaluation purposes to ensure the quality of radiomics research [8]. In addition, the factors that affect radiomic features include image preprocessing (filtering or discretization of gray values) and image reconstruction. At the same time, the naming of features, the definition of feature formulas, and programming software used will affect the inconsistency of radiomics features [24]. Therefore, the implementation procedures of features, naming rules of features, use of programming software, and corresponding algorithms should be standardized. Meanwhile, the process of dimensionality reduction of image features should be clearly described to ensure its repeatability [8]. Consideration of the best overall nature of the model, clinical information, treatment information, and biological/genetic information should be included in the radiomics analysis. Different modeling methods have their own strengths and weaknesses, so a variety of modeling methods should be tried and compared in radiomics research. The value of unverified models is limited. Therefore, verification is an indispensable part of the complete radiomic analysis. The model must be verified internally and, ideally, externally. Many published predictive models have identified lots of factors related to disease and treatment, but there is no standardized evaluation of their performance [25]. The above key contents of radiomics research need to be standardized.

5.2.3 Fundamentals of medical big data

Professor Lambin, one of the proposers of the radiomics concept, has pointed that the development of radiomics relies on big data and the "four Vs": volume, variety, velocity, and veracity [8].

Researchers and clinicans should be aware that data from multiple centers and countries should be integrated. However, there are some challenges in the process of data integration, such as a lack of human resources to integrate the data, linguistic and cultural differences in the collection of data from multiple countries, different ways of storing data, and data privacy/security concerns [26−28].

Data standardization will be key to the progress of radiomics. Data acquisition, analysis, and data sharing should be standardized. In addition, the clinical decision-making system should be repeatedly evaluated and revised using a large number of clinical verifications [8]. Finally, the naming of data and features should be unified to promote the interoperability of the whole research field. When obtaining data, each center should consider the principle of unified naming so that the management of data can be more standardized.

It is expected to establish a large medical imaging database from millions of patients to form an integrative healthcare network. However, at the same time, this will face considerable data management obstacles [8,29].

With the increasing demand for medical imaging, hospitals at all levels continue to produce a large amount of imaging data, and the routinely used picture archiving and communication system (PACS) and digital imaging and communications in medicine (DICOM) need to organize the imaging data to facilitate the data access. Concretely, dataset access should be improved to encourage the legal sharing of data between medical institutions and governments to support the development of radiomics. This requires overcoming many technical, legal, and ethical issues [30].

5.2.4 Lesion segmentation algorithms

At present, the majority of research about lesion segmentation is focused on exploring the impact of different segmentation methods on the stability of radiomic features [31]. The movement of organs and the expansion or reduction of the region of interest will increase the instability of radiomic features, which seriously hinders the clinical application of radiomics [32]. Besides, the automatic lesion segmentation algorithm based on deep learning has developed rapidly in recent years, but the realization of its clinical application still requires further research. We expect that the powerful automatic segmentation can greatly reduce the labor cost of manually labeling the lesions during the radiomics research.

5.2.5 Reproducibility of the experiment

In a radiomics study, the reproducibility of the experiment is important so that other research teams produce the same results using the same data and methods. Therefore, to illustrate the validity of the finding, the used image acquisition parameters should be documented along with the protocol of the segmentation of the regions of interest.

When calculating the radiomic features, features with the same names may be obtained differently across studies. It is important to carefully analyze the effects of feature implementation and calculation methods on the predicted values of radiomic features to ensure the reproducibility of experiments [6].

Regarding retrospective studies, a lack of standardization of data acquisition and management may negatively impact the reproducibility, robustness, and stability of the results [33]. Therefore, prospective studies should be encouraged for strict research design, in which the optimal scheme of data acquisition and management can be planned, and model verification can be further achieved.

Many radiomic studies have a small sample size, but the number of radiomic features is large, making it a challenge in big data research. Due to the extraction of a large number of features in radiomics research, a small dataset degrades its performance and increases the risk of overfitting [34], which ultimately leads to the non-repeatability in the external validation set.

Besides, there is an urgent need to solve the interpretable problems for radiomics, because the interpretability of radiomics is the basis of its clinical application. In addition, the diagnosis of the disease not only depends on imaging but also the molecular characteristics or tumor biomarkers. Therefore, it is of great significance to construct radiomics models combined with clinicopathological data. The data collected from wearable devices, mobile phones, and social media are expanding rapidly, and all of them can be included in the radiomics model.

Furthermore, radiomics research should be supervised by governments. With the emergence of new technologies, it is necessary to ensure that the artificial intelligence (AI) diagnosis model is based on real data and examine its real effect before it is approved. At the same time, due to the continuous learning and training of radiomic models with newly added samples, the regulatory review should be continuous. Furthermore, clinical applications of radiomics must be strictly tested, including quality control and risk assessment. As cloud computing technology is increasingly used to deal with medical data, it is bound to pose a threat to data security and privacy. At present, the field of network security has begun to provide early solutions. Moreover, from an ethical point of view, the role of an automated intelligent auxiliary diagnosis system in a doctor—patient relationship needs to be further clarified.

Finally, the main criticism of radiomics is that the association between radiomic features and biological characteristics is ambiguous [34]. Most radiomics studies have shown that there is a statistical correlation between radiomic features and genes or prognosis. However, such correlations do not necessarily mean the causality. The establishment of this link is necessary for the personalized treatment of patients based on tumor images [31].

5.2.6 Influence of machine parameters

In modern medicine, imaging examinations (such as X-ray, CT, MRI, ultrasound, and nuclear medicine) have become routine to determine clinical diagnosis and treatment planning. Imaging is particularly important for the detection of neoplastic diseases, characterization of lesions, clinical grading and staging of cancer, formulation of clinical treatment plans, and judgment of the curative effect and prognosis prediction [30]. Radiomics here is used to build a bridge between medical imaging and individualized diagnosis and treatment [8]. In radiomics research, X-ray, CT,

MRI, nuclear medicine, and ultrasound images can all be used for image feature mining. Studies believe that radiomic features and screening are affected by machine parameters [35]. The data used in the experiments of radiomics research are often collected from multiple machines or even multiple hospitals. Therefore, it is important to study the influence of machine parameters on experiments.

Different imaging devices and images have different scanning parameters. For CT images, many machine scan parameters affect medical image analysis, such as enhanced and non-enhanced CT images, reconstruction thickness, and reconstruction nucleus [36]. Meanwhile, some studies consider the voltage of CT as a machine parameter and as one of the features included in the modeling [37]. He et al. [36] used a solitary pulmonary nodule as the research object, with different reconstruction slice thicknesses, contrast-enhancement and convolution kernel as variables, and explored the effects of different parameters on the radiomic features when constructing a differential diagnosis model. The experiment collected a total of 240 CT scans (there are 180 and 60 patients with malignant tumors and benign tumors, respectively). Each patient had both enhanced and non-enhanced CT. In each type of CT, there were thin- (1.25 mm) and thick-slice images (5 mm), as well as standard and lung convolution kernels. All groups used lasso-logistic regression for feature selection and model construction. The experimental results showed that for the classification of lung nodules, the models constructed by the non-enhanced CT cohort, thin-slice image cohort, and standard convolution kernel cohort were better than the comparison models. Non-contrast CT is better than contrast-enhanced CT because the intravenous contrast material perhaps confused the biological heterogeneity within the tumor described by radiographic features [38]. Compared to thin slice images, thick slice images will bring in larger partial pixel artifacts [39]. For the reconstruction kernel, a lung convolution kernel will be generated when a high-pass filtering algorithm is used, and it has a higher spatial frequency and noise. The low-pass algorithm can generate standard kernel images, has a higher spatial frequency contribution, and reduces noise, which is most suitable for tissue with low inherent contrast, such as lung tissue [40]. In addition to comparing the results of different radiomic models, Roberto et al. [41] carried out a study on the reproducibility of radiomic features under different machine parameters. Their study used two phantoms to test the reproducibility of radiomic features. The radiomic features were evaluated through the consistency correlation coefficient and the coefficient of variation. The experiment evaluated a total of 177 radiomic features, including intensity, shape, and texture features. For retest analysis experiments, 91% of the radiomic features (161 out of 177) could be reproduced according to the agreement correlation coefficient. For intra-CT experiments, the reproducibility of the radiomic features ranged from 89.3% (151 of 177) to 43.1% (76 of 177). For the inter-CT experiment, the results showed that there was no difference between the five scanners, while the type of material had a great influence on the reproduced results. In general, an analysis of the machine parameters is required in radiomic research, which can make multi-center research a significant challenge. At the same time, we can also alleviate potential image discrepancies by drawing up an image acquisition protocol [41].

5.2.7 Integration of radiomics and multi-omics

As a complex disease, cancer involves many aspects of the human body's malfunction, which can be interpreted by multi-omics data at different levels, such as molecular, cellular, tissue, and patient levels. Using data from a single level is often insufficient in cancer research, as these levels are mutually associated and one level cannot fit the reality of cancer. Hence, to deal with the complexity of cancers, researchers have made efforts to integrate data from multi-omics profiles [42].

Although there are published radiomics-only predictive models that are capable of prediction tasks, the potential of radiomics has not been fully explored and there still remain key problems that are unsolvable. Integrating radiomics with other omics can provide a large amount of information related to specific types of biological features. The information generated between radiomics and other omics can strengthen the predictive models and offer alternative novel insights.

The motivation of the integration of radiomics and other omics data is obvious for the following two reasons. First, besides radiomics data, other kinds of biological omics data are often available in clinics as well. It is helpful to take these data into consideration during the radiomics model construction. The second reason is that clinical imaging is noninvasive and has become routine practice in oncology, and integration of biological omics data and radiomics data can potentially improve the prediction accuracy.

There have been reports about survival prediction using radiomics and other omics; most of them were motivated by the poor performance of single-omics predictive models, like a weak predictor developed from genomics data or an unsophisticated model built based on radiomics data [43,44]. These researches compared the multi-omics models with the single-omics models and the results showed that the multi-omics model outperformed the other models, indicating the advantages of multi-omics integration in survival analysis and the useful complementary information between radiomics data and other kinds of omics data [44].

However, research about radiomics and multi-omics integration is still limited. The current research on integrated radiomics with multi-omics only utilized a small part of biological omics data, such as genomics and pathology images, because these data came from classical genome testing and biopsy methods. But, there have been many studies that concentrated on integration of various biological multi-omics data, including genomics, transcriptomics, proteomics, and metabolomics, and the results were satisfactory in cancer pathogenesis analysis and improvement of targeted therapy [45]. Therefore, many other kinds of biological omics data that have been proved to be associated with cancer can be integrated with radiomics and need further exploration.

The applications of multi-omics data integration strategy emerge as important research tasks for translational cancer research. We found that most current researches integrated radiomics and multi-omics for survival prediction. As a wide application of biological omics data in many kinds of oncology studies, with the leverage of radiomics data, it could be a new target to test the usage of radiomics data in other tasks besides survival analysis.

Finally, radiomics showed prosperous capability for the joint analysis with other omics profiles. Although it is still under experimental design, it is cost-efficient to integrate radiomics data with biological omics data to construct a more suitable model , improve the performance of the existing methods, and explore the potential correlation between radiomics and other omics.

5.2.8 **Prospective study**

A prospective cohort study is defined to be conducted by researchers according to the requirements of research topics and experiments. It has a clear research purpose, a careful research plan, reasonable obse rvation and evaluation indicators, and detailed clinical data records. Prospective studies usually focus on outcomes during the study period, such as the development of the disease, and associate it with clinical factors or treatment schemes. Lambin et al. [8] mentioned that it was critical that prospective studies fully related radiomics data with clinical results in an appropriate patient group.

Generally, prospective studies are conducted with a clear purpose, using the same data collection and experimental methods to check the progress of the participants on a regular basis. Once the participants who meet certain criteria are enrolled in the study, they are followed for a period of time to observe the outcomes.

The opposite is a retrospective study, which collates and analyzes similar clinical data accumulated in a certain period of time from previous clinical work, sums up the experience, finds rules, and guides practice. In other words, researchers conducting retrospective studies recruit people who already have the disease or condition for analysis. If prepared high-quality data are available, a retrospective study is the quickest to perform. However, if there is a lack of high-quality and reliable data, a prospective study is necessary [46].To some extent, prospective design has been ranked higher in the hierarchy of evidence than a retrospective design [47].

The quality of prospective clinical research mainly depends on the topic selection and design, as well as whether the clinical implementation is carried out completely in accordance with the design, and whether the statistical processing of data is reasonable. Prospective clinical studies are often related to the methods used, conditions, equipment, and other factors.

Prospective validation of a radiomics model in an appropriate trial provides the highest level of evidence supporting the clinical validity and usefulness of the radiomics biomarker [8]. In a prospective multi-center study [48], in order to quantitatively analyze liver fibrosis stages, the authors constructed a deep learning radiomics model based on shear wave elastography (DLRE). Comparing DLRE with 2D shear wave elastography (2D-SWE) images, the study found that DLRE performed better. Therefore, it can be applied to noninvasively predict the stage of liver fibrosis in patients with hepatitis B virus infection [48].

Prospective studies also have some shortcomings. It is expensive and time-consuming. Also, the incusion of specific groups of patients may lead to potential selection bias. Therefore, all deficiencies are supposed to be avoided as far as possible, such as individuals who did not follow-up in the course of the study. In prospective research, all findings should be made public, including true-negatives, false-negatives, false-positives, and so on, so that the negative effects of negative results should be mitigated because of the inclusion of material biases and the risk of distorting radiomics prospects.

5.2.9 Distributed learning in medical research

The privacy protection of medical data is crucial. Therefore, hospitals tend to store their medical data on their servers. Regrettably, sharing medical data between different hospitals is hampered by legal, administrative, ethical, and political barriers. However, a large amount of data sampling is necessary for generating a robust deep learning model using medical image analysis. One of the biggest medical imaging datasets available to the public only contains 65,240 records, which is still extremely limited [49]. On the contrary, the ImageNet dataset, which is a natural image dataset created for object recognition subject, has more than 14 million images. Meanwhile, more than 20,000 categories have been annotated in the ImageNet dataset. Federated learning (FL) [50], split learning (SL) [51], and distributed asynchronized discriminator GAN (AsynDGAN) [52] strategies were introduced to address the privacy issue around medical records.

FL models tend to cooperate with local clients in the distributed model to learn a global model without sharing any data. Instead of directly exposing user data, FL mechanism only transfers model information (parameters, gradients) with a privacy method to protect the users' privacy information. However, communicating gradients are dimension dependent, which is still not economical for large models. Interestingly, SL can separate shallow and deep modules in every deep learning model. The central processor only preserves several shallow layers which are a few blocks away from the input of the model, and only the information of interlayer is transferred from local clients to the central model. Therefore, privacy information is protected because the processor in the center cannot come in contact with the data directly. The cost of communication is cut down from a model-consuming level to a layer-consuming level while protecting the privacy of the local information. However, such a mechanism cannot be adopted to deep learning models with skipped connections. The novel AsynDGAN mechanism utilizes a central generator and several local discriminators to learn the comprehensive distribution of the distributed datasets. This mechanism has the ability to concentrate information from medical data of numerous hospitals to generate a robust estimation of the distribution of the overall data. The central generator does not have to communicate with each hospital for obtaining the local information of raw images. Instead of generating a specific model, AsynDGAN produces a central generator which gathers all the information from local discriminators. More importantly, AsynDGAN learns the distribution of multiple distributed datasets using a central generator to generate plentiful synthetic images for future use without worrying about losing privacy of datasets. When the central generator communicates with local discriminators, such mechanism only transmits the information of the synthetic images. It can effectively avoid direct access between the central generator and raw data of local hospitals; thus, privacy is protected. Moreover, the communication cost of each iteration is low.

In one study, the authors utilized a public dataset (BraTS2018 and Multi-Organ) to implement segmentation tasks [52]. The results showed that the performance of distributed learning was comparable to that obtained by all of the real datasets. In addition, the authors found that the AsynDGAN framework helped build an accessible and reliable public medical dataset, which could benefit scientists and boost the development of AI in the medical field [52].

In another study, the authors collected data from 287 patients with lung cancer that had been treated with curative intent with chemoradiation or radiotherapy from five different medical institutes [53]. A Bayesian model was used to create the distributed learning models to predict dyspnea, a side effect after radiotherapy in the lung cancer group. The results of this study showed that the distributed learning model could extract and utilize knowledge from routine medical data of different hospitals [53].

In conclusion, distributed learning architecture overcomes the issues around small data volumes and single data distribution, and obtains a more robust and higher performance model for healthcare applications (e.g., diagnosis, prognosis, lesion segmentation, and tumor detection). Furthermore, distributed learning enables smaller hospitals to effectively serve a central model while also benefiting from the distributed network.

5.2.10 Interpretability of radiomics

Every step of the radiomics pipeline should be clinically interpretable, including feature extraction, feature selection, and model establishment.

Interpretability is an urgent focus in AI-based research, especially in medical applications. Although the radiomics method has demonstrated its ability to quantitatively characterize lesions in many clinical problems, it failed to establish the correlation between most texture features and biomarkers. So far, no robust histopathological interpretations of radiomics and the extracted features have been explicitly developed. Many studies have found a correlation relationship between radiomicfeatures and prognosis or genes, rather than a causation relationship [2,5,8]. This implicit and indirect relationship leads to the interference of radiomics in clinical applications.

A handful of studies have attempted to reveal the interpretability of radiomics pipelines to address these issues. Kumar et al. proposed an interpretable computer-aided diagnosis system named CLEAR-DR, which was based on class-enhanced attentive response discovery radiomics to help diagnose diabetic retinopathy [54]. Based on the discovery of the deep radiology sequencer, the system not only generated distinguishable radiological sequences for the classification of diabetic retinopathy but also provided a mechanism for visually explaining its decision-making process. In another study by Kumar et al., an end-to-end interpretable discovery radiopharmaceutical-driven lung cancer prediction framework was introduced, which uses the proposed deep-level interpretable sequencing cells composed of interpretable sequencing cells [55].

Li et al. extracted features from multiphase CT and proposed an interpretable radiological model for identifying clear cell renal cell carcinoma (ccRCC) from non-ccRCC subtypes [56]. They investigated the biological significance of radiology by evaluating possible radiogenomic links between radiological features and key ccRCC driver genes. Their results showed that the radiation model was accurate and interpretable because its imaging features reflected the underlying molecular basis of cancer. Similarly, Kuthuru et al. developed a method that could identify regions of medical images to potentially influence the prediction process [57]. They used dictionary learning methods to derive visually interpretable MRI radiological features related to genetic changes, thereby predicting two essential biomarkers of low-grade glioma. Besides, the visual areas related to these dictionaries showed the relevance of critical molecular pathways related to the occurrence of glioma [57].

Li et al. developed an MRI-based radiotherapy model to classify gliomas and explained the radiological characteristics used in this model [58]. They discovered the interaction pattern between the radiological characteristics and the pathological grades learned by the model, which may indicate the interpretability of the model and contribute to the high-throughput computer-aided diagnosis system for glioma [58].

Despite preliminary results, there is still a lack of widely recognized research to promote the interpretability of radiomics. Overcoming the challenge of interpretability is important before radiomics can be broadly used in clinical applications.

5.2.11 Advancement in clinical guidelines

The National Comprehensive Cancer Network (NCCN) is one of the world's top cancer centers and a nonprofit academic consortium [59]. This center is dedicated to patient healthcare, treatment, and research [59]. Over the past two decades, the NCCN has developed an integrated manual to improve the quality of treatment in cancer. The NCCN guidelines provide a scientific consensus to benefit patients [59]. The clinical practice guidelines developed by the NCCN are the main reference guidelines for the diagnosis and treatment of tumors in many countries. Furthermore, the American Joint Committee on Cancer (AJCC) staging manual is used for diagnosing patients with cancer, determining the schedule of treatment, and determining the best diagnosis. Particularly for tumors, lymph nodes, and metastases, the staging manual evaluates and guides individualized treatment [54].

However, with the rapid development of knowledge, improving the accuracy of analyzing biological factors that predict cancer outcomes and response to treatment in clinically personalized medicine remains a significant challenge.

The AJCC has acknowledged that the manual is a never-ending work that will need to be continuously updated to reflect changes [54]. For individualized treatment, the AJCC personalized medicine core committee asserts that we should realize the importance of the intelligent method (e.g., radiomics method) based on the machine learning algorithm for more accurate prediction in combination with the existing cancer staging systems based on the experience of clinical experts [60]. Lambin et al. [2] showed that the radiomics method digitally decoded medical images with rich information related to the tumor phenotype, which were transformed into quantitative high-dimensional features. The information can be used in various decision-making systems to improve the management of patients [8].

Although radiomics can establish risk models, to better promote the improvement of clinical guidelines, we need to establish standards for radiomic models to assist clinical decision-making. We should formulate strict inclusion and exclusion evaluation criteria for risk models [60].These formulated criteria will help to accelerate the facilitation of individualized risk prediction for cancer patients. To enable the radiomics method to be used in clinical practice, attention should be given to performance metrics. Moreover, these criteria might be helpful when trying to assess the potential use of a published risk evaluation tool [60].

For example, if we want to utilize a model for clinical use, and the guidelines accept the model, it should include correlated and key predictors, and show the detailed reasons for its inclusion. The model should be approved by most clinicians. If the modeling team needs to remove some predictors due to their poor predictive performance, an evaluation should be conducted by a clinician with disease management expertise [60].

Bi et al. asserted that overdiagnosis exists for nodule detection and that attention should be given to this issue [30]. Clinical guidelines show great significance to offer reasonable suggestions to assess the nodules, but do not predict the outcomes automatically for diagnosis and prognosis. Radiomics can be developed as an AI tool to provide more intelligent and convenient approaches to identify biomarkers that avoid overdiagnosis. AI tools will lead to more accurate and robust prediction, which will assist the application of clinical guidelines [30]. In the future, with the development of imaging technology, the radiomics method should lead to more user-friendly clinical guidelines to improve cancer treatment and decision-making.

5.3 **Conclusion**

We believe that based on standardized medical imaging data, the use of radiomics will be key to the development of individualized medicine in the near future.

Innovation and development in the imaging field, with the collaboration of clinicians, radiologists, and AI engineers, is expected. Further radiomics developments will help to promote the realization of precision medicine.

References

[1]   Aerts HJWL, Velazquez ER, Leijenaar RTH, et al. Decoding tumour phenotype by noninvasive imaging using a quantitative radiomics approach. Nat Commun 2014; 5(1):1−9.

[2]   Lambin P, Rios-Velazquez E, Leijenaar R, et al. Radiomics: extracting more information from medical images using advanced feature analysis. Eur J Cancer 2012;48(4): 441−6.

[3]   Kumar V, Gu Y, Basu S, et al. Radiomics: the process and the challenges. Magn Reson Imag 2012;30(9):1234−48.

[4]   Haase AT, Henry K, Zupancic M, et al. Quantitative image analysis of HIV-1 infection in lymphoid tissue. Science 1996;274(5289):985−9.

[5]   Lambin P, Van Stiphout RGPM, Starmans MHW, et al. Predicting outcomes in radiation oncology—multifactorial decision support systems. Nat Rev Clin Oncol 2013;10(1): 27−40.

[6]   Yip SF, Aerts HJWL. Applications and limitations of radiomics. Phys Med Biol 2016; 61(13):R150.

[7]   Gatenby RA, Grove O, Gillies RJ. Quantitative imaging in cancer evolution and ecology. Radiology 2013;269(1):8−14.

[8]   Lambin P, Leijenaar RTH, Deist TM, et al. Radiomics: the bridge between medical imaging and personalized medicine. Nat Rev Clin Oncol 2017;14(12):749−62.

[9]   Aerts HJWL. The potential of radiomic-based phenotyping in precision medicine: a review. JAMA Oncol 2016;2(12):1636−42.

[10] Lambin P, Zindler J, Vanneste BGL, et al. Decision support systems for personalized and participative radiation oncology. Adv Drug Deliv Rev 2017;109:131−53.

[11] Parmar C, Grossmann P, Rietveld D, et al. Radiomic machine-learning classifiers for prognostic biomarkers of head and neck cancer. Front Oncol 2015;5:272.

[12] Parmar C, Leijenaar RTH, Grossmann P, et al. Radiomic feature clusters and prognostic signatures specific for lung and head & neck cancer. Sci Rep 2015;5:11044.

[13] Avanzo M, Stancanello J, El Naqa I. Beyond imaging: the promise of radiomics. Phys Med 2017;38:122−39.

[14] Rosenstein BS, West CM, Bentzen SM, et al. Radiogenomics: radiobiology enters the era of big data and team science. Int J Radiat Oncol Biol Phys 2014;89(4):709−13.

[15] Rutman AM, Kuo MD. Radiogenomics: creating a link between molecular diagnostics and diagnostic imaging. Eur J Radiol 2009;70(2):232−41.

[16] Okada H, Weller M, Huang R, et al. Immunotherapy response assessment in neurooncology: a report of the RANO working group. Lancet Oncol 2015;16(15):e534−42.

[17] Coulie PG, Van den Eynde BJ, Van Der Bruggen P, et al. Tumour antigens recognized by T lymphocytes: at the core of cancer immunotherapy. Nat Rev Cancer 2014;14(2): 135−46.

[18] Schumacher TN, Schreiber RD. Neoantigens in cancer immunotherapy. Science 2015; 348:69−74.

[19] Rooney MS, Shukla SA, Wu CJ, et al. Molecular and genetic properties of tumors associated with local immune cytolytic activity. Cell 2015;160(1-2):48−61.

[20] Mellman I, Steinman RM. Dendritic cells: specialized and regulated antigen processing machines. Cell 2001;106(3):255−8.

[21] Demaria S, Golden EB, Formenti SC. Role of local radiation therapy in cancer immunotherapy. JAMA Oncol 2015;1(9):1325−32.

[22] Leijenaar RTH, Nalbantov G, Carvalho S, et al. The effect of SUV discretization in quantitative FDG-PET radiomics: the need for standardized methodology in tumor texture analysis. Sci Rep 2015;5:11075.

[23] Fave X, Zhang L, Yang J, et al. Delta-radiomics features for the prediction of patient outcomes in non−small cell lung cancer. Sci Rep 2017;7(1):1−11.

[24] Hatt M, Tixier F, Pierce L, et al. Characterization of PET/CT images using texture analysis: the past, the present… any future? Eur J Nucl Med Mol Imag 2017;44(1):151−65.

[25] Vickers AJ. Prediction models: revolutionary in principle, but do they do more good than harm? J Clin Oncol 2011;29:2951−2.

[26] Deasy JO, Bentzen SM, Jackson A, et al. Improving normal tissue complication probability models: the need to adopt a "data-pooling"culture. Int J Rad Oncol Biol Phys 2010;76(3):S151−4.

[27] Skripcak T, Belka C, Bosch W, et al. Creating a data exchange strategy for radiotherapy research: towards federated databases and anonymised public datasets. Radiother Oncol 2014;113(3):303−9.

[28] Budin-Ljøsne I, Burton P, Isaeva J, et al. DataSHIELD: an ethically robust solution to multiple-site individual-level data analysis. Pub Health Genomics 2015;18(2):87−96.

[29] Roelofs E, Dekker A, Meldolesi E, et al. International data-sharing for radiotherapy research: an open-source based infrastructure for multicentric clinical data mining. Radiother Oncol 2014;110(2):370−4.

[30] Bi WL, Hosny A, Schabath MB, et al. Artificial intelligence in cancer imaging: clinical challenges and applications. CA Cancer J Clin 2019;69(2):127−57.

[31] Larue RTHM, Defraene G, De Ruysscher D, et al. Quantitative radiomics studies for tissue characterization: a review of technology and methodological procedures. Br J Rad 2017;90(1070):20160665.

[32] Balagurunathan Y, Kumar V, Gu Y, et al. Test−retest reproducibility analysis of lung CT image features. J Dig Imag 2014;27(6):805−23.

[33] Scalco E, Rizzo G. Texture analysis of medical images for radiotherapy applications. Br J Rad 2017;90(1070):20160642.

[34] Napel S, Giger ML. Special section guest editorial: radiomics and imaging genomics: quantitative imaging for precision medicine. J Med Imag 2015;2(4):041001.

[35] Mackin D, Fave X, Zhang L, et al. Measuring computed tomography scanner variability of radiomics features. Invest Radiol 2015;50(11):757−65.

[36] He L, Huang Y, Ma Z, et al. Effects of contrast-enhancement, reconstruction slice thickness and convolution kernel on the diagnostic performance of radiomics signature in solitary pulmonary nodule. Sci Rep 2016;6:34921.

[37] Roger S, Elaine JL, Maria V, et al. A radiomics approach to assess tumour-infiltrating CD8 cells and response to anti-PD-1 or anti-PD-L1 immunotherapy: an imaging biomarker, retrospective multicohort study. Lancet Oncol 2018;19(9):1180−91.

[38] Ganeshan B, Miles KA. Quantifying tumour heterogeneity with CT. Cancer Imag 2013; 13:140−9.

[39] Zhao B, Tan Y, Tsai WY, Schwartz LH, Lu L. Exploring variability in CT characterization of tumors: a preliminary phantom study. Transl Oncol 2014;7:88−93.

[40] Weiss KL, et al. Hybrid convolution kernel: optimized CT of the head, neck, and spine. Am J Roentgenol 2011;196:403−6.

[41] Berenguer R, del Rosario Pastor-Juan M, et al. Radiomics of CT features may be non-reproducible and redundant: influence of CT acquisition parameters. Radiology 2018; 288(2):407−15.

[42] Zanfardino M, Franzese M, Pane K, et al. Bringing radiomics into a multi-omics framework for a comprehensive genotype−phenotype characterization of oncological diseases. J Transl Med 2019;17(1):337.

[43] Lin P, Wen D, Chen L, et al. A radiogenomics signature for predicting the clinical outcome of bladder urothelial carcinoma. Eur Radiol 2020;30(1):547−57.

[44] Feng L, Liu Z, Lou X, et al. A radiomics-based multi-omics integration model to predict the therapeutic response to neoadjuvant chemoradiotherapy of rectal cancer. Int J Rad Oncol Biol Phys 2019;105(1):S119.

[45] Lu M, Zhan X. The crucial role of multiomic approach in cancer research and clinically relevant outcomes. EPMA J 2018;9(1):77−102.

[46] Mann CJ. Observational research methods. Research design II: cohort, cross sectional, and case-control studies. Emer Med J 2003;20(1):54−60.

[47] Vandenbroucke JP. Observational research, randomised trials, and two views of medical science. PLoS Med 2008;5(3):e67.

[48] Wang K, Lu X, Zhou H, et al. Deep learning radiomics of shear wave elastography significantly improved diagnostic performance for assessing liver fibrosis in chronic hepatitis B: a prospective multicentre study. Gut 2019;68(4):729−41.

[49] Irvin J, Rajpurkar P, Ko M, et al. CheXpert: a large chest radiograph dataset with uncertainty labels and expert comparison. Proc AAAI Conf Artif Intel 2019;33:590−7.

[50] McMahan B, Moore E, Ramage D, et al. Communication-efficient learning of deep networks from decentralized data. Artif Intel Stat 2017:1273−82.

[51] Vepakomma P, Gupta O, Swedish T, et al. Split learning for health: distributed deep learning without sharing raw patient data. arXiv preprint arXiv:1812.00564. 2018.

[52] Chang Q, Qu H, Zhang Y, et al. Synthetic learning: learn from distributed asynchronized discriminator GAN without sharing medical image data. Proc IEEE Comput Soc Conf Comput Vis Pattern Recognit 2020:13856−66.

[53] Jochems Λ, Deist TM, Van Soest J, et al. Distributed learning: developing a predictive model based on data from multiple hospitals without data leaving the hospital−a real life proof of concept. Radiother Oncol 2016;121(3):459−67.

[54] Kumar D, Taylor GW, Wong A. Discovery radiomics with CLEAR-DR: interpretable computer aided diagnosis of diabetic retinopathy. IEEE Access 2019;7:25891−6.

[55] Kumar D, Sankar V, Clausi D, et al. SISC: end-to-end interpretable discovery radiomics-driven lung cancer prediction via stacked interpretable sequencing cells. IEEE Access 2019;7:145444−54.

[56] Li ZC, Wu G, Zhang J, et al. Towards an interpretable radiomics model for classifying renal cell carcinomas subtypes: a radiogenomics assessment. IEEE 16th Int Symp Biomed Imag (ISBI 2019) 2019:1288−92. IEEE.

[57] Kuthuru S, Deaderick W, Bai H, et al. A visually interpretable, dictionary-based approach to imaging-genomic modeling, with low-grade glioma as a case study. Cancer inform 2018;17. 1176935118802796.

[58] Ma L, Xiao Z, Li K, et al. Game theoretic interpretability for learning based preoperative gliomas grading. Future Gener Comp Systs 2020;112:1−10.

[59] Wood DE, Kazerooni EA, Baum SL, et al. Lung cancer screening, version 3.2018, NCCN clinical practice guidelines in oncology. J Natl Compr Cancer Netw 2018; 16(4):412−41.

[60] Kattan MW, Hess KR, Amin MB, et al. American joint committee on cancer acceptance criteria for inclusion of risk models for individualized prognosis in the practice of precision medicine. CA Cancer J Clin 2016;66(5):370−4.

Index